Tips for Better Point-and-Shoot Pictures

Improve your photographs with these simple tricks:

- **Always lock the focus before taking a picture.** (See Chapter 6.)
- **Frame, don't aim.** Use the whole viewfinder to compose your shot. With people pictures, place heads near the top rather than dead-center. (See Chapter 9.)
- **Get closer.** In most photographs, the main subject is too small — and getting closer when you shoot is the best way to make the subject bigger. (See Chapter 9.)
- **Use flash outdoors.** Set your point-and-shoot's fill-flash mode whenever possible. It softens the unflattering facial shadows created by direct sunlight and brightens a subject lit from behind without washing out the background. (See Chapter 7.)
- **Use a fast film.** *ISO 400 print film should be your standard film.* If you like to zoom your lens way in to make the subject bigger, use ISO 800 film instead. These super-quality films lessen picture-wrecking blur and improve background detail in flash shots. (See Chapter 2.)
- **Shoot from a different angle.** Eye level is often not the best height from which to take pictures. Try squatting for a low angle, or standing on a chair for a high one. (See Chapter 9.)
- **Place the subject off-center.** This is an easy way to make your pictures more interesting. But off-center composition makes locking the focus all the more imperative! (See Chapter 9.)

Making Point-and-Shoot Pictures Sharper

Got fuzzy pictures? Here are the symptoms of that common photographic affliction — and how to diagnose and cure it.*

- *Symptom:* **Something other than the main subject is sharp — usually the background.**
  - *Cause:* Camera focused on the wrong thing.
  - *Solution:* Lock the focus on the main subject before shooting. (See Chapter 6.)
- *Symptom:* **Overall unsharpness, often with a glowing quality or a slight halo around light areas of the subject.**
  - *Cause:* Smudge on the lens.
  - *Solution:* Clean the lens with lens cleaning tissue and solution. (See Chapter 6.)
- *Symptom:* **Overall unsharpness in nonflash pictures, sometimes with visible blur or streakiness.**
  - *Cause:* Involuntary camera shake.
  - *Solution:* Use a faster film (ISO 400 or 800) or set fill-flash mode to force the flash to fire. (See Chapters 2 and 7.)
- *Symptom:* **The main subject is unsharp, but things right behind it are sharp.**
  - *Cause:* Subject too close.
  - *Solution:* With autofocus models, make sure that the viewfinder's focus-OK lamp glows steadily before shooting — and back up a little if it's blinking. With non-autofocus (focus-free) models, stay at least four feet from the subject. (See Chapter 6.)
- *Symptom:* **The scene through a window is unsharp.**
  - *Cause:* Camera focused on the window, not the scene.
  - *Solution:* Set infinity lock or landscape mode — or just open the window! (See Chapter 4.)

If none of these solutions helps, the problem may be with your lens or focusing system — and may require repair. Also see Chapter 6 for autofocusing tips.

For Dummies™: Bestselling Book Series for Beginners

BESTSELLING
BOOK SERIES

Photography For Dummies®

Cheat Sheet

If Your Point-and Shoot Won't Let You Take a Picture. . . .

Sometimes you bear down on the shutter button with all your might, and the camera still won't let you take a picture. When that happens, try these suggestions — and see Chapter 20 for even more.

- **Reload the film.** The camera tells you it's having trouble engaging the film by flashing an *E* (for empty) or *0* on its display panel after you close the camera back. (See Chapter 1.)
- **Reinstall or replace the battery.** You may have put the battery in backward; refer to diagrams or symbols inside the battery compartment for correct installation. If the battery is too weak to power the camera, it alerts you to this problem with a "low battery" symbol (on models with display panels). (See Chapter 1.)
- **Wait until the viewfinder's red or orange flash-ready lamp stops blinking and glows steadily.** The flash takes several seconds to charge (when you turn the camera on) or recharge (after you take a flash picture) — and it won't let you shoot while it's charging. (See Chapter 7.)
- **Step back from the subject.** An autofocus lens can't focus if you're too close — and if the lens can't focus, the camera won't let you take a picture. The camera tells you that you're too close by rapidly blinking the viewfinder's focus-OK lamp, which is usually green. (See Chapter 6.)
- **With a digital point-and-shoot, wait for the camera to finish "saving" the picture to its memory.** This process can take as long as ten seconds, during which the camera won't let you shoot. (See Chapter 15.)

Locking the Focus

The only way to make sure an autofocus point-and-shoot focuses correctly — especially if the main subject isn't centered in the frame — is to lock the focus before you take a picture. Here's how:

1. **Look through the viewfinder and place its focus point (the marks in the middle) on the main subject.**

   (Doing this centers the subject in the frame.)

2. **Press the shutter button halfway down to lock the focus.**

3. **Holding the shutter button halfway down, compose the shot the way you want.**

4. **Press the shutter button all the way to take the picture.**

(See Chapter 6 for more details on locking the focus.)

Making Point-and-Shoot Pictures More Colorful

Got muddy pictures? Here are the most common causes of dull color, lack of detail, and flat gray or brown tones.

- *Symptom:* **Can barely make out the main subject in a flash picture taken at night or by artificial light (such as in a sports stadium).**
  - *Cause:* Subject was too far away for the flash to reach.
  - *Solution:* Get closer to the subject (within 15 or 20 feet), if possible; if not, turn off the flash and use a faster film (ISO 800). (See Chapter 7.)

- *Symptom:* **Colors are washed out, tones weak in a nonflash shot taken in dim light.**
  - *Cause:* Film did not receive enough exposure to light.
  - *Solution:* Use a faster film (at least ISO 800). Or, if the subject is close enough, set fill-flash or slow-sync flash mode. (See Chapter 7.)

Other problems may be due to photofinishing errors. See Chapter 3 to find out when to ask for a reprint.

For Dummies™: Bestselling Book Series for Beginners

Praise for Photography For Dummies and Russell Hart

"What a wonderful book for beginners in photography. Russell Hart covers all aspects of photography with great simplicity. Why take a basic course in school when you can learn all about it from this book? I wish I'd had a book like this when I started in photography some 25 years ago."
— John Isaac, Chief Photographer, United Nations

"Russell is that rare commodity among photography writers: He addresses technique and the philosophy behind that technique in clear, direct terms. The book is a wonderful compendium of information for both the beginner and advanced photographer."
— Joe McNally, Award-Winning Photojournalist

"Russell Hart's *Photography For Dummies* is like the Rosetta Stone for anyone trying to decipher the mysteries of the craft. The book is chock-full of solid advice on everything from composing pictures to dealing with photofinishers to understanding all those little icons on your point-and-shoot camera. Although clearly aimed at beginners, even experienced photographers will pick up some valuable tips and techniques."
— Bob Krist, Contributing Editor and Photography Columnist for *National Geographic Traveler* magazine

"As the author of 20 books myself, I know the importance of communicating ideas effectively and easily. Russell Hart accomplishes this goal, by making the alphabet soup jargon of photography easy to digest. With chapters like "Ten Simple Ways to Make Your Pictures Better," this book gets a "10" in my opinion."
— Rick Sammon, Photographer and Internationally Syndicated Photocolumnist

"Russell Hart has written a book filled with information that will enable everyone to make images that equal their memories."
— Elaine O'Neil, Director, School of Photographic Arts and Sciences, Rochester Institute of Technology

"Russell Hart has a special talent for explaining and connecting technique and aesthetics — for bridging photography and art. *Photography For Dummies* is a very valuable resource for anyone who takes photography seriously and considers it an important part of their life."
— Mark Seliger, Chief Photographer, *Rolling Stone* magazine

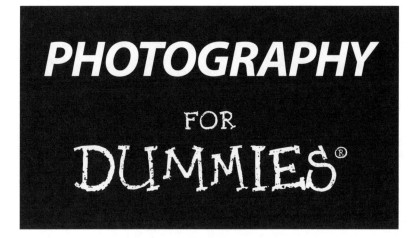

PHOTOGRAPHY
FOR
DUMMIES®

by Russell Hart

With additional writing
by Dan Richards

IDG
BOOKS
WORLDWIDE

IDG Books Worldwide, Inc.
An International Data Group Company

Foster City, CA ♦ Chicago, IL ♦ Indianapolis, IN ♦ New York, NY

Photography For Dummies®

Published by
IDG Books Worldwide, Inc.
An International Data Group Company
919 E. Hillsdale Blvd.
Suite 400
Foster City, CA 94404
www.idgbooks.com (IDG Books Worldwide Web site)
www.dummies.com (Dummies Press Web site)

Library of Congress Catalog Card No.: 98-85431

ISBN: 0-7645-5065-9

Printed in the United States of America

15 14 13 12 11 10 9 8 7 6

1O/QX/QX/QQ/IN

Distributed in the United States by IDG Books Worldwide, Inc.

Distributed by CDG Books Canada Inc. for Canada; by Transworld Publishers Limited in the United Kingdom; by IDG Norge Books for Norway; by IDG Sweden Books for Sweden; by IDG Books Australia Publishing Corporation Pty. Ltd. for Australia and New Zealand; by TransQuest Publishers Pte Ltd. for Singapore, Malaysia, Thailand, Indonesia, and Hong Kong; by Gotop Information Inc. for Taiwan; by ICG Muse, Inc. for Japan; by Intersoft for South Africa; by Eyrolles for France; by International Thomson Publishing for Germany, Austria and Switzerland; by Distribuidora Cuspide for Argentina; by LR International for Brazil; by Galileo Libros for Chile; by Ediciones ZETA S.C.R. Ltda. for Peru; by WS Computer Publishing Corporation, Inc., for the Philippines; by Contemporanea de Ediciones for Venezuela; by Express Computer Distributors for the Caribbean and West Indies; by Micronesia Media Distributor, Inc. for Micronesia; by Chips Computadoras S.A. de C.V. for Mexico; by Editorial Norma de Panama S.A. for Panama; by American Bookshops for Finland.

For general information on IDG Books Worldwide's books in the U.S., please call our Consumer Customer Service department at 800-762-2974. For reseller information, including discounts and premium sales, please call our Reseller Customer Service department at 800-434-3422.

For information on where to purchase IDG Books Worldwide's books outside the U.S., please contact our International Sales department at 317-596-5530 or fax 317-572-4002.

For consumer information on foreign language translations, please contact our Customer Service department at 1-800-434-3422, fax 317-572-4002, or e-mail rights@idgbooks.com.

For information on licensing foreign or domestic rights, please phone +1-650-653-7098.

For sales inquiries and special prices for bulk quantities, please contact our Order Services department at 800-434-3422 or write to the address above.

For information on using IDG Books Worldwide's books in the classroom or for ordering examination copies, please contact our Educational Sales department at 800-434-2086 or fax 317-572-4005.

For press review copies, author interviews, or other publicity information, please contact our Public Relations department at 650-653-7000 or fax 650-653-7500.

For authorization to photocopy items for corporate, personal, or educational use, please contact Copyright Clearance Center, 222 Rosewood Drive, Danvers, MA 01923, or fax 978-750-4470.

About the Author

Technology Editor at *American Photo* magazine, **Russell Hart** takes more pictures with his point-and-shoots than with the assorted professional cameras he has accumulated in over 20 years as a working photographer. Also a contributing editor to *Popular Photography*, he has been senior editor at both magazines, and has written for most other major photo magazines. He is also the editor of *American Photo On Campus*. Russell has written about photography for *The New York Times*, *Men's Journal*, and *Us* magazines, and is the author of a number of books on photographic subjects, including *The Photographic Essay* (Bulfinch Press), *Photographing Your Artwork* (North Light), and *The New Joy of Photography* (Addison-Wesley).

But Russell would rather take pictures than talk about them. Before he began writing about photography, he made a living with it, shooting for publications such as *Boston* magazine, *The Boston Globe Magazine,* and *Inc.* magazine, as well as various advertising clients. His landscape photographs have been shown in galleries and museums across the country, and are in the permanent collections of Boston's Museum of Fine Arts; New York's Hudson River Museum; Lincoln, Massachusetts' DeCordova Museum; and the Reader's Digest Collection. He has been awarded several fellowships in photography, and has taught photography at Tufts University, the Boston Museum School, and Mount Ida College.

Eastman Kodak Company has provided technical information for this book. However, the opinions expressed are those of the author and are not necessarily those of Kodak.

ABOUT IDG BOOKS WORLDWIDE

Welcome to the world of IDG Books Worldwide.

IDG Books Worldwide, Inc., is a subsidiary of International Data Group, the world's largest publisher of computer-related information and the leading global provider of information services on information technology. IDG was founded more than 30 years ago by Patrick J. McGovern and now employs more than 9,000 people worldwide. IDG publishes more than 290 computer publications in over 75 countries. More than 90 million people read one or more IDG publications each month.

Launched in 1990, IDG Books Worldwide is today the #1 publisher of best-selling computer books in the United States. We are proud to have received eight awards from the Computer Press Association in recognition of editorial excellence and three from Computer Currents' First Annual Readers' Choice Awards. Our best-selling ...For Dummies® series has more than 50 million copies in print with translations in 31 languages. IDG Books Worldwide, through a joint venture with IDG's Hi-Tech Beijing, became the first U.S. publisher to publish a computer book in the People's Republic of China. In record time, IDG Books Worldwide has become the first choice for millions of readers around the world who want to learn how to better manage their businesses.

Our mission is simple: Every one of our books is designed to bring extra value and skill-building instructions to the reader. Our books are written by experts who understand and care about our readers. The knowledge base of our editorial staff comes from years of experience in publishing, education, and journalism — experience we use to produce books to carry us into the new millennium. In short, we care about books, so we attract the best people. We devote special attention to details such as audience, interior design, use of icons, and illustrations. And because we use an efficient process of authoring, editing, and desktop publishing our books electronically, we can spend more time ensuring superior content and less time on the technicalities of making books.

You can count on our commitment to deliver high-quality books at competitive prices on topics you want to read about. At IDG Books Worldwide, we continue in the IDG tradition of delivering quality for more than 30 years. You'll find no better book on a subject than one from IDG Books Worldwide.

John J. Kilcullen
John Kilcullen
Chairman and CEO
IDG Books Worldwide, Inc.

**Eighth Annual
Computer Press
Awards ≥1992**

**Ninth Annual
Computer Press
Awards ≥1993**

**Tenth Annual
Computer Press
Awards ≥1994**

**Eleventh Annual
Computer Press
Awards ≥1995**

IDG is the world's leading IT media, research and exposition company. Founded in 1964, IDG had 1997 revenues of $2.05 billion and has more than 9,000 employees worldwide. IDG offers the widest range of media options that reach IT buyers in 75 countries representing 95% of worldwide IT spending. IDG's diverse product and services portfolio spans six key areas including print publishing, online publishing, expositions and conferences, market research, education and training, and global marketing services. More than 90 million people read one or more of IDG's 290 magazines and newspapers, including IDG's leading global brands — Computerworld, PC World, Network World, Macworld and the Channel World family of publications. IDG Books Worldwide is one of the fastest-growing computer book publishers in the world, with more than 700 titles in 36 languages. The "...For Dummies®" series alone has more than 50 million copies in print. IDG offers online users the largest network of technology-specific Web sites around the world through IDG.net (http://www.idg.net), which comprises more than 225 targeted Web sites in 55 countries worldwide. International Data Corporation (IDC) is the world's largest provider of information technology data, analysis and consulting, with research centers in over 41 countries and more than 400 research analysts worldwide. IDG World Expo is a leading producer of more than 168 globally branded conferences and expositions in 35 countries including E3 (Electronic Entertainment Expo), Macworld Expo, ComNet, Windows World Expo, ICE (Internet Commerce Expo), Agenda, DEMO, and Spotlight. IDG's training subsidiary, ExecuTrain, is the world's largest computer training company, with more than 230 locations worldwide and 785 training courses. IDG Marketing Services helps industry-leading IT companies build international brand recognition by developing global integrated marketing programs via IDG's print, online and exposition products worldwide. Further information about the company can be found at www.idg.com. 1/26/00

Dedication

To Rena and Rachel, who endured it all, with my deepest love.

Acknowledgments

A book is a miracle. The miracle is that all its pieces ultimately come together to create something meaningful and attractive. But like most miracles, a book takes hard work. For all its simplifying, *Photography For Dummies* is the sum of many people's hard work, and I'm grateful to them all. Families usually get thanked last, but mine comes first: my wonderful wife Rena, who sustained and organized me through unending months of double shifts, and my resilient daughter Rachel, who now gets back her silliest play-mate. Thanks and love also to my forbearing parents, Lorena and Francis Hart, who provided a writer's hideaway and commented on early text in their uniquely intelligent way.

Great thanks to *everyone* at IDG Books: most of all to my editor Kelly Ewing, who knew better than me how to structure the book, and whose unfailing good humor and organization are both powerful editorial tools; to Tami Booth, my Executive Editor, without whose encouragement, understanding, and perspective I could not have finished the job; to the book's many sharp-eyed copy editors, including Kim Darosett; to the equally sharp-eyed Shelley Lea, who oversaw the color section; and last but not least, Karen York, Project Coordinator. My agent, Mark Reiter of IMG Literary — as affable as he is connected, a rare combination — made the whole thing possible by calling me first.

Huge thanks to the able writers and photo industry friends who contributed to the book, including *Popular Photography* Senior Editor Pete Kolonia and Technology Editor Mike McNamara; Web maven Mason Resnick; and the inventive Elinor Stecker-Orel. But my biggest debt of gratitude is to *Popular Photography* Senior Editor Dan Richards, whose way with words is matched only by his point-and-shoot comprehension. Also many thanks to *Popular Photography/American Photo* Publishing Director Burt Keppler for his continuing help and wisdom, and to my good friend Dave Schonauer, Editor-in-Chief of *American Photo* magazine, who gave me the opportunity to learn all about this stuff, and who shares my skewed view of the photo world.

I'm extremely grateful for the generous support of the Eastman Kodak company, which supplied not just film, cameras, and pictures from its remarkable KINSA archive, but also the amazing expertise of its people. Such help always comes through individuals: among them, Michael More, whose love of culture makes him a corporate asset, and Terry McArdle, who threw his great intelligence and considerable energy behind the book. Thanks also to the many other helpful photo companies in this really not-so-big business; their dedicated press people provided both cameras and answers.

And last but decidedly not least in my gratitude are the many photographers who contributed pictures to *Photography For Dummies*. They are my friends, not just col-leagues — and all of them superb artists. They include John Isaac, Henry Horenstein, Allen Green, Jody Dole, Amos Chan, Shellburne Thurber, Bill Neill, Chris Rainier, Franklin Berger, Pete Kolonia, and Mark Ewing. Mark Harris shot top-notch example pictures at a moment's notice, and the gifted Pat O'Hara let me keep his lecture slides for months. This book is a tribute to the power of these photographers' vision — and to the simple pleasures of photography.

Publisher's Acknowledgments

We're proud of this book; please register your comments through our IDG Books Worldwide Online Registration Form located at http://my2cents.dummies.com.

Some of the people who helped bring this book to market include the following:

Acquisitions, Editorial, and Media Development

Senior Project Editor: Kelly Ewing

Executive Editor: Tammerly Booth

Copy Editors: Kim Darosett, Stacey Riebsomer

General Reviewer: Dan Richards

Editorial Manager: Colleen Rainsberger

Editorial Assistant: Darren Meiss

Production

Project Coordinator: Karen York

Layout and Graphics: Steve Arany, Lou Boudreau, Linda M. Boyer, J. Tyler Connor, Kelly Hardesty, Angela F. Hunckler, Jane E. Martin, Drew R. Moore, Brent Savage, Janet Seib, Michael A. Sullivan

Proofreaders: Christine Berman, Kelli Botta, Michelle Croninger, Rachel Garvey, Nancy Price, Rebecca Senninger, Ethel M. Winslow, Janet M. Withers

Indexer: Sharon Hilgenberg

General and Administrative

IDG Books Worldwide, Inc.: John Kilcullen, CEO

IDG Books Technology Publishing Group: Richard Swadley, Senior Vice President and Publisher; Walter R. Bruce III, Vice President and Publisher; Joseph Wikert, Vice President and Publisher; Mary Bednarek, Vice President and Director, Product Development; Andy Cummings, Publishing Director, General User Group; Mary C. Corder, Editorial Director; Barry Pruett, Publishing Director

IDG Books Consumer Publishing Group: Roland Elgey, Senior Vice President and Publisher; Kathleen A. Welton, Vice President and Publisher; Kevin Thornton, Acquisitions Manager; Kristin A. Cocks, Editorial Director

IDG Books Internet Publishing Group: Brenda McLaughlin, Senior Vice President and Publisher; Sofia Marchant, Online Marketing Manager

IDG Books Production for Branded Press: Debbie Stailey, Director of Production; Cindy L. Phipps, Manager of Project Coordination, Production Proofreading, and Indexing; Tony Augsburger, Manager of Prepress, Reprints, and Systems; Laura Carpenter, Production Control Manager; Shelley Lea, Supervisor of Graphics and Design; Debbie J. Gates, Production Systems Specialist; Robert Springer, Supervisor of Proofreading; Trudy Coler, Page Layout Manager; Troy Barnes, Page Layout Supervisor, Kathie Schutte, Senior Page Layout Supervisor; Michael Sullivan, Production Supervisor

Packaging and Book Design: Patty Page, Manager, Promotions Marketing

◆

The publisher would like to give special thanks to Patrick J. McGovern, without whom this book would not have been possible.

◆

Contents at a Glance

Introduction 1

Part I: What You Need to Take Pictures 7
Chapter 1: Getting to Know Your Point-and-Shoot 9
Chapter 2: Choosing a Film 37
Chapter 3: Working with Your Photofinisher 67

Part II: Getting the Most from Your Point-and-Shoot 103
Chapter 4: Pictures à la Mode 105
Chapter 5: Optical Options: Seeing through Your Camera 131
Chapter 6: The Lens and Focusing 151
Chapter 7: A Flash of Inspiration 167

Part III: The Art Part 189
Chapter 8: The Light Fantastic 191
Chapter 9: Composition 101 (Suitable for Framing) 209

Part IV: Don't Stop, I'm Shooting 225
Chapter 10: Capturing Your Life on Film 227
Chapter 11: Snapping Action 261
Chapter 12: Photographing Landscapes 281
Chapter 13: Have Camera, Will Travel 295

Part V: Into the Future: New Age Point-and-Shoots 309
Chapter 14: The Advanced Photo System 311
Chapter 15: Photography and Your Computer 329

Part VI: The Part of Tens 343
Chapter 16: Ten Things to Think about When Buying a Point-
and-Shoot Camera 345
Chapter 17: Ten Simple Ways to Make Your Pictures Better 353
Chapter 18: Ten Great Photographic Web Sites 357
Chapter 19: Ten Favorite Places to Take Pictures 363
Chapter 20: Ten Things to Try If Your Camera Won't Shoot.............................. 371
Appendix A: Impress Your Friends! A Short Glossary of Photo Jargon 375
Appendix B: Manufacturers, Distributors, and Retailers 383

Index 387

Book Registration Information .... Back of Book

Cartoons at a Glance

By Rich Tennant

page 103

page 7

page 189

page 309

page 225

page 343

Fax: 978-546-7747
E-mail: richtennant@the5thwave.com
World Wide Web: www.the5thwave.com

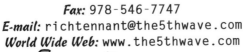

Table of Contents

Introduction 1
   About This Book 1
   Conventions Used in This Book 2
   Foolish Assumptions 3
   What You Can Skip 3
   How This Book Is Organized 3
      Part I: What You Need to Take Pictures 3
      Part II: Getting the Most from Your Point-and-Shoot 4
      Part III: The Art Part 4
      Part IV: Don't Stop, I'm Shooting 4
      Part V: Into the Future: New Age Point-and-Shoots 4
      Part VI: The Part of Tens 5
   Icons Used in This Book 5
   Where to Go from Here 6

Part I: What You Need to Take Pictures 7

   Chapter 1: Getting to Know Your Point-and-Shoot 9
   Point-and-Shoot Cameras 10
      35mm point-and-shoots 10
      Advanced Photo System point-and-shoots 10
      One-time-use point-and-shoots 10
      Digital point-and-shoots 12
   The Parts of Your Camera 12
   Batteries: The Pluses and Minuses 13
      Lithium batteries 14
      Pack an extra 15
      Recycling woes 15
      The good old AAs 16
      Loading batteries 16
   Loading Film 19
      Counting up — and down 24
      Fogging film 25
      Loading film into an Advanced Photo System camera 26
      Loading digital cameras 29
   Turning the Camera On — and Off 29
   Get a Grip: Holding Your Camera 30
   Rewinding Film 33

Chapter 2: Choosing a Film **37**

What's Your Film Type? 38
   Color print film 38
   Color slide film 41
      Getting good results with slide film 43
      Slide rules and exposure compensation 45
   Black-and-white film 46
      Which black-and-white film to choose? 48
      Chromogenic black and white 49
      The Ektamax option 50
A Question of Speed 51
   Film speed and grain 54
   Film speed and panoramic prints 55
   Film speed and shake 56
   Film speed and focal length 57
How Long a Roll Should You Buy? 58
Which Brand Should You Buy? 62
   Premium films 63
   Private label films 64
   Mail-order films and processing 65

Chapter 3: Working with Your Photofinisher **67**

Some Day My Prints Will Come 68
Types of Photofinishers 72
   Mass-market photofinishing 72
   The minilab 74
   The mail-order option 76
How to Get Good Prints 78
Finding a Lab 80
Photo Communications 101 82
Things That Can Go Wrong — and Do 83
Getting Reprints 90
The Match Game: Finding the Right Negative for a Reprint 92
Getting Enlargements 95
The Electronic Photofinishing Revolution 97
The Photo Kiosk 101

Part II: Getting the Most from Your Point-and-Shoot **103**

Chapter 4: Pictures à la Mode **105**

The Great Button Bazaar 105
Mastering Your Camera's Modes 107
Buttons to Push and Dials to Turn 108
Millions of Modes? 110
   Flash modes 111
   Print-format modes 113
   Drive modes 114

Focusing modes 119
Subject or picture modes 122
Metering modes 125
Creative modes 128
Getting in the Mode 129

Chapter 5: Optical Options: Seeing through Your Camera **131**
Changing the Picture 132
Do you have a zoom lens? 132
Zooming in versus zooming out 133
Going to Great Lengths 135
Going Wide — and Long 138
The whole wide world 140
The normal view 142
The telephoto touch 142
Getting close at telephoto settings 144
Telephoto settings and the lens aperture 146
Types of Point-And-Shoot Cameras — by Their Lenses 147
The single-focal-length (nonzoom) point-and-shoot 147
The compact-zoom point-and-shoot 148
The standard-zoom point-and-shoot 149
The long-zoom point-and-shoot 149

Chapter 6: The Lens and Focusing **151**
What Is Autofocusing? 152
Autofocus versus Fixed-Focus 153
The Focus Point: Where Your Camera Focuses 154
Locking the focus 155
Making sure your focus is locked 157
If you move, the focus doesn't 160
Infinity Lock: Focusing Far Away 160
Widening the Autofocus Horizon 161
The Commandments of Good Autofocusing 162
With all types of autofocus 162
With active autofocus 163
With passive autofocus 165

Chapter 7: A Flash of Inspiration **167**
Autoflash: No-Fault Photo Insurance 168
Button, Button, Where Is the Button? 170
Flash to Fill Shadows 172
When to use fill flash 173
When not to use fill flash 176
Flash-Off Mode: To Flash or Not to Flash 177
Slow Sync Is Not the Kitchen Sink 181
Red-Eye Reduction: Getting the Red Out 184
Preflash red-eye reduction systems 186
Prelamp red-eye reduction systems 187

Part III: The Art Part **189**

Chapter 8: The Light Fantastic **191**
How Light Creates Mood and Atmosphere 191
    The quality of light 192
    The direction of light 193
    The color of light 195
Coping with Hard Light 196
    Shooting in direct sun 197
    Preserving detail in hard light 197
        Use fill flash 199
        Increase the exposure 199
        Use a reflector 200
Capturing Light at the Right Time 201
    Midday blues 201
    Shooting early or late in the day 202
    Cloudy is beautiful 202
Shooting in Special Kinds of Light 202
    Window light 203
    Artificial light 205
    Backlight 207

Chapter 9: Composition 101 (Suitable for Framing) **209**
Composition Rules 210
Aiming versus Framing 210
Filling the Frame 212
Zooming versus Moving 213
Balancing Foreground and Background 216
Composing Off-Center 218
Changing Your Angle 219
Shifting Sideways 221
Rotating the Frame: Horizontals versus Verticals 221
Working the Subject 222

Part IV: Don't Stop, I'm Shooting **225**

Chapter 10: Capturing Your Life on Film **227**
Why Take Pictures? 228
Pictures Are for Sharing 229
Film Is Cheap 230
When to Shoot? 232
What You Need for Great People Photos 232
Expression and Gesture 234
    Relaxing your subject 235
    Getting formal 238

Planning your candids 241
    Make candids tell a story 242
    Candids and backgrounds 244
Use Flash for People Pictures 246
Zoom Settings for Portraits 246
    Long focal length portraits 246
    Wide-angle portraits 248
Photographing Children 248
    Know your child — and be ready 250
    Should kids look at the camera? 252
    Shoot from eye level — theirs 253
    Photo fashions for photogenic kids 254
Photographing Pets 254
Photographs as Family History 256
Ten Lame Excuses for Not Taking Along Your Camera
    (And Why They're Lame) 259

Chapter 11: Snapping Action **261**
You Don't Need Fancy Equipment to Shoot Action 261
Your Dawdling Point-and-Shoot Camera 262
The Anticipation Game: The Art of Prefocusing 263
Frozen or Blurred Action? 265
    Freezing action with fast shutter speeds 266
    Finding the decisive moment 269
Tips for Better Action-Freezing 270
    Capturing action with panning 272
    Freezing action with flash 273
    Showing action with blur 275
    Combining stop action and blur 276
The Last Word on Action 277

Chapter 12: Photographing Landscapes **281**
Landscapes Close to Home 282
The Lens and Landscapes 283
    Capturing more background with a wide-angle focal length ... 284
    Shooting wide-open spaces without wide-angle 285
Landscapes and Composition 286
    How to place the horizon line 286
    Move yourself for a better view 287
    Should you shoot a horizontal? Or vertical? 287
Choosing a Landscape Print Shape 288
    A print shape for wider scenes 288
    A print shape for panoramic views 288
Adding a Sense of Scale 289
Seeing the Light 290
Exploring Seasonal Changes 290
Shooting Cityscapes 292

Chapter 13: Have Camera, Will Travel 295

Planning Your Trip 296
Weather or Not. . . . Finding Out about Your Destination 296
Deciding What to Bring 298
   Taking the right camera 299
      Don't forget to test your camera 300
      Don't succumb to New Camera Syndrome! 300
   Film for wanderers 301
   Tripods: Three legs are better than two 302
   Don't pack it, bag it 303
Scenes from a Voyage 303
   Choosing what to photograph 304
   Good things to shoot in bad weather 304
   Photographing the locals 305

Part V: Into the Future: New Age Point-and-Shoots 309

Chapter 14: The Advanced Photo System 311

Advanced Photo System Advantages 312
Advanced Photo System Print Formats 313
   How to select your print format 315
   What shape will my pictures be? 316
   Which format to choose? 317
APS Printing and Reprinting 319
   How APS lets you change your mind about print shape 320
   Finding the right negative the painless APS way 320
Loading Advanced Photo System Film 323
Types of Advanced Photo System Film 324
The Mid-Roll Change Feature 325
APS Printing Refinements 327
The Advanced Photo System and Your Computer 327

Chapter 15: Photography and Your Computer 329

The Digital Details 330
Getting Pictures into Your Computer 332
   Having your photofinisher scan your pictures 332
      Floppy disks 332
      CD-ROMs 333
      The World Wide Web 333
   Scanning photos yourself 333
Taking Pictures with a Digital Camera 334
Downloading Photographs from a Digital Point-And-Shoot 337
Imaging Software: Digital Magic 337

Getting Pictures out of Your Computer 341
    E-mailing pictures 341
    Putting pictures on the Web... 341
    Printing digital images yourself 342

Part VI: The Part of Tens 343

Chapter 16: Ten Things to Think about When Buying a Point-and-Shoot Camera 345

Don't Buy More Camera Than You Need 346
How Much Do You Want to Spend? 346
Who Will Be Using the Camera? 347
What Subjects Will the User Be Shooting? 348
Do You Want a Digital Camera or a Film Camera? 348
Do You Want a 35mm Point-and-Shoot or an APS Point-and-Shoot? 349
Do You Want a Zooming or Nonzooming Model? 349
What Zoom Range Do You Need? 350
What Features Do You Want? 351
Is the Camera Comfortable to Hold and Operate? 352
Is the Viewfinder Easy to Look Through? 352

Chapter 17: Ten Simple Ways to Make Your Pictures Better 353

Capture the Moment 354
Don't Use the Viewfinder like a Gun Sight 354
Get Close 354
Shoot from a Low or High Angle 355
Use Flash Outdoors 355
Keep Flash Backgrounds Close 355
Use a Fast Film 356
Place the Main Subject Off-Center 356
Move from Side to Side 356
Experiment with the Horizon Line 356
Take Lots of Pictures 356

Chapter 18: Ten Great Photographic Web Sites 357

Kodak's Guide to Better Pictures 357
Popular Photography Online 358
The Family Photo Historian 358
Kodak Picture Network 359
The Mining Company 360
Phil Greenspun's Guide to Point-and-Shoot Cameras 360
Collected Visions 361
Fodor's Focus on Photography 361
PhotoNet 362
Photography Information Council (PIC) 362

Chapter 19: Ten Favorite Places to Take Pictures 363

Chincoteague Island, Eastern Shore, Virginia 364
Cadillac Ranch, Amarillo, Texas 364
Bryce Canyon National Park, Utah 365
Las Vegas, Nevada 365
White Birch Forest, Pictured Rocks National Lakeshore, Michigan 366
The Staten Island Ferry, Battery Park, New York 367
Paradise Meadow, Mount Rainier National Park, Washington 368
Vietnam Veterans Memorial, Washington, D.C. 368
Lucy the Elephant, Margate City, New Jersey 369
The Santuario de Nuestra Señor de Esquipulas, Chimayo,
    New Mexico 369
Anhinga Trail, Everglades National Park, Florida 369
The Salton Sea, Southern California 370

Chapter 20: Ten Things to Try If Your Camera Won't Shoot 371

Turn the Camera On Correctly 372
Reload the Film 372
Replace the Battery 372
Make Sure the Battery Is Correctly Installed 372
Clean the Battery Contacts 373
Check the Flash-Ready Lamp 373
Step Back from the Subject 374
Make Sure Your Digital Camera Has Finished Saving the Previous
    Picture 374
Rewind the Film and Insert a New Roll 374

Appendix A: Impress Your Friends! A Short Glossary
of Photo Jargon 375

Appendix B: Manufacturers, Distributors, and Retailers 383

Index 387

Book Registration Information .... Back of Book

Introduction

. . . .

*I*f I asked you to name your most valuable possession, what would you choose? At first, you might say your wedding ring, your car, or your house. But after further thought (and a little coaxing from me), you would probably arrive at this conclusion: your photographs. Unlike most other earthly belongings, your personal photographs have a worth that can't be measured in dollars and cents. They're the one thing you would grab on the way out of a burning house — an irreplaceable record of the life you lead, of friends and family, and of the occasions with which you mark passing years. Photographs are the visual handmaiden to memory. They let you possess that elusive property called time.

The funny thing is, most people aren't entirely happy with their photographs. You may be one of these slightly disheartened shooters. You probably think your pictures could be better — if not more artistic, then more colorful, more interesting, or just plain sharper. You may wonder why you're not getting better results with your point-and-shoot camera, one of those auto-everything models that are supposed to make photography foolproof.

But if you've been blaming your camera for your photographic unhappiness, I'm here to tell you that it's the least likely culprit. Today's point-and-shoot cameras are remarkably reliable devices, especially considering all the stuff that they do, and yours is probably doing its job pretty well. So why aren't your pictures better? You may just not know the right button to push — and believe me, your point-and-shoot has a magic button or two. You may just not be using the right kind of film. Or you may not be getting the most from your photofinishing, a process that you have more control over than you think. But the main secret to better photographs is knowing what to shoot, when to shoot it, and how to shoot it: how to squeeze your subject meaningfully into the little patch of visual real estate called a print. You need *Photography For Dummies* because it lets you in on this secret.

About This Book

If you think you can't get better pictures from your point-and-shoot, consider this: The most important photographs in this book were made with point-and-shoot cameras and reproduced directly from 4 x 6-inch commercial prints. You do *not* need a fancy single-lens reflex (SLR) camera — those bulky, system-style models that take interchangeable lenses — to get good photographs. The problem is, nearly every book on how to make better pictures assumes that you're using a single-lens reflex. This focus on SLRs is a mystery to me, given that point-and-shoot cameras now outsell those models by close to 15 to one.

This book is different. *Photography For Dummies assumes that you're using a point-and-shoot camera for all your pictures.* In fact, this book may well be the most complete guide available to taking pictures with a modern point-and-shoot camera (if I do say so myself). But even if you *are* an SLR user — and some avid point-and-shooters still like to get out their big guns — you can actually get more help from this book than from techier volumes. Why? Because most SLR cameras can now be operated in an entirely "point-and-shoot" manner, and that's the way most people use them. And because the better part of photographic skill has nothing to do with pushing buttons or turning dials.

Conventions Used in This Book

When I use the term *point-and-shoot,* I mean any of four different types of cameras. One is the 35mm point-and-shoot, which takes those familiar, funny-looking little cassettes with the spool and film strip poking out of them. (35mm is by far the most popular film in history, and most point-and-shoots are 35mm models.) The second type of camera in this book's mix is the Advanced Photo System (APS) point-and-shoot, which combines the best of point-and-shoot operation with an ingenious new interlinked film and photofinishing system. The third camera type is the one-time-use point-and-shoot, a streamlined model designed to expose a single roll of film, available in both 35mm and APS versions, and in stock almost anywhere chewing gun is sold. And the fourth camera type is the digital point-and-shoot, which, unlike the other three types, creates its pictures electronically — that is, without film.

This is important: Much if not most of what you read in this book applies to *any* of these four types of cameras.

If you read anything else about point-and-shoot cameras, you may notice two other terms for them kicking around. One term is *compact* cameras. The other is *lens/shutter* cameras. Neither term is as apt as *point-and-shoot,* and I don't use either one in this book. Point-and-shoot cameras sometimes aren't that compact, and plenty of non-point-and-shoot models have shutters in their lenses. (What's a shutter? See Chapter 2.)

Foolish Assumptions

Photography For Dummies assumes that you're using a point-and-shoot camera for your photographs. But this book is just as noteworthy for what it *doesn't* assume. This book does not assume that you have any prior knowledge of photography. It does not assume that you know the difference between a shutter speed and the speed of light. It does not assume that you know the difference between telephoto and television. This book just assumes that you want to take better point-and-shoot pictures.

What You Can Skip

This book is not a novel. You don't have to read it from cover to cover to get better pictures. Open it to any page, and you can find useful information that doesn't presume any prior reading, let alone prior knowledge. So you can skip around. And you can skip the sidebars and the parts marked "Technical Stuff" entirely, if you like. I've made the book this way for two reasons: One, because my editors told me to; and two, because it's actually how I like to read novels.

How This Book Is Organized

If you want to take better pictures, you have to take lots of pictures. And taking lots of pictures is the *only* way that you can see for yourself the actual effect of the things this book asks you to try. So before I get into the nuts and bolts and pushbuttons of photographic craft, I do the basics, giving you just enough to get started shooting. Then after the nuts and bolts — after I basically tell you how many nuts and bolts you need, and how many you can stick in your mental basement — I get into the art and adventure of point-and-shoot photography, and how to shoot what you love.

Part I: What You Need to Take Pictures

This part helps you through the steps and choices that go into just taking that first picture on a roll: how to choose a film (much simpler than you'd think), how to load the film cassette into the camera (no big sweat), and even how to hold the camera and press the shutter button. (Yes, there are right ways and wrong ways!) It also offers a complete guide to dealing with your photofinisher — a far more important factor in getting good results than most people realize.

Part II: Getting the Most from Your Point-and-Shoot

Read this part, and those buttons and dials you may now be afraid to push and turn won't intimidate you any more. Here, you find out about *modes* — the different settings that make your camera do different things. But you also discover, depending on your particular point-and-shoot model, that many modes are best ignored! The exception is flash modes, the most important modes of all — which is why your camera's built-in flash gets a whole chapter to itself. Of course, you can't get a picture at all without a lens, so your lens gets two chapters of its own. In one, I explain why you have to *help* your autofocus camera focus the lens. In the other, I answer the important question "To zoom or not to zoom?"

Part III: The Art Part

More than anything, photographic artistry depends on these two skills: recognizing and exploiting the opportunities that light presents every day, and applying design strategies that give your subjects a visually appealing form. Think light is beyond your control? It isn't, and this part explains how to work with it. Think you can't compose in a way that's suitable for framing? You can. In this part's two chapters, you find powerful but simple suggestions for photographic "seeing."

Part IV: Don't Stop, I'm Shooting

This part gets more focused, explaining how to shoot specific kinds of subjects — your own life first and foremost. And because people are probably the most important thing in your life, I begin with them. You *can* get shots that both flatter people and capture their personalities, and this part is where you find out how. (Just don't tell your local portrait photographer!) And because some people in your life may be moving pretty fast (kids, for example), this part is also where you find out how to stop action — photographically, at least. More contemplative photographers can seek this part's guidance on shooting landscapes. And because nearly everyone travels, whether across state lines or to the far side of the world, the special considerations of travel photography — visual and practical — are also covered.

Part V: Into the Future: New Age Point-and-Shoots

And now for a forward look at the new directions point-and-shoot photography is taking with both the Advanced Photo System (APS) and the link between your pictures and your home computer. In this part, you get the full scoop on the features and benefits of the Advanced Photo System — how APS point-and-shoots and photofinishing not only improve the quality of your photography, but make it easier and more fun, too. You also find out how digital point-and-shoots dispense with film altogether, allowing you to put your pictures directly into your computer for retouching and printing, not to mention e-mailing and posting to the World Wide Web for all to see.

Part VI: The Part of Tens

The glue that holds this part together is tens: everything from ten great places to take pictures to ten great photographically oriented Web sites. Troubleshooting tips and camera-buying tidbits are also here for the plucking. Last but not least: the top ten ways to make your pictures better. You also find out how to contact camera makers with your questions and problems, and I translate some of those funny-sounding photo terms into plain English.

Icons Used in This Book

The margins of this book are wide for a reason: They contain icons — cute little symbols — that identify particular kinds of photo hints and help. (No connection to the icons that your camera uses to indicate settings!) Here's what each icon means:

Follow this icon's advice (always simple and straightforward), and your pictures should hit the mark.

This icon's fuzziness suggests one possible consequence (blurred pictures) of committing the sorts of photographic *faux pas* that it describes.

I recommend picture-taking experiments throughout this book, highlighted by this icon. Call them exercises — sort of like photo aerobics.

Information for people who want to know photography's *whys* along with its *hows,* this stuff is really never very technical — so I hope everyone reads it.

The standard symbol for the Advanced Photo System (you find it on all APS point-and-shoots), the APS icon highlights text about this exciting new way of taking pictures.

Last but decidedly not least, this icon directs you toward the book's color section, and to a great picture illustrating that particular point.

Where to Go from Here

Where to go from here depends on where you are — both physically and photographically. If you're sitting on a plane heading toward a vacation destination, you could start with Chapter 13, which is dedicated to travel photography. (You could also check out Chapter 12 for tips on shooting exotic landscapes.) If you're sitting in your kitchen, and never seem to get away, try Chapter 10, which is about all the photographic possibilities of staying at home.

If you're truly a photographic novice, or if you've just bought your first serious point-and-shoot camera, then start with Chapter 1 (and don't forget the film and batteries). If you're an old point-and-shoot hand, you can skip the hands-on stuff in the first half of the book (Parts I and II) and go straight to the art and applications of photographic craft (Parts III and IV). Just want to have fun? Go directly to The Part of Tens, where you'll find photographic hot spots (both real and virtual) and pointers (both amusing and practical).

Oh, and any time you need help with a photo term, turn to Appendix A for a definition — but don't think you have to master the medium's unique language. Fortunately, you don't have to know much more than the equivalent of *Hello, Goodbye, Please,* and *Thank You* — and sometimes *Smile* — to get the most from your point-and-shoot camera.

Part I
What You Need to Take Pictures

The 5th Wave   By Rich Tennant

"I know I don't need a flash in this light, but it stuns them into inactivity long enough for me to compose subsequent shots."

In this part . . .

You need three things to take pictures: your point-and-shoot camera, some film, and photofinishing. So this part's three chapters introduce you to those three things. Of course, your camera may need no introduction — but I still take you through the steps required just to get to that first frame. Why? Because if you're like most photographers, you find some aspect of the process intimidating, and I want to unintimidate you.

I also talk about what film you should buy. Those of you whose eyes glaze over as you stand in front of a camera store film counter will be shocked — *shocked* — at the simplicity of the choice. And you'll be at least *surprised* by how much control you have over the way that your pictures are printed, even though the printing is done by a machine. Hey, machines are meant to work for *people* — your point-and-shoot included!

Chapter 1

Getting to Know Your Point-and-Shoot

· ·

In This Chapter

▶ Installing batteries

▶ Loading film

▶ Turning on the camera

▶ How to hold your camera

▶ What to do if you accidentally open the camera back

▶ Rewinding do's and don'ts

· ·

*Y*our point-and-shoot camera is practically an invitation to just start taking pictures. A wonder of automation, it uses advanced electronics and tiny motors to quickly execute the many separate steps that photographers used to have to do manually each time they wanted to take a picture. Point-and-shoots automatically advance the film from shot to shot. They automatically compute the correct exposure — the exact amount of light that your film needs to properly record the subject — and adjust camera settings accordingly. They automatically turn on the flash in dim light. And they automatically focus the lens.

Actually, your particular point-and-shoot may not perform every one of these functions. And which ones it does perform depends partly (though not entirely) on what type of point-and-shoot you have. So I begin this chapter — a chapter otherwise devoted to getting you started taking pictures as quickly as possible — by describing the four different types of point-and-shoot cameras. The good news: You really don't need to know what kind of point-and-shoot camera you have to make it point and shoot. But knowing what kind of point-and-shoot you have can actually help you make better pictures. That is, after all, why you're reading this book — right?

Point-and-Shoot Cameras

Like people, point-and-shoots have more in common than they do differences. This is especially true of the way you operate the cameras — what you push, slide, or twist to make them do specific things. But while they're operated in pretty much the same way, point-and-shoots differ both in the way the image is captured and in the mechanical and electronic complexity they bring to the job. Those differences make it possible to divide these cameras into four main types.

35mm point-and-shoots

Granddaddy of the point-and-shoot movement, the 35mm point-and-shoot uses 35mm film — the film that comes in the funny-looking little cassette with the perforated tongue sticking out at you. You grab that tongue of film to start the roll through the camera, as this chapter explains in detail. 35mm point-and-shoots come in every form from cheapo check-out counter specials to expensive, full-featured models that rival 35mm single-lens reflexes (those professional-style system cameras) in their sophistication.

Advanced Photo System point-and-shoots

The next generation of point-and-shoot camera, Advanced Photo System (APS) models usually look just like their 35mm counterparts. They take a special, smaller-than-35mm film cassette that not only lets manufacturers create smaller cameras, but that also simplifies film loading, improves the quality of photofinishing, makes storage and reprinting easier, and (most fun) gives you a shot-by-shot choice of three different print sizes, which you actually select with a switch on the camera. See Chapter 14 for complete details on the Advanced Photo System.

One-time-use point-and-shoots

They're everywhere. From drugstore counters to Disney World, one-time-use cameras are by far the most popular type of point-and-shoot, outselling reloadable models by more than six to one. These inexpensive (usually $7 to $15, depending on the type) models are in some respects the ultimate point-and-shoot. You don't have to figure out how to insert film, for example, because they come preloaded with a roll. (In fact, you can get them in both 35mm and Advanced Photo System versions.) The same goes for batteries, also preinstalled. You needn't master any pushbuttons except for the shutter button and the flash button, if your model has a flash at all. You don't even have to remember to bring your camera along, because you can buy a one-time-use camera on the way or on the spot. After you finish shooting a roll, you just give the camera to the photofinisher — no rewinding necessary. And last, but not least, one-time-use cameras are the only cameras with complete instructions printed on them! (See the sidebar "The pros and cons of one-time-use cameras" for details.)

TIP

The pros and cons of one-time-use cameras

Did you accidentally leave your regular point-and-shoot at home? Don't want to subject it to sand or salt spray? Is someone else in the family using it? Don't want to risk theft? Then get a one-time-use camera. One-time-use cameras are worry-free and convenient, and now come in many varieties: underwater models, sports models, panoramic models; models with or without built-in flash; 35mm or Advanced Photo System models (see figure). (One-time-use Advanced Photo System models now give you a shot-by-shot choice of the system's different print shapes!) And here's good news: According to Kodak, more than 80% of one-time-use cameras are recycled, including the battery, flash, and most of the plastics.

For all their fun and convenience, one-time-use cameras don't offer the automation, versatility, or quality of most reloadable point-and-shoots. They don't have a film-winding motor, for example, so you have to advance the film manually each time that you take a picture; you simply turn a grooved thumbwheel to the right until it stops. And unlike most reloadable point-and-shoots, a one-time-use camera can't decide when flash is needed. (Some models don't even *have* a built-in flash because they're intended for outdoor use.) *You* have to decide if flash is necessary, and then if it is, push a flash-activation button that is usually on the front of the camera. For more on one-time-use cameras and flash, see Chapter 7.

Yet the point-and-shoot simplicity of a single-use camera makes it the ultimate test of your photographic eye. Because you have little or none of the control possible with reloadable point-and-shoots, the success of a picture depends almost entirely on nontechnical things: the moment that you capture; the colors, tones, shapes, and textures that describe it; and the effectiveness of your composition.

Even if you're planning to shoot outdoors with a one-time-use camera, I suggest getting a model with a built-in flash. (See the figure in the "The pros and cons of one-time-use cameras" sidebar.) Firing the flash when you're shooting in bright light helps lighten dark shadows, for more flattering pictures of people. (See Chapter 7 for details on using flash.) And having flash available lets you keep shooting when outdoor light gets low or you move into deep shade.

Don't buy and shoot with a one-time-use camera simply because you're too intimidated by your regular, reloadable point-and-shoot. Read this chapter, and your regular point-and-shoot won't scare you anymore!

Digital point-and-shoots

Unlike the other types of point-and-shoot cameras, a digital point-and-shoot neither contains nor accepts film. How can it capture photographs without film? The same way video camcorders do: With a permanently-installed electronic light-sensing "chip." But unlike most camcorders, a digital camera stores photographs as digital files that can be downloaded directly to a computer for retouching, e-mailing, and printing out. Yet in terms of actual operation, digital point-and-shoots are essentially like film-using cameras — and again, most of the shooting advice in this and other chapters applies to them as well. For specifics on working with digital models, see Chapter 15.

The Parts of Your Camera

Here are a couple of things to remember whenever you feel you're not quite getting the hang of operating your camera. First, for all its pushbuttons, dials, windows, and flashing lights, your camera is basically a lightproof box. It's lightproof to protect the film inside from any light other than what the lens gathers from the subject and uses to form a picture on the film's surface. And second, the camera is basically an extension of your eye — a window on your subject. In fact, to view your subject you look through a little window on the camera back called the *viewfinder*. For more about what you see when you look through the camera's viewfinder, read Chapter 5.

Now for those pushbuttons. When it comes to the design and location of your point-and-shoot's controls, little standardization exists. In pictorial terms, two very different-looking controls in two very different places may do pretty much the same thing. But whatever the control configuration, all but the least expensive models usually have an LCD panel — a digital display on the top or side of the camera — that indicates what settings you're making. Figures 1-1 and 1-2 show the location of camera controls and other basic camera features for a typical Advanced Photo System point-and-shoot and a typical 35mm point-and-shoot. The purposes of these controls and features are spelled out in Part II, and you can refer back to these figures for help in locating specific parts and buttons. But your camera may be different from the models shown — and the only way to know is to check your camera manual.

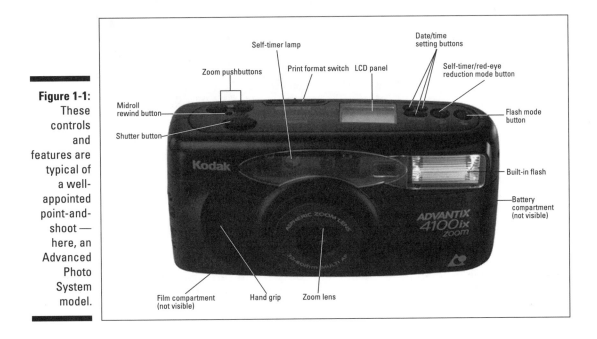

Figure 1-1:
These controls and features are typical of a well-appointed point-and-shoot — here, an Advanced Photo System model.

Your camera manual shows you which controls do what, and where they are. Sometimes it loses a little in translation, but your manual is an important photographic tool. It doesn't tell you how to take better point-and-shoot pictures; that's the job of this book. What it does tell you is where to find and how to operate the camera controls that can *help* you take better pictures.

Batteries: The Pluses and Minuses

Point-and-shoot cameras are chock full of little motors that do everything from advancing and rewinding your film to zooming your lens. These motors are highly efficient, but they consume quite a bit of electricity. Makers of kids' toys have a simple solution — just use more batteries. But because a point-and-shoot camera must remain compact, manufacturers have devised a different strategy: use smaller, more powerful, longer-life batteries.

Figure 1-2:
The photographer's view of a point-and-shoot's controls and parts — here, on a typical full-featured 35mm model.

*Labels in figure:*
Red-eye reduction mode button
Flash mode button
Date/time setting button
Drive mode button
LCD panel
Midroll rewind button
Shutter button
Diopter-adjustment dial
On/off switch
Zoom lever
Viewfinder eyepiece
Focus-OK lamp (green)
Flash-ready lamp (red or orange)
Camera back latch
Camera back   Panorama switch   Tripod socket (not visible)   Film check window

Lithium batteries

Many, if not most, point-and-shoots are powered by special *lithium batteries.* Made for use in cameras, these cells are shorter than the familiar AA battery, but a lot more expensive.

The most common type of lithium battery, a three-volt cell that goes by proprietary designations such as KL123A, CR123A, or DL123A (a 123A is always in there), costs as much as $7. The shorter, thinner three-volt CR2 lithium battery — not as common but used by more and more ultracompact point-and-shoots — costs about the same. What's more, some cameras need two three-volt lithium batteries. And some take double-barreled six-volt batteries, either the 223A or, infrequently, the bigger 2CR5. These batteries cost a whopping $13. Their prices can go even higher, depending on what the market will bear — and in tony or touristy areas, it will bear a lot.

Fortunately, lithium batteries last longer than AA cells. (See the section "The good old AAs," later in this chapter.) But the number of pictures you actually get out of a lithium battery depends on the power needs of your camera; the more motorized it is, the fewer the rolls. Most models give you within the range of 10 to 25 24-exposure rolls per battery, assuming that you use flash about half the time. (Lithiums also don't conk out in freezing weather as fast as regular AAs, a good thing if you like taking pictures in the snow.)

When you need to buy a new battery, always bring the old one — or better yet, your camera — to the store. Given all the different types of batteries, not knowing which type you need can drive clerks crazy. And by bringing your camera to the store and putting in the new battery there, you're immediately reassured that the new battery brings your camera up to snuff.

Unfortunately, lithium batteries are hard to find in out-of-the-way places. Suburban camera shops carry them (though even in the suburbs, you may have trouble finding the CR2). But if your camera loses power in Timbuktu, you're in trouble. Even if you can find the right lithium battery, you may have to pay a black-market price for it.

Pack an extra

If your point-and-shoot takes lithium batteries, you should always keep an extra one (or two, if that's what the model requires) on hand. To prolong the battery's shelf life, keep it in the refrigerator, in its original packaging inside a baggie. (Never freeze it.) Just avoid putting the battery straight into your camera from the refrigerator; give it a half hour to warm up.

Take an extra battery with you to weddings, graduations, bar mitzvahs, or any other occasions that you want to photograph. These events are flash-intensive, and using flash a lot reduces the number of pictures you get from a battery. If you take an extra battery along, you don't have to stop shooting if the one in your camera peters out. Just be sure to refresh your memory about how to install it, in case you need to do it fast. (See "Loading batteries," later in this chapter, for the details.)

Recycling woes

As a battery weakens, your camera's flash takes longer to *recycle* — to recharge itself for the next flash picture. (See Chapter 7 for more on flash recycling.) This sluggishness becomes a practical problem if, as with most point-and-shoots, your camera won't let you shoot until the flash has mostly recycled. Have you ever tried to take a picture right after turning on the camera or to take flash pictures in quick succession, only to find that when you press the shutter button it just doesn't respond — and you have to keep pressing and pressing to get it to fire the camera? Sometimes the problem is due to the camera's inability to focus, but more often than not, it's caused by an overly long recycling time — the direct result of a low battery.

You can turn off the flash (which otherwise powers up automatically every time you turn on the camera) to sidestep this problem. But I think flash is one of the most valuable photographic tools on your point-and-shoot, and I encourage you to use it generously — even outdoors! So please read Chapter 7 for ways to deal with flash recycling woes and to find out about the flash-ready lamp, which alerts you when the flash is ready to fire again.

If your camera's shutter button won't let you take a picture, don't keep bearing down on it. The camera may still be recycling the flash, preventing you from shooting to reduce the chance of a bad picture. Release the pressure, wait a few seconds, and then press again.

The good old AAs

Some point-and-shoots use AA (or AAA) batteries, the same size that goes into most battery-powered gizmos. These models tend to be the less expensive variety, and they economize further by avoiding the need for special lithium cells. If you have such a camera, be sure to use alkaline AA (or AAA) batteries rather than the standard cheapo batteries. Alkalines last many times longer than regular batteries. Some models actually accept both AA alkalines *or* three-volt lithiums. Now *there's* a great idea, especially if you're going to Timbuktu. (Pack extra AAs anyway.)

If your camera takes AA batteries and you feel guilty about throwing them away, you can get rechargeable AA cells. Some digital point-and-shoots actually come with rechargeables and a charger. (A few models use video-style rechargeable batteries, avoiding the problem altogether.) Purchase an inexpensive plug-in AA recharger and at least two sets of cells — four cells if your camera takes two batteries, eight cells if it takes four. That way, you can alternate charging them and always have a freshly charged set.

Loading batteries

If you've ever had to figure out where to stick batteries in your child's latest electronic acquisition, then loading batteries in your point-and-shoot shouldn't be a challenge. Turn off your camera when you install the batteries; otherwise, it may go crazy opening and closing its lens. (Some cameras turn themselves off after you install new batteries, so you have to turn them back on to shoot.)

With big point-and-shoot models, you typically have to open a latched cover on the camera bottom to install batteries. On more compact models, the battery compartment is often under a door or flap incorporated into the side or grip of the camera (see Figure 1-3). Sometimes you have to pry open such doors with a coin. This design is annoying when you don't have any change and break a fingernail trying to do it.

Figure 1-3:
This point-and-shoot's battery compartment is on the side; others' are in the bottom.

AA batteries and digital point-and-shoots

AA batteries have found a new home in digital point-and-shoot cameras, which usually need four of them. (Check out Chapter 15 for more on digital point-and-shoots.) The reason digital point-and-shoots don't take the kinds of lithium batteries used by film models, as far as I can tell, is that these newfangled cameras have enormous power needs — so special lithium batteries would make them prohibitively expensive to operate. As it is, most models eat alkaline AAs like they're going out of style.

The big power drain in these cameras is their external, video-style color LCDs — in effect, little flat-screen TVs. These mini-monitors are designed not just for video-style playback of pictures that you've already shot, but also for viewing and composing your subject while you're shooting. With some models, you *have* to use the monitor for shooting — and every minute it's on, even if you're not actually taking pictures, it's sucking your batteries dry. So if your model makes you shoot with the color LCD, turn the camera on *only when you're ready to take pictures*. Turn it off as soon as you're done shooting. This habit extends the life of the batteries.

Other digital point-and-shoots have both a regular window-type viewfinder *and* a color LCD. If your camera has both and you want to get more life out of your batteries, shoot with the regular viewfinder and save the color LCD for playback. Oh, and if you're taking your digital point-and-shoot to an occasion — or on a trip — pack at least two changes of batteries.

Actually, you can do something else about that digital drain: Get *lithium* AA batteries. They look the same as regular AA batteries, but they last up to three times as long. Alas, they're also three times as expensive as alkaline AAs. But you don't have to change them half as often, which means you're less likely to see a great photo opportunity disappear before your eyes as you struggle with batteries. Lithium AAs are especially valuable with digital cameras that have color LCDs, but you certainly can use them in your regular film point-and-shoot if it accepts AAs.

When you use flash with digital point-and-shoot cameras that have external color monitors, they consume batteries even more quickly. But the ten or more seconds digital point-and-shoots often make you wait before taking the next shot isn't usually battery-related: During this interval, the camera is processing the information from the light-sensing "chip" that actually captures the image.

More annoying are camera-bottom battery covers that you open by loosening a screw. (You need a coin for this type, too.) And most annoying are battery covers that aren't hinged. They come off completely when you unscrew them. If you have one of these covers, don't change batteries when you're standing over a sewer grate, in a field of tall grass, or on a pier!

Whether you're loading four AA cells or just a single lithium, make sure that the batteries are correctly oriented as you insert them. You'll find a diagram and/or plus and minus markings, usually within the compartment or on the inside of the door. The bump end of the battery is its positive (+) terminal; the flat end is its negative (–) terminal. The batteries also have plus and minus symbols on their sides. AA (and AAA cells) usually don't go in all facing the same way; you may have to reverse every other cell. Always follow your camera's diagram.

If you don't install batteries in their correct orientation, your camera won't start up when you try to turn it on. If this happens, remove the batteries, reinsert them correctly, and then try to turn the camera on again.

If your camera doesn't turn on and you're sure the batteries are correctly installed, then the problem may be that the batteries have lost their punch from sitting on a shelf too long. Which brings me to the battery icon. If your camera has an LCD panel, the icon tells you when battery power is low.

After you turn on your camera or load film, your camera may display a battery-shaped icon, usually in a corner of the LCD panel, if it has an LCD panel. (See Chapter 4 for more on the LCD panel.) If the icon's shape is fully darkened, the battery has sufficient power. If it's half darkened, you've already used a good portion of its juice — and may have noticed already that the flash recycling time is increasing. If the icon is barely filled in and/or blinking, you need a new battery. (See Figure 1-4.) Many models won't display the icon at all until the battery is on its way out.

Figure 1-4:
Typical battery power icons.

Power sufficient

Power low

Change battery

Some models may display battery status all the time. And other models may have a pushbutton battery check. Pushing the button makes a light glow. But however your camera displays battery status, if it does, check the status regularly. If you're planning to shoot a special event or going on a trip, check it before you go. If the battery needs replacing, do it now.

By the way, changing batteries when film is in the camera is perfectly okay. The LCD panel goes blank during the change. Even though the LCD is battery-dependent, the camera "remembers" how many pictures you've taken — or how many are left, depending on your model — and restores the display after you power up again. Models with mechanical counters remain unaffected. The camera ordinarily *doesn't* remember specific settings that you previously made, however. (See Chapter 4 for more on setting camera modes.)

If you have a roll of film in the camera, be sure to leave the old battery in it until you're ready to put in a new one. Left too long without a battery, the camera may forget how many pictures have been taken.

Models with *quartz date capability,* which allows them to imprint the time and/or date on your prints, generally do not use the camera's main battery to keep time. They use a tiny *button cell* — a watch battery — that either comes with the camera or is factory-installed. This battery usually lasts many years. You can replace it after it dies, though some models may need to be returned to the manufacturer for this service. Check your manual! (And see Chapter 3 for the pros and cons of putting the time or date on the front of your pictures.)

If you don't use your camera for long periods of time — a couple of months or more — remove the batteries to prevent the possibility that they start to leak corrosive fluids. (Just remember that you lose the frame count — but then you shouldn't be leaving film that long in the camera anyway!) Leakage, most likely with AA batteries, can seriously damage your camera's innards. The solution: Take pictures more often!

Loading Film

Probably the single greatest source of photographic anxiety, loading film is much easier than it used to be — and, thanks to point-and-shoot innovation, easier than most people think. The Advanced Photo System's near-foolproof film cassette and drop-in automatic loading makes something easy even easier, and I get to those advantages shortly. (Also see Chapter 14 for more on the Advanced Photo System.)

But first, here's all that you ever need to know about loading film into a 35mm point-and-shoot. Nothing gives away an amateur like tentative or prolonged film loading. Master this stuff, and you'll look like a pro.

Most 35mm point-and-shoots have automatic film loading. After you close its back, the camera automatically advances the film to the first frame. But what cows people is the film *leader* — the little strip of film that protrudes from the cassette's lightproof lip (see Figure 1-5). The leader starts out perforated on both sides (as is the film inside the cassette), but tapers to a short half-width strip with perforations only on one side. After the cassette is in position inside the camera, you pull the leader across to the film *take-up spool,* which automatically engages it after you close the camera back.

Figure 1-5:
An Advanced Photo System film cassette (left) and a 35mm film cassette (right).

Here's how 35mm loading works:

1. **Open the camera back.**

   You do this with a latchlike sliding switch (usually marked with an arrow or the word *open*) on the side or back of the camera. Sometimes you have to hold down a locking button as you move the switch; this double catch lessens the chance that the back would accidentally pop open and ruin your film when you're shooting. The back clicks open on the latch side; lift it up so that you can put in the film. (The camera can be off or on when you load the film.) (See Figure 1-6.)

   In the middle of the inside of the camera is a rectangular opening though which you can see the back of the lens. This rectangular opening is where each frame of film rests as you shoot it. On either side of this rectangle are two chambers. The large, empty one is where the film cassette goes. With some models, it's on the left; with others, it's on the right.

Figure 1-6:
The view
inside an
open 35mm
point-and-
shoot. The
loaded
cassette's
film leader
has been
extended
to the film
tip mark.

Film cassette chamber

Film take-up chamber

Film take-up spool

Camera back latch

Film tip mark   Film leader   Film cassette   Camera back

2. Nestle the film cassette into the empty chamber.

You can't just drop the film cassette in. Notice that the cassette has a small cylindrical protrusion at one end, called the spool hub. This protrusion must fit into a small recess in the film chamber. Notice, too, that there's a little spindle extending into the film chamber, from the top or bottom. You have to slip the flat end of the cassette — the end opposite the spool hub — over this spindle as you fit the cassette into the chamber. The process sometimes takes a little nudging and wiggling.

3. Grasp the leader and pull enough film from the cassette so that the leader's front edge lines up with the *film tip mark* in the opposite chamber.

The film tip mark is often, though not always, colored orange or red. Pull gently on the leader, keeping a finger on the cassette itself so that it doesn't lift out of the chamber. Lie the film flat across the rectangular opening to see if it reaches the mark. If it doesn't, pull it out a little more.

After you get more comfortable pulling film out of the cassette, use your thumb to press against the top edge of the film and push it along its path, as shown in Figure 1-7. This technique helps you gauge how much film to pull out. Just be sure not to press against the rectangular opening.

With compact cameras, you don't need to pull the film out more than a few perforations' worth; with bigger models, rarely more than $^1/_2$ or $^3/_4$ of an inch. But you don't have to be especially precise about the amount of film you pull out. Some models seem more able than others to handle excess film. None, however, can grab the leader if it's physically too far away. So err on the side of more film rather than less.

Figure 1-7:
One way to extend 35mm's film leader is to slide it across with your thumb.

4. **Now press the whole film strip flat against the rectangular opening, double-check that the cassette is snugly seated, and then close the camera back with firm pressure until it clicks.**

The camera's take-up mechanism and winding motor should engage the film and advance it to the first frame. The camera's frame counter or LCD panel then displays the number *1*.

If nothing happens after you close the camera back, your camera may be the type that must be turned on to advance the film. Turn it on. If it still doesn't advance the film, try pressing the shutter button once. (A few inexpensive models may require that you push the shutter button repeatedly until the number *1* appears in the frame counter.)

If you pull too much film out of the cassette when loading it — or not enough — the camera may not advance the roll to the first frame (see Figure 1-8). If this happens, you must open the back and reload the film.

Figure 1-8:
Don't pull too much film out of a 35mm cassette when you're loading it — or too little.

Right   Wrong

Fortunately, a 35mm point-and-shoot tells you (after you close the back and it attempts to engage the leader) if you pulled out too much film — or if you didn't pull out enough. It gives you this warning, if it has an LCD panel, by blinking an icon of the film cartridge and/or the number *1* or an *E* (for empty). Models without LCD panels simply fail to move their mechanical frame counters to 1.

To fix the problem, open the camera back. Pressing the film flat against the camera, check again to see whether the leader lines up with the film tip mark. If it's short, just pull out a little more film and close the camera back again.

If you pulled out too much film, take out the cassette. Hold the cassette between the thumb and fingers of one hand and point the spool hub toward you. Grasp the spool hub with the thumb and forefinger of your other hand and rotate it counterclockwise *to draw the leader back into the cassette* (see Figure 1-9). This rotation may not appear to have an effect until the coil of film inside the cassette begins to tighten up. Continue to turn the spool hub until the half-width portion of the film is a few perforations away from the cassette's lip. Rotate it *slowly,* so that you don't accidentally pull the whole leader back into the cassette.

Now load the film as I describe earlier in this section. If you pull out too much film again, just repeat the process.

Do not rotate the film cassette's spool hub in a clockwise direction. It puts up a lot of resistance if you try, and doing so may cause damage to the film.

Some 35mm point-and-shoot brands use a drop-in loading system that is fairly foolproof, as such things go. The cassette slips into a shaped compartment on the *bottom* of the camera. You do have to pull out the film leader a bit so that the camera can engage it after you close the door, but the compartment is shaped so that you can clearly see how to insert the cassette.

Figure 1-9:
To draw
excess film
back into
a 35mm
cassette,
rotate the
spool hub
slowly
counter-
clockwise.

Counting up — and down

After you load the film, the camera automatically advances it from one shot to the next. If your camera is an inexpensive model, you may have to advance the film by rotating a thumbwheel after every shot. You can't overwind: The wheel, which is located in the upper right of the camera back, stops when the next frame is lined up.

Most 35mm models count exposures upwards — 1, 2, 3, and so on, all the way to the last frame on the roll. (Rolls of 35mm film come in 12, 24, and 36-exposure lengths.) Displayed either by a mechanical counter under a small window (usually on the camera top) or by the camera's LCD panel (if it has one), the frame number is actually the number of the frame that you're *about* to shoot (see Figure 1-10). If it says 18, you've taken 17 pictures and are about to take number 18. To know how many pictures are left on the roll, you have to know the length of the roll, and deduct this number from it. If you've forgotten the length of the roll that you loaded, don't worry: With almost all 35mm point-and-shoots, a narrow vertical window on the camera back lets you read vital statistics off the side of the loaded film cassette, including the length of the roll. (See Figure 1-11.)

Figure 1-10: To display the frame count, your point-and-shoot uses either its LCD panel (left) or a separate window (right).

By contrast, some 35mm models count down — 24, 23, 22, and so on, all the way to 0. The number that they display actually tells you how many frames you have left on the roll.

If you mistakenly open your camera in the middle of a roll (thinking it's empty or that the film has been rewound), *close it immediately.* Your cue to close the camera is if you see *any* actual film at all; if the film has been rewound, it should *all* be back inside the cassette. (See the following section.)

Figure 1-11:
You can tell whether 35mm film is loaded by looking at a window on the camera back.

Fogging film

When you open the camera back before the film has been fully rewound, the resulting exposure to incoming stray light is said to fog the film. *Fogging* basically clouds up, discolors, mars with streaks, or completely obliterates the pictures that you've shot — assuming that you go on to get them developed.

Fogging almost certainly ruins your most recent shots. But if you close the camera back quickly, some of the earlier pictures on the roll may be salvageable. They may be okay because the film is opaque before development and forms a tight coil on the take-up spool as you shoot — the top loop or loops protecting the film beneath. But the longer you leave the back open, the more damage is done. And the brighter the surrounding light, the more immediate the damage. You don't know how bad the damage is until you have the film processed, which is worth doing. The photofinisher does not print badly fogged frames, so you don't have to pay for them.

If you open the camera in the middle of the roll, the film you *haven't* used yet is still safe in the cassette and, with the exception of a frame or two, should be unfogged. In fact, after you reclose the back, the camera might behave as if you've loaded a new roll and advance the film to what it thinks is the first frame — in the process pulling out enough film to reach the unfogged portion. But just to be safe, fire off a few blank frames (shots of nothing in particular) to advance the roll farther, and you're ready to continue shooting. (That is, if you're not so anxious to assess the damage that you choose to rewind the film and have it processed immediately!) Keep in mind that because the frame counter is reset to 0 after you open and close the back, unless you can remember how many frames were left on the roll, you don't know exactly when it will end.

35mm models that count frames *down* rather than up may actually prewind the film. *Prewinding* means that right after you load the cassette and close the camera back, these models advance the film all the way to the *last* frame. You hear their motors whirring for quite some time, and you may see their counters counting up along the way. Then, as you take each picture, they draw the film, a frame at a time, back into the cassette. (Rewinding is short, because at the end of the roll only a few inches of film are left!)

The thought behind prewinding is sensible: Should you open the camera back accidentally in the middle of the roll or should you drop the camera and the back pops open, the frames that you've already shot are safe inside the cassette. With a prewinding camera, the only film that would be fogged by the light you let in is the film that's still *outside* the cassette — which has no pictures on it.

So if you have a prewinding camera and accidentally open the back in the middle of a roll, close it and rewind the film. (Check out "Rewinding Film," later in this chapter, for instructions on midroll rewinding.) Do *not* shoot any more pictures; you'd be taking them with fogged film, and they probably wouldn't come out. If you shut your camera really fast, you may have a few good frames toward the end of the roll, but why take the chance? The photofinisher doesn't print what you don't shoot and certainly doesn't print fogged negatives. And at the risk of repeating myself, film is cheap.

Loading film into an Advanced Photo System camera

Being well thought-out machines, APS cameras make loading film effortless. Photographers who move from a 35mm point-and-shoot to an APS model may notice that the APS model doesn't have a camera back to open up for film insertion, only a small door. This door — call it the *film-compartment door* — is usually on the bottom of the camera (see Figure 1-12). On a few models you may find it finagled into the side or even the top. You open it with a latchlike sliding switch or a flat lever, though I've actually seen one model with which you open the door by pushing a button — which activates yet another motor.

With some models, you have to press a button to unlock the switch; with others, you must push the switch up or sideways before it fully slides to open the film-compartment door. Such designs are meant to protect against accidental opening of the door, which would fog your film. In fact, if you open and close the door without rewinding the film (or with some models, even if you move the switch), the camera may go ahead and rewind the film for you as insurance against any possibility of shooting on fogged film. (See "Fogging film" for more details.)

Figure 1-12:
The
Advanced
Photo
System
cassette
usually
loads into
the camera
bottom.

By the way, I've found that the film-compartment switch or lever on APS cameras often takes more pressure to move than the camera-back switch on 35mm models.

As for the APS cassette, you'll notice not only that it's smaller and differently shaped than a 35mm cassette, but that it lacks 35mm's leader — the annoying little strip of protruding film. (Are you happy?) The film is entirely within the cassette and is actually *pushed* out of the cassette to the take-up spool (which you can't even see) after you close the film-compartment door. Loading an APS cassette is as simple as sliding a VHS cassette into your TV's VCR.

As you throw the switch, the door pops open. Lift the door up if it doesn't open all the way on its own. Then just push the film cassette into the camera, end first. If one end doesn't fit, put in the other end first.

You can't accidentally load an Advanced Photo System film cassette backwards. The cassette is specially shaped so it fits only one way.

With some APS models, you may encounter a slight, springy resistance as you slide in the cassette. If you do, push the cassette all the way down; it may click into position. But if the cassette rides up a little in the compartment, just push it down with the film-compartment door when you close it.

After you close the film-compartment door, which takes firm pressure, the camera automatically advances the film to the first frame. Most APS models automatically advance the film whether they're on or off. They take more time than 35mm cameras to accomplish this task — quite a long time, which can be frustrating if you're in a hurry to get more pictures. But don't let all this motorized whirring and whining lead you to think that the film is being prewound. You may get that idea because most APS cameras (though not all) count frames *down,* starting at 15, 25, or 40 frames — the standard APS roll lengths.

The Advanced Photo System cassette

Part of the Advanced Photo System's appeal is that its film cassette has no visible leader — so you don't have to worry, as you do with 35mm, about engaging a leader to load the film. But this lack of a visible leader also means that you can't tell with a quick look whether you've shot a roll of film. Instead, you have to look at icons on the end of the cassette. These icons are especially useful because with the Advanced Photo System, your processed film is returned in the original cassette, where it remains for long-term storage and future reprinting.

The icons — a circle, a half circle, an *X,* and a rectangle — surround the opening in the middle of one end of the cassette (see figure). To keep their proper sequence perfectly clear, they are numbered 1, 2, 3, and 4 (respectively), and arrows point from one icon to the next. The icons are actually small, shaped cutouts in the cassette surface, and a white indicator

appears beneath the appropriate cutout to tell you the roll's status. With a new, unexposed cassette, the circle appears white (left cassette in figure). With a cassette in which only a portion of the roll has been shot, the half circle appears white. (This status is only possible with the few APS models having mid-roll film change capability, which I explain in the section "Rewinding Film.") With a cassette that is fully exposed (that is, all the frames have been shot) but unprocessed, the *X* appears white (center cassette). And with a processed cassette, the rectangle appears white (right cassette).

If you inadvertently load either an exposed but unprocessed APS cassette or a processed APS cassette, your APS camera does not advance the film. This protection, which prevents double-exposure and shooting pictures that would not come out, is typical of the foolproof design of the system.

Loading digital cameras

Digital cameras don't need film, silly. That's why you can't hear the familiar whir of the film winding motor after you take a picture. The silence of digital point-and-shoots is disquieting to some film-oriented photographers. I've facetiously suggested to manufacturers that they put a little computer chip into these cameras to fake this noise, just to make it seem as if something is really happening. Something is happening, of course — quietly and electronically. (See Chapter 15 for the lowdown on digital cameras.)

Turning the Camera On — and Off

Most point-and-shoots, whether Advanced Photo System or 35mm models, are turned on with a single pushbutton on the top or back of the camera, marked on/off. (Certain fashionable models put it on the front, just to be different.) You push it once to turn the camera on and again to turn the camera off. Other models may turn on and off with sliding switches, also placed on the top or back. Some switches have two positions; others have a spring mechanism that returns them to a single position. (You slide them once to turn the camera on and again to turn the camera off.) Some cameras have sliding on/off switches on the front, usually below the lens. These switches also open the camera's built-in protective lens cover, so you must slide them back to close the cover and turn off the camera.

Still other models are turned on and off with a large, sliding front panel that doubles as a lens protector. It's sometimes called a *clamshell* cover, a term inherited from older cameras that actually had swing-out front covers. This design is very sensible. To open up and turn on the camera, you simply use the flats of your fingers to slide the cover to the side. (The cover usually has a ridge to help you grasp it.) To turn off the camera, you slide the cover back over the lens. With some designs, you have to wait a moment for the lens to retract into the camera before you can slide the cover all the way over.

One other style of on/off switch is increasingly common. It is built into a thumb-controlled dial on the back or top of the camera. The dial has various settings on it, but rotating it one click away from its off position, to a setting marked *A* or *Auto,* or sometimes just plain *On,* turns on the camera. (This setting may be color-coded green, for *go.*) Rotating the dial back to *Off* turns the camera off.

As you turn the camera on, the first thing that happens is that the lens is uncovered. This function may be strictly mechanical, as it is with sliding front panels or below-the-lens sliding switches. In other cases, it's accomplished with motor-driven spring action.

Some lens covers are just large, flat doors that are flush with the front of the camera; after you turn off the camera, they hide the entire lens, cylindrical barrel and all, within the camera body. (You find them mainly on nonzooming models.) Other lens covers are made of delicate blades that are built into the lens barrel and spring open to uncover just the glass portion of the lens. Whatever the design, the lens cover protects the front glass surface of the lens from smudges or scratches. But if your camera has a bladed cover, be advised that if you leave it in a purse or carryall, the cover blades can catch on something and be pulled open, subjecting the lens to scratching from keys and so on. If you stash your camera in a bag, keep it in a fitted pouch.

Point-and-shoot cameras with sliding front covers are a smart idea. The lens is more protected than with other designs, making the camera ideal for slipping into a pocket or purse.

Some models dispense with moving lens covers altogether. They use a clear, flat piece of glass to protect the more delicate glass of the lens itself. This glass cover remains in place whether the camera is on or off, so it's very susceptible to smudging when you're *not* shooting — just holding or carrying the camera. Whether they're on a cover glass or on the lens itself, smudges are one of the main causes of unsharpness in photos.

If your camera lens has a permanent glass cover, inspect it for smudges regularly. If you see any, clean them off the same way that you would clean a lens. (See Chapter 6 for detailed instructions on cleaning your lens.) And consider keeping the camera in a fitted pouch when you're not using it.

After you turn your camera on, it may extend the lens, especially if it's an autofocus model. (Many cameras extend the lens as the cover is opening.) The lens is extended with a small motor. Extending the lens readies the camera for shooting, and with zoom models, sets the lens to its shortest (most wide-angle) focal length — which is generally 35mm or 38mm, though sometimes 28mm. (Note that these settings are different for APS cameras; for more on focal lengths, check out Chapter 5.) You can then zoom to the setting of your choice. If your camera does not have autofocus capability, the lens may not need to move at all.

Get a Grip: Holding Your Camera

Point-and-shoot cameras are often so small — and therefore so crowded with buttons, dials, windows, and other doodads — that you usually don't have much leeway in terms of how to hold them when you're taking pictures. You basically have to pinch each end of the camera between your thumb and fingers, except that with the right hand, your index finger must rest on the shutter button, on top of the camera. Your remaining three right-hand fingers form a sort of wedge against the front of the camera. Many models incorporate a curved or ridged grip on the right side, which makes for a more secure grasp and, coincidentally, a nice little space for the battery compartment.

Your right thumb should rest vertically against the back of your camera. With most zooming models, you find the zoom control at the tip of your thumb, in the upper right of the camera back. But some models have their zoom controls on the top of the camera, where they must be operated by the right index finger. You have to get used to moving your finger back and forth between these zoom controls and the shutter button. You will.

You have a little more flexibility in how you use your left hand, though the best way depends partly on the specific design of your camera. The worst thing that you can do is to stick a finger over the flash, which definitely ruins indoor pictures (see Figure 1-13, top left). Find a comfortable way of grasping the camera that avoids this problem and use it consistently.

An easy way to determine whether you're covering the flash when you hold the camera — a real no-no — is simply to look at yourself in a mirror while sighting through the camera's viewfinder.

Figure 1-13: The steadiest grip on the camera is often the most comfortable one, but there are right ways and wrong ways — and you should never cover the flash (top left). See text for details.

As far as your left thumb goes, one thing that you can do with it is pretty much to match the position of your right thumb: point it up and slightly inwards. The front of the camera then rests against the side of your index finger (see Figure 1-13, top right). But my preferred left-hand grip places the thumb against the bottom of the camera, and, preferably, the index finger across the top (see Figure 1-13, bottom left). You just have to hold your other fingers away from the camera (again, to avoid blocking the flash) either by folding them in tightly or splaying them out, which looks a little ornate.

I think this technique is more secure, lessening the chance that hand tremors will make your pictures unsharp. However, if your camera has a flash that pops up from the top of the camera or it has pushbuttons there that you may accidentally press, you can't use this technique, so go back to Plan A. For vertical shots with flash, try to place the camera's built-in flash at the top rather than the bottom; this creates a more flattering effect with people pictures (see Figure 1-13, bottom right).

Alas, there's no such thing as a left-handed point-and-shoot: The shutter button is always on the right. But I can't think of any absolute reason to use your right eye when you hold the camera to your face for viewing and shooting. The only possible argument is comfort; many if not most viewfinder windows are on the *left* side of the camera back, which means that if you use your right eye for viewing, the body of the camera extends away from your face to the right. If, on the other hand, you use your left eye for viewing, the camera body sits across your nose. Whether this arrangement is comfortable depends, quite honestly, on how much your schnozz sticks out.

How to press the shutter button

Don't treat your shutter button like a hot potato! Many point-and-shooters wait for pictures with their finger hovering above the shutter button, "stabbing" it to take the shot. This bad habit causes you to jerk the camera — and that unintended movement is one of the main causes of unsharp pictures.

Instead, keep your finger resting lightly on the shutter button. When you want to take a picture, slowly, smoothly bear down on the button until you hear the shutter click. Then release the button without completely removing your finger from it. Get yourself to do this by pretending that your shutter-button finger is glued on: Keep it there before, during, and after snapping a picture.

This technique is also crucial to mastering the shutter button's two-step operation — pressing it halfway to lock the autofocus and then all the way down to take the picture. See Chapter 6 for more on the shutter button two-step.

Rewinding Film

When a point-and-shoot camera reaches the end of a roll of film, it automatically *rewinds* it — that is, the camera draws the entire roll of exposed but undeveloped pictures back into the cassette. (Less expensive models may require manual rewinding with a crank; read on.) Sometimes the camera squeezes in an extra shot or two at the end of a roll, depending on the brand of film and the winding system; you may get 37 exposures instead of 36. The standard roll lengths in 35mm are 12, 24, and 36 exposures; in the Advanced Photo System, 15, 25, and 40.

If you have a 35mm camera, it has a little window on the back through which you can see a small portion of the outside of the loaded film cassette. This window allows you to read the number of frames off the cassette, should you forget the length of the roll that you loaded. If the camera counts exposures upwards (1, 2, 3, and so on), as most do, this information lets you determine when you're nearing the end of the roll. If you have an Advanced Photo System camera, you probably don't have to figure out how many frames you have left, because most APS models count frames *down* — in other words, they tell you how many exposures are *left* on the roll.

Knowing how many frames are left on a roll is useful, not because of anything to do with rewinding — the camera rewinds the film only after it senses the tug at roll's end — but because it lets you plan your shooting. If you're about to leave for a wedding with a 24-exposure roll in your 35mm point-and-shoot and the frame counter says 23, you know you're not going to have enough film to get the pictures you want. At the very least, you should bring an extra roll.

I say at the very least because I have a better idea: Put a new roll of film in your camera *before you go*. That way, you won't have to stop and reload after shooting two frames — possibly just when you have a perfect picture in sight. It's not worth losing a great picture to save a frame or two of film. Film is the cheapest part of photography, and photofinishers don't print frames that you don't shoot — nor can they charge you for prints that they don't make.

To put in a new roll of film before the last one is finished, you have to push the rewind button. With most point-and-shoot cameras, it is a tiny pushbutton (usually the smallest of any button on the camera) that is recessed to prevent accidental rewinding. Its location varies totally from camera model to camera model; yours may be on the bottom, sides, back, or top. (The only place that you won't ordinarily find it is the front.) The button is almost always marked with a symbol that combines double arrows and a stylized film cassette (see Figure 1-14). The capability is often called *midroll rewind*.

Figure 1-14:
The film
rewind icon.

There are other reasons to rewind film before roll's end. For one, you can get pictures back sooner — for example, to be able to send out promised prints of a special event. Even if you waste five or ten frames (a buck or two's worth of film), it's worth the satisfaction of sharing those important images when the event is still fresh in peoples' minds.

Another good reason to rewind film before the end of a roll is to switch to a different type of film for a different purpose, occasion, or lighting condition. The switch can be aesthetically motivated — a change from color to black and white, for example. Or it can be practical — switching to a faster film (one with a higher ISO number) when you want to take pictures by low existing light. (Read Chapter 2 for more on different types of film.)

To rewind your film:

1. **Turn the camera on, if it's not on already.**

   Some models may be able to rewind when they're off, but turn them on anyway.

2. **Push the rewind button.**

   To push the rewind button, you probably need a pencil or pen or bobby pin, though some cameras may incorporate a little groove that allows you to use your fingernail. After you push the button, the camera starts rewinding the film with its motor, just as if it had reached the end of the film on its own. Most but not all models count down the exposures. If you have a mechanical frame counter, you see it slowly move backwards from the last exposure (say, 24) to 0; if your camera displays frame numbers on its LCD panel, it counts backwards frame by frame.

   After the camera rewinds the film all the way back into the cassette — and with some models, this process can take as long as 45 seconds with a 36-exposure roll — the motor stops. (Cameras having an LCD panel usually blink the icon of the cassette with the number *0* or the letter *E* — for empty, not error.)

If pressing the rewind button doesn't start the rewind motor or if the winding stops in the middle, *do not open the camera.* First, if the camera is off, turn it on and push the button again. If that procedure doesn't work, replace the battery. You don't have to hurry to replace it; the film is safe. If replacing the battery doesn't get the rewind going (push the button again, if need be, after it's installed), bring the camera to your local photo dealer or photofinisher to have the film rewound. (See Chapter 3 for more on choosing a photofinisher.)

3. After the motor stops, open the camera back or film compartment and take out the film.

With 35mm, rewinding draws the film entirely inside the cassette, leaving no film leader outside. In fact, that's how you can tell if a 35mm roll has been shot: If the perforated film leader is visible, the roll is ready to shoot; if the film leader is not visible, the roll is exposed and ready for processing. (See Figure 1-15.)

Figure 1-15:
If a 35mm cassette's film leader is visible (left), the roll is ready to shoot; if the leader's inside the cassette (right), the roll has been shot.

Some rewind variations

A few point-and-shoots replace the single rewind button with a sliding switch that clicks back into position when you open the camera back to remove the rewound film. And a few use a two-button combination for rewinding. With one of my favorite models, actually, you have to hold down what is normally the self-timer button for a couple of seconds to make the LCD panel's rewind symbol flash, and then you push the *shutter button* to start the rewind. I definitely needed my manual to figure this one out. So if you can't find a rewind button anywhere on your camera, check your manual!

If you have a bare-bones 35mm point-and-shoot, it may not have a rewind motor at all — just a manual crank on the camera bottom. You flip out the crank and rotate it to rewind the film into the cassette. In order to start rewinding, you usually first have to push a small (and sometimes recessed) button, normally on the camera bottom. Pushing this button unlocks the film-advance mechanism. Be sure to turn the crank in the direction of its indicating arrows (usually, but not always, counterclockwise). Hold the camera body firmly (keep those fingers off the lens!) and rewind smoothly and slowly until you feel a little tug or click, which is the film leader disengaging from the take-up spool. Then you feel a reduction in the pressure needed to turn the crank. Turn the crank a few more times to draw the film completely into the cassette. (Don't worry — you can't overdo it.) Finally, open the camera back to remove the film.

One final rewinding note. A few high-end Advanced Photo System cameras have a special feature called *mid-roll change* (MRC). This feature allows you to swap film cassettes without wasting a single frame. How? When you put a previously rewound roll back into your camera, the camera actually remembers where you left off — advancing the film to the first unexposed frame beyond. It does so by reading information from the APS film's unique magnetic layer. You can find out more about this capability in Chapter 14.

If you've read this chapter and still face the ultimate frustration — your camera just won't shoot — go directly to Chapter 20. There you find ten succinct suggestions for getting your point-and-shoot shooting again.

Chapter 2

Choosing a Film

- -

In This Chapter

▶ The advantages of color print film

▶ Understanding the film cassette

▶ Choosing a roll length

▶ What's your film type?

▶ Experimenting with black and white

▶ Choosing a film speed

▶ The relationship between film speed and grain

▶ Offsetting shake with film speed

▶ Choosing a film brand

- -

*F*ilm is the magic substance that captures the moments, people, and places that you choose to photograph — the recording medium to which all your camera's pushbuttons and dials are dedicated. Unlike video-tape and the digital media that have invaded your audiovisual world, film records an image that you can directly *see,* however small. Simply put, to take pictures you must have film.

Actually, if you're using a digital point-and-shoot, it makes pictures without film — so you don't have to read this chapter. But I hope that you do anyway, because film creates a photographic image that is far superior in quality to what's produced by the imaging "chip" in a digital camera. Film is cheap, but cheap as it is, it delivers a quality of photographic detail and richness that digital cameras costing thousands of dollars can't match! (See Chapter 15 for more information on digital point-and-shoots.)

Kodak says that the average snapshooter spends at least two minutes agonizing at the store over what kind of film to buy. But you can whittle that time down to about two seconds if you know what to look for. The choice begins with the *type* of film — though for the most part, you'll only use one type. And each type of film is usually available in different *speeds* — degrees of sensitivity to light, indicated by something called an ISO number. (Though by the time I'm through with you, you may only be using one speed!) Using different types of film can make your point-and-shoot experience more fun; using different film speeds can enhance your ability to capture certain kinds of subjects, and also affects image quality. Film brand and roll length are also part of the equation. So in choosing a film for your photography, you really have to consider four things: type, speed, length, and brand. Fortunately, these decisions are not complicated, and this chapter guides you through them.

What's Your Film Type?

The photographic image formed by most commonly used films is a *color negative:* a tiny, transparent picture in which tones and colors are the opposite of what they were in the original subject. After developing your film to make this negative visible, your photofinisher enlarges the negative to make a positive image — the print that you get back. Because it's meant for making prints, film that produces a color negative is usually called *color print film.* That's the term I use for it in this chapter and throughout the book.

Nearly 99 percent of all film used is color print film, and point-and-shoot cameras are made to order for it. But you can get other types of film (see Figure 2-1) and use them in point-and-shoot cameras with varying degrees of success.

 Photofinishing has as big an influence on the quality of your prints as the film you choose — sometimes bigger. Lack of care or attention, whether on the part of a minilab or a mass-market processor, can make prints from a great film look terrible. Good photofinishing, on the other hand, can pull excellent prints from run-of-the-mill film. A good, brand-name film — Kodak Gold Max, for instance — should be giving you rich color and detail, even with a pretty inexpensive camera. If it's not, then you should consider switching to a different photofinisher or minilab. (See Chapter 3 for more on choosing a photofinisher.)

Color print film

Most snapshot photographers use color print film because it gives them both color and prints — color for the sake of realism, prints for the sake of viewing convenience and ease of sharing. Therefore, color print film is the film on which both minilabs and mass-market photofinishers base their voluminous business. It is also the film in which manufacturers invest the most money, time, and effort. So color print film is, generally speaking, the most technologically advanced film you can buy.

Figure 2-1:
Films come
in various
types.
Kodak's
Select line
includes
Royal Gold,
a top-
quality
color print
film; Elite
Chrome, a
fast-
process
color slide
film; and the
venerable
Kodachrome.

This superb quality is, in fact, what has made the Advanced Photo System both possible and good. This new system's negative is considerably smaller in physical size than the 35mm negative; the downsizing allows for smaller cameras, among other advantages, but would also diminish picture quality if current color print film were not so good.

Color print film is also known as a *forgiving* film. This description means, basically, that it's good at backing up your point-and-shoot camera, like a catcher who can pull in a pitch from way outside and make it look like a strike. Even if your camera doesn't expose color print film perfectly — that is, if it doesn't get the right amount of light from the subject to the film — you can still get a print of acceptable quality. This ability is called *exposure latitude,* and color print film has more of it than either color slide or black-and-white film. (For more about film exposure, see the section "A Question of Speed," later in this chapter.)

Fortunately, you don't have to know what exposure latitude means to benefit from it. But as an example of its worth, imagine shooting a landscape at dusk. Even if your point-and-shoot opens up the little window in its lens as much as possible (that is, sets its widest *lens aperture*) and keeps the window open for as long as possible (that is, sets its slowest *shutter speed*), it may not get enough light to the film for a correct exposure. (See the sidebar "How your camera gets the right amount of light to the film.")

With slide film, which I tell you about in the next section, you'd get an overly dark result. But with color print film, the resulting underexposed negative may produce an acceptable print, if your photofinisher takes care. And, in fact, color print film actually gives *better* results when it is somewhat overexposed. (I talk more about the pluses of overexposure in Chapter 8.)

So in some situations, too much or too little light pushes your camera to its limits. Sometimes, though, your camera just makes a mistake and doesn't get the exposure quite right — and this is when color print film's exposure latitude is most valuable. Color print film's flexibility extends to the actual *color* of the light, too. The film is able to cope well with subjects in which the lighting is different from the daylight for which the film is technically designed. It provides accurate, or at least acceptable, color in a variety of lighting situations.

Color negatives have a strong reddish or reddish-orange cast to them. (35mm users can see this cast because they must handle actual negative strips; Advanced Photo System users cannot, because the processed film remains inside the cassette.) Formed by dyes during processing, this odd tint actually helps the printing paper produce more faithful color.

How your camera gets the right amount of light to the film

Some subjects are bright and others are dim, but for best results a specific film needs to receive pretty much the same amount of light every time you take a picture. Your point-and-shoot knows how much light the film needs — an amount called the *correct exposure* — and does its best to get that quantity to it. (The light entering your camera is actually an image of the subject, with brighter and darker areas, but the light's overall brightness is variable.) The camera automatically controls the amount of light reaching the film with a tiny, adjustable window in the lens. Two things determine how much light gets through the window: the shutter speed and the lens aperture.

✔ **Shutter speed:** The shutter speed is the length of time the window in the lens remains open. Because today's photographic film is so sensitive to light, the window doesn't have to stay open very long — usually somewhere between 1/60th and 1/500th second.

✔ **Lens aperture:** The lens aperture is basically the size of the window in the lens, when it is open. The opening can be enlarged or reduced to let more light or less light into your camera. (Regardless of the opening's size, the lens still forms a full image of the subject on the film.) As with the shutter speed, your point-and-shoot camera automatically controls the lens aperture, though some high-end models allow you to choose it yourself.

Print problems? Try, try again.

If you get a print from a photofinisher that is too light or too dark or in which the color is way off, take it back and ask for a new, corrected print. The photofinisher should redo it for free. If they manage to convince you that they aren't responsible, paying for a reprint may be worthwhile — on the condition that they try to do a better job. If they refuse, or try and don't succeed, take the negative to a different photofinishing service — especially if the print is important. But in fairness, remember that some negatives simply don't print well.

You'll probably have more difficulty getting satisfaction on such second tries from mass market, drugstore- and discount-store-type photofinishing services. If you want this kind of special attention, you're better off patronizing a minilab or other facility that does its work on the premises so you can convey your wishes directly to the technician who operates the printing machinery. For more information on setting up such a relationship, see Chapter 3.

Part of color print film's forgiving nature has to do with the fact that, unlike color slides, the negative must be printed to produce the final positive result. And in printing, exposure adjustments and *color filtration* (adding or subtracting color from the light used to make the print) make each print the best that it can be — theoretically. Photofinishers actually have a lot of leeway in this process. Their mechanized, automated printing machinery may not produce a good print, especially from an iffy negative, on the first try — that is, the first print that you get back. But getting a better result is usually possible. (See the sidebar "Print problems? Try, try again.")

Color slide film

In terms of sheer visual impact, few prints can compare to the beauty of a projected slide. In the '40s, '50s, and even the '60s, before cable and video rentals and the Internet — and, I might add, the loss of family togetherness — slide shows were the height of audiovisual entertainment. (The audio was provided by family and friends who loved to talk about the people and places shown in the slides.) Unfortunately, viewing slides requires an expensive projector and, for best results, a special screen. A few people still have these unique appliances; others may find them in their attics or basements. But most people don't have them and are unprepared to make the considerable investment in them.

Perhaps more of an obstacle in this hurried, convenience-driven culture is that slide-projection equipment takes time to set up — much longer than popping a cassette into your VCR or, for that matter, getting out a stack of prints. You can buy special hand and tabletop viewers for slides; these viewers backlight and magnify the image, sometimes projecting it on a small built-in screen. But much can still be said for sitting in a darkened room and watching the play of projected color on the wall. The experience commands your attention in a way no TV screen, nor any print, quite can.

If you grew up after the heyday of slide shows, think of a color slide as a *positive transparency* of the subject. A color slide represents the subject's colors and tones pretty much as you originally saw them through the camera (as opposed to reversed, as they are in a color negative) and on a completely clear, rather than tinted, base (the plastic on which the image rests). In fact, the slides that you get back from the color lab or photofinisher, which are mounted in two-inch square plastic or cardboard frames with rectangular windows (see Figure 2-2), are the same film that actually went through your camera. The images are cut up individually rather than into strips (as they are in 35mm) or left as whole rolls (as they are with the Advanced Photo System).

You can usually tell slide film by its name. Most brands use the suffix *chrome,* as in Agfa's Agfachrome, Fuji's Fujichrome, or Kodak's Ektachrome.

Figure 2-2:
Color slides have a richness all their own, but they are best seen either projected or printed by a good custom lab.

TECHNICAL STUFF

Better photography through chemistry

Color print film is by far the easiest type of film to get processed. The series of chemical solutions that bring out its hidden negative image, which go by the rather dry name *C-41,* are relatively easy to control and have become a worldwide standard. C-41 is the universal designation for color negative processing, whether you're in Boston or Beijing.

The chemical process for developing slide film, which actually reverses the exposed film's hidden negative image, is called *E-6.* Like color negatives' C-41 process, it's a worldwide standard. But regular minilabs don't offer it, so you either have to have them send slide film out for processing by a larger lab or take it yourself to a photo lab that specializes in E-6 processing on the premises. (See Chapter 3 for details.) Labs offering in-house E-6 processing have a more professional orientation, because slide film is mostly used by working professional photographers.

Then there's good old Kodachrome film. Introduced in 1936, it was the first commercially successful color film — the stuff of family lore and Paul Simon lyrics. Whereas almost all common color slide films (Ektachrome and its ilk) use the universal standard E-6 chemical process, Kodachrome must be processed in its own special machinery and chemicals (designated K-14 — you had to ask). But Kodachrome's uniquely rich colors and crispness make it beloved to this day by both serious amateur and professional photographers. (Turn to the color section to see an example of a Kodachrome slide.)

You *can* get prints from color slides, by the way. Your minilab or other photofinisher can send your slides out for prints, a service that is usually somewhat more expensive than getting reprints from negatives. Or you can go to a custom photo lab, which uses special processes and/or materials to print your slides — and charges you accordingly. (See Chapter 3 for details.)

Getting good results with slide film

For good results with slide film, you can't depend on a point-and-shoot that comes in a blister pack — you know, those molded plastic packages that you see hanging on drugstore display racks. Generally, you need to spend close to $100 to get a model that has a good enough *light meter* (the device that measures the subject's brightness) and adequate *exposure control* (the ability to adjust its shutter speed and lens aperture over a wide range) to ensure that the film is properly exposed — that is, neither too light nor too dark.

Proper exposure is more important with slide film than with color negative film because problems are harder to correct when printing slides. With slide film, what you see in the processed slide is pretty much what you get, to borrow that photographically relevant expression. If highlights are all washed out, you cannot restore them. If shadows are so dark that you can't see into them, a print usually cannot salvage detail from them.

You may be able to tell whether your 35mm point-and-shoot is up to the challenge of slide film just by looking. Open the back — make sure that the camera is empty! — and look in the film chamber. (The film chamber is the bigger of the two compartments; see Chapter 1 for details.) Inside the chamber you should find a row of small, silver-colored, springy metal contacts. These contacts allow the camera to read the film cassette's DX bar code and set the correct *ISO speed* — the number that tells the camera how sensitive the film is to light, information it needs to ensure correct exposure. (See the section "A Question of Speed," later in this chapter, for more information about ISO numbers.)

How many contacts do you see? If you see less than four, your camera has a pretty simple exposure system, and using slide film is probably not a good idea. If you see four or more contacts, your camera probably has the degree of exposure control needed for slide film.

You can't do a quick check like this for Advanced Photo System cameras, although APS slide film is somewhat hard to find anyway. Instead, check the specifications section of your manual for the camera's acceptable range of speeds. If the camera accepts a limited range of film speeds — say ISO 100 to 400 — it probably doesn't have enough exposure accuracy to shoot slides. If it accepts a wider range of speeds — say ISO 50 to 3200 — chances are it can handle slide film.

If your 35mm camera has four or more contacts, or if your APS camera accepts a wide range of speeds, continue your test by shooting a 24-exposure roll of slide film. (A camera shop or a discount store with a large photo department should stock major brands of slide film, such as Kodak Elite Chrome.) Be sure to ask for *ISO 100* slide film; the meaning of the ISO number is explained in "A Question of Speed," but you don't need to under-stand it for this test. Now load up your camera and have a go at it. Shoot a variety of outdoor scenes in light ranging from bright sun to dark overcast or shade. Take both people pictures and scenes of greenery and flowers. Take a few flash shots, too, but be sure to stay within your camera's flash range, as I describe in Chapter 7.

When you're finished, drop the film off at your photofinisher. If you're using your regular photofinisher, be sure to remind the clerk that it's slide film. He or she has to send it out for processing, and you may have to wait at least a couple of days for it.

When you get the slides back, a simple way to view them is to tape a piece of thin white paper to a window that faces a bright patch of sky (not direct sun), to diffuse the light for viewing. Hold the slides up to the paper. If you have a good magnifier, use it to make the tiny slide image bigger. You'll quickly find out the right way and wrong way to look at slides; if the scene is backwards (flopped), just flip the slide over.

Do you like what you see? Do the slides look crisper and more satisfying than what you're accustomed to getting with prints? Are most of them pretty well exposed — that is, not too light, not too dark? If the answer to these questions is yes, then you and your camera are good candidates for slide film. If, on the other hand, many of the slides are too dark or too light, your camera's exposure system may not be accurate enough for slide film. This inability to handle slide film isn't a defect, mind you. It just means your camera has been designed for that so-very-forgiving color print film.

Slide rules and exposure compensation

Remember the strictest teacher that you had? The one who never believed that Bowser ate your homework? The one who never accepted answers that were *almost* right? Slide film is like that teacher.

Unlike color print film, color slide film needs very precise exposure — in other words, your camera has to get just the right amount of light to the film. Too little, and the slide is too dark. Too much, and it is too light. Period.

Before I scare you away from slide film, let me reassure you: Most point-and-shoot cameras above the $100 mark can take pretty good slides, most of the time. In fact, the exposure systems on middle-of-the-road point-and-shoots are often more sophisticated than were those on the *best* cameras of the pre-point-and-shoot era. But the problem is that these systems are part of totally automatic cameras. They're robots. And robots need a predictable environment. In the case of a point-and-shoot camera, this means a subject with a good mix of tones — blacks, whites, and miscellaneous grays. (Of course, most of these tones are actually colors, but point-and-shoot exposure systems only see in black-and-white.)

 If the camera doesn't see this sort of scene, it usually can't get the exposure right. Shoot friends standing in shade under a tree in front of a brightly lit landscape, and they end up mere silhouettes of themselves. Shoot musicians in spotlight on a dark stage, and the camera tries desperately to find detail in the shadows, washing out the main subject. In these instances, with slide film, *exposure compensation* may be necessary. This fancy bit of photo jargon means that you force your camera to nudge the exposure one way or the other — to make the picture lighter or darker than the one that your robot exposure system would have given you. But how, if the camera's fully automatic?

By using a special exposure compensation mode, also sometimes called EV compensation. Your camera may not have this feature — it tends to be reserved for more expensive models — but if it does, you access it with a pushbutton or dial, as I describe in Chapter 4. After you get your camera in this mode, you again poke a button or twist a dial to add or subtract chunks of exposure called *EV*, short for *exposure value*. They're pretty big chunks: Adding one EV (shown on the LCD panel as *+1 EV*) doubles the amount of light getting to the film; taking away one EV (shown as *–1 EV*) halves the amount of light. Most point-and-shoots with this feature let you make this adjustment in half or full EVs, so you can set +1.5 EV, for example, or –0.5 EV. With slide film, making adjustments in *small* increments is prudent.

Generally, you want to use exposure compensation when you see a big difference in tone or brightness between what's in the middle of the frame — the main subject, ordinarily — and what's in the surrounding area. If the middle of the scene is substantially *darker* than the surrounding area (those friends in the shade), then you want to *increase* exposure by setting +0.5 EV, +1 EV, or even +1.5 EV, depending on how extreme the difference is. If the middle of the scene is substantially *lighter* than the surrounding area (that spotlighted performer), you want to *decrease* exposure by setting –0.5 EV, –1 EV, and so on.

Always be sure, though, to take the same shot with no exposure compensation whatsoever. The camera may, after all, be right! Many professional photographers routinely *bracket* their slide-film exposures in this way, shooting extra frames with more and less exposure. Also keep in mind that *fill flash* (forcing the flash to fire in bright light, which you can read about in Chapter 7) may in some cases be a better remedy than exposure compensation for an overly dark or heavily shadowed subject. Those friends in the shade, if they're close enough, can be brightened with a blast of flash — bringing them into better balance with the background. But a blast of flash probably can't brighten the dark stage around that spotlighted performer, because it's just too far away!

Most point-and-shoots with exposure compensation automatically cancel any adjustments that you make immediately after you take the shot. But a few do not. If you have a model that maintains the exposure compensation setting until you change it, be sure to set it back to normal as soon as you don't want it. You don't even have to fiddle with the mode button to set the EV back to 0; you can usually just turn the camera off and on again. But if you forget, you may shoot the rest of the roll with a setting that ruins your remaining shots.

Black-and-white film

Color pictures have become the norm pretty recently in the grand sweep of photographic history. Before color became practical and affordable, black and white *was* photography. The great photo-essays that appeared in the first decades of *Life* magazine were all in black and white — and no one questioned their realism. In its grittiness, black and white actually seemed more true-to-life — less decorative — than color. That perception persisted even after color became the norm for magazine reproduction.

Now, though, black and white seems a bit exotic to the eyes. By reducing a subject's colors and textures to shades of gray, and in the process making the subject more abstract, black-and-white film seems to take the photograph a step away from reality. For most people, the very absence of color gives black and white the stamp of art. But that absence also demands special visual attention when you're shooting black and white. (See the sidebar, "Tone and texture: Thinking in black and white.")

Compare the way that black-and-white and color films render the same subjects. Before loading a roll of black and white, save a few frames at the end of the color roll that's already in your camera. Choose a couple of subjects around your house and yard — be sure to include some nonflash subjects — and then finish off the color roll on them. Immediately load the black-and-white film and reshoot the same subjects. Examine the prints that you get back. Which do you prefer?

Tone and texture: Thinking in black and white

Color is often the first way that you describe the world around you. A car is red; a shirt is green; eyes are blue or brown. Color tends to overwhelm all other visual properties. And its very absence is what makes black-and-white photography such a great medium.

Yet the absence of color also makes black and white a great photographic challenge. Not everything lends itself to black and white: Fall foliage, an intense sunset, wildflowers, and a brightly frosted birthday cake just don't cut it without color. Point-and-shoot flash pictures may look especially bad in black and white because their frontal light can't provide the range of grays on which it mostly depends. If dim light forces you to use flash with black and white, set your camera to its slow-sync flash mode (or if it has none, to fill-flash mode). (See Chapter 7 for more on flash modes.) This flash mode causes more of the existing light to be included in the picture, not only improving background detail but giving a better sense of shape to things in the picture.

Light is especially important in black and white. Look for light that has character but is neither too strong nor too flat. Good light for black and white is directional enough to make textures stand out and give shading to things in the picture; a subject that doesn't show any sense of light's direction tends to look flat in a commercial print. Just as with flash, getting a good black-and-white picture of a subject in direct, hard sunlight is difficult. Part of the problem is that commercial prints often don't retain detail in both the brightest and darkest parts of the subject.

Composition is also key to black and white. In my experience, black-and-white photographs must have a clear visual structure — more of a design aspect than with color. Yet you can experiment with abstract, strongly graphic composition more easily in black and white than in color. With only tones to go on, people tend to read black-and-white photographs less quickly and easily — which can actually make them more interesting to look at!

Which black-and-white film to choose?

Just as with color print films, most black-and-white films are made to produce a negative. This negative must then be printed. (A few black-and-white slide films exist, but they require special processing that you must either do yourself or that is available only at very few specialty photo labs.) But unlike color print films, you first have to choose between two different kinds of black-and-white print film (see Figure 2-3).

One option is to use a black-and-white film that must be processed in conventional black-and-white chemicals, a classic such as Kodak's Tri-X Pan film. Black-and-white chemicals are quite different from those used for color processes, and minilabs don't have them. So whether you take your exposed roll of Tri-X to a minilab or a drugstore that uses mass-market processing services, it has to be sent out for processing. The Kodak Premium Processing service does a creditable job with black and white; other outfits are a mixed bag, some decent, some lousy. The truth is that getting good conventional black-and-white processing is a gamble.

Your usual processing outfit may even bounce you and your roll of Tri-X to a custom black-and-white lab, one that specializes in black-and-white developing and printing. Don't go unless you're very serious about your black-and-white work — enough to spend some money on it. A custom lab may develop the film for a reasonable sum, but it probably won't have the automated machinery needed to make large numbers of inexpensive prints. Each print is basically handmade and priced accordingly. For more about custom labs, see Chapter 3.

Figure 2-3: Black-and-white print film comes in two basic versions, conventional (right) and chromogenic (left).

Knowing the quality gamble and costs involved — and wanting more creative control — I process and print all my own conventional black-and-white film. I always rented an apartment and (eventually) bought a house with an extra bedroom so I could have a darkroom without appropriating my family's bathroom on Sunday afternoons. But I don't get into the darkroom much these days, and I do love black and white. So here's what I do: I shoot _chromogenic_ black-and-white film. (See the following section to find out more about this film.)

Chromogenic black and white

Chromogenic black-and-white film is a much easier way than conventional black-and-white film to get black-and-white pictures. Three such films now exist: Kodak Professional T-Max T400 CN, Ilford XP-2, and Konica VX Pan 400, all of very good quality. The only black-and-white film sold for Advanced Photo System cameras (Kodak's Advantix Black-and-White+ 400, for example) is, in fact, chromogenic.

Don't be alarmed by the term chromogenic; _chromo_ is just old Greek for color. In fact, chromogenic black-and-white film is designed to be processed in the very same chemicals that minilabs and other photofinishers use for color print film. You can give the photofinisher a roll of chromogenic black-and-white film and a roll of color print film, and he or she can send both rolls through the processing machine at the same time. One roll comes out as color negatives and the other as black-and-white negatives.

The problem with conventional black-and-white processing is that you can actually go about it in a lot of different, legitimate ways, using different chemicals and different procedures. What's more, the process is often not as carefully controlled as with color, because the very absence of color tends to make some darkroom technicians think of black and white as a less demanding medium. Unfortunately, the end result is that four different custom labs can run the same roll of conventional black-and-white film and come up with four different-looking sets of negatives and prints.

By contrast, the processing for color print film is highly standardized — no two ways, or four ways, about it. So chromogenic black-and-white film, processed just like color print film, actually gives you more dependable, consistent negatives than conventional black-and-white film.

Because chromogenic black-and-white film uses color technology to create its black-and-white negative image, it also benefits from many of the same characteristics as color print film. For example, it's more forgiving of exposure errors than conventional black-and-white film, and it actually gets finer grain and better shadow detail with deliberate _or_ inadvertent overexposure.

Here's an easy way to give chromogenic black and white a try — without ever taking the color film out of your point-and-shoot. Get a black-and-white one-time-use camera. These cameras are now available from both Ilford and Konica, and they're preloaded with chromogenic black-and-white film. All you do is shoot the roll and hand the camera over to your photofinisher. He or she should know what to do with it!

As for making prints from chromogenic black-and-white negatives, you have two choices. Both are as cheap, per print, as your usual color prints, and both should be available from your minilab or photofinisher. One is to have the prints made on color paper, the same paper used for printing color negatives. Because the negatives don't have any color in them, you don't get any in the pictures. Well, almost none. You may get *one:* a reddish-brown, yellowish, or (worst case) greenish or bluish cast. But a good lab should be able to get the color out altogether, for a strictly neutral tone. If you're told that getting all the color out is impossible, the truth is just that it's too much trouble — requiring some extra twiddling of dials to tweak color settings. Just tell the folks at the lab that I sent you and that I expect them to make neutral prints for you, if that's what you *do* want. In fact, a little brown or yellowish cast can be nice, similar to the effect of sepia-toned prints (that warm coloration you sometimes see in very old family pictures). It's probably not the right feeling, though, for pictures of a new baby or the stealth jet at the air show.

The Ektamax option

Another option is to ask the minilab or photofinisher to do your black-and-white prints on *Ektamax* paper instead of regular color paper. This unique Kodak paper makes a strictly colorless black-and-white print when processed in the same chemicals the lab uses for color paper. (Those chemicals are called RA-4, in case you have to discuss the matter with your photofinisher.) In other words, Ektamax does on paper what chromogenic films do on film. Unlike printing your chromogenic black-and-white negatives on color paper, printing on Ektamax eliminates the risk of getting ghoulish color casts, and often its effect is crisper and snappier than with color paper. But you may have to convince the minilab or the photofinisher to use Ektamax, because it involves changing paper. Suggest to the minilab that they wait until the end of the day or anytime they have a lull in volume.

Keep in mind that with Ektamax paper, you won't get prints back in one hour, or maybe even one day. But if you want it and the minilab or photofinisher won't give it to you, take your business elsewhere. Switching to Ektamax paper isn't much more trouble than changing the paper in a photocopy machine; it just takes time away from cranking out those color prints.

If you have existing 35mm black-and-white negatives that were processed *conventionally,* you can have your minilab print them on either Ektamax or color paper. If you come across a stash of old family negatives, for example, you can get prints from them for family keepsakes, albums, and so on. For details, see Chapter 3.

A Question of Speed

Probably the most frequently asked question about film is "What speed do I need?" Your choice of film speed can have both practical and visual consequences for your picture-taking, but the answer is simpler than you may expect. First, a definition and some reassurances.

A film's *speed* is photo jargon for its sensitivity to light. This sensitivity is indicated by its *ISO rating,* which is printed on the box and on the film cassette itself. The higher the number, the more sensitive the film and the less light the film must gather from the subject to create an acceptable image of it. With color print film, these speeds are typically ISO 100, ISO 200, ISO 400, and ISO 800, though oddball speeds such as ISO 50, ISO 160, ISO 640, ISO 1000, ISO 1600, and even ISO 3200 are also available (see Figure 2-4).

 Film speed numbers are surprisingly straightforward in their meaning. ISO 200 film is twice as sensitive to light as ISO 100 film. ISO 400 film is twice as sensitive to light as ISO 200 film. And ISO 800 film is twice as sensitive to light as ISO 400 film. (ISO 800 film is therefore *eight* times as sensitive to light as ISO 100 film.) And the higher the number, the more easily you can get pictures without flash in dim light.

Figure 2-4: Standard 35mm color print films are available in ISO 100, 200, 400, and 800 speeds, APS films in ISO 100, 200, and 400.

Not to worry. *You yourself don't have to set the film's ISO speed on your point-and-shoot.* The camera does it for you, by reading a metallic bar code on the film cassette. Using this *DX code,* the camera can calculate how much light the film needs for a *correct exposure* — again, to produce a negative or slide that makes the subject neither too dark nor too light, and in the case of color print film, to create a negative that would make the best possible print. The camera gets the right quantity of light to the film by adjusting the size of the lens aperture (the window in the lens) and the shutter speed (the length of time that window is open).

For example, the camera usually sets a higher shutter speed if you're using a higher-speed film because the film needs less light for a correct exposure than a lower-speed film. Most point-and-shoot cameras don't let you manually control lens aperture or shutter speed settings, of course. But your choice of film speed is still very important in terms of getting the best picture quality.

Before I tell you more, let me make an important suggestion — possibly the most valuable point-and-shoot suggestion this book has to offer. Ordinarily I just drop in tips unannounced, but this one deserves a fanfare. *Use ISO 400 film as your standard print film.* Use films of other speeds only for particular situations, lighting conditions, and printing requirements (see Table 2-1).

Well-intentioned photo store clerks may try to dissuade you from using ISO 400 film, which along with ISO 800 film is called a *fast* film because of the speed with which it reacts to light. They may tell you that you need a *slower* film — ISO 200, even ISO 100 — for best results. They may argue such advantages as finer grain, better color, and greater sharpness. But this advice is largely outdated, lingering from times when using fast films involved considerable compromise in picture quality.

In truth, you're unlikely to see much, if any, difference in quality between a snapshot-sized print from an ISO 400 film and the same from an ISO 100 or ISO 200 film. ISO 400 color print films are just so spectacularly good that using them involves little tradeoff. For specific technical reasons, in fact, you usually get *better* results than with slower film — greater overall sharpness, improved color, and richer detail. In truth, you can even use the sensational new ISO 800 color print films as your standard film; in fact, the preloaded film in most one-time-use cameras is ISO 800 film. Even in bright light, the camera's lens aperture and shutter speed range are such that overexposure is unlikely to be a problem — and the film tolerates overexposure very well anyway. (Note that the highest speed available in Advanced Photo System color print film and chromogenic black-and-white film, both APS and 35mm, is ISO 400.)

Table 2-1	Film Speed Buying Chart (Color Print Film)		
Film Speed	*Pros*	*Cons*	*Best Subjects/Light*
ISO 100	Finest grain of all; improves smoothness and detail in big blow-ups (11 x 14 and larger); helps soften distracting backgrounds in outdoor portraits	Increases the risk that hand tremors blur or soften the entire picture; reduces flash range and background detail in indoor flash shots; may not stop action outdoors	Landscapes in sunlight; beach and snow scenes; portraits in bright light; close-ups with flash
ISO 200	Reasonable compro-mise between fine grain and speed; less risk of blur due to hand tremors than with ISO 100 film; increases flash range by 40 percent over ISO 100 film	Still too slow for much low-light shooting; considerable risk of blur due to hand tremors at long zoom settings	All-around out-door shooting in moderate over-cast to bright sun; outdoor portraits in soft light; flash shots at medium distances
ISO 400	Best all-purpose film; fine-grained but *fast,* provides excellent picture quality in standard-sized prints; permits higher shutter speeds for better action stopping and reduced risk of blur from hand tremors; more faithful color in mixed (indoor/ outdoor) light; doubles the flash range of ISO 100 film	May suppress flash in indoor shots, making you *force* the flash when you don't want to shoot by existing light; shows grain in big blowups (11 x 14 and larger)	All-around shoot-ing in conditions ranging from deep shade and existing indoor light to bright sun; indoor flash shots at greater distances from subject
ISO 800	Excellent all-purpose film combining high speed and surprisingly fine grain; good fail-safe film for must-get shots; provides two-and-a-half times the flash range of ISO 100 film; offsets hand tremors due to long zoom settings; best film in mixed light	Expensive; may sup-press flash in indoor shots or create flash *ghosts;* shows grain in blowups (8 x 10 or larger)	All-around outdoor shooting from dawn to dusk; outdoor portraits in less favorable light; indoor existing-light shots; distant flash subjects

Switching to a fast film (perhaps to do some low-light shooting without flash) may mean that you have to get that slower film (ISO 100 or 200) out of your camera. But don't shoot off the remainder of a roll on any old thing — subjects you wouldn't ordinarily shoot — just to use it up. You have to pay for the prints, and you don't pay for prints of negatives that you don't shoot. Get over it and push the midroll rewind button. (It's marked with a double arrow/film cartridge symbol and is usually recessed or otherwise squirreled away so you don't push it accidentally.) And as you do this, remind yourself that film is photography's cheapest ingredient. (For more on midroll rewinding, see Chapter 1.)

Film speed and grain

One thing that does differ from one film speed to another is the film's *graininess*. Grain refers to the clumps of silver crystals that form the image during the film's development. Faster films (again, those with higher ISO numbers) have larger grain than slower films (those with lower ISO numbers), allowing them to capture light quickly. (A wide bucket catches more rain than a narrow one.) And the larger a film's grain clumps, the more visible their texture is in the print. Thus, fast films are said to be *grainier* than slow films. But the new ISO 400 films still have exceptionally fine grain, and most photographers are blithely unaware of the texture their larger grain produces.

With color film, the silver crystals that form the image during development are bleached out before processing is completed. This chemical action leaves only color dyes to reproduce the image. But these dyes "remember" the silver crystals' pattern, creating a texture that is visible in the print — though with fine-grained films, not all that visible!

Not too long ago, knowledgeable photographers shot as slow a film as conditions permitted. Faster films — ISO 400 films, I admit — used to be quite toothy in the texture created by their relatively coarse grain. Indeed, making the grain bigger is still the main way a manufacturer gives a film greater sensitivity to light. But my point, again, is that you're unlikely to notice the difference in grain texture between your photofinisher's prints from ISO 400 film and those from slower film. In fact, I think that you'll hardly notice any texture at all.

The main reason you won't notice much difference is that the negative doesn't have to be *enlarged* very much to make a 4 x 6- or 4 x 7-inch print. So the grain's texture isn't enlarged very much either. But ultimately, you must be the judge of that. You shouldn't let me stop you from using ISO 100 or 200 film if you really feel it makes a difference in your pictures.

Experiment to see the difference

If you're nearing the end of that roll of ISO 400 or ISO 800 color print film that I encouraged you to get, buy a short (12- or 15-exposure) roll of ISO 100 film and have it on hand. Then choose a subject and shoot the last few pictures of the ISO 400 or ISO 800 roll. After rewinding the roll, immediately load the ISO 100 roll and shoot some pictures of the same subject, or subjects, in the same lighting conditions. Try to include a smooth area in the pictures — a blue sky or a colored wall, or even just a prominent face. Smooth areas are where a film's grain is most visible.

After you get the prints back, first mark the film speed on the back of every print. Then shuffle them thoroughly. Now, compare: Decide which prints you like better and/or which have finer grain. I think you'll be hard pressed to tell the difference. I have a feeling you'll like the ISO 400 shot better, for reasons unrelated to grain!

You're more likely to see differences in quality between different speed films if and when you make a big blowup of your picture — 8 x 10 or 11 x 14 inches. In addition to making everything in the picture bigger, enlargements also make the grain bigger. Personally, I'm more than happy with big prints from my ISO 400 negatives; I can see the grain, but it doesn't bother me or interfere with the sense of detail in the image. And I'd rather not limit myself to slower film just for the sake of the occasional negative that I may want to blow up bigger than 4 x 6 or 4 x 7 inches.

Film speed and panoramic prints

One place that you may notice the effect of a film's grain is in a panoramic print. (You can find out more about getting panoramic prints in Chapter 3.) The grain is larger because panoramic prints, which measure either 4 x 10 or 4 x 11$\frac{1}{2}$ inches (depending on who does the printing), require a much higher degree of enlargement of the negative than 4 x 6- and 4 x 7-inch prints — in fact, about as much enlargement as a full-sized 8 x 10-inch print. (Think of a panoramic print, basically, as an 8 x 10- or 8$\frac{1}{2}$ x 11-inch print with the top and bottom cut off.)

I am most aware of grain with panoramic prints from ISO 400 Advanced Photo System film. (Because the APS negative is smaller, it must be enlarged more, so the grain is enlarged, too.) But only if the film is underexposed, or the printing is sloppy, does it really bother me.

The thing is, unless you're doing a side-by-side comparison of the sort that I suggest in the previous section, you're unlikely even to notice such things. And there is much more to print quality than just fineness of grain. A mediocre lens or inaccurate autofocus is likely to be a bigger factor, causing a loss of sharpness especially noticeable in enlargements. And even those factors aren't the biggest threat to image quality!

Film speed and shake

Far more important than film speed's effect on overall picture quality is film speed's effect on overall *sharpness*. In general, the faster (higher ISO) the film you use, the *sharper* your point-and-shoot pictures will be.

This relationship between film speed and sharpness has nothing to do with the lens or its focusing accuracy. It has to do with *shake* — camera movement due to your involuntary hand and body tremors.

Shake can cause an unwanted blurring of your pictures. But the effect is not always an outright blur. It's often just an annoying lack of crispness — an unexplained softness. My experience tells me that unsharp point-and-shoot pictures are more often due to shake than incorrect focus or a third-rate lens.

How does a faster film lessen the risk of shake? By making the camera set a higher shutter speed — that is, shorten the length of time the window in its lens stays open for the exposure. The longer the window stays open, the greater the chance that shake will blur the image (see Figure 2-5).

Figure 2-5:
Even in reasonably bright light, shooting with a slow film — ISO 100 or 200 — can cause camera shake to blur the image (left). Shooting with an ISO 400 film (right) lessens that risk, making pictures sharper.

ISO 100 film　　　　**ISO 400 film**

© Mark Harris (2)

Here's how to tell whether a picture's lack of sharpness is due to shake or incorrect focus. If the main subject is unsharp but the background or foreground (or any other part of the picture) is sharp, then the problem is due to incorrect focus. (See Chapter 6 for ways to ensure correct focus.) If, on the other hand, the entire image is unsharp or blurry, the problem is usually due to shake. At its most severe, shake creates a streaky, directional blur.

Using a faster film is all well and good, but don't let it make you lazy about holding your camera as steady as possible. Steadying the camera may take concentration and practice. You can even brace the camera by resting it on or pressing it against something.

Shake is personal. Some people are steady as a rock; others, like me, are the jittery type. Shake's effect also depends on the individual specs of your point-and-shoot — how slow a shutter speed it can set, for example, or at what light level it turns on the flash. Because a flash burst is so short, flash pretty much kills shake; in fact, if you're at all shaky about shake, just force the flash (see Chapter 7 for details). Of course, there may be times when you want to turn *off* the flash to keep it from firing and overpowering the quality of the existing light. And that situation is when a fast film makes all the difference.

Film speed and focal length

Your lens's focal length plays a big part in shake. *Focal length* is a number used to describe both a lens's *magnification* (how big or small it makes the subject) and its *angle of view* (how much or how little of the scene it puts on film). The farther in you zoom (that is, the longer your focal length), the more your lens magnifies the subject — pulls in your novice soccer player or the steeple on an old cathedral, for example. But the more the lens magnifies your subject, the more it also magnifies your shake. (See Chapter 5 for more on focal length.)

Point-and-shoot cameras hit you with a double whammy here. At longer zoom settings, the lens is forced to use a smaller aperture (that is, it reduces the size of the window that admits light to the film). The camera has to make up for the resulting reduction of light by setting an even slower shutter speed (that is, it increases the length of time the window is open). It does this, alas, just when it's most harmful — when you're zoomed way in.

Basically, the more you zoom in to fill the frame with a subject, the greater the chance shake will make your picture unsharp. So if you're in the habit of taking pictures with the lens zoomed way in, keeping a fast film in your camera — at least ISO 400, and maybe even ISO 800 — is all the more important (see Figure 2-6).

Figure 2-6:
Long zoom settings (left, 135mm) increase the risk that shake will blur your pictures. Shorter settings (right, 38mm) reduce that risk, resulting in sharper pictures. But if you like to zoom in a lot, use an ISO 800 film.

at 135mm

at 38mm

I know, I'm harping on the fast film. But with point-and-shoot photography, it solves a *lot* of problems. In its efficiency and quality, fast film gives your little camera a big advantage.

How Long a Roll Should You Buy?

A roll of film is measured not by the yard but by how many pictures fit on it. For this purpose, each frame of film is called an *exposure*. (Exposure is also the term used to describe the quantity of light that strikes the film when you take a picture.) The available roll lengths for 35mm cameras are 12 exposures, 24 exposures, and 36 exposures. (Types of 35mm film other than color print film may not come in 12-exposure rolls.) With 35mm rolls, you sometimes get an extra exposure or two at the end of a roll. Don't worry if your roll seems to be going a shot or two longer than its official length. If your camera is working properly, it automatically rewinds the film when it senses the tug at the end of the roll.

If your frame counter indicates that you've reached the end of the roll but the camera keeps taking picture after picture, its end-sensing mechanism may not be working. If this situation occurs, don't take any more pictures; they probably won't come out. Push the rewind button to rewind the whole roll. (See Chapter 1 for more on midroll rewind.)

One-time-use 35mm cameras, which come with a roll of film already loaded, have odd roll lengths, by the way. The shortest length is usually 15 exposures; the longest is usually 27 exposures. (Basically, you get three extra shots.) You can't get 35mm one-time-use cameras in 36-exposure models. Shorter roll lengths make sense for one-time-use cameras, because these models are best used occasionally. You buy them to shoot a particular event or place or to temporarily fill in for your regular point-and-shoot.

Film for Advanced Photo System point-and-shoot cameras comes in different roll lengths than 35mm. You can get rolls of 15 exposures, 25 exposures, and 40 exposures. One-time-use models using APS film usually come in 25-exposure models — no bonus shots included.

What roll length should you buy? You need to consider two things: cost and convenience. Film is like hamburger or laundry soap: The more you buy, the cheaper it is, per pound or per exposure. A 36-exposure roll of 35mm film selling for a typical $6.89 costs just over 19 cents per exposure. A 24-exposure roll selling for a typical $5.49 costs almost 23 cents an exposure. And a 12-exposure roll selling for a typical $4.19 costs about 35 cents per exposure. (Where I live, the local tax is over two cents per exposure on that roll of 12!) But you shouldn't buy long rolls just to save money on film. If you want to save money on film, buy multiple-roll pack deals.

Keep unused extra rolls in the refrigerator, in their original box, in a plastic bag or container. Refrigeration extends the shelf life of film and actually protects it in hot climates without air-conditioning. When you plan to do some shooting or are coming up to the end of a roll, get a new roll out of the fridge and let it warm up for an hour or more before loading it.

Convenience and practicality are more important considerations than cost. Say that you promised to send photos of your 40th-anniversary outing to your children. Now, because I firmly believe that the more pictures you take the better you get, I'd prefer that you shoot off an entire 36-exposure roll on such an occasion. But I'll be realistic. If the film that's already *in* your camera is a 36-exposure roll on its 25th exposure or a 25-exposure roll on its tenth exposure, you probably have enough film left to take the pictures you need. So you can finish off the roll, get it processed right away, and send those prints off. (Not to needle you, but there's always that chance you'll see a great picture after you've used the last exposure. So bring an extra roll.)

If, on the other hand, you have just a few shots left on the roll in your camera, or if your camera is empty, you may want to buy a 12- or 15-exposure roll and dedicate it entirely to your anniversary. Why? Because even if you only shoot ten pictures, you can have the roll processed right after the occasion, instead of waiting weeks to finish it. And you can get the prints off to your children before they start nagging you.

If you still have a few extra frames at the end of a roll you devote to an occasion, shoot them off if you can find worthy subjects — but remember that you don't *have* to. The photofinisher or minilab doesn't print frames that you don't shoot, and you only pay for pictures that get printed. To get the film to rewind before the end of the roll, push the midroll rewind button (see Chapter 1). Wasting a few frames of film on a short roll of film is still cheaper than buying a 36- or 40-exposure roll and "using it up" to get your money's worth.

Film is much cheaper, per shot, than prints. Don't take pictures that you don't need or want!

Now that I've told you when and why it's okay to use a short roll of film, I confess that I myself never, ever, shoot rolls shorter than 36 exposures. I shoot so many pictures that the film never stays in my camera for very long. And I'm talking about pictures that I take around the house and in the neighborhood. But you're not me, and the right roll length for that kind of all-around shooting depends on your personal photographic habits. If you're really trying to keep a visual diary or if you're in no particular hurry to get particular pictures back, then go with longer rolls. If you're the photographer about whom the staff at the local minilab jokes — the sort with two different Christmas trees on either end of the roll — then stay with shorter rolls. You don't want to be the brunt of that joke. Leaving film in the camera for that long, however, may cost you more than a few barbs from photofinishers.

Don't leave film in your camera for extended periods, especially if it's already exposed. Process film within a month or two of shooting it. Leaving film exposed and unprocessed for longer than that period may cause a deterioration in picture quality.

If you don't plan to have a roll of film processed fairly soon after removing it from your camera, store it in the refrigerator, in its original canister, in a plastic bag or container. No pockets, purses, or glove compartments, please! Keeping exposed film in the refrigerator doesn't just preserve the quality of its pictures; you also know exactly where to find it when you're ready to have it processed. Take the canister out of the refrigerator an hour or so before you deliver it to the photofinisher so that it can warm up.

Is your film fresh?

When I buy a carton of milk, I dig around for the one that's stamped with the latest "sell by" date. Actually, film has similar dating information stamped right on the box. Called the *expiration date*, it appears next to printed words such as *Develop before*.

You should definitely shoot and develop a roll of film before the date stamped on it. If you don't, it may not give you the best quality, diminishing your pictures' contrast and color brightness. Some merchants discount film that's past its expiration date; if I were you, I wouldn't buy it. It's not worth gambling on your pictures to save a buck.

Refrigeration can help keep film "fresh" both before and after you actually shoot it. But never, ever store film in a place it can get hot; this actually accelerates its aging, and may even cause prints to be discolored or otherwise flawed.

Whatever your day-to-day picture-taking routine, you should certainly buy a long roll or rolls for a once-in-a-blue-moon expedition — a whale watch, perhaps. Otherwise, you may find yourself reloading film just as that long-awaited humpback is breaching.

And buying long rolls for your vacations and travels goes without saying. But don't kid yourself into thinking a single 36- or 40-exposure roll is all the film that you need. Always keep two or three extra rolls of film on hand. You never know when you're going to have a shooting spree.

On the other hand, short rolls allow you to switch more regularly between different types, speeds, or even brands of film. This flexibility may give you more creative freedom — the ability to mix in black-and-white pictures with your color shots or to experiment with different film brands. Or you can switch to film of a different speed to suit different kinds of subject matter and lighting conditions, or specific printing and display purposes.

If you still can't decide what film roll length is best for your purposes, check out Table 2-2.

Table 2-2	Film Length Buying Chart	
Length	*Purpose*	*Advantage*
12-exp. rolls *(35mm)* 15-exp. rolls *(APS)*	One-time events; quick results; low shooting volume	Ability to finish the roll and get prints quickly; allows more frequent switch from one film type or speed to another

(continued)

Table 2-2 (continued)

Length	Purpose	Advantage
24-exp. rolls *(35mm)* 25-exp. rolls *(APS)*	All-around shooting; moderate shooting volume	Good compromise between convenience and cost; you're less likely to run out of film at inopportune times
36-exp. rolls *(35mm)* 40-exp. rolls *(APS)*	Diary-keeping; vacation and travel photography; high shooting volume	Encourages you to shoot more and to take many pictures of a single subject; cheapest per shot; my personal choice

Which Brand Should You Buy?

In choosing a film, you have to decide what type, speed, and roll length you want. But you also have to make one more decision: which brand to buy. I save this decision for last because in my view it's probably the least important. I can tell you, with little reservation, to shoot 36-exposure (40-exposure, if you have an APS camera) rolls of ISO 400 color negative film, for reasons of cost, picture quality, practicality, versatility, and motivation. But I can't tell you that one brand of film is necessarily better than another.

I'm not saying, however, that film manufacturers don't compete to make their films better than their competitors' film. They do so aggressively, and the results have been very, very good for photography — to the extent that truly bad films are few and far between.

In fact, film manufacturers hold endless focus groups to figure out what their customers look for in a film. Those qualities seem obvious enough. People want their pictures to be sharp, brightly colored, as detailed as possible, and to have realistic skin tones. Getting all those features in a single film is not easy, but current color print films — especially the fast ISO 400 and ISO 800 films that I recommend — come pretty darn close.

Once upon a time, different manufacturers' film tended to have different personalities — to render color and detail in visually distinctive ways. Modern film technology has minimized those differences, but that doesn't mean they don't exist. Those differences in color and detail are more evident in slide films than color print films, but it's still worth experimenting with various brands of print film to see whether one in particular gives you results that are more to your taste. For most purposes, you'll probably find little visible difference in sharpness or graininess between one maker's film of a particular speed and type and another's. Where you may see subtle differences, however, is in the films' contrast or color saturation.

Contrast refers to the tonal scale of a photographic image — specifically, the difference between light and dark values. That difference is easier to discern in black and white than in color, though you may see it especially in the ability of a film to render textures. But color *saturation* — the overall intensity with which a film renders color — is another story. Some films appear to produce redder reds, greener greens, and bluer blues than other films and are said to have *higher* color saturation. It sounds great, but higher saturation can come at the expense of a loss of texture and detail in brightly colored areas, and it may even cause an unattractive ruddiness in skin tones. Color saturation, the sense of texture, and the fidelity of skin tones are important qualities to evaluate in your pictures. Because they're more variable than graininess and sharpness, they're really *more* important.

Buy two short (12-exposure for 35mm, 15-exposure for APS) rolls of ISO 400 print film, each a different brand. Load one and do your usual all-around shooting, saving the last few frames. For those frames, choose a subject that has a variety of colors, tones, and textures. If you like, choose two subjects close by — one for a shot with flash, one for without. (Throw in a person for some skin tones.) Shoot the subject(s) with the last few frames of the roll.

Immediately load the other roll and shoot the same subject(s). (You can even put a card in each shot with the film brand written on it, so you don't have to look at negative strips to get that information.) Have your usual photofinisher process and print both rolls, and then compare the prints from each. Do you like one better than the other? If so, then stick with that brand — but just to be fair, periodically shoot another brand to confirm your preference!

Premium films

If you buy your film at photo shops rather than in drugstores and supermarkets, you may have noticed that the big-brand films sometimes come in pre-mium versions. Kodak has Royal Gold film in addition to its standard Gold line, for instance (see Figure 2-7). Available in more or less the same choice of speeds as the standard line, premium films are often marketed as special-purpose or special-occasion films — films for once-in-a-lifetime sorts of pictures.

Suspicious consumers may dismiss premium film as a marketing scam, but it really isn't. Real differences exist between a given maker's premium and standard films. The question, as usual, is whether you can see those differences; I think you'll be hard pressed to in a standard 4 x 6-inch print. Differences are more visible, if you have an attentive eye, in an 11 x 14-inch blowup for your family room wall. And, after all, important shots are the ones that you're more likely to be enlarging. But if you don't want to pay the price premium for premium films, don't feel as if you're taking chances with your most important pictures. Photofinishing often has more to do with the quality of the results than differences between films — certainly between films that are already very good (see Chapter 3).

Figure 2-7:
The high quality of premium films, such as Kodak's Royal Gold, makes them a good choice for pictures you want to blow up.

Private label films

Private label films are the films that big drugstore and supermarket chains sell under their own names, so I call them store-brand films. Rest assured that Well-Mart and Pharmaceuticals R Us don't have a thing to do with the actual manufacturing of the films. In most cases, reputable photo companies make these films. Eliminate the big two film manufacturers (hint: yellow and green boxes), and you can figure out which three companies provide the bulk of private label films (hint: German, Japanese, and American). It goes without saying that they make very good products.

Store-brand films can be very attractive because they're often part of a discount pricing scheme in which you get cheap processing, sometimes double prints for free or just a little extra, and perhaps a new roll of film each time that you drop off a roll for processing. In fact, the idea is to get you to keep coming back to the store — to buy more film, to drop it off for processing, and to pick up the processing. That's three chances to sell you lawn chairs.

You don't have to have store-brand color print film processed by the store where you buy it. You can give it to any minilab or other photofinisher.

If you've been using store-brand films and are happy with your results, then don't let me dissuade you from continuing — especially if the low cost encourages you to shoot more, which is my main agenda. But these stores do rely on mass-market photofinishing, which is variable in quality. If you feel that your store-brand pictures aren't turning out as well as they should or are even just a little dull-looking, consider a foray to a reputable minilab or an outfit that sends its film to labs directly associated with the name-brand film companies. Getting good photofinishing is especially important if you're handing in once-in-a-lifetime pictures or if you want big blowups.

Keep an eye out for *gray-market film*. This film is manufactured in various countries other than the U.S. and then imported when currency exchange rates give it the highest profit margin. You can tell gray-market film by the box, which is printed in other languages along with English.

The film itself may be fine to begin with; indeed, it's usually the same brand-name film that you ordinarily use. But gray market film's global wanderings may subject it to less-than-ideal storage conditions and improper handling, and you won't discover such ill effects until you shoot and process the film. At the very least, you shouldn't pay the same price for gray-market film as you do for the U.S. version of same film, because the dealer usually gets it at a considerable discount.

Name-brand films sold in the U.S. are, of course, often made in other countries — Fuji in Japan, Agfa in Germany. But they're made for immediate import under ideal conditions, rather than shipped around according to financial whim or stockpiled until the dollar is strongest. Here's the bottom line: If a film's box indicates that it's manufactured outside the U.S., shoot it only if it says "made for sale in the U.S." and has a U.S. proof of purchase.

Mail-order films and processing

You may have seen ads in photography magazines for mail-order film companies such as Seattle FilmWorks and Dale Labs. Though these outfits process your regular film, too, their business really revolves around a special movie film that is respooled for 35mm use. The process is unique in that you get back both slides and prints (see Chapter 3 for more details).

It bears repeating that good film is worthless if you don't get good photofinishing — good, rich prints. And just as you have choices with film (surprise!), you have choices with photofinishing. Literally and figuratively, it completes the picture. To find out how you can be more involved in your photofinishing, see Chapter 3.

Chapter 3

Working with Your Photofinisher

· ·

In This Chapter

▶ What is photofinishing?

▶ Getting a good negative

▶ Finding a good lab

▶ Talking to your lab

▶ Troubleshooting bad prints

▶ Matching negatives to prints

▶ Getting enlargements and reprints

▶ Restoring damaged pictures

▶ Keeping prints and negatives safe

· ·

*T*here comes that time when you press the shutter button, take a picture — and hear the telltale *whirrr* of the camera rewinding. You've finished the roll.

In fact, though, you've hardly started the roll. Because then you must take that little film cassette to a business — aptly named a *photofinisher* — that transforms it into an envelope full of bright, colorful pictures.

At least, you *hope* that's what happens.

Because if you're like many picture-takers, what really happens between handing your film over to a lab and getting your prints back might as well be voodoo. What mysterious processes go on once your film cassette is pried open? And how many times, after taking important or memorable photographs, have you crossed your fingers and prayed under your breath, "I just hope the pictures come out"?

Well, I'm here to tell you that photofinishing is not voodoo. It is magic, like all of photography. But it is dependable, repeatable, easily understood magic.

It is also magic that you, the photographer, can help perform. Your involvement with your pictures shouldn't end when the rewind motor kicks in at the end of the roll. If you dutifully follow this book's advice — or at least its most important suggestions, like locking the focus and using fill flash and shooting fast ISO 400 or 800 film — you'll see a noticeable improvement in your pictures. But believe me, there's a good bit you can do *after* you've pressed the shutter button to get better pictures, too.

This chapter goes into detail about how prints are made from your film. Having this understanding should help you figure out how bad prints happen, and how to get more good prints.

Some Day My Prints Will Come

The pictures you've taken on the roll of film in your camera are invisible until you get the film processed. Even if you could look at the film after you snap a picture (you can't, because opening up the film cassette to light would obliterate the pictures), you wouldn't see anything anyway. Well, yes, you'd see a piece of film with perforations, and a grayish coating all over it — but certainly no pictures.

The picture you took is present on the film only as an invisible image, known in photo jargon as a *latent image*. When you pressed the shutter button, the light that entered your camera caused an invisible chemical change in the film's light-sensitive coating, known in photo jargon as the *emulsion*. Think of the latent image as kind of a shadow on the film. It's the job of the photofinisher to turn that shadow into a visible, permanent image called a *negative*.

Photofinishing is the broad term covering everything that goes into making the film you've shot into prints and/or other visible, usable forms. Photofinishing has two main components. The first, *development,* is the chemical process that makes your film's invisible images visible and then makes these images permanent. In other words, it changes the film into negatives — those translucent reddish-orange strips you get back in the envelope with your prints, or, if you're using an Advanced Photo System camera, the single strip that comes back rolled up inside the cassette (see Figure 3-1). The other major photofinishing step, printing, is the process of taking those negatives and reproducing their tiny images in a bigger size on photographic paper, either as standard-sized prints or blowups (more correctly known as *enlargements*). The combination of film development and printing is also sometimes referred to as *processing,* and I sometimes refer to it that way, too.

Figure 3-1: The envelope, please. If you have a 35mm camera, the photo-finishing envelope comes back with both prints and strips of negatives. If you have an APS model, it contains prints and your film cassette, which houses the negatives.

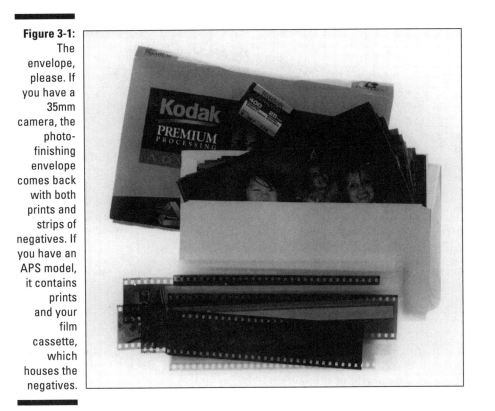

Several things make color-print photofinishing highly reliable. For one, the development process for color print film, which goes by the bland designation C-41, is a universal, worldwide standard. The C-41 process is the same in Bangkok as in Brooklyn. For another, developing and printing are highly automated, controlled by sophisticated computers. To develop a roll of film — 35mm or APS — a photofinishing technician needs to do little more than put the cassette into a machine, which, after chugging and churning, spits out a sparkling strip of negatives. Printing is likewise performed and monitored by very smart machines.

All this motorized magic may lead you to think that humans have no say in the process. Not true. Photofinishing isn't entirely robotized, nor can it be. At the very least, its processes must be watched by people who make sure the machines are operating correctly, that the chemicals are fresh, and that the film and paper are running through the system smoothly.

Which print surface to choose?

Unless you tell him otherwise, your photo-finisher ordinarily prints your negatives on *glossy* paper — that is, paper with a shiny surface. You can also ask for nonglossy paper, which usually goes by the name *matte.* Technically, matte paper has no shine whatsoever, but some brands may in fact have a bit of luster to them. Matte paper may also have a slight texture, as opposed to glossy's glassy smoothness.

A matte surface seems artier — somehow less commercial-looking — than a glossy surface. And it definitely hides greasy fingerprints. But glossy prints are the standard in photofinishing because they usually make your photographs look better than matte prints. The extra shine brightens colors, adds crispness to the subject's tones, and makes the picture actually appear sharper.

You may have a particular reason for wanting a matte print. It could have just the right look for a homemade greeting card, or lend a more impressionistic feeling to a particular image. But otherwise, I'd stick with glossy. In fact, if your pictures ever come back on matte paper when you didn't ask for it, it usually means the photofinisher either ran out of glossy or is trying to use up his excess supply of matte! Request that the roll be reprinted on glossy paper.

And during printing, human operators — call them photofinishing technicians — can exert still more control. They can even override the decisions of the machines' computers, if need be. In fact, the technicians fiddle with those decisions on a regular basis. This brings me to an important point — the most important point of this chapter, really, and one that many people often overlook.

There is no one, single way to print a color negative. Prints from the same single negative can be made lighter or darker. They can have their colors changed — made less blue, for example, or more reddish. Prints are not simply copies of the original negative; they are more like interpretations of the negative. And you, as a photofinishing customer, can request a different interpretation, when you first get prints made, or anytime later.

The negative is the very picture you shot — the physical film that ran through the camera when you were photographing. The camera took those big, real-world scenes you "framed" and recorded them as little rectangles on that strip of film. Again, development just makes all those little pictures visible and safe to handle in the light of day. But after development is done, the negative can't be changed. Prints are a different story. Prints are en-larged versions of that negative — with the difference that tones and colors are reversed to recreate your original subject. But you can think of printing really as taking a *picture* of the *negative,* much like taking a picture of a scene with your camera.

Just as you can shoot two, three, or more pictures of a scene with your camera, the printing machine can be set to shoot multiple prints of a negative, or of all your negatives. (That's how it does those double-print orders I suggest getting in the sidebar "Double your pleasure," later in this chapter.) You can get prints made right after you've had the film processed, which is the usual practice. Or you can get them made 25 years later. (In fact, getting a new print from an old negative is the best way to "restore" faded pictures — see the sidebar "Everything old can be new again: Picture restoration.")

But keep in mind that whenever you choose to make another print, *the printing machine can be told to make it differently.* The printing machine's computer brain — or the human operator — can command the machine to alter the light that makes the print, so that the print comes out lighter, or darker, or different in color.

Everything old can be new again: Picture restoration

You're looking through an old photo album, and there it is: That picture you asked Great Aunt Gretyl to shoot of you with your parents at your high-school graduation. But it has faded, and the color has taken on a weird pinkish hue. Can this photograph be saved?

If you have the original negative, almost always. Negatives usually withstand the ravages of time better than prints. If you can dig up the negative, just take it to a photofinisher and get a new print. Even if there's some fading or color change in the negative itself, a photofinisher can usually adjust for it quite well in printing.

Can't find the negative? The computer can come to the rescue. Digital print restoration services are increasingly available through local labs or mail-order. They scan your old print and then use special photographic software to get colors back to their old selves; remove marks, stains, creases, and cracks; or even sharpen up the picture a bit. They then print the retouched image file on a photographic-quality color inkjet printer or color laser printer. Quite frankly, the results can be amazing.

By the way, it's now perfectly feasible for you to do this electronic photo restoration yourself, on a moderately capable home computer. If you have one, but don't have a scanner for it, you'll need to have a photofinisher scan the print for you and "write" it on a Kodak Photo CD or other digital storage source that you can access with your computer. Once this is done, you can do restoration work on that old picture with inexpensive programs like Kodak Picture Easy Software and Adobe PhotoDeluxe. If your computer setup doesn't include a printer that gives you high-quality color output, you'll also have to find a lab or service bureau to print your digital file. (Good copy shops may offer this service.) For more on this, see Chapter 15.

Think of a color negative as a musical score: It contains the clef, the notes, and the time signatures needed for your photographs. (After all, people call photographs compositions!) The print, then, is like a *performance* of that score. Just as the most brilliant piece of music may sound off-key and lifeless in the hands of unskilled musicians, a superb negative can look bad in a print made by a careless photofinisher. And just as the World's Best String Quartet can make a mediocre piece of music sound sensational, good photofinishing can wrest a pretty good picture out of a so-so negative.

Your role in all of this? You guessed it: You're the conductor — and, of course, you also composed the score! So here's how you and your negatives and your photo lab can make beautiful music together. The first step is to look for some good performers.

Types of Photofinishers

Three kinds of businesses do color-print photofinishing: mass-market labs, minilabs, and custom labs. Amateur photographers use mass-market or minilab processing (or a combination of the two) almost exclusively, so this chapter concentrates mainly on them.

Custom labs cater to professional and advanced amateur photographers, so they're expensive. They may also be hard to find. The work of top-notch custom labs, though, is routinely superior to the best automated photofinishing. Custom labs also provide services that are unavailable at popularly priced labs. If you think you might want to use a custom lab, refer to the sidebar "The customs of the country" later in this chapter.

Mass-market photofinishing

Mass-market labs are what they sound like: industrial-sized places that develop and print lots and lots of film. Many of you are familiar with their services as "drugstore" photofinishing, not because the drugstore actually does the work but because you drop off your film at a retail store like a drugstore or, these days, perhaps a supermarket or discount store. From there, your film is picked up by van and whisked away to the big lab, developed and printed, put in envelopes, and then sent back to the retail store. These facilities may also be known as regional labs because they serve entire regions, perhaps several states. One of the biggest and best known of mass-market labs is Qualex, which is owned by Kodak and provides what's known as *Kodak Premium Processing*.

The processing offered by merchants of store-brand films (see the sidebar "Store-brand photofinishing") is mass-market photofinishing. Drive-through, drop-off photo booths in shopping-mall parking lots are the retail outposts of mass-market photofinishers.

Store-brand photofinishing

One of the more economical ways to buy film is at a store that sells film under its own brand name. These private label films, which I describe in Chapter 2, are made by major manufacturers and are usually quite good in quality. Stores that sell private-label films usually offer photofinishing, too, often at a deep discount. The work is done by a mass-market lab under contract to the store.

One argument for store-brand photofinishing is that the store's lab may do a better job with store-brand film because it's more familiar with it. A lab that processes thousands of rolls of store-brand film every week may optimize its methods to do a more consistent job with this film than would another mass-market lab, or even a minilab.

I've seen good results from store-brand processing, and the price is right. If you're satisfied with this combination, stick with it. But I've also seen plenty of mediocre (and worse) store-brand photofinishing. Keep in mind that you don't have to get store-brand film processed by the store; you can take it to a minilab, and you might try getting a roll (or a few reprints) done there just to see the difference. I know people who economize on film by buying store brands and then splurge on good minilab processing — at least for important pictures.

The great advantage of mass-market processing is low cost: High volume allows these outfits to do photofinishing at very competitive prices. For the same reason, mass-market labs almost always offer good deals on double-print orders, as well as frequent promotions — free or low-cost reprints and enlargements if you have them process a certain number of rolls, for instance. These labs' drop-off points are probably also very convenient for you. They may be in the supermarket where you always shop, or in the shopping mall you pass every day on your way to work.

These labs do take a day (or two, or three) to process film. (Some drugstore and photo-booth operations offer same-day service if the film is in by a certain time, but you still have to make two stops.) Picking up your prints may be an inconvenience if you don't have food shopping or mall errands to do. And while most mass-market labs are careful about handling film, the possibility of loss is greater with them than it is with minilabs (see the following section), which do their processing right in the store.

But by far the greatest disadvantage of mass-market labs is that you get no personal service. You may hit it off with the sales clerk at the counter, but that person is just a sales clerk. If you ask to get a print redone — and if I have any say in the matter, you'll be asking more often — the negative goes back into an envelope and is returned to that big, anonymous lab. There, a person you'll never meet reads your instructions (or whatever else the sales clerk has scribbled on the envelope) and takes a guess as to how much lighter or darker or less blue you want your print. And then the negative and print make yet another trip back to the store.

Double your pleasure

Sharing pictures with family and friends is easier if you take advantage of photofinishers' doubles service. For $2 or $3 more a roll, typically, photofinishers make two prints of every frame at the time that you have your film processed. (Some photofinishers give free doubles as a promotion; others may charge as much as half of the original price on the second set of prints.)

If you get doubles, you can immediately send off or give away the extra prints of shots that are worth sharing — and have copies for yourself as well, no reprinting required. Otherwise, given your busy schedule, you may never get around to having reprints made. Or by the time you find the time, the pictures may seem outdated, and you won't bother.

Of course, you end up with two prints of some less good, or even not-so-good, pictures. Throw the extra print away if it bothers you. Or give it away. After all, its recipient doesn't have the better shots to compare it to and should be more than satisfied.

Getting doubles of a whole roll is no more expensive than getting several reprints — and if the roll is full of great pictures worth reprinting, it's cheaper. But the real point is that you don't have to go to the extra trouble of ordering reprints. Of course, if you want to send print copies to two or more people, you have to deal with reprinting, not such a big deal when you know what you're doing.

The minilab

If you have a minilab in your neighborhood or town — and chances are you do — you've probably noticed that it has its own developing and printing machinery right on the premises. You drop off film there, it's processed there, you pick up your prints there. As a result, minilabs tend to provide much faster service, typically an hour or two. (That's not hard and fast; I've used a few pokey minilabs that take a full day to get the job done.) The real tipoff of the minilab, though, is not turnaround time but equipment. The printing machine is almost always right out in the open. It's about the size of a large office photocopier, with a place at one end for an operator to sit at a kind of control panel and viewing screen. Some minilabs arrange their hardware so that you can see the uncut strip of fresh prints feeding into a bin in the store window!

And right there is the great advantage of the minilab: Your prints are done in-house, not at some factory-sized lab 50 miles away. If you're dissatisfied with a print and want to get it reprinted, you can get it done there and then, right after you've looked through your envelope of prints. You can probably even talk to the person who was running the printing machine. If you have a question, or a complaint, or a suggestion, or just want to chew the fat about film and cameras, the minilab is where it's at. Photography is the minilab's business, not lawn chairs or cosmetics or groceries.

People like minilabs for their fast service. It's great to drop off film on your way to lunch and pick up prints on the way back. I like this, too, but another big selling point of the minilab is quality. Overall — and as with everything in photography, there are lots of exceptions — minilabs do a better job of printing than mass-market labs. And even if a minilab print doesn't look so hot, it's a simpler, faster, and more personal process to get it reprinted. Should a negative really prove impossible to print well — it happens — a good minilab operator will take the time to explain it to you, perhaps even showing you what's wrong with the negative.

What you get with a good minilab, to put it plainly, is a relationship. A good minilab operator wants your business and wants your pictures to improve, because that will only increase his or her business. And you want good printing (including courteous reprinting) and knowledgeable service. When you find the right minilab, you've found a partner in good picture-taking. So a minilab may be worth the search.

Minilabs have some drawbacks, of course. You may have to go out of your way to get to a good one. Minilabs are typically more expensive than mass-market labs, anywhere from a few cents more per print to twice as much. (The average seems to be about 30 to 40 percent higher, which, for a 36-exposure roll of film, may put a bite in your wallet.) Minilabs usually don't offer the cut-rate promotions common with mass-market labs, although they do offer double-print orders for a small premium, and sometimes freebies like an 8 x 12-inch enlargement with every roll of film processed. Minilabs also have to send out for some services, like big blowups: Anything over 8 x 12 almost always goes to a mass-market lab, although minilabs tend to use the better services such as Kodak Premium Processing. A fair number of minilabs can't make prints any bigger than a standard 4 x 6. And while minilabs usually sell a good variety of film and batteries, and often have a nice selection of frames and albums and other picture paraphernalia, these items may be more expensive than at the discount store.

 If you're a new user of an Advanced Photo System point-and-shoot, I'd suggest you take your film to the minilab that has given you good service on 35mm film in the past. If the minilab doesn't have the special machinery needed to process APS film and prints on the premises — many still don't — it will have to send it out to a mass-market lab anyway. But the minilab may well send APS film to a Kodak Premium Processing lab, which in my experience does very good work and offers an excellent fixed-priced deal on APS processing. (See the sidebar "A prints-ly sum: How much it all costs.") Minilabs throughout the country are slowly but surely installing APS photofinishing machines. So even if your preferred minilab doesn't have the machinery yet, stick with it anyway if you like the service you get.

It is now my sad duty to report that there are crummy minilabs, too. I've dealt with minilabs for whom customers are merely another jingle of the cash-register bell. They're the ones who blame obvious bad printing on you or your camera. Or refuse to do makeup reprints at no extra cost. Or charge you plenty, but make prints no better than the cheapest drugstore service. Or give you back whole rolls of film printed off-color or too light or too dark. And so on. My advice in these circumstances is to make your objections known, find another lab pronto, and don't hold the actions of such a business against the many conscientious minilab operators out there.

The mail-order option

Astute shooters may be thinking, hey, he's left out another kind of photofinisher: mail order. Well, not really. Mail-order photofinishing is simply a variation of mass-market photofinishing. The only difference is that you send your stuff to the processing lab directly, via the mail, rather than using the intermediary of a drugstore or supermarket. In most instances, mail-order labs provide you with *mailers* for your film. (You frequently find them bound into magazines as promotions). These mailers may be *prepaid,* which means you buy empty envelopes at retail (or by mail order) and then send in your film as you shoot it. The envelope itself is your proof of payment. Lots of Kodak Premium Processing is done through prepaid mailers.

Although the mail-order approach has all the disadvantages of mass-market photofinishing (including increased possibility of film loss and an even greater time delay), it has some real advantages. Mail-order photofinishing is convenient for people who live far away from a photofinishing service. (The turnaround time is usually a week, though that depends on what kind of week the post office is having.) And some people just see mail-order photofinishing as less of a fuss. In fact, many travelers enjoy dropping film in the mail as they shoot it, so that prints are waiting for them when they get home. (This saves you carrying around exposed rolls of film, though mailing film is ill-advised in corners of the world with dicey postal services.)

A prints-ly sum: How much it all costs

Most photofinishers use à la carte pricing — that is, you pay for processing on an item-by-item basis. A 24-exposure roll of 35mm film costs me $10.66 (plus taxes) to have developed and printed at my favorite minilab, or $8.99 at the local supermarket that sends out to a mass-market lab. (These are fairly typical big-city prices for these services; prices may vary in your area, but probably fall within this range.)

Those prices break down this way. The minilab charges $2.50 to develop the film, plus 34 cents for each print. The supermarket also charges $2.50 to develop the film, but only 27 cents for each print. The supermarket price, though, includes a "free" second set of prints as a special promotion.

Prices for Advanced Photo System processing are a different story. For developing and printing a 25-exposure roll, my favorite minilab charges me $13.49. A seemingly whopping $4.99 of that price is for the developing, but also includes an index print. (See Chapter 14 for more on the APS index print.) The per-print price is actually the same as with 35mm: 34 cents for either C or H format. And the supermarket? It charges $10.78 for a 25-exposure APS roll, but again, the index print ups the price. Prints are the same price as with 35mm.

Panoramic prints skew the picture, though. My minilab charges a lot more than the supermarket for panoramic prints on the original order — $1.00 apiece versus 52 cents. So if ten of the pictures on a roll are panoramic shots, the minilab charges me $20.09, while the supermarket is quite a bargain at $14.28.

When the supermarket charges for second prints, they are generally about seven cents each — $1.68 extra on a 24-exposure roll. My minilab charges 10 cents extra for second prints, or $2.40 more for a 24-exposure roll. With APS film, C or H second prints are 17 cents at the minilab, 13 cents at the supermarket. So whatever type of lab you use, double prints are the best bargain in photofinishing.

This is especially clear when you look at prices for reprints from already-processed film (your existing negatives). My minilab charges 50 cents for a 4 x 6 reprint from a 35mm negative, the supermarket 35 cents. Why more for a reprint than the original print? One argument is that the negatives are now cut into short strips, so they require more handling to print. But the real reason is that the labs get a bigger markup on the smaller orders. APS reprints take a major jump: At the minilab, they are 89 cents for C reprints, 99 cents for H reprints, and $1.98 for P reprints! Think the supermarket will be cheaper here? Guess again — its prices are 89 cents, 99 cents, and $2.29!

Note that most mail-order labs also have à la carte pricing, even if you pay a set price for a roll up front. To reimburse you for negatives they can't print (or for a roll you didn't fully shoot), these labs usually include credit vouchers for reprints in your returned order. So if you have a high proportion of unprintable negatives per roll and don't cash in these vouchers on later rolls, you may not be getting much of a bargain!

Some photofinishers offer true fixed-price processing: One price covers developing and printing, no matter what the final assortment. Kodak Premium Processing offers a widely available deal for Advanced Photo System film of $8.95 for a 25-exposure roll — any combination of print formats. Is this a good price? Yes, especially if you shoot a lot of panoramic pictures. In fact, if you shoot the whole roll as panoramas, you save $13.83 over the aforementioned supermarket processing, and $21.04 over the minilab! If you shoot the whole roll as C prints, the savings is less, but still a savings.

The bottom line? Check prices before you assume mass-market labs are cheaper. If you're an APS fan, check out the one-price-fits-all deals such as that from Kodak Premium Processing. And get double prints. If you give prints away (of course you do!), you'll save a fortune in the long run.

Oddball films

A number of mail-order photofinishing companies promote their own "brand" of films by offering them as a package deal with inexpensive processing that may include both prints *and* slides from the negatives. These films are usually respooled 35mm movie film — and cannot be developed with the universal C-41 process for color print film. To get them processed, you must return them to the same company for photofinishing, a closed loop sometimes known in photo jargon as *captive processing.*

Photo magazines occasionally test these films against conventional color print films, and they prove anywhere from okay to very good, depending on the type of film and the lab. The consensus is that they may be a touch grainier and less bright in color than the best conventional films, but that they deliver more than acceptable prints and slides.

Some big captive-processing outfits like Dale Labs and Seattle FilmWorks get good marks from their customers for reliable and consistent service. These labs also offer conventional C-41 processing, and many folks use them just for that. But keep in mind that their services aren't really unique. Most mass-market labs can make slides from your existing negatives, for example, and if you actually shoot slide film, your minilab can send it out for Kodak Premium Processing. Remember, too, that after films requiring special processing are developed into negatives, you can have them reprinted at any other lab, mass-market or minilab.

Many mail-order outfits offer aggressive promotions, like cheap or free film, or extra reprints or double prints at low cost. But again, if you want a reprint, or have some other problem, Who you gonna call? Some mail-order photofinishers do have customer-service phone lines. But nothing beats face-to-face service.

How to Get Good Prints

Getting good prints starts with taking the pictures. Here are the four most important ways to get the technically good negatives on which good printing depends:

- ✔ **Lock the focus.** If your negative isn't focused on what you want sharp, the best photofinisher in the world can't make it look sharp in a print. (See Chapter 6 for more on focusing.)

- ✔ **Use fast film.** I mean ISO 400 as standard, ISO 800 if you're shooting a lot of pictures in dim light, or of moving subjects, or with a long zoom setting. If your negative is blurry due to movement (either in the subject or the camera), a photofinisher can't sharpen it. Fast film is the best insurance against this kind of blur. (See Chapter 2 for more on film.)

✔ **Stay within flash range.** Your built-in flash has limited power; even with ISO 400 film, the greatest distance at which it can light a subject is usually around 20 feet, if that. Take a picture from farther away and too little light will come back to the film, producing a muddy-looking print that lacks detail. This is a *very* common cause of bad prints. (See Chapter 7 for more on flash.)

✔ **Use fill flash.** Even outdoors on a bright day you can get pictures that lack detail in critical areas — people's faces in particular. This often happens with backlit subjects, those in which strong light is coming from behind. The best cure for it is to set your point-and-shoot to fill-flash mode (also known as "flash-on mode"), which adds light to your subjects' faces. (See Chapter 7.)

The last two items on that list are remedies for what is far and away the most common kind of unsatisfactory print: the so-called *muddy* print. You've seen muddy prints, and you know them when you see them. But it's important to define the problem clearly.

The term *muddy* is pretty descriptive as it stands, but it has a distinct meaning when applied to color prints. First of all, muddy prints have very poor *contrast;* in other words, there's not much difference in tone between areas that were bright and areas that were dark in the original subject. Both come out as dull, in-between tones, neither bright nor dark. A muddy print also has muted colors, typically brownish-beige (like mud). Muddy prints lack detail — a sense of texture and dimensionality — especially in parts of the scene that were in shadow. (Muddy prints have little sense of *light* in them.) Finally, muddy prints look much more "grainy" than you'd expect, with an unattractive gritty appearance to them.

Most muddy prints are the result of underexposure: Not enough light made it to the film when the picture was taken, so the film couldn't produce enough detail in the processed negative. (Imagine trying to see at night through dark sunglasses, and you'll know how underexposed film feels!) This shortage of light results in a thin negative. If you hold a thin negative up to the light, it will look quite transparent, except for its overall reddish-orange cast. You may even have a hard time telling where the picture area ends and the clear edges of the film begin. When a photofinisher tries to print a negative like this — even tries very hard — the print will end up muddy. Most of what shows up in the print is, in fact, the actual grain texture of the film, rather than subject details.

Two mistakes are responsible for almost all muddy prints. Number one is taking a flash picture of a subject beyond the limited range of your built-in flash. (I discuss this topic in Chapter 7.) Number two is taking pictures in light too dim for your camera or film to record. A common example is shooting the end of a sunset with a fairly simple camera loaded with ISO 100 speed film. This slow film needs a lot of light to make a good picture, but the sunset can't provide it — nor can a basic model point-and-shoot keep its shutter window open long enough to get enough light to the film. Result: Those beautiful reds look soupy beige in the print.

Finding a Lab

Got your shooting procedures in order? Now it's up to the lab. Do you have a good one? Chances are, you've been going to a certain photofinisher because it's convenient, or your friends and family have been going there for years, or it's in the drugstore and you assume that's where you're supposed to take film. If you're satisfied with your prints, by all means stay with the photofinisher you're using. If not, maybe you should look for another. Or maybe, just maybe, you don't know how good photofinishing can be — and should try out another lab, just to see how its work compares with that of your usual place.

You can generally find or identify a good photofinisher in three ways, as follows. (Note that the communication involved in some of these suggestions makes them applicable mainly to minilabs.)

- ✔ **Word of mouth:** Somebody you know shows you some prints, and they look better than yours. Ask her where she gets her film processed and give the place a try when you're finished with your next roll. Or test the photofinisher with a few reprints.

- ✔ **Step right up:** One way to tell whether a minilab is good is simply if it does a good business. Busy labs are usually good labs. Walk in, say you're looking for a new photofinisher, and ask to see sample prints. While you're looking them over, check out the store, too. Is it neat, well-organized, clean? If an operator is actually working at the printing machine, does he appear to fuss a lot with the controls? (That's a good thing.) Is the store stocked with a good variety of film? Do the customers seem satisfied with their prints? You might even ask one or two customers what they think of the lab's work. Most people are happy to answer, and may even show you some of their pictures. (I won't be held responsible for delays caused by doting grandparents!)

- ✔ **Test prints:** Probably the best method. Somewhere in your possession you should have some prints you think are top-notch, with rich color and crisp detail. Now dig up the negatives for them. (See the section "The Match Game: Finding the Right Negative for a Reprint," later in this chapter, if you're having trouble figuring out which negative goes with which print.) It's best to choose four or five such negatives, taken of different subjects in different kinds of light. Now bring them to the lab you want to try and ask for 4 x 6-inch reprints. This test will cost you no more than a few dollars, and regardless of the outcome you'll have some reprints of favorite pictures.

By the way, it's okay to tell the lab people that you're testing them — that you're looking for a good lab and want to see how they do. Why not? You want the best work they can do, so put them on their toes!

Several things can happen with your test negatives. First (the best!) is that the prints come back and they're simply smashing. If the shop's prices are within your means, try them for your next full roll.

You might also get prints back that are quite good overall, with maybe one that's not quite up to snuff. One bad print is no reason to reject the lab. Go back, show the lab the print, and ask whether it can improve upon it. (The section "Photo Communications 101" tells you how to make such a request.) If the lab is good, its staff should try hard to get you a better print. If the lab's employees say they can't make a better print, ask them to show you the problem with the negative. Good labs do that, too. If the second try is up to your satisfaction, again, give the lab your next full roll. And if that's printed well, you just may have found your lab.

By now a nagging little voice in your head may be saying, "Gee, I remember those pictures of Uncle Clive that were all blue . . . maybe they shouldn't have been" or "I was wondering why those last vacation pictures were so light . . . could they have been fixed?" Indeed, maybe they could have been.

Which brings me back to the central point of this chapter. There is no single way to print a negative. If you are dissatisfied with a print for some reason — you feel that it's too light, or too dark, or that the color is off — you can request that the lab make a reprint. But there are limitations to what you can get in a reprint, and there's one limitation you need to under-stand right off.

A minilab or mass-market lab can only make prints lighter or darker overall or change the color overall. A print-machine technician can't make one part of the print darker and another lighter. She can't make one part of the print less blue and another part more blue. (Custom labs, on the other hand, can do some of these things. See the sidebar "The customs of the country," later in this chapter.)

A printing machine's controls are a little like the tint and brightness controls on your TV. When you turn the brightness down to make one part of the picture to your liking — a face, perhaps — you may make some other parts too dark. If you adjust the color to get the western sky a brilliant blue, you may make John Wayne's face look a little blue, too.

This all-or-nothing photofinishing principle is behind a number of annoying print problems. I describe these problems later in this chapter, in the section "Things That Can Go Wrong — and Do," a list of common printing snafus. This list should help you identify your prints' problems. But to get those problems fixed, you have to know how to talk to your photofinisher (see the following section).

Photo Communications 101

Let's face it — a lot of people are meek consumers. They usually take what they get. But as a photo consumer advocate, I have an obligation to discourage you from caving in when it comes to your important photographs.

As a photofinishing customer, you have a right to prints as good as can be made from your negatives.

Some photofinishing companies make a big deal about good print guarantees — that they'll reprint a picture at no extra charge if you're not satisfied with the print. Well, they're *all* supposed to do that. Satisfactory prints are what you're paying for when you hand your money to a photofinisher.

But just to reiterate, bad negatives do happen to good people. And when negatives are bad, it's impossible to get a good print. Photofinishers see a lot of bad negatives.

This is where that minilab relationship I keep talking about can come in handy. If you go to a minilab on a regular basis, it knows you. It knows you can take pretty good pictures. It knows you're not a crank. If you have a not-so-good but important negative, the minilab should be willing to try a couple of print variations for you to see what looks best to you. For your part, if the lab gives the print its best effort, there comes a time to acknowledge that the picture may not be a "keeper." Even professional photographers have their share of "dumpers."

And *good* negatives can be hard to print. A classic problem is a picture with bright sky above green foliage. A print with lots of leafy detail and bright color in the foliage will probably have a blank white sky. A print with a nice blue sky tone may have dark, nearly black trees. Here, a good photofinisher can compromise — adjusting the print's exposure to give you a reasonable balance between the two areas.

As with any relationship, the key is communication. Based on my experience with good minilabs, I've put together these guidelines.

- ✔ **Always bring the negatives!** The negatives are the real pictures, remember? The print is just one rendition of the negative. How do you know whether it's a bad rendition of a good negative (the lab's fault) or a pretty good rendition of a bad negative (your fault, or your camera's)? You don't. The only way to troubleshoot a bad print is to look at the original picture — the negative — with the help of your friendly lab staff. (Looking at the negative is really only an option with 35mm, because APS film is hard to withdraw from that little cassette.)

✔ **Be specific about your complaints.** Point out the exact objections you have to a print. This doesn't require any technical lingo. Use direct visual descriptions: "too yellow," or "too blue," or "too light," or "too dark," or "I can't see any detail in my aunt's face," or "My Uncle Clive just came back from Florida, and he's nowhere near that pale" are just fine. (Being explicit is particularly important with mass-market photofinishing, because you will have to write reprint instructions on the envelope. "Print is no good" is not a very clear set of instructions.)

✔ **Ask to be shown the problem.** If your photofinisher says a negative can't possibly print any better, ask him to show you, in the negative, exactly what's not up to snuff. The photofinisher may be right. Then again, when he looks at the negative, he may see detail that can be brought out in a print.

✔ **Be firm, but reasonable.** If you really don't like a print or reprint, say so. Labs depend on satisfied customers, and good labs will want a second chance. At the same time, don't throw a fit because one or two prints are a little off in a batch of 72. No lab is perfect all the time.

✔ **Warn the lab about unusual shooting circumstances.** If you've shot a roll almost entirely under household light or office fluorescents — both of which can produce color casts — be sure to inform the lab when you drop off the film. This way, the machine's operator will know to watch for these pictures and adjust the color to make the prints look more natural. Likewise, if you have a 35mm camera that can shoot panoramic pictures and you've taken some shots in this format, tell the lab beforehand so that the technicians can retool and print them in the correct shape and size. That way, you get panoramic prints with your original order and don't have to have them reprinted at extra cost.

✔ **Learn from mistakes — yours *and* the lab's.** If you've gotten some muddy prints because you've taken flash pictures from too far away, get closer for your next flash shots. (Or use a faster film, ISO 800 instead of ISO 400.) And if your lab made an honest goof in printing some beach pictures — say it made them too dark, so that the sunny scene looked overcast — you can alert them next time you take similar pictures so they print them accurately.

Things That Can Go Wrong — and Do

Here's a rundown of common problems with color prints, their likely cause, and suggested remedies, if any. Remember, if you're going back to the photofinisher, always bring along the negatives.

✔ **Problem: Outdoor daylight picture is too light. This problem is common with subjects having a lot of foliage.**

- *Likely cause:* The printing machine (or its operator) tried too hard to hold detail in the leaves and overdid it.

- *Can print be fixed?* Almost always.

- *What to do:* Go back to the photofinisher and ask for a darker reprint. It might help if you bring along another print of the same scene that you think looks right and leave that as a guide.

- *Note:* Don't confuse this kind of print with a muddy print. What I'm talking about is a print with lots of detail that's just very light, but with good bright colors. A muddy print has dull colors and poor detail.

✔ **Problem: Outdoor daylight picture is too dark — it looks like it's overcast instead of sunny. Especially common with beach pictures.**

- *Likely cause:* Photofinishing machine saw very large, bright areas and tried to compensate for them by making the print darker.

- *Can print be fixed?* Almost always.

- *What to do:* Go back to photofinisher and ask for a lighter print. Tell her it was a bright scene.

- *Further glitch:* A lighter print might have a hint of muddiness because it's possible your camera didn't get quite enough light to the film.

- *Note:* Scenes like this benefit from fill flash when parts of the scene (or people) are within flash range. (See Chapter 7 for more on fill flash.)

✔ **Problem: Picture taken of a snowy scene is grayish and muddy.**

- *Likely cause:* A double whammy. Your camera's light meter was fooled by all that white stuff and gave the negative too little exposure. Then the printing machine saw the same thing and made the print darker still.

- *Can print be fixed?* Only a bit.

- *What to do:* Go back to the photofinisher and ask whether any improvement is possible. The print usually can be made a little lighter, but it won't be bright and snappy (see Figure 3-2).

- *Further glitch:* The lighter you make the print, the muddier the shadows and other dark areas will look.

- *Note:* When shooting snow scenes or other predominantly light-toned subjects, add exposure with backlight compensation or exposure compensation, if your camera offers these modes. (Check out Chapter 4 for more on exposure compensation.) Always use fill flash with people pictures. (This problem also occurs when you shoot people standing in front of a very light background such as a sunlit white church.) (See Chapter 7 for more on flash.)

Figure 3-2: Snow trips up your light meter, causing a grayish print (left) that can be lightened in a reprint (right).

© Russell Hart (2)

🗸 **Problem: Indoor shot has funny yellowish, reddish, or brownish overall color.**

- *Likely cause:* You were taking pictures with fast film indoors under conventional household light. Your flash didn't fire because the light was sufficient — or else you deliberately turned off the flash for a natural light effect. (Household tungsten bulbs produce a very warm color on film.)

- *Can print be fixed?* Pretty much, although not always totally.

- *What to do:* Take the negative back to the photofinisher and ask for a reprint. The printing machine's color filtration can be adjusted to make a new print less yellow, more natural-looking.

- *Further glitch:* Sometimes the negative has recorded so much yellow and so little light of other colors that you can't get it all the way back to a normal color rendition without muddying dark parts of the picture.

- *Note:* Some people like the added warmth.

🗸 **Problem: Indoor picture has an objectionable green cast.**

- *Likely cause:* You were shooting without flash under fluorescent lights.

- *Can print be fixed?* Pretty much, though not always totally.

- *What to do?* Ask your photofinisher for a redo with different color *filtration* to make the print less green. (This means that he will change the color of the actual light used to make the print.)

- *Further glitch:* Sometimes the negative has recorded so much green and so little light of other colors that you can't get it all the way back to a normal-looking rendition without muddying dark parts of the picture.

If you're shooting people under fluorescents, set your point-and-shoot to its fill-flash (flash-on) mode. This will add light of a more normal color to people's faces, though the background may still end up green. (For more on flash, see Chapter 7.)

✔ **Problem: Person's face in the foreground or bottom of a flash shot is *burned out* — that is, too light.**

- *Likely cause:* The printing machine saw all the dark area above or behind the person and overcompensated by making the picture too light (see Figure 3-3).

- *Can print be fixed?* Almost always.

- *What to do:* Ask the photofinisher for a darker reprint. Explain that you want the person's face to be normal in tone.

- *Further glitch:* Making the person's face darker will make the background, or the top of the print, darker as well. If no one is visible in these areas, the darkness makes no difference. But anyone above or behind the main subject will appear darker in the reprint.

- *Note:* This is a very common problem in group shots made with flash. One way to avoid it is to move people around or reposition yourself so that everybody is about the same distance from the camera. (See Chapter 10 for more on positioning subjects.)

✔ **Problem: Outdoor nighttime flash shot is very muddy, lacks detail.**

- *Likely cause:* You were just too far away. The built-in flash in your camera has limited reach; most run out of steam by 20 feet, some even less.

Figure 3-3:
A flash subject against a dark background can end up too light in the print (left), but is easily darkened in a reprint (right).

© Russell Hart (2)

- *Can print be fixed?* Almost never.

- *What to do:* Ask your photofinisher if a slightly lighter or darker print would look better. You may see a small improvement.

- *Further glitch:* If you simply leave your camera set on autoflash mode to take pictures outdoors in low light, it curses you with a double whammy. Autoflash usually won't allow the camera's shutter — the window in the lens — to stay open very long. So besides the inadequate illumination on your main subject, the background of the picture doesn't get enough light, either.

- *Note:* This is probably the most common cause of muddy prints among amateur photographers. Your point-and-shoot's built-in flash may be the best thing about it, but it isn't a cure-all. In this case, deliberately setting the slow-sync flash mode (also called night flash), or even turning off the flash entirely (hold the camera steady!), will probably give you a better print. (See Chapter 7 for more on flash techniques.)

✔ **Problem: Picture of person against a bright background is near-silhouette, has almost no detail in face.**

- *Likely cause:* Strong backlight told your camera's meter that there was lots of light, so it automatically reduced the amount of light reaching the film. As a result, the picture's darker areas — including the person's face — didn't get enough light.

- *Can print be fixed?* Sometimes.

- *What to do:* Ask your photofinisher to make a reprint, this time with reduced exposure to lighten the person's face or figure. Sometimes the face or figure has enough detail to allow a decent rendition, though if the backlight was strong the detail may appear quite muddy.

- *Further glitch:* Even if the photofinisher can salvage some detail in the face, this will make the rest of the print much lighter and possibly washed out.

- *Note:* The best way to keep detail in a backlit portrait is to use fill flash, as I describe in Chapter 7. You can also add exposure — that is, get more light onto the film — by using either the backlight compensation or exposure compensation modes, if your camera offers them. (See Chapter 4 for more on modes.)

✔ **Problem: Print has small, randomly scattered white shapes — sometimes spots or blobs, sometimes hairlike.**

- *Likely cause:* Dust on the negative. Dust blocks the light with which the printing machine exposes the print, whiting out whatever part of the subject it lands on.

- *Can print be fixed?* Nearly always.

- *What to do:* Take negative back to photofinisher, point out dust spots, get a redo.

- *Further glitch:* If dust falls on negatives while they're still wet out of the processing machine, it can get embedded in the film. Special film cleaner may be required; consult your photofinisher.

- *Note:* If you have a recurring problem with dust spots on your prints, it's time for a serious talk with your photofinisher. Or maybe an introductory conversation with a new photofinisher. The same holds true if you seem to be getting frequent scratches in your negatives; see the following two problems.

✔ **Problem: Thin, straight white or black lines run lengthwise through the picture.**

- *Likely cause:* Scratches due to grit inside the camera or in the processing machinery; may also be caused by metal burrs or nicks inside the camera or processing machinery.

- *Can print be fixed?* Sometimes.

- *What to do:* If lines are white, they're on the back of the film and may be lessened in a reprint with an application of *nose grease.* (No, I'm not making this up. Printers have been doing it for years.)

- *Further glitch:* If lines are black, they're on the film's emulsion side, in the image itself. In this case, your only recourse is retouching — if the picture is worth it. (Consider digital retouching software, if you're computer-ready; see Chapter 15.)

- *Note:* Here's what to do to avoid the problem in the future. First, buy a small can of compressed air from your photo shop, open your camera's back or film compartment, and carefully blow out its interior to remove any grit or dirt. (Don't tilt or shake the can or you'll squirt propellant.) If the scratches persist, then they may be due to poor maintenance of the photofinishing machinery. Try another lab to see whether the problem goes away, and if it does, stick with the new lab.

✔ **Problem: White or black line(s) or gouges run through picture, often at a diagonal.**

- *Likely cause:* Scratches due to mishandling of negatives, by you or the lab.

- *Can print be fixed?* Sometimes.

- *What to do:* If lines are white and not too thick, try the nose grease remedy (see the preceding problem).

- *Further glitch:* If lines are thick or black, retouching may be the only way to save the picture.

- *Note:* Handle 35mm negative strips with extreme care.

✔ **Problem: People photographed against a colored wall or strongly colored background have a weird cast in their faces.**

- *Likely cause:* The printing machine saw lots of one color in the negative, thought it was a problem, and tried to fix it by making it more neutral.

- *Can print be fixed?* Almost always.

- *What to do:* Ask your photofinisher to reprint with more attention to the face tones in the picture.

- *Note:* This phenomenon is often called the *red barn effect* because it often shows up in pictures of people standing in front of big, brightly colored things like red barns. The printing machine looks at all that red, thinks it's a problem, and then tries to reduce the red. This results in people looking pallid, or even a bit blue, in pictures. But a careful print-machine operator won't let prints like this through.

✔ **Problem: Outdoor shot has great sky, but the ground (or water) below is too dark. Or the opposite — the ground (or water) looks fine, but the sky is nearly white.**

- *Likely cause:* The printing machine identified the predominant tone in the print and made it look the best. If a picture has lots of light sky, a printing machine makes the print darker to richen it — and the lower part of the image will look too dark. If a picture has lots of dark ground (or water), a printing machine makes the print lighter to preserve its detail — resulting in a washed-out sky.

- *Can print be fixed?* Sometimes.

- *What to do:* Ask your photofinisher to print for more tone in the area you want. Keep in mind that if the photofinisher lightens the ground (or water), the rest of the print gets lighter. If the photofinisher darkens the sky, the rest of the print gets darker.

- *Further glitch:* If your camera exposed the film properly for a big expanse of sky, the negative may actually be underexposed in the ground (or water) areas. If this is the case, adjusting the print to make these areas lighter can make them muddy.

- *Note:* Extreme differences in tone are a recurring problem with prints of landscapes. If a scenic shot is really important to you, and you want a print with good tones in both sky and ground, you might want to take your negative to a custom lab. (See the sidebar "Customs of the country.")

Getting Reprints

Possibly the most underused service at the photofinisher, *reprinting* just means getting another standard-size print (usually 4 x 6 inches, or, with Advanced Photo System cameras, usually 4 x 6 or 4 x 7 inches) made from the original negative. (A few labs still do the old 3^1/$_2$ x 5-inch prints.) Reprints are inexpensive — mostly under 50 cents apiece. In my experience, reprints also tend to get a bit more attention from minilabs than prints made in the first develop-and-print order. There's a good chance you'll actually get a better print when you get a picture reprinted.

One reason people shy away from getting reprints is that they're intimidated by the business of figuring out which 35mm negative matches up with which print. (Reprinting has been hugely simplified with Advanced Photo System film; see Chapter 14 for information on getting APS reprints.) That reluctance is understandable, given those loose strips of negatives stuffed into the envelope holding your prints.

Most minilab staffers will help you figure out which negative should be used to make the reprint you want. If you use mass-market photofinishing, the counter people may have some idea how to match negative to print — though they may not always pick the right one. With mail-order, of course, you're going to have to figure it out for yourself.

 You can get reprints made from prints. If you've lost the negative for a print — or can't bear the thought of rummaging through a dozen shoeboxes to find it — any photofinisher, minilab or mass-market, can make a print directly from an existing print.

It's a straightforward process: The lab literally takes a picture of your picture, develops the film, and then makes a print from that new negative. (Photo kiosks, described in the section "The Photo Kiosk," later in this chapter, make it even simpler. They work much like a photocopier, but give you photo-quality results within a minute or two.)

As easy as these reprinting methods are, they can't give you the picture quality that your original negative would provide — though they may come close. On the other hand, big enlargements made from prints rather than original negatives will be noticeably poorer in quality.

The customs of the country

If your local minilab or favorite mass-market lab is like a good family-style restaurant, a custom photo lab is like a gourmet chef you personally hire for a special dinner.

Good custom labs can cook up color enlargements that will give you a new appreciation for the limitations of automated photo processing. The key to custom printing is that it foregoes rapid-fire printing machinery, instead using old-fashioned enlargers — essentially precision projectors. (You may have seen one of these, or at least a picture of one. They were the major appliance of the home darkroom, once commonplace in this country!) An enlarger allows a custom lab technician to make *local* adjustments to your print. Unlike the operator of an automated printing machine, she isn't limited to making the whole print lighter or the whole print darker. The custom printer can make one part of the picture lighter and another part darker, to get every part of the print perfect, and not just a compromise.

A good example is that scenic shot on a brilliant day with blue sky at top and dark foliage below. If your regular photofinisher prints this picture, you'll get either a nice blue sky with nearly-black trees, or detailed, richly-colored trees with a chalky sky. A custom printer, though, will expose the print to get good tree tones and then *burn in* the sky — that is, allow more light to hit just the sky part of the print, to make it darker. Result: A beautiful print with a blue sky and green trees.

Now suppose that you had someone posing in the foreground of that picture, in shadow. The preceding enlargement might leave the person's face a little too dark. So the custom printer can hold back or *dodge* the face — that is, allow less light to hit that one small area. Result: The tones in the face are lightened enough to retain some detail.

Custom lab printers can also make very fine adjustments in color. And labs offering black-and-white services can make prints in which the overall contrast — the degree of difference between various tones — is adjusted to suit your taste. Custom labs offer a range of other services, notably in-house slide processing (often in less than three hours).

Before you run out and get all your negatives done up at a custom lab, remember that there's a price for this sort of mastery: A standard 8 x 10-inch custom color print can run $15 to $20, or more. An 8 x 10 done to exhibition standards can cost as much as $75. You're paying not just for manual labor, but for a practiced photographic eye.

Custom labs are really not the place to bring bad negatives. A custom printer may be able to wring a somewhat better print out of an underexposed *(thin)* negative, but unless the photograph is extremely important, I hardly think it's worth it. You should use a custom lab to get the best print out of a really good negative of a special picture.

Custom labs tend to be concentrated in cities with a substantial professional photo trade. You won't find them everywhere. If you're looking for one, start with the Yellow Pages, but you might also check with professional photographers in your area to see whether they know of one close by. (Some custom labs will work by mail or overnight delivery services.)

Finally, a warning: The word custom is a very popular marketing buzzword. Some run-of-the-mill mass-market photofinishers advertise custom hand enlargements. But if they can't offer lightening or darkening of individual areas of the prints, custom they ain't.

APS and PQI

One of the selling points of the new Advanced Photo System is a serving of alphabet soup called PQI, for Print Quality Improvement.

Most APS cameras above the very basic level have a magnetic head akin to that in a video- or audiocassette recorder. This head can record various sorts of information on APS film's transparent magnetic layer: the date and time, captions, and the print format you choose for the picture.

On midlevel and better APS cameras, the head also records information about the conditions in which you took the pictures. If you used flash, for example, the head marks that frame as a flash shot. If the scene had a high level of artificial light, that's recorded, too. Other things that can be recorded include whether a subject was very bright, or dark, or in-between.

When you get your APS film processed, this print-quality improvement information is read by the printing machine, which automatically adjusts its settings to make a better print. If the machine knows it's printing a flash picture, for example, it won't try too hard to lighten the print to hold background detail, because it knows this would make your main subject washed out. If the machine is printing a picture in which the subject is illuminated mainly by artificial light, it fiddles with the print's color to make it look more natural. If the machine knows that a picture was shot under very bright conditions, it won't darken it too much — because it may be a beach scene that should stay bright in the print.

In a sense, PQI does many of the things that a conscientious human operator will do from experience. And from the APS prints I've seen, PQI does boost the percentage of prints that are keepers on the first pass. This seems true of mass-market APS processing as well as that done by minilabs. But whether at the mass-market lab or the minilab, nothing compares to a human touch. So yes, PQI is a good thing — and it's even better in experienced hands.

The Match Game: Finding the Right Negative for a Reprint

Okay, you have a great 35mm picture of Great Aunt Gretyl with her prize-winning quilt, and you want six reprints of it, one for each branch of the family. You find the envelope from your original photofinishing order, no small task in itself. But the envelope contains nine orange strips — each with four negatives on it. How do you figure out which negative is the one you need for the reprints?

Thankfully, 35mm negatives are numbered. The numbers are on the edge of the film, right next to the perforations. (Some brands of film have numbers running along both sides.) These numbers are called *frame numbers*. If you hold up a negative to a window, you'll see frame numbers running in this sequence: 1, 1A, 2, 2A, 3, 3A, and so on up to the total number of exposures on the roll. Each strip picks up where the previous strip leaves off; one ends with 12A and the next begins with 13, for example. Some brands may start with zero, but otherwise they work the same. (If the numbers are backwards, just flip the negative strip over.)

You'll notice a couple of other things. One is that an awful lot of frame numbers are on the negatives — about twice as many numbers as there are frames! Another is that the frame numbers don't always line up very well with the pictures. They might be at the edge of a frame or at the mid-point of the frame or anywhere in-between. Don't wonder why!

Now, about that negative of Great Aunt Gretyl and the quilt. Finding it is truly easy if your photofinisher prints the frame numbers on the back of the print. (I commend this practice highly!) In this case, you'd simply flip the print over and look for printing that reads something like <No. 13A>. Now go through the negatives and find the strip that has 13A on it. At the photofinisher, simply present the negative and request six reprints of number 13A. It's also not a bad idea to offer your original print as a reference and say whether you want any adjustments on the reprints.

It's not always this easy. Many photofinishers don't print frame numbers on the backs of prints (or offer index prints), in which case you'll have to match negative and print by looking at the actual picture. First of all, check whether your negatives are in protective sleeves. Most photofinishers use transparent or frosted sleeves that let you see the negative pretty clearly. If that's what you've got, there's no reason to take the negatives out. Some photofinishers, however, just put the bare negatives into your print envelope. (I do not commend this practice!) If this is what you find, handle the negatives very gingerly, by their edges only.

Handle unsleeved negatives by the extreme edges only; never put fingers on the picture area. Greasy fingerprints will cause dust to adhere to the film, which will mar your reprints. Even more injurious, the oils in your skin can discolor or fade the image. (Eventually, perfect FBI-style fingerprints may be etched into the negative!) Always wash your hands thoroughly (with soap, please!) before handling negatives. That way, if you do accidentally touch the picture area, you won't be leaving as much of a damaging residue behind.

Now, hold each negative strip up to a bright window or other wide, even light source (lampshades work well). After you get used to the reversed tones and weird colors, you can tell which negative produced which print by looking at shapes and position. If there is only one negative of Great Aunt Gretyl, for example, it will be easy to identify. Now note the frame number. My practice is to pick the number that is as close as possible to the very middle of the frame. (Depending on how your camera winds film, the numbers may be upside-down in relation to the image.) If you're going to a minilab, bring the original print for reference, if you still have it.

Things can get trickier. Suppose that you're an enthusiastic shooter and you took six or seven very similar frames (see Figure 3-4). To find the right one for the reprint, you'll have to rely on subtle visual clues. Gretyl's head may be tilted a slightly different way in each frame. Or her hands may be in different places on the quilt. Or you may have composed some frames a little differently; Gretyl could be more to one side, or higher or lower in the frame. You may need your reading glasses — or a magnifier — to really spot the differences.

Once you've determined what you think is the right negative, note the frame number. Once at the photofinisher, physically point out the negative to the counter person, to see whether he agrees with your choice.

I hate to bring this up, but you can run into another problem. Suppose that you separated your picture of Gretyl from the envelope of prints — you put it in an album or on your refrigerator. And when you opened up the desk drawer to look for the negative, you found 17 envelopes of prints. In this case, you'll have to go though considerably more negatives. You can narrow your search by checking the dates on the envelopes — they're almost always dated — and you can usually recognize the right roll after looking at a few prints in an envelope. But you can prevent this drudgery.

Be a matchmaker with 35mm prints and negatives. Before you separate any print from its envelope and negatives, put a reference code on the back of the print and on the envelope. (Use a china marker, also known as a *grease pencil,* to mark the print. Felt-tip markers can bleed through to the front of the print, and ballpoint pens can emboss it.) You might mark an envelope Vacation/Birthday 1998 and then mark the same on the back of the print. If you have more than one envelope of the same subject, distinguish them with A and B or some such designation. Now when you flip over the print, you'll know right off in which print envelope you'll find the negatives.

Figure 3-4:
To pick the right 35mm negative for a reprint, study each frame for slight differences.

For a small extra charge — usually around $2 — some photofinishers will make an *index print* for a roll of 35mm film. (Not all photofinishers provide this service, but those that do may even offer it free, as a promotion.) Created by digital scanning of processed negatives, the index print is a sheet the same size as the prints themselves containing tiny, numbered "positive" images of every shot on the roll. Because each image's number corresponds to the frame numbers on 35mm film strips, negatives can be quickly and easily identified for reprinting and blowups, with no need to scrutinize them. You simply look at the index print for the picture you want reprinted, and note the frame number beside it. Index prints are a standard part of both Advanced Photo System processing orders (see Chapter 14 to find out what an index print looks like) and Kodak Photo CDs (see the section "The Electronic Photofinishing Revolution," later in this chapter).

Never cut 35mm negative strips into single frames! If you do, your photofinisher may refuse to reprint them. Negatives must remain in strips of four or more for handling purposes during printing.

Getting Enlargements

Enlargements — popularly known as blowups — are simply reprints made in a bigger size. They're great for display purposes: propped up on your desk, hanging on the wall, in big albums. (Gifts, too.) To get an enlargement made, you need to find the right 35mm negative, of course. (See the preceding section.)

Because the Advanced Photo System makes keeping track of negatives much easier than in 35mm, getting enlargements is much easier, too.

Because blowups are just big reprints, all the problems and remedies described in the section "Things That Can Go Wrong — and Do," earlier in this chapter, apply to enlargements as well. The main decision you have to make concerning blowups is how big they should be — a simple function of how and where you want to display them.

Don't blow up too much! What looks like a minor flaw in a 4 x 6-inch print (or something not visible at all) can turn into a big wart in a big print. Even fast films now have incredibly fine grain, so grain is usually not the problem but, rather, sharpness. (See Chapter 2 for more on film grain.) Something a bit out of focus on a 4 x 6 can look annoyingly unsharp in an 8 x 10- or 11 x 14-inch print. Slight blur from subject motion or camera shake will likewise be magnified as you go up in size. So before you get carried away and make a super 20 x 30-inch blowup, check the negative — not the print — with a strong magnifier. A minilab should have special magnifiers, called *loupes,* that are made for looking at negatives. Ask your photofinisher to help you evaluate the negative's enlargeability.

Standard enlargement sizes (for both 35mm and APS) include 5 x 7, 6 x 8, 8 x 10, 8 x 12, 11 x 14, 12 x 18, 16 x 20, 16 x 24, 20 x 30, and 24 x 36 inches. Most minilabs can make enlargements to 5 x 7 or 6 x 8, a few to 8 x 12, with same-day or overnight service. If you want larger sizes, they have to send out your negative to a mass-market lab (for example, Kodak Premium Processing), and it will be gone at least a couple of days. Really big sizes (20 x 30 or 24 x 36 inches) are typically special orders and can take as long as ten days, depending on where they're printed.

You may have noticed those differing print size shapes — 8 x 10 and 8 x 12 inches, for example. The 8 x 10-inch size is traditional, but it isn't a very good fit either for a 35mm negative or the APS *C* format, let alone the even-longer APS *H* format. Because an 8 x 10's proportion of length to width is less elongated than that of these negatives, a negative blown up to fit the 8-inch side of the print will make an image too big for the long side — sort of like a tall person's feet overshooting the bed. The photofinisher will have to *crop off* the short sides of the picture — that is, leave out a portion of the actual image — to fit it onto the 8 x 10-inch printing paper. And so the 8 x 12-inch print size — which fits the 35mm frame and APS *C* format just about perfectly — has become very popular. The same holds true with 16 x 20 and 16 x 24; the longer print shape allows a more full frame print of your 35mm negative.

A number of 35mm point-and-shoots allow you to take panorama format pictures. Some photofinishers print panoramas as a narrow strip on standard 4 x 6-inch paper, with dark bands above and below — the image itself relegated to a tiny area. True panoramic prints (4 x 10 or 4 x 11½ inches) are really enlargements, so you need to find out whether your photofinisher can make them, at least on the premises. Always alert the photofinisher when you bring in a roll of 35mm film with panoramas on it. The lab technicians will have to print the regular-shape pictures (if there are any on the roll) and then switch to another machine to make the panoramic prints.

Always mark 35mm rolls containing panoramic shots. If you have a 35mm point-and-shoot that shoots panoramas, get yourself a writes-on-anything fine-point marker. Keep it handy so that you can mark the cassette with a *P* when you finish shooting the roll. Then you'll remember to alert the photofinisher about the panoramas.

Getting panoramic prints with Advanced Photo System cameras and photofinishing is no sweat. APS photofinishing machines automatically make the correct-sized print (again, 4 x 10 or 4 x 11¹/₂ inches) with any pictures for which you set the camera to the *P* print format. Even though panoramas are one of the new system's standard print formats, they do require a greater degree of enlargement than the other APS print formats, which is why I mention them in this section.

Just as you can get full frame enlargements from your negatives, you can get both 35mm and APS panoramic shots enlarged. These prints are available in sizes such as 6 x 18 and 8 x 24 inches. Their effect can be dramatic indeed.

A point to keep in mind, though, about panoramic blow-ups: Because the top and bottom of the negative area must be cropped to create them (whether physically, as in a 35mm camera, or just in printing, as with APS), a standard 4 x 11¹/₂-inch panoramic print requires about the same degree of enlargement as an 8 x 12-inch blowup. And an 8 x 24-inch panoramic blowup is the equivalent of a 16 x 24! So it's especially important to make sure your negative is sharp. You may even want to shoot slightly slower films (like ISO 200) than my recommended ISO 400 if you intend to get big panoramic enlargements, because the film's grain texture will be less visible with them. (See Chapter 2 for more about film speeds.)

You can buy special *chromogenic* black-and-white film that can be processed and printed with standard color-print photofinishing machines, both at minilabs and mass-market labs. (See Chapter 2 for more on this unique material.) Chromogenic black-and-white film is available in both 35mm and Advanced Photo System cassettes. Some photofinishers are now offering enlargement service as well for these films.

The Electronic Photofinishing Revolution

The digital revolution in photography isn't limited to people who have filmless digital cameras. All sorts of electronic fun can now be had with pictures from conventional film cameras, as I describe in Chapter 15. The key is *scanning* your photographs — either negatives or prints. Scanning is the process that translates a photograph into an electronic form that can be understood by your computer, stored on special Kodak CD-ROMS, floppy disks, or other removable media (such as Zip disks), and even e-mailed.

The dating game

Many point-and-shoot models have the ability to automatically print all sorts of things on the front or back of your pictures. The most common way of doing this is with the so-called *date back* or data back, found on 35mm point-and-shoots. In fact, some 35mm models can be bought either with or without a date back.

A date back is basically a built-in quartz watch (in fact, these models' names often have "Quartz Date" or "QD" attached to them) that imprints the date, the time, or both in the picture area each time you take a shot. Some models also let you choose one of a half-dozen or so standard captions, like Happy Birthday or Happy Holiday. The printing is done with tiny lights (actually, light-emitting diodes, or LEDs) that expose the numbers onto the light-sensitive emulsion of the film. The numbers usually appear in the lower right corner of the image — and cannot be removed. In my opinion, these numbers ruin good photographs.

But many photographers, especially those for whom the picture is really just a record, love having that date on there. If you're one of these people, consult your manual to see which buttons must be pushed to set the right date and/or time. You usually refer to a small adjacent LCD panel to do this.

If you have a date-back model and don't want the date or time on your pictures, be absolutely sure to turn off the imprinting. (I've had whole rolls imprinted with an incorrect date by date backs that were set wrong. A few years from now, that's bound to be confusing!) To turn it off, you have to toggle through the settings until the LCD panel shows a series of dashes, like this: - - - - -. This does not mean a series of dashes will print. It means nothing will print. Needless to say, that's where my date-back cameras are set!

Advanced Photo System imprinting is an entirely different story. Most good APS cameras come with a built-in, quartz-controlled date feature — but, mercifully, the system puts the date and/or time on the back of the print, not in the picture itself. These models record the date and time electronically, on the film's invisible magnetic layer, using their built-in magnetic recording head. When you get your APS film processed, the printing machine reads the stored date and time and imprints it onto the back of the print. Captioning, if your APS camera offers it, works in a similar way; you use pushbuttons to choose from a menu of titles and sentiments. You can even express these in different languages. *Bonne anniversaire.*

A fair number of photofinishers, minilab as well as mass-market, now routinely imprint the date on the backs of prints. This date is the date of processing, not the date an individual picture was taken. But as with other photographic record-keeping and organizational features — at least those that don't mar photographs — it's still a very useful thing in my book.

Now here's one last weird one. A few inexpensive APS cameras don't have electronic date recording, but are equipped with conventional date backs that imprint permanently on the film, in the picture area. So be forewarned and check your manual to find out what your APS camera is printing where.

A growing number of photofinishers offer inexpensive scanning services in conjunction with regular film processing:

✔ **Scan-to-floppy:** An extra-cost option in which a photofinisher, as part of a regular develop-and-print order, scans the negatives and saves them to a standard computer floppy disk, which is returned with your negatives and prints. These scans are usually of quality that is fine for viewing on your computer screen, sending by e-mail, and so on. The scans won't make a very good print if produced on digital printers — but then again, that's what your negatives are for! For this reason, though, floppy scans are not good for pictures you'd like to digitally retouch or restore on your computer.

Mostly mail-order and mass-market labs offer scan-to-floppy service; Kodak Premium Processing has its "Picture Disk," for example. But minilabs are getting on the bandwagon, too.

✔ **Kodak Photo CD and FlashPix CD:** This is basically a compact disc on which your pictures are stored, and from which you can retrieve pictures with your computer's CD-ROM drive (see Figure 3-5). It has much, much greater storage capacity than a floppy disk. This means not only that you can put more pictures on it, but that you can store them at much higher resolution — at a much higher level of quality. Because of this high quality, the files on a Photo CD can be used for serious retouching with your home computer, and for digital printing.

Labs that offer this service generally scan a roll of film to a Photo CD or FlashPix CD as a package deal with develop-and-print orders. You can add images to the disc at a later date. (An index print is included inside the Photo CD's jewel case — see Figure 3-5.) Photo CDs and FlashPix CDs are more expensive than floppies, and you need a computer CD-ROM drive to view pictures on them.

Figure 3-5:
Left, the Kodak Photo CD is an affordable way to get digital files of pictures into your computer. Right, its jewel case and index print.

✔ **Photo networks:** The newest example of photo networks is the Kodak Picture Network, available through stores that offer Kodak Premium Processing. Your pictures are scanned, again as part of a develop-and-print order. But instead of coming back to you on a disk, the scans are transmitted to a Web site, where you can view them online after entering a password (see Figure 3-6). You can give the password to friends and relatives, too, so that they can visit the site and look at the pictures. You can use the site to send the pictures by e-mail and also get a regular print of a shot mailed to anyone who isn't wired. And you can download the scans to your home computer for storage and manipulation.

A number of other companies are developing their own online photo networks. So this may become a very common option at photofinishers — perhaps as common as double-print orders!

Figure 3-6:
Kodak
photofinishers
can transmit
your pictures
to the Kodak
Picture
Network
Web site,
where you
can view
them with a
password.

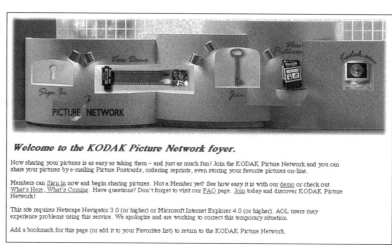

Welcome to the KODAK Picture Network foyer.

Now sharing your pictures is as easy as taking them — and just as much fun! Join the KODAK Picture Network and you can share your pictures by e-mailing Picture Postcards, ordering reprints, even storing your favorite pictures on-line.

Members can Sign in now and begin sharing pictures. Not a Member yet? See how easy it is with our demo or check out What's Here, What's Coming. Have questions? Don't forget to visit our FAQ page. Join today and discover KODAK Picture Network!

This site requires Netscape Navigator 3.0 (or higher) or Microsoft Internet Explorer 4.0 (or higher). AOL users may experience problems using this service. We apologize and are working to correct this temporary situation.

Add a bookmark for this page (or add it to your Favorites list) to return to the KODAK Picture Network.

The Photo Kiosk

Yet another photofinishing option is the do-it-yourself booth, or *kiosk*. The best known of these is the Kodak Picture Maker, which is found in some photo shops and well-equipped minilabs.

With these computerized machines, you put a negative into a slot or a print onto what looks like a photocopier window. Then you view your picture on a video screen and use the machine's controls to make various modifications.

For example, you can crop the picture (that is, cut out unwanted parts of it to concentrate on the important area), remove red-eye (that devilish glint caused by the reflection of flash in your subject's eyes), or do other simple retouching. You can set up the sheet so that you get one large picture or a page of smaller or different-sized ones. Other options include adding fancy borders or printing your photograph as a greeting card or calendar.

If you're new to photo kiosks, you're best off having a store clerk guide you through the process. In fact, most stores with these machines routinely have a clerk help you with the button-pushing. The great advantage of these systems is speed. Depending on the machine, you might be able to get an enlargement, with retouching, in just minutes.

Keeping them forever (or nearly forever)

Nothing is forever, and photographs are no exception. Over time your prints (and to a lesser extent, your negatives) can suffer a considerable amount of deterioration — even if they're safely tucked away in an album.

Most deterioration takes two forms. One is fading, in which the print gets lighter and loses color and contrast. (Basically, it starts to look like a muddy print, as described earlier in this chapter.) The other is staining, in which the print starts to pick up some unwanted color, especially in irregularly shaped patches. (Yellow is a frequent intruder.) Prints can also dry up and crack. They can even get mildewed from damp storage conditions.

Part of the problem is stuff in the prints themselves. The leftover chemicals in prints can, over time, injure the photographic image. The other part of the problem is environmental. Sunlight, humidity (or lack of it), air pollutants, temperature, and substances in albums, boxes, and envelopes can either attack prints directly or accelerate the chemical damage already going on in them.

The good news is that modern films and papers are far more long-lived than they were 20 or even 10 years ago. But it's still worth taking some steps to keep your prints from deteriorating prematurely.

✔ **Never use any kind of sticky stuff on the surface of a print.** I've seen prints fading and crumbling in albums with transparent overlay stickum pages after a year. Choose albums that have separate sleeves for the prints — and are made of archival materials. (See the following item.)

✔ **Use archival materials.** *Archival* is photo jargon that means a storage material or system that is minimally injurious to photographs. To be archival, for example, an album must have acid-free paper, if it has paper pages. (Acid is a prime culprit in print deterioration, and cheap paper contains lots of it.) If the album has plastic sleeves, they should be made from chemically inert plastics such as polyethylene,

(continued)

(continued)

polypropylene, and polyester. (Never buy storage sleeves made of polyvinyl chloride, also known as PVC — it's the stuff that smells like your kids' pool toys.) Any other materials you use with albums — mounting corners, glues, slipcases, and so on — should be labeled acid-free or archival quality, too.

By the way, shoeboxes are about the worst place you can put prints or negatives. They're usually made from pulp cardboard, which is full of acidic sulfur compounds. Use plastic boxes, ring binders, or recipe-card boxes instead. Or order special archival storage boxes from companies such as Light Impressions. (See Appendix B.)

✔ **Keep the negatives safe.** If the negative is safe and sound, you can always get a new print from it should your existing one fade, discolor, or be damaged. Photo shops and companies that sell archival storage and album materials also carry clear, photographically correct plastic pages with sleeves for individual negative strips. I transfer my negatives into these from the photofinisher's sleeves, which you never really know the content of.

You can get sleeved pages that fit three-ring binders. And if you happen to keep your prints in plastic pages in three-ring binders, this is also a great way to store negatives and prints together; just keep the negatives right behind the pages holding the prints for that roll. (Then there are the advantages of the Advanced Photo System, in which your negatives are safeguarded in a cassette of inert plastic.)

If you're especially anxious, like me, about the security of your negatives, you might also consider getting a fireproof safe. Special models are available specifically for *media* (often called media safes), which, in addition to photographic materials, include floppy disks and magnetic tape.

✔ **Keep pictures out of the sun.** The ultraviolet component of sunlight is incredibly injurious to photographic prints, as it is to human skin. It's fun to hang pictures on the wall, yes — but try to place them so that they aren't in direct sun at any time of day. And look for frames with anti-UV (ultraviolet) glass or acrylic cover plates, which help filter out light's most photographically harmful components.

Part II
Getting the Most from Your Point-and-Shoot

In this part . . .

Your point-and-shoot camera is made to point and shoot. Turn it on, point it at something, press the shutter button — and it focuses automatically, figures the exposure, fires the flash if needed, and speeds the film to the next frame, ready to start all over again. You can get acceptable pictures this way, but they often won't be the best pictures that you can get. And this is where those little pushbuttons come in. If you know which buttons to push, you can get a *good* picture, and maybe even a *great* picture, instead of a merely acceptable one.

Pushbuttons control modes, and modes are what make the camera do your visual bidding. But even if your point-and-shoot has many modes — and Chapter 4 describes just about all you can possibly have — you really only need a few. Which few? The flash modes, which is why that little built-in flash gets special attention in Chapter 7. Everything in between those two chapters concerns the lens — the little glass sandwich that actually forms the image on film, and without which those pushbuttons would be like the light switches in your basement that turn nothing on.

Chapter 4

Pictures à la Mode

. . . .

In This Chapter

▶ What is a mode?

▶ Making a mode map

▶ Setting modes

▶ Exploring different modes

▶ Getting creative with modes

▶ Avoiding *moditis*

. . . .

A funny thing happens when you show good pictures to people. Ever notice it? You take out some well-focused, colorful, nicely composed photos, pass them around to your friends, and they oooh and aaah. "Wow!" they say. "What a great camera you have!"

As if you, the one pushing the button, had nothing to do with it. But be honest with yourself. How many times have you excused your not-so-good pictures the same way? "Oh, geez," you say. "Would you look at what this lousy camera did again!"

The fact of the matter is that your camera has a great deal to do with how your pictures turn out. And so do you. You and your camera are a partnership. But you have to be the major partner. You can't always leave all the decisions up to your minor partner, the camera, if you want to get beyond okay-but-not-great pictures. *You* have to call the shots — or should I say, push the buttons.

The Great Button Bazaar

You have a lot more say than you might think in the many decisions your all-automatic camera makes each time you take a picture. And the way you get your say, on most point-and-shoots, is with those pushbuttons.

Most point-and-shoots have several buttons that you can push besides the most obvious one, the shutter button. You frequently find these buttons right next to the camera's *LCD panel* — the silvery little screen that shows you, among other things, how much film you've used. (LCD stands for *liquid crystal display.*) This panel is commonly on the top of the camera, but you may also find it on the camera's back. Regardless of the panel's location, you'll probably find additional buttons in other places — next to the camera's viewfinder, on the side of the camera, or even squirreled under a sliding or hinged cover. Figure 4-1 shows a typical array of pushbuttons. Some models have buttons on nearly every flat surface!

Dials are now replacing buttons on many point-and-shoot cameras. They do the same thing as buttons. Dials simply show you more of your optional settings at a glance (see Figure 4-2).

Why all the extra buttons or dials? To let you get out of the camera's default settings and set modes according to your pleasure, creative needs, and photographic purposes.

Default in photography doesn't mean that you've missed a credit-card payment on your camera. Default refers to a setting, or a group of settings, that the camera always returns to on its own — if you don't deliberately set it to do something else. For example, almost all point-and-shoots default to *autoflash* mode after you shut them off and turn them on again.

Time/date setting button   Shutter button

DATE

Figure 4-1: Pushbuttons on a typical point-and-shoot let you set everything from flash modes to the self-timer.

Midroll rewind button | Panorama switch   Drive mode button

Red-eye reduction mode button

Flash mode button

Figure 4-2:
Many point-
and-shoots
now
substitute
dials for
pushbuttons,
part of a
"retro"
trend.

I can hear you griping already. You're saying, what's the point of getting this newfangled, auto-everything camera if you actually have to understand something about how it works?

Look at it this way. A car with automatic transmission, power everything, and cruise control is also a marvel of computer automation — but it can't drive itself. You still have to make a lot of decisions and operate a bunch of controls (even push some buttons!) to get where you're going.

The deal is pretty much the same with point-and-shoot cameras. Now, if you use your point-and-shoot wrong, it won't crash and burn, though some of your more photophobic subjects may threaten you with mayhem. But understanding its different modes, features, and functions allows you — with no muss or fuss — to get a much higher percentage of keepers. Those people looking at your pictures may actually exclaim, "What a great photographer your camera has!"

Mastering Your Camera's Modes

Mode is a modish word in photography today. Even a fairly simple point-and-shoot can have several flash modes, and focusing modes, and drive modes. . . . So just what is a mode anyway, and why is it important?

A *mode* is simply a set of instructions that tells the camera to operate in a certain way. (See the sidebar "That's an order, camera!") Point-and-shoot cameras may seem pretty smart, but like computers, they're really very dumb. Cameras, like computers, have to be *told* to do every single thing they do — every time they do it. In fact, a small computer in your point-and-shoot actually carries out a mode's electronic instructions. You could just as easily call modes *programs,* and some camera makers do just that!

That's an order, camera!

Like any self-respecting mode, autoflash — the default mode on your point-and-shoot camera — issues instructions. Here's pretty much what it tells the camera:

✔ Hey you! Camera! Focus the lens and measure the brightness of the light.

✔ Shoot without flash if possible, but don't set a shutter speed so slow that the picture will be blurred.

✔ Turn on the flash if the light is too dim!

✔ Advance the film one frame after the picture is taken.

✔ If this shot is the last one on the roll, rewind the film. Then display a blinking icon and refuse to do anything else until that human takes out the cassette.

Pretty thorough instructions, right? And they aren't even half of the camera's marching orders, just the major stuff. When you switch a mode, you're just changing some of those instructions. Not all of them, mind you — some modes change only one little instruction, nothing more.

Even if you've never touched any control except the on/off switch and the shutter button, you've already set the camera to a mode — many times, in fact. When you first turn your camera on, it sets *itself* to its default mode. This mode is usually called *autoflash* because it automatically fires the camera's built-in flash, if it's needed. You can also call the mode *all-auto* because everything else is automated, too. Either way, the default mode is probably the one that you'll be using the most.

Buttons to Push and Dials to Turn

The most typical way to change a mode is to press a button on the camera and watch as different symbols or words representing each mode appear on the LCD panel. Repeatedly pressing the button to move through the modes is called *toggling*. If you keep pushing the button, you eventually return to the default mode and can start all over. You can toggle through the modes as many times as you like to arrive at the one you want.

An *icon* is a symbolic representation of a specific point-and-shoot mode — not to be confused with the icons used in this and other *...For Dummies* books! An icon can appear on an LCD panel, beside a button, or along the edges of a dial. But modes may be represented by words or letters, too, so for the purposes of this book, icon simply means any representation of a mode that your camera uses.

If your point-and-shoot uses a dial (or dials) rather than pushbuttons, the mode icons are printed around the edge. This arrangement lets you see all the icons at once, instead of having to view them sequentially as you do with a pushbutton. You simply rotate the dial to the icon for the mode that you want. Another kind of dial actually changes the icon on the LCD display or moves an LCD pointer from icon to icon as you rotate it.

Mode buttons on some point-and-shoots are so small that they're hard to press, especially for ham-handed photographers. If your fingernails don't do the job, try a pen or pencil. Better yet, get yourself a paper clip — not a regular-size one, but one of those two-inch jobs — and loop it around your camera's neck or wrist strap. When you want to change modes, unbend the free end and use it as a button-poker.

A fairly common arrangement on point-and-shoots is to have one button that toggles through the flash modes and a second one that toggles through all the remaining modes. Some cameras have a dial only for flash modes (because they're so important and should therefore be easier to access), relegating other modes to a button. Some cameras have two dials. Some have two dials and a button. Some have four, five, or six buttons. . . .

Alas, no standard point-and-shoot control configuration exists; every manufacturer uses its own arrangement. Nor have camera manufacturers ever settled on standard icons for different modes — which means that one model's icon for landscape mode may look suspiciously like another model's icon for backlight mode, and one's slow-sync flash may look an awful lot like another's flash-off. The only surefire way to find out what the icons on your particular camera mean is to check the manual.

Map your modes! Get out your camera and its instruction manual, plus an index card and a pen. Push every button and turn every dial on the camera. As you do, refer to the manual and to the rundown of different modes that follows in this chapter. On the index card, write down the location of each button or dial, and underneath, list the modes it toggles or rotates through in the order they appear. Next to each mode, write a brief description of what it does and what it's good for. For example: "Fill flash: Fires flash all the time. Portraits in bright sun; backlit subjects." If you can't find your way out of a mode, just turn the camera off and on again.

You can also add little customized reminders and bits of advice about using each mode (see the sidebar, "Mode map for Zarkon SuperBlitzmatic 90 Zoom"). After you complete your mode map card, keep it in your camera case or slipped into a wallet or pocketbook so that you can refer to it "in the field," as pros say. This project may sound a bit like schoolwork. But you won't need to use the card for long before you know exactly which button does what and when to use a specific mode.

Mode map for Zarkon SuperBlitzmatic 90 Zoom

No, there is no Zarkon camera. I simply made up a typical fair-to-middling zoom point-and-shoot, much like one you may already own. Here's a typical personalized "mode map" that a user of this camera might jot down on an index card to take along when shooting. The instructions describe what each mode is good for as well as precautions to take when using them.

Flash button

Auto: Fast shooting on the run; always-ready position. (Turn camera off and then on to get back to this mode!)

Fill flash: Fires flash all the time. Portraits in bright sun; backlit subjects.

Flash-off: Prevents flash from firing. Dark scenes far away; existing light shots with fast film. (Hold camera steady!)

Night flash: Fires flash all the time, together with slow shutter speed. Outdoor portraits in evening; indoor shots with distant backgrounds. (Hold steady!)

Red-eye reduction button

Red-eye reduction on: Fires rapid preflashes before the flash for the actual picture. (Tell subjects to wait for final flash!)

Red-eye reduction off: Kills annoying preflashes.

Clock face button

Self-timer: Takes picture ten seconds after shutter button is pressed. (Watch flashing light!)

Remote control ready: Sets up camera for hands-off firing. (Keep remote in camera case!)

Infinity lock: Far-away focus; use to shoot through window. (Turn off after use!)

Millions of Modes?

I've actually counted all the modes that you can find on current point-and-shoots, and they add up to about 30. Fortunately, no one camera has them all, though some fancier models come pretty close.

You can divide modes into groups, depending either on what part of the camera they control or what kind of picture they're designed to help you take, and I've done just that in the following explanation of different modes. *Note that words (or letters) in quotes are actual words (or letters) that may appear on the camera's LCD display or dial(s).* Refer to Chapter 7 for more specifics on all-important flash modes. And again, remember that camera makers can and do use all sorts of nonstandard icons — so let your manual be your guide!

Most point-and-shoots have no more than a half-dozen modes. Even if your camera has more, you'll use only a few with any regularity. I mark these modes with an asterisk (*) in the following list. Some modes, on the other hand, you may never use at all. But to find out which modes you can ignore, you first have to figure out which ones your particular point-and-shoot has and what they're good for, or at least intended for. So now's the time to sit down with your camera and manual. Do it, and you can skip the descriptions of modes that your camera doesn't have!

Flash modes

Flash modes let you change how and when the flash fires — or let you turn it off entirely. If a point-and-shoot has any modes at all, the flash modes usually get their own button or dial. They're that important. Find out how to use flash modes well, and you'll see noticeable — maybe even astonishing — improvements in your pictures. Flash modes are by far the most useful modes on your camera. For this reason, I devote Chapter 7 to them.

✔ **Autoflash mode.*** *Typical icons: no icon at all; lighting bolt with "Auto"; "Auto"* (see Figure 4-3). You find this mode on just about any camera above the one-time-use level. Autoflash is the universal default mode. Autoflash gives you flash when needed, turns the flash off when the light is bright, and does its best to keep shots from blurring. When in doubt, leave your camera in autoflash mode. It's the grab shot mode — just turn on the camera and shoot!

Figure 4-3:
Typical
icons for
autoflash
mode.

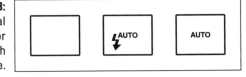

✔ **Fill-flash or flash-on mode.*** *Typical icons: plain lighting bolt; lightning bolt with sun symbol; "Fill-flash"; "Flash-on"* (see Figure 4-4). Fill-flash mode is present on point-and-shoots above the most basic level. This mode turns on the flash and keeps it on, no matter what the lighting conditions — whether you're shooting in the dark or by blazing sun. Fill flash is the mother lode of modes — perhaps the single most important camera setting within your control. It's essential for lightening harsh shadows in outdoor portraits and the best choice for brightening subjects lit from behind.

Figure 4-4:
Typical
icons for
fill-flash
mode.

✔ **Flash-off mode.*** *Typical icons: lighting bolt with cancel sign through it; moon and star(s); "Flash-off"* (see Figure 4-5). Found on most models above the very basic, this mode turns off the flash and keeps it off no matter what the lighting. Use it to preserve interesting natural light when flash would overpower it. Of course, if the light is bright enough, the flash turns itself off in autoflash mode. But flash-off mode is a way of ensuring that the flash won't fire. Definitely set it for low-light scenes that are beyond the range of flash — a sunset, for example.

Figure 4-5:
Typical
icons for
flash-off
mode.

On some camera models, the flash-off icon may be combined with other symbols — and if it is, setting it may do more than just turn the flash off. If the flash-off icon is paired with a sun symbol, it probably means you're getting backlight compensation. If it's paired with a mountain symbol, you may be getting a landscape setting.

✔ **Slow-sync flash mode or night flash mode.*** *Typical icons: lightning bolt with moon and stars; "Night"; "Slow sync"* (see Figure 4-6). A feature on many cameras at the $100 and higher level, slow-sync flash mode works just like the fill-flash mode, except that it's designed specifically for low light. (*Night flash* is the increasingly popular name for it, though the mode is just as valuable indoors during the day, as I explain in Chapter 7.) In addition to firing the flash, slow-sync allows the shutter (the window in the lens) to stay open longer than usual — helping the film capture more of the existing light behind and around your subject. In practice, this mode improves background detail. (On some cameras, slow-sync flash automatically adds red-eye reduction.) Great use: a portrait in front of city lights or a sunset.

Figure 4-6:
Typical
icons for
slow-sync
flash mode.

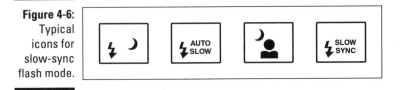

✔ **Red-eye reduction mode.** *Typical icons: an eye; a double lightning bolt* (see Figure 4-7). Present on most cameras above very basic models, red-eye reduction is designed to lessen the reddish glint a subject's eyes often pick up in a flash picture. With many models, you can add it to any other flash mode (autoflash, fill-flash, and so on), in which case it may have its own on/off button. Red-eye reduction usually takes one of two forms, depending on the brand of camera (see Chapter 7).

Figure 4-7:
Typical
icons for
red-eye
reduction
mode.

Print-format modes

Everyone's familiar with the 4 x 6-inch shape of standard commercial prints. (The $3^1/_2$ x 5-inch size, once the standard and still available, has similar proportions.) But a few 35mm cameras and *all* the new Advanced Photo System cameras (with the exception of some one-time-use models) let you choose a differently shaped print called a *panorama*. Panoramic prints are long and narrow — 4 x 10 inches or 4 x $11^1/_2$ inches, depending on who does the photofinishing. With the right subject, an occasional panorama can be lots of fun. (Try verticals!) But for most of your picture-taking, the 4 x 6-inch size, or with APS, either the 4 x 6- or standard 4 x 7-inch size, is best — and the most economical choice. Chapter 14 helps you figure out when to switch print formats.

✔ **Panorama mode (on 35mm cameras).** *Typical icons: "Panoramic"; "P"; a long, narrow rectangle* (see Figure 4-8). You see this mode on a handful of current 35mm cameras; you set it by sliding or rotating a marked switch. With most models, doing so immediately reshapes the viewfinder to match panoramic-format prints, allowing you to compose accordingly. (With some models, you have to compose using lines within the viewfinder frame.) Note that the panorama setting on 35mm cameras physically blocks off the top and bottom of the negative, so after you shoot a picture this way, you can't go back and get a normal full-frame 4 x 6 print from this negative. Shoot a second, nonpanoramic picture if you have second thoughts. Depending on your photofinisher, getting panoramic prints can also be a bit of a hassle (see Chapter 3).

Figure 4-8:
Typical
icons for
panoramic
mode.

C, H, P switch (on APS cameras). *Typical icons: choice of "C," "H," and "P"; rectangles of each format's respective shape* (see Figure 4-9). Advanced Photo System (APS) cameras let you choose from three different print formats for each picture you take; you change formats by sliding a switch or rotating a small dial to the desired selection. The choices are Classic *C* (a 4 x 6-inch print), HDTV *H* (a 4 x 7-inch print), or Panoramic *P* (a 4 x 10-inch or 4 x 11½-inch print, depending on photofinishing). Unlike the panorama switch on 35mm models, changing APS print size does not change the actual negative, only the way it's first printed. If you decide your panoramic composition of Uncle Clive sacked out on the sofa would be better as a regular old 4 x 6, you can get it reprinted that way. (See Chapter 14 for details on having APS pictures redone in different-shaped prints.)

Figure 4-9:
Typical
icons for
APS print
format
modes.

Drive modes

Most point-and-shoots above the $50 mark now have motorized film winding, and most people take it for granted. Shoot a picture, and the camera goes "BZZZZT," speedily advancing the film to the next blank frame. But drive modes, if your model offers a choice of them, let you alter the way the camera goes about the business of winding. They also include ways to fire your camera without your finger on the shutter button, such as the self-timer.

✔ **Self-timer mode.*** *Typical icons: clock face; "Self"* (see Figure 4-10). Found on nearly all point-and-shoots other than one-time-use models, the self-timer mode just delays the picture by a set interval, typically 10 or 12 seconds. You place the camera on a nearby secure surface — a table (indoors) or a rock (outdoors), for example — aim it, and then press the shutter button and double-step to get into the picture yourself. The ability to include yourself in your pictures makes the self-timer much beloved by vacationers and party-goers, but it's useful in another way, too: It lets you keep your hands entirely off the camera when it fires. It's a good handmaiden to the flash-off mode, because it eliminates the risk that your shaky hands will blur the picture when the camera sets slow shutter speeds for low-light shots.

Figure 4-10:
Typical
icons for
self-timer
mode.

Try a fun shot with your self-timer

If you've never used your camera's self-timer for a low-light shot, now's the time. Load up your camera with fast print film (ISO 400 or 800) and find a scene that you've always wanted to capture in low light. It may be the sun setting behind a patch of woods, the twinkling lights of a downtown skyline, or maybe just your house at dusk. Turn on the camera and set it to flash-off mode. Then place it on a solid support — a fence railing, car top, or window sill is fine, as long as you can see through the camera well enough to aim it. Now set the camera to self-timer, press the shutter, and hands off! You'll probably be pleased with the result.

The self-timer isn't just for group shots and travel photos. Use it for more mundane pictures, too — the kind that you'd take for the visual diary I propose in Chapter 10. Get a shot of yourself going about holiday dinner preparations. Or with Bowser on your front porch. Or with a toddler in your lap. Or with your freshly waxed sports car.

✔ **Sequential self-timer or multi-self-timer mode.** *Typical icons: overlapped clock faces; a clock face with a numeral next to it* (see Figure 4-11). You find this feature on many point-and-shoots in the middle-to-high price range. It works just like the self-timer, except that it takes one or two more shots after the first one, spaced apart by a second or two. (With flash pictures, the spacing may be lengthened by the time needed for the flash to recharge.) This mode is great for group shots — take one formal shot and then act up for the second!

Figure 4-11:
Typical icons for sequential self-timer mode.

✔ **Remote control mode.** * *Typical icons: remote controller shape with waves or beams coming out of it; "Remote"* (see Figure 4-12). This mode is available on many cameras over $100, though the remote controller itself is usually an extra-cost accessory. Remote control functions much like the self-timer, eliminating the need for hands-on firing of the camera. It works like your TV remote: You take the picture by pointing the remote controller at the camera and pushing a button, which fires the camera almost immediately rather than after a delay. Setting the remote control mode activates the camera's *remote receptor* (that's a little electric eye on the front of the camera that can see the beam from your remote controller) and tells it to look out for incoming photons.

Figure 4-12:
Typical icons for remote control mode.

Steady the camera on a rock or branch, and you can use remote control to get candid shots of local fauna in your backyard, as you hide behind a tree or look through a window. But keep in mind that the remote's beam range is usually limited to 20 feet or so, and the controller must be in a direct sight line with the camera. (Some remotes even allow you to zoom the lens back and forth.)

You can use your remote control to steady the camera for any low-light photograph, just as you would with the self-timer, by placing and firing the camera on a secure surface rather than holding it. And remote control is faster: You don't have to wait 10 or 12 seconds for the camera to fire as you do with the self-timer.

✔ **Step zoom mode.** *Typical icons: a lens zooming; three different-sized figures superimposed; "Step"* (see Figure 4-13). This mode is present on a few feature-packed point-and-shoots at the middle-to-high price range. It works just like the sequential self-timer, but automatically zooms for each picture — for example, it may take a wide view, an in-between one, and a tight one, advancing the film between shots. This feature can be fun, but it's probably a good idea to take a look through the viewfinder at each lens setting first and compose for the shot where you're zoomed in the most. Otherwise, you may accidentally behead your subjects! (Your manual, or even your camera's LCD, tells you what lens settings the step zoom mode uses.)

Figure 4-13:
Typical
icons for
step zoom
mode.

✔ **Continuous wind mode.** *Typical icons: "C"; "Cont"; three overlapping rectangles* (see Figure 4-14). Found on a fair number of cameras, this mode sets the camera to keep shooting picture after picture (automatically advancing the film after each shot) for as long as you hold down the shutter button. Normally, to take more than one shot you have to release pressure from the shutter button and press down again, which causes the camera to refocus. Because continuous wind eliminates the need for the camera to refocus for each shot, you can take sequences of pictures a bit faster than you can by shooting a single picture at a time — which is why this mode is good for fast-changing action. (Did you say kids acting up in the pool?) But you do have to make sure that your subject is approximately the same distance away for all your sequence shots. And how fast you can really capture the action is limited in other ways.

Figure 4-14:
Typical
icons for
continuous
wind mode.

Even in continuous wind mode, most point-and-shoots can't take pictures at an especially fast rate to begin with. They chug along at maybe a picture per second — one frame-per-second (1 fps), in photospeak. Some models can do a frame-and-a-half per second (1.5 fps). And the occasional model has a special *burst* capability that allows perhaps four shots — bam bam bam bam — in a second. But generally, you're better off developing a ready eye and quick finger than depending on the law of averages to get a few good shots out of a rapid-fire sequence.

✔ **Interval timer or intervalometer mode.** *Typical icons: "Int"; "Interval"* (see Figure 4-15). You find this somewhat obscure mode on feature-packed point-and-shoots at midrange price and above. It takes a sequence of shots, unmanned or unwomanned, one at a time at specific intervals. For example, you may be able to set the camera to take eight pictures over two hours, one every 15 minutes. (You usually can set intervals anywhere from ten seconds to one hour.)

Figure 4-15:
Typical
icons for
interval
timer mode.

Typically, you ready the camera for interval shooting by pressing a button to toggle through drive modes until you get to the intervalometer mode. Then you use a separate button (or, on some cameras, the zoom lever) to toggle through different intervals, which are displayed on the LCD screen — 10 sec, 20 sec, and so on. You set the number of frames that you want in the same way. The procedure is very much like setting a VCR or a digital watch (simple, right?), but you'd better have your manual handy!

Most cameras with this feature also cleverly shut themselves off between shots to conserve power. An interval timer can be fun for time-lapse photos of that prize bloom opening in the backyard. Also a gas at parties: Set the camera up in a busy corner to take a shot every few minutes!

Focusing modes

Less expensive point-and-shoots use a fixed-focus lens design that basically tries to make everything reasonably sharp from around four feet on out. These focus-free models, as they're often sweetly called, do eliminate the need to think about focusing. You get better results with cameras that focus their lenses automatically. But you have to give focusing some thought — and know when to push the right button — to fully reap their benefits. (See Chapter 6 for more on focusing.)

Autofocus cameras usually have a central focus point in the viewfinder, marked with lines or brackets. You place the focus point on the most important part of the scene (the main subject) to make the camera focus there. When you press the shutter button halfway, the camera locks the focus on that part and holds it until you release pressure. If you want your main subject to be off-center, you may have to recompose before shooting. But increasingly point-and-shoots have wide-area autofocusing systems that allow them to correctly focus subjects that are a little off-center in the frame. Even if your camera fits this description (check the manual), locking the focus is a good idea (see Chapter 6). And whether your camera has this feature or not, it may have other focusing modes that let you tinker with how it goes about focusing.

✔ **Infinity lock mode or landscape mode.** * *Typical icons: a mountain(s); the sideways-8 infinity sign; "Landscape"* (see Figure 4-16). Infinity lock sounds like a doohickey on the warp drive of the Starship Enterprise, but it's actually a feature on most autofocus point-and-shoots and really a very simple thing. It basically overrides the camera's autofocus, setting the lens to focus far away — no ifs, ands, or buts. *Far away* in photographic terms just has a fancy name: *infinity.* Infinity is the distant point beyond which an autofocus camera doesn't have to fiddle with focus anymore. Use this mode when photographing a landscape that doesn't have any important foreground detail or when shooting through glass, which can confuse many autofocusing systems. (Infinity lock/landscape mode also turns off the flash because it might reflect in a window — and isn't powerful enough to light a distant landscape anyway.)

Figure 4-16:
Typical
icons for
infinity lock
mode.

✔ **Spot autofocus mode.** *Typical icons: Small, solid circle inside a rectangle; "Spot"; "Spot AF"* (see Figure 4-17). Many point-and-shoots now feature *wide-area* or *multipoint* autofocus. In this default focusing mode, the camera can often tell when the subject is not perfectly centered in the frame, correctly focusing it when other models may mistakenly focus on the background. But what if you're a Nervous Nellie (or Ned) and want to be absolutely sure that the camera focuses exactly where you tell it to? Setting spot autofocus disables the wide-area autofocus and limits the focus point to a smaller, central area instead, giving you greater precision in the placement of the focus point. (Note that spot autofocus is often automatically set in tandem with another mode, spotmeter.)

Figure 4-17: Typical icons for spot autofocus mode.

✔ **Snap mode.** *Typical icon: "Snap"* (see Figure 4-18). You find this mode on very few point-and-shoot cameras. It overrides the autofocus, like infinity lock, but instead of focusing the lens far away the camera sets it to a medium distance (usually in the six- or eight-foot range), which is where the main subject is likely to be in a typical quick snapshot. The point? Snap mode lets you shoot faster because the lens doesn't have to refocus for each picture. Some snap modes set the camera to continuous wind; zoom models may also keep the lens locked at its most wide-angle setting, where you have a better chance of getting sharp pictures. If you're interested in the sort of quick, off-the-cuff candid photography of people that enthusiasts call *street shooting,* snap may be your mode. Remember, though, that your subjects may have to be in that snap range of 6 to 8 feet to be acceptably sharp.

Figure 4-18: A typical icon for snap mode.

✔ **Macro mode.** *Typical icons: tulip; "Macro"* (see Figure 4-19). Still present on a fair number of mid- to high-priced cameras, macro mode lets the camera focus closer than it ordinarily can at standard settings — call it a close-up mode. To use macro mode, you normally have to stay within a certain narrow distance range from your subject. You can stay within this range by looking through the viewfinder and pressing lightly on the shutter button while watching the green focus-OK lamp, which blinks if you're too far or too close. Some macro modes also trigger the flash — even when the subject is pretty bright — to make sure it gets enough light.

Figure 4-19:
Typical
icons for
macro
mode.

If macro mode sounds like kind of a pain, well, it is. More and more cameras simply shift automatically into a macro-type range when you aim the camera at a close object — a much more convenient system. But if your camera does have macro mode, check the manual carefully to determine how to use it.

✔ **Manual focus mode.** *Typical icons: "manual focus"; "MF" with numerical readout of the distance* (see Figure 4-20). You're unlikely to see this mode on your camera unless you have a pricey designer model. It allows you to manually focus at, say, 3 feet or 5 feet or 7 feet. On a couple of models (those made by Contax), the autofocus system helps by indicating whether your manual-focus setting is correct. Although not especially useful, manual-focus capability does let you set focus on a certain distance and keep it there for a series of shots without refocusing, which is useful if you're taking a lot of shots of the same scene or portrait. This is focusing the old-fashioned way, except that you're likely to have to do it with pushbuttons or a dial instead of the focusing ring found on the lenses of traditional, non-autofocus cameras.

Figure 4-20:
Typical
icons for
manual
focus mode.

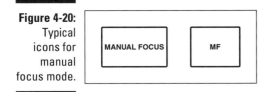

Subject or picture modes

The idea behind subject or picture or program image modes (all three mean the same thing) is simple: Optimize the camera's various settings for a certain kind of subject, whether portraits, action, or landscapes. In practice, though, using subject modes can get kind of complicated. Usually what the camera is doing here is setting several modes in combination — a combination that you may not necessarily want. And in most cases, the camera isn't doing anything that you can't do by adjusting the individual modes. But don't let me turn you off subject modes. If you're still puzzling over all your camera's flash and drive and focus modes, setting, for example, portrait mode when you're taking a portrait gives you a quick starting point without fussing and fuming over a bunch of buttons. So if you try a subject mode and really like how it works, use it!

✔ **Action mode.** *Typical icon: running man* (see Figure 4-21). You find this mode on a number of higher-priced point-and-shoots, and it's one of the few modes that has a nearly standardized icon. Too bad the mode itself isn't standardized: How it works varies widely from camera to camera. With almost all models, action mode sets the drive mode to continuous wind. With some models, it also turns off the flash, which makes sense; waiting ten seconds for the flash to recharge is hardly the way to snap fast sequence pictures.

Figure 4-21:
A typical icon for action mode.

If the light is low, on the other hand, having no flash may very well result in blur with a fast-moving subject. Contrary to what that running man icon may lead you to think, action mode does not usually make the camera set a higher, more action-stopping shutter speed. Point-and-shoots are pretty much designed to set as high a shutter speed as they can *in any mode,* given the light level and the film speed.

The best way to stop action is not by setting action mode. Action mode can help you capture moving subjects, but the only surefire way to get your point-and-shoot to set a higher, more action-stopping shutter speed is to use a faster film (see Chapter 2).

On a few high-end models, action mode does trigger a special auto-focusing trick. In it, the camera focuses continuously — that is, it keeps readjusting the focus to keep a moving subject sharp. Such models may even have *predictive* autofocus, which actually anticipates the subject's distance at the moment the shutter fires — and focuses accordingly! Check your manual for details.

✔ **Portrait mode.** *Typical icon: person's head and shoulders* (see Figure 4-22). Often found on the same upper-crust cameras that have action mode, portrait mode is another anything-goes mode that varies in operation from model to model. But with many models, this mode sets an *autozooming* or *autoframing* function. (Some models even call it "Autozoom" mode.) Autozooming? Yes. Touch the shutter button lightly to focus and the lens automatically zooms to produce a half-height portrait. It basically frames your subject for you, from about the waist up — though the smaller your subject, the more you get. (With toddlers, you may even get the whole kid!) Having the zoom lens zip in and out on its own is a little disconcerting, I find. Anyway, who says a waist-to-head shot is always the best portrait framing?

Portrait mode may, in some cameras, also automatically trigger fill flash, which is usually a good thing — but what if you think the portrait would be better with existing light? Something else to keep in mind: Portrait mode is designed for photographing people. Focus on a tree at a middling distance, and it will zoom in to get a shot of the trunk, which can drive you a little crazy after a while. So make sure to switch your camera out of portrait mode after you're done with the people shots!

Figure 4-22:
A typical
icon for
portrait
mode.

Use portrait mode when you're handing the camera to someone else to take your picture or perhaps when you let a child use the camera. Other times you're usually much better off making your own decisions about zooming and flash.

✔ **Take my picture mode.** *Typical icons: camera being handed off; "Take my picture"; "Thank you"; "Easy pic"* (see Figure 4-23). You find this mode on just a few models. It's much like autoflash, but with special precautions thrown in for when you hand the camera to someone to take your picture. For example, most models limit the focusing distance to within a certain range — perhaps 6 to 15 feet — so that if your designated photographer accidentally lands the viewfinder's focus point on the Eiffel Tower instead of you, chances are you'll still be pretty sharp. Some Take my picture modes also autozoom. Use this mode only for its intended purpose, and nothing more! (Some icons for this mode look a lot like icons for infinity lock/landscape mode, but the difference is that they have people in them.)

Figure 4-23:
Typical icons for Take my picture mode.

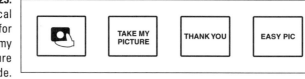

✔ **TV mode.** *Typical icon: TV screen* (see Figure 4-24). Once found mainly on cameras made by Ricoh, this mode now turns up on a fair number of models at various prices. TV mode turns off the flash and adjusts the exposure settings to get a shot of a TV screen without the diagonal bands (invisible to the naked eye) that might otherwise mar the picture. It works pretty well with computer monitors, too. Make sure that you use fast film and hold the camera steady — or even better, support it on a secure surface.

Figure 4-24:
A typical icon for TV mode.

✔ **Fuzzy logic mode.** *Typical icons: "Fuzzy"* (see Figure 4-25). You may find this mode if you have a camera from Samsung or Rollei. (At the moment, several dozen such models are on the market at a variety of prices.) The mode's name confuses people, and I can see why. Its usual icon is simply the word *fuzzy* — leading people to think, geez, why would I want fuzzy pictures? But fuzzy logic mode doesn't blur your pictures. It actually does something quite complex and fascinating: It's a mode that automatically sets modes! And it does so differently than a subject mode, which always goes to the same settings regardless of what you're actually photographing.

Figure 4-25:
A typical
icon for
fuzzy logic
mode.

FUZZY

Using fuzzy logic (computerese for humanlike calculation) the camera analyzes the light level, the subject's distance, and the zoom setting and then chooses a mode or a combination of modes that it "thinks" best suits the subject. The camera does this analysis every time you take a picture. If you focus on something at a middling distance in good light, for example, the camera may say, "Aha! A portrait!" — autozooming closer and triggering fill flash. If you focus on something far away, the camera may say, "Yes! A landscape," turning off the flash and setting infinity focus.

My advice about fuzzy logic mode is simpler than that explanation. Every once in a while, set your empty camera to it and watch what happens as you shoot different things. Fuzzy logic is really a sort of super-default mode — an insurance mode similar to the Take my picture mode. But I feel strongly that you should know how to set modes for yourself. That is, after all, why you bought this book!

Metering modes

Using its built-in light meter, your point-and-shoot actually measures the light level in the scene you're photographing. The meter uses this information to set the camera so that the film (or in the case of a digital camera, the light-sensing chip) receives the amount of light it needs for a correct exposure. Point-and-shoot meters can be quite sophisticated; they may be able to detect strong backlight, for example, and automatically tell the camera to fire the flash or add exposure to compensate for it. But in certain lighting situations, the camera may botch the exposure. And in other situations, you may just want the picture to look different — to be a silhouette, for example, or a *high key picture* (the sort where all the tones are light, for a soft, airy look). Metering modes allow you to change the way that the camera evaluates light or to actually second-guess that evaluation.

✔ **Spotmeter mode.** *Typical icons: small, solid circle in a rectangle; "Spot"* (see Figure 4-26). This mode sets the camera's light meter so that it reads just a small area of the scene, rather than the whole thing. The area is almost always in the center of the viewfinder frame, often indicated with a little circle surrounding the central focus point. After you set the camera to spotmeter mode with the correct button (and the LCD icon), you place the spotmeter circle over the area you choose — usually the most important part of the scene — and press the shutter button halfway to lock in the exposure settings. Then you frame up your final composition and press the shutter button all the way to take the picture.

Figure 4-26:
Typical icons for spotmeter mode.

SPOT

The spotmeter mode is most useful for fussy shooters. If your subject has strong sunlight coming from behind, for example, you can place the spotmeter circle directly on his or her face to make sure that the camera measures that exact tone, not the brighter sun behind. Spotmetering can also be valuable with slide film, which requires more accurate exposure than easygoing print film. Its drawback: It's almost always set in conjunction with spot autofocus.

If your camera pairs spotmetering with spot autofocus (check the manual), you can make a big boo-boo if you don't pay attention. Suppose that you're shooting a portrait against some beautiful fall foliage in the distance. You want to be sure the trees are properly exposed, so you aim the spotmeter at them and press the shutter halfway to lock exposure. Then you recompose to take the portrait. What do you get? A beautifully exposed picture with your main subject out of focus, because the camera also *focused* on those distant trees when you locked in the exposure. This example is one reason why I prefer point-and-shoots that have just a plain spotmeter function, but those models are few and far between.

✔ **Manual backlight compensation mode.** *Typical icons: sun behind a person; "+1.5 EV"; "BLC"* (see Figure 4-27). Some point-and-shoots automatically compensate for backlight by increasing the exposure — the amount of light the film receives. But this mode, found on a fair number of point-and-shoots, allows you to make sure that it's happening. By pressing this marked button (or rotating a dial to the icon), you make the camera add a certain amount of exposure. The amount is almost always 150 percent more, which is expressed photographically as +1.5 EV. (For more on backlight compensation, see Chapter 8.)

Figure 4-27:
Typical icons for manual backlight compensation mode.

↙ **Exposure compensation mode.** *Typical icon: "EV" and a plus- or minus number* (see Figure 4-28). This mode, seen on some high-end point-and-shoots, does backlight compensation one better. It lets you dial in (or press in) a specific amount of variation from what the camera says is correct exposure — twice as much (indicated by +1 EV), half as much (indicated by –1 EV), and so on. Exposure compensation is mainly useful for photographers who are experimenting with slide film (see Chapter 2). Most others should leave this mode alone.

Figure 4-28:
A typical icon for exposure compensation mode.

↙ **Aperture-priority autoexposure mode.** *Typical icons: "AV"; "Aperture" plus an f-stop number* (see Figure 4-29). This advanced mode lets you set the exact size of the lens aperture, the window in the lens that lets light into the camera. (A specific-sized window is called an *f-stop.*) One thing is certain: Aperture-priority autoexposure mode gives the advancing shooter a new level of camera control. But because you find this mode on only a few high-end point-and-shoots and you don't *have* to use it with them, I suggest not worrying about it for now.

Figure 4-29:
Typical icons for aperture-priority autoexposure mode.

Creative modes

Modes can't really be creative — you're the creative one, right? But when you're feeling inspired, so-called creative modes let you play with exposure, or flash, or focus, for unusual, arty, or just plain far-out effects. The effects are quite tasty, but a steady diet can lead to pictorial indigestion. You find most modes that I list here on just a few cameras in the mid-to-high price range.

✔ **Bulb mode.** *Typical icons: "Bulb"; "B"* (see Figure 4-30). Named after the old-time airbulb cables with which our photographic forefathers often snapped their shutters, this simple mode opens the shutter after you press the shutter button and keeps it open for as long as you bear down. It closes the shutter only after you let up on the shutter button. Bulb mode lets you take time exposures of ten seconds, ten minutes, or more. If you put the camera on a steady support and photograph moving traffic at night, for example, it gives you those saucy red and white streaks of glowing spaghetti. If you live or work near an airport, it's also interesting for shots of planes landing at night. Best bet: Use print film, because it forgives exposure errors.

Figure 4-30:
Typical icons for bulb mode.

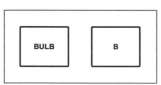

A *time exposure* is a picture made with the shutter kept open deliberately for a long time — usually more than one second. Long exposure times allow nonflash photography of a very dark scene or create interesting streaky effects with moving objects.

✔ **Multiple exposure mode.** *Typical icons: two frames overlapping one another; "Multi"* (see Figure 4-31). In a way, this feature can also be considered a drive mode. What it does is actually stop the film from advancing so that you can deliberately expose one piece of film with two or more different scenes. Depending on your tastes, you may like what you get — somebody's face hovering in the sky, or your wife standing on two sides of the same tree. And depending on your eye, you can actually plan the exposures so that they work together. (For that shot of your wife standing on both sides of a tree, for example, you have to keep the camera in the same position for both exposures. Keeping the camera in one exact place is best done with a tripod, although positioning the camera carefully on some other firm support would work, too.)

Figure 4-31:
Typical
icons for
multiple
exposure
mode.

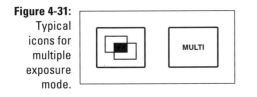

If multiple exposure sounds like a dicey mode, you're right. All cameras that have it immediately default back to the previous mode after you've made two exposures, which, as you may guess, is called a *double exposure.* However, most such models let you take still more exposures on the same frame, as long as you keep resetting the multiple-exposure mode.

✔ **Multiple flash mode.** *Typical icons: lightning bolt with "Multi"; other icons or words* (see Figure 4-32). This unusual mode makes a strobo-scopic multiple exposure on a single frame of film by rapidly firing the flash several times. Multiple flash mode can be a fun technique at, well, discos, or parties, or for capturing a superimposed sequence of your Little Leaguer's swing. But it works best in pretty dark surroundings.

Figure 4-32:
Typical
icons for
multiple
flash mode.

Getting in the Mode

Phew! If you perused the previous section on all the different modes you might find on a point-and-shoot camera, you may have gotten the idea that point-and-shoots are pretty darn complicated. Trust me, they're really not. I made that long list only so that you can go back and refer to the specific modes your camera has and understand what your model can and cannot do. An important suggestion, though: Familiarize yourself with how your camera cancels or doesn't cancel mode settings. Some cameras cancel infinity lock mode, for example, after one shot. Others stay in infinity lock until you change the mode or turn off the camera. Do yourself a favor: With your empty camera, set each mode and snap the shutter to see whether the mode remains active or is canceled.

You may also be muttering to yourself, "Gee, they put all these modes on the camera and a lot of them are no big whoop." Exactly. Much of current camera design, unfortunately, is the result of marketing considerations rather than concern for user-friendliness. The thinking is that a camera with 12 modes is better (both more salable and more profitable) than a camera with six modes. But *you* know that it isn't better if those half-dozen extra modes do things you'll never need.

Do you suffer from *moditis?* This affliction comes from taking a picture with an unwanted or incorrect mode setting. For example, if you shoot a portrait in infinity lock mode, your main subject will be utterly unsharp. If you leave the camera in action mode when you come indoors, you may miss a great shot because the flash won't fire. Keep in mind that most cameras reset themselves to default mode(s) after you turn them off and on again. If you're in doubt about the modes you're using, don't hesitate to do this.

So just don't fret about modes. And don't get button-happy, either. Photography is mostly about *seeing* and self-expression, not pushing buttons. Think about changing modes when you're in specific situations: When the light is very bright, or very dark, or the difference between what's bright and what's dark is big, or when something like a window comes between you and the picture. Your most important weapons are the flash modes, infinity lock, and the self-timer. If you get adept at using a few other modes for creative effect, that's gravy. And don't forget: You always have autoflash!

Shoot first and ask questions later. Don't miss a picture because you're worrying about what mode to use. If you see a picture possibility, grab the camera, turn it on, and take the shot — in autoflash. Autoflash covers most photographic situations. After you're sure you've gotten a shot, slow down and think what else you could do. Would fill flash add detail to the picture? Would the scene be more dramatic in panoramic form? Then set that mode and take another picture. After a while, your second guess will come faster and faster. And you'll see the change in your pictures.

Chapter 5

Optical Options: Seeing through Your Camera

In This Chapter

▶ What the viewfinder sees

▶ Does your camera zoom?

▶ When feet are better than a zoom

▶ Zooming for more reach and extra space

▶ Seeing through wide-angle, normal, and tele zoom settings

▶ Shooting up close at tele settings

▶ What different zooms are best for

▶ What focal lengths do with different formats

You've probably noticed that when people ask to see your camera, the first thing they do is look through the viewfinder — not *at* the camera. It's a reflex. They seem to understand that the viewfinder is your window on a world of photographic possibilities, and far more important than any button or dial on the camera.

Within this window's frame, of course, is where you arrange your pictures. In some cameras, that frame is defined by the opaque black edges that you see when you look through the viewfinder. In other cameras, it may be indicated with light or dark lines just inside the black edges; these are called, fittingly, *frame lines*. And in some very simple cameras (one-time-use models, for example), the frame may be nothing more than a rectangular opening in a piece of cardboard or plastic — quite literally, a window without glass.

However it's indicated, the viewfinder frame has but one purpose: to show you what part of a scene your camera's lens will put on film when you press the shutter button. Of course, you're the one who really determines what the lens puts on the film, by looking through the viewfinder and moving yourself and the camera, and, in some cases, by zooming the lens. This process, and its result, is called *composition*. (For more about the art of framing your subject, see Chapter 10.) But before you can even think about composition, you have to understand just what the viewfinder and the lens do, and that's what this chapter, and the next, are all about.

Changing the Picture

You can change the view through your point-and-shoot's viewfinder window in a variety of ways. Move closer to something, and that object gets bigger in the viewfinder. Move back, and the object gets smaller. The object's appearance also changes when you tilt the camera up or down from a low or high position, which of course requires a little squatting or scrambling. But if you have a *zoom lens* on your point-and-shoot, you can change the view through the viewfinder window in another way — without moving at all.

When you turn on a point-and-shoot with a zoom lens — call it a zoom point-and-shoot — it starts out just like a nonzoom model. Look through the viewfinder, and you see that it's filled with a good-sized chunk of the scene in front of you. By zooming, you can get a closer view of parts of that scene. First, though, you have to figure out where your zoom controls are. Perfectly smart people own point-and-shoots for years without ever touching these controls!

Be sure that you know where your frame edges are. (See Figure 5–1.) In cameras that have frame lines, you must compose a picture within the lines. If you don't, you may inadvertently cut off part of the subject. (The top of someone's head is the most common casualty.)

Do you have a zoom lens?

If you don't know already, first make sure that you *have* a zoom point-and-shoot. Turn the camera on. Generally, zoom lenses protrude a little more than nonzoom lenses when the camera starts up, though that's not a hard-and-fast rule. And zoom models have writing on their lenses with two numbers rather than one: *35–70mm* or *38–115mm* is a zoom; just plain *38mm* or *35mm* or *32mm* is not a zoom (see Figure 5-2). But the giveaway is a control lever or buttons for the zoom lens. Here's what to look for; check your manual if you're still not sure.

Most zoom point-and-shoots' zoom controls take the form of a rocker or toggle switch, usually on the back of the camera behind the shutter button. You operate this kind of switch by rocking or sliding it from side to side with your right thumb. But some models have two little buttons on the right side of the camera top, near the shutter button; you press one and the other

Figure 5-1:
With some
point-and-
shoot
viewfinders,
you use the
opaque
black edges
of the
window to
"frame"
your subject
(left). With
others, you
use "frame
lines" just
inside the
black edges
(right).

alternately with your shutter-button finger to adjust the zoom. (Using these buttons requires that you remove your finger from the shutter button, obviously.) And some models have similar buttons on the left side of the camera top, designed to be operated by the forefinger of your left hand. (You can press these buttons without removing your finger from the shutter button, not a bad idea.) A few cameras have a little nub near the shutter button; you wiggle it back and forth to adjust the zoom. (See Figure 5-3 for typical zoom controls.)

No matter what shape or form your zoom control takes, rocking or sliding or pressing or wiggling it causes the lens to extend or retract, most often by way of telescoping tubes. If you look through the viewfinder window while you're adjusting the control, you can see that the view changes: Things seem to get closer or farther away, depending on which way you move the zoom switch or which button you press — without even moving your feet!

Zooming in versus zooming out

Adjusting a zoom lens to make things look bigger in the viewfinder is called *zooming in,* because its effect is something like physically moving in toward the subject. Adjusting a zoom lens to make things look smaller in the viewfinder is called *zooming out,* because its effect is something like physically moving out, away from the subject.

Figure 5-2:
If your lens has one number (left, 34mm), it's not a zoom. If it has two (right, 30–60mm), it's a zoom.

 What's confusing is that when you zoom in — that is, adjust the zoom lens to make the subject bigger in the frame — the lens actually extends farther *out.* And when you zoom out — that is, adjust the zoom lens to make the subject smaller in the frame — the lens actually pulls back *in,* retracting toward the camera body. My suggestion: When I talk about zooming in and zooming out, ignore what the lens is physically doing. Just pay attention to what's happening in your viewfinder!

Though you can plainly see these changes through your viewfinder, the zoom controls are often marked to tell you which direction or button makes the subject bigger or smaller. Many models use tree symbols. Slide a zoom rocker switch toward a single, large tree symbol, and it zooms the lens in, making your subject bigger in the frame. Slide a zoom rocker switch toward a cluster of (usually) three small trees, and it zooms the lens out, making your subject smaller in the frame. Some models' zoom controls are marked with the letters *T* and *W,* which stand for *tele* and *wide,* terms that I explain later in this chapter. And some zoom controls are imprinted with those full words. Slide the switch toward *T* or Tele, or push the button marked *T* or Tele, and your subject gets bigger. Slide the switch toward *W* or Wide, or push the button marked *W* or Wide, and your subject gets smaller. Again, though, the best way to see what happens when you zoom is to just look through the viewfinder.

Figure 5-3:
Zoom controls come in all shapes and styles, from rocker switches (left) to push-buttons (right).

Going to Great Lengths

On zoom point-and-shoots, your viewfinder window is really just like a small, second zoom lens. When you zoom your camera's lens to make things bigger or smaller, the viewfinder zooms right along with it. This way, it can show you what the lens sees at every zoom setting. And here's the good part: You can take a picture at *any* of those settings — zoomed all the way out, zoomed all the way in, or anywhere in between. These different settings are called *focal lengths*.

Focal length is a number used to describe both a lens's *magnification* (how big or small it makes the subject) and its *angle of view* (how much or how little of the scene it puts on film), two closely related photographic properties. The number is always followed by *mm,* which stands for millimeters.

Please don't choke on the term *angle of view.* I'm not talking philosophy or politics here. For photographic purposes, angle of view simply refers to how big a piece of the scene the lens takes in. If it takes in a big piece — as a zoom lens does when it is zoomed out — it has a wide angle of view. If it takes in a smaller piece — as a zoom lens does when it's zoomed in — it has a narrower angle of view.

A short focal length — say, the 38mm setting on your zoom point-and-shoot — reduces magnification, giving the lens a wider angle of view. In other words, by making everything in the scene smaller, it can put more of it on film. (Sort of like looking out through the peephole on an apartment door.)

A long focal length — say, the 105mm setting on your zoom point-and-shoot — increases magnification, giving the lens a narrower angle of view. In other words, by making everything in the scene bigger, a long focal length can't fit as much of the scene on film. (Sort of like looking through a telescope or binoculars.) Keep in mind, though, that focal length numbers can mean different things depending on what kind of camera you have — 35mm, Advanced Photo System, or digital. (For the full scoop, see the sidebar, "The long and short of different film formats," later in this chapter.)

Don't confuse focal length numbers (which are always followed by mm, for millimeters) with the 35mm film format used by most point-and-shoot cameras. When a camera is said to be a 35mm model (as opposed to an Advanced Photo System or digital model), 35mm simply refers to the width of the strip of film in the standard cassette that it's designed to accept.

When a camera is said to have a 35mm lens (as many nonzoom 35mm point-and-shoots do) or to have a 35–70mm zoom lens, 35mm is a reference to the lens's focal length. Focal lengths come in all different numbers; 35mm is just one of them, but the main source of this confusion. So when I talk about a 35mm point-and-shoot, that's simply a reference to the film the camera uses.

And when I talk about a point-and-shoot with a 35mm lens, that's a reference to the camera's focal length. In fact, I may even talk about a 35mm point-and-shoot with a 35mm lens, which happens to be a very popular combination!

The long and short of different film formats

Point-and-shooters have three vast photo systems available to them: the traditional 35mm film system, which has been around for decades; the Advanced Photo System (APS), with its smaller, encapsulated film; and digital cameras, which don't use film at all. Each system offers much choice in lenses. And the area of lenses is where their differences are most confusing. To whit: A 38mm focal length on a 35mm camera is moderately wide-angle. On an APS camera, it's a normal focal length. And on a digital camera, 38mm would be a super telephoto focal length!

Isn't a wide-angle a wide-angle a wide-angle? Nope. The angle of view of a lens depends not only on its focal length, but on the size of the piece of film (or the light-sensing chip) that it is expected to fill. Of the amateur photo systems, 35mm uses the biggest piece of film, comparatively huge at an inch by an inch and a half per frame. The smaller APS film frame is about two-thirds that size. And a chip commonly found on digital point-and-shoot cameras is a sub-dinky $^3/_{16}$ x $^1/_4$ inch — not quite the size of the fingernail on your pinky!

The bigger the piece of film, the more of the lens's image it can record. Imagine the postage-stamp-sized piece of film in a 35mm camera, with an image formed by the lens projected on it. Now imagine the smaller piece of Advanced Photo System film in the middle of the 35mm film. It records a smaller section of the lens's image than the 35mm film, and if you were to print that image as a standard-sized print, it would show a narrower slice of the subject than the 35mm film. Next, imagine a digital point-and-shoot's tiny digital chip sitting in the middle of the APS film. (You could fit 15 or 20 chips on it!) The chip records only a very small center portion of the lens's image, and if you were to print *it* as a standard-sized print, it would look like a big blowup of the center portion of the APS or 35mm print.

As a result, the normal focal length for a small digital chip — in other words, one that would produce a middling angle of view, not a super telephoto one — is around 8mm. Normal for Advanced Photo System film is around 40mm. And normal for 35mm film is around 50mm.

When you go to buy an APS or digital camera, in fact, you will often see the lens's focal length expressed as an *equivalent*. This terminology means the manufacturer has figured out what focal length it is closest to in the familiar 35mm system — the one that gives you about the same angle of view. To further that effort, check out the following table of typical focal lengths that you find on these three kinds of point-and-shoot cameras, and their equivalents.

Format	Wide-Angle	Moderate Wide-Angle	Normal	Tele	Long Tele
35mm	28–30mm	34–45mm	45–55mm	60–100mm	105–160mm
APS	22–24mm	26–35mm	35–45mm	48–80mm	85–125mm
Digital	*	4.5–6.5mm	6.5–8mm	8.5–14mm	15–23mm

*Digital point-and-shoots currently don't come with lenses having true wide-angle focal lengths.

Remember that even nonzoom point-and-shoots have a focal length — one focal length. For this reason, they get the gee-whiz name of *single-focal-length* models. This term is just a fancy way of describing what is, in camera terms, the plain-vanilla version. If you want, you can call a zoom model a multiple-focal-length or a variable focal-length camera. But you don't have to, because that jazzy little word *zoom* says it all.

An important note to folks with nonzoom, single-focal-length point-and-shoot cameras: There's no need for zoom-lens envy! A zoom is a great tool for picture-taking, as this chapter explains. But you can vary your lens's view enormously with a single-focal-length camera. You just have to use that most valuable of photographic accessories, your feet. In fact, a serious *disadvantage* of zoom cameras is that they encourage photographic laziness: People plant their two feet wherever they may be, hoist the camera to their eyes, and just stand there and wiggle their zoom levers (in public, no less) to change the picture in their viewfinder frames. This is why the little exercise in the sidebar "Using your own built-in zoom — your feet" is just as much for zoom shooters as nonzoom shooters.

Using your own built-in zoom — your feet

No matter what kind of lens you have on your camera — zoom or nonzoom — that lens can provide you with all sorts of different views of a single subject. Turn on your camera and look through the viewfinder at a scene that you want to photograph — something simple like a friend in your backyard, an unusual house on your street, or your kids in a local park. (If you have a zoom model, leave the zoom controls alone for now.) Frame the scene in the viewfinder the way that you normally would. All set?

Now do everything that you usually *wouldn't* do. Get low to the ground — I mean low — and see how that changes the scene in the viewfinder. Get up high — maybe stand on a chair or step stool, or the ladder of your kids' slide, or a deck or balcony — and see how that changes the picture. Move in closer. Now closer than that. Move back. Now farther back. See something that looks interesting, or

even a little strange, from one of these different positions or angles? Take the picture! The point here is to discover how many different ways you can frame a picture, regardless of what kind of point-and-shoot you have. Even the simplest camera gives you a lot of framing options. (And check out Chapter 9 for framing tips that apply to *any* kind of camera.)

If you do this exercise thoroughly, though, you'll notice that you can't get some pictures simply by changing your position or angle. That curious architectural detail just below the roofline of your neighbor's house? You can't get close enough to fill the viewfinder with it just by moving yourself. (Maybe you can do this with a long ladder, but unless you're a house painter or roofer you're unlikely to have one — and your neighbor may be suspicious!) With subjects like this, a zoom lens does come in handy.

But sometimes changing position just can't change your angle of view as much as you want. Say that you're trying to get your whole backyard in the viewfinder. You probably keep stepping back and stepping back until your back is against the side of the garage. Even when you can get as close as you want, it's sometimes too close. If you want a close-up of your daughter's face as she concentrates on a chess match, you can move the camera until it's right in her face — but that would destroy the moment, let alone her concentration. Or if, being a more athletic type, she's playing catch, you can move the camera in until you're right next to her — but you would interfere with the game, and quite possibly get bonked.

These situations are when you want to change focal length: to slide or push those zoom controls, if your camera has them. To capture that gargoyle on your neighbor's house, the solution is to zoom in. (In photo jargon, you're changing to a longer focal length setting, same thing as telephoto.) If you want to get more of your backyard in the viewfinder frame, you need to zoom out as much as possible. (In photo jargon, you're changing to a shorter focal length setting, same thing as a wider angle of view.) For that close-up of your chess whiz, zooming in is also the way to go — in this case, not because you can't get closer but because you want to keep a greater distance between the two of you so as not to distract her. And you can stay clear of that game of catch, and still get your shot, by zooming in. In giving you all these other chances for a picture, zoom lenses are like magic feet.

Going Wide — and Long

Once upon a time, if you wanted to change the angle of view of your camera's lens, you had to have a camera with interchangeable lenses. You had to twist off one lens and replace it with another one having a different angle of view. Replacing the lens was the only way you could switch from the short focal length that was best, say, for scenic photos, to the long focal length that was best for the close-up portrait that you now wanted to shoot. Many a good picture was lost in the time you spent making the switch.

The zoom lens put an end to that struggle. More than a convenience that lets you change your angle of view without changing lenses, it also lets you fine-tune your focal length. Say you have a 38–90mm zoom, very common on 35mm point-and-shoots. You can zoom to, and take pictures at, 38mm and 90mm, of course. But you can also shoot at 45mm or 70mm or any other intermediate setting. Even $56^{1}/_{2}$mm. And these multiple settings can help you not just fit the subject in the frame, but quickly tweak composition when you can't take the time to move in and out.

A zoom lens is described by its *focal length range,* an indication of its shortest and longest focal length settings. A 38–90mm zoom point-and-shoot has a focal length range of 38–90mm; you would say this aloud as "38 to 90 millimeters," or for short, just "38 to 90." A 38–105mm zoom point-and-shoot is said to have a focal length range of "38 to 105," with the 105 pronounced "one-oh-five." (Focal lengths beyond 100mm are pronounced this way; 135mm would be "one-thirty-five," for example.)

Keep in mind that when you turn on a zoom camera, its lens starts out just like the lens on a single-focal-length camera. It has the same, or a very similar, focal length setting — perhaps 35mm or 38mm for 35mm cameras, 28mm or 30mm for APS cameras — as a single-focal-length model's single focal length.

Smart thinking is at work here. This moderate wide-angle setting is extremely useful for most kinds of pictures snapshooters take. You can take pretty close shots with it; you can step back a bit and still get all of a nice big landscape in the picture. It's a fine focal length for group shots and grab shots. It works as well on vacations as around the house. In short, it's a good compromise.

Like any compromise, though, a moderate wide-angle setting doesn't serve every purpose. If you want to fill the frame with a subject, you do have to be physically pretty close. (You have to use those feet of yours, and walk right up.) Moving in close is no problem if you're photographing blossoms in your backyard garden. People, on the other hand, aren't so thrilled when you put a camera inches from their nose, especially if they're crocheting a sweater or changing spark plugs. What's more, the picture you get when you photograph someone that close will more than likely be unflattering — marred by a big-nose effect that I tell you about shortly.

This sort of situation is when zooms are so useful. Fine, you're thinking, but how do I know when to zoom the zoom? Do I just zoom back and forth until the subject looks right?

Well, the fact of the matter is some focal length settings are better for certain kinds of pictures than others. You'll begin to understand which focal lengths are better for certain subjects as you shoot more pictures with a zoom point-and-shoot. Choosing an appropriate focal length quickly becomes second nature.

The easiest way to understand focal length numbers is to break them up into three categories: wide-angle, normal, and telephoto (or just the abbreviation *tele*).

- ✔ Wide-angle focal lengths are the smaller numbers.

- ✔ Normal focal lengths are the in-between numbers.

- ✔ Tele focal lengths are the numbers that are bigger still.

With 35mm point-and-shoots, for example, the widest focal length available is 28mm, the longest tele, 200mm. (This range is different for Advanced Photo System and digital models, as you see in the sidebar "The long and short of different film formats.") Wide-angle, normal, and tele focal lengths each take a different view of things (see Figure 5-4). Here's the long and short of it.

The whole wide world

Any fan of *National Geographic* magazine has seen photos along these lines: a white-water raft and its struggling crew against a background of towering Grand Canyon cliffs; the interior of a huge cathedral, from nave to chapel; a window view of a teeming street. These kinds of pictures are what you can get with a short focal length, also known as a wide-angle focal length.

A wide-angle focal length lets you take pictures when you're short on space — when backing up any further is impossible because you're against a wall, or on the edge of a cliff, or actually *in* that raft on the Colorado River. Thinking of these lenses as *reducing* lenses may help, because they make things look smaller than things do to your naked eye, and can therefore squeeze more stuff into the picture. As I mention earlier in this chapter, what wide-angle focal lengths do is sort of like looking through one of those peephole viewers in a door. The shorter the focal length setting, the more the lens can squeeze into the picture; a 28mm focal length on a 35mm camera can squeeze in much more than a 38mm, just as a 24mm focal length on an Advanced Photo System camera can squeeze in much more than a 30mm.

A wide-angle focal length's mission in life may be to get more stuff on your film, but it does other things, too. For one, it tends to exaggerate the size of objects or people in the foreground, and to make things in the background look farther away than they actually are. (See Chapter 9 for an example of this.) In producing this effect, a wide-angle focal length can help create a strong sense of depth or three-dimensionality. In extreme cases, foreground objects, photographed up close with a wide-angle lens, may seem to bulge out of the picture at the viewer.

You may think this is some weird optical effect, but it's actually the way your eyes work, too. Don't believe me? Recruit a cooperative family member or friend and put your face right up to his or her face. See the bug eyes and bulging nose? That's what the lens sees, too — and it's a good reason not to take close portraits of people with a wide-angle focal length.

But wide-angle focal lengths are supremely useful for all sorts of point-and-shoot pictures: the four kids and three pets acting up in the backyard, the (big) family gathering in the dining room, the den by window light, and, of course, your vacation shots.

Figure 5-4:
When you turn on your point-and-shoot (here, a 38–105mm model), you see a pretty big piece of the scene through the viewfinder. The lens auto-matically sets its shortest focal length — in this case, 38mm — to provide the widest view of your subject (top pair). Zoom the lens to the 70mm setting, and you get a tighter shot — one that looks as if you'd moved closer (center pair). Zoom to 105mm, and the framing is tighter still (bottom pair).

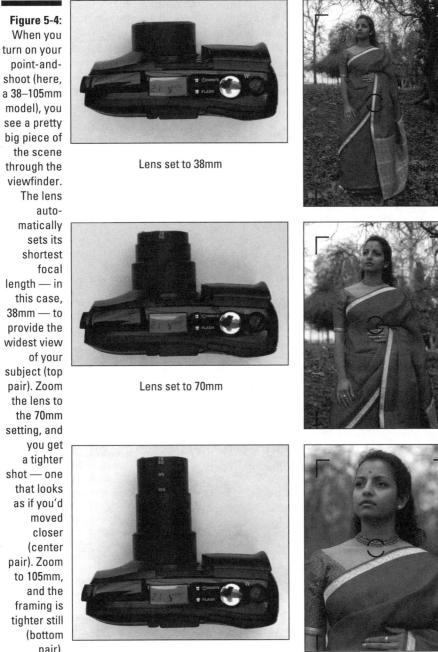

Lens set to 38mm

Lens set to 70mm

Lens set to 105mm

© *Mark Harris (3)*

Indeed, if you have a nonzooming (remember, single-focal-length) point-and-shoot, or if your zoom is set to a wide-angle focal length, you can still take good portraits — provided you shoot from the waist up, and no closer. In fact, the wide-angle is often the focal length of choice for a special type of people picture called an *environmental portrait*. No, it's not an ecological statement. It's simply a portrait photograph that includes a meaningful background or surroundings — an environment that says something about the person.

A picture of Grammie surrounded by the well-seasoned iron pots and pans of her cluttered kitchen tells you something about who she is, not just what she looks like. A picture of Uncle Clive seated at his workshop table with various parts for his vintage radio collection makes him more of a personality than if he were just standing by the garage door. Because people's personal environments are often small and enclosed, a wide-angle focal length helps show the main subject more in context.

The normal view

As you zoom your point-and-shoot's lens to slightly longer focal lengths, you get into the *normal* range — on 35mm models, about 45mm to 55mm, and on APS models, 35mm to 45mm. The term normal actually has a technical meaning that I won't bore you with. Easier and more useful, just think of it this way: Normal focal lengths give you the most natural-looking rendition of the subject. Pictures taken at normal focal lengths appear neither magnified nor reduced. They neither exaggerate depth, like a wide-angle focal length, nor flatten the scene, as happens with tele focal lengths. And precisely because normal focal lengths give you no visual gimmicks to fall back on, you have to work especially hard with what's inside the viewfinder frame. You have to arrange the elements of the picture in an interesting way, or wait for the telling gesture, or take the shot in just the right light.

Many point-and-shooters, though, have the habit of using their zoom lenses at only two settings — zoomed all the way out and zoomed all the way in. They completely ignore the focal lengths in between, which include the normal range.

The telephoto touch

Long focal length settings — those beyond 60mm on a 35mm point-and-shoot, or about 50mm on an Advanced Photo System model — are also known as *telephoto* focal lengths. You use them when you need to capture a subject that's at a distance, either because you can't get closer or because getting closer would call too much attention to your photographic intentions.

Tele focal lengths magnify the subject — that is, they make it look bigger than it does to your naked eye. The longer the focal length, the greater the magnification. Think of looking through binoculars (basically, a pair of matched telephoto lenses).

Professional 35mm sports and wildlife photographers use telephoto lenses with focal lengths way longer than the longest one on your point-and-shoot's zoom — often 300mm, 400mm, and beyond. These high-powered, high-priced lenses allow them to fill the frame with a subject even though they must remain at a considerable distance from it.

When you zoom in with your camera, you're simply changing the focal length to a telephoto setting. But more is going on than simple magnification. Telephoto lenses tend to *flatten* or *compress* a scene. Things behind your main subject, in the background, seem to move up closer to it. Those greeting-card shots with a huge sun or moon looming on the horizon behind the lighthouse are extreme instances of this effect. (See Chapter 9 for other examples.) Telephoto compression is, in fact, the flip side of the effect that you get with a wide-angle focal length, in which the background seems to shrink in comparison to the main subject.

When what you see is not what you get

You may have noticed that when you look through your point-and-shoot camera's viewfinder, you're looking through a window that is above and/or to the side of the lens. This separation doesn't seem like much — maybe an inch — but it's enough to make the slice of the scene that you get on film a slightly *different* slice than what you see through the viewfinder. In extreme cases, things or people can be unexpectedly cut off. This effect is called *parallax error.*

For a quick demonstration of parallax error, close your left eye and look at something in the distance with your right eye. Now raise a hand to block your view of that distant object. Then close your right eye and open your left eye. See how your view shifts so that you can see the distant object again? Basically, that's parallax error. With your eyes, its effect is beneficial because it allows you to see things in stereo — three dimensions. But imagine what would happen if one eye were the viewfinder of your camera, and the other eye — with a very different view of things — were the lens.

The longer your lens zooms, the worse parallax error gets. And it's compounded when you're shooting something at a fairly close distance. In tight portraits taken with a point-and-shoot zoomed way in, you can end up cutting off part of the person's face in the picture — even though you can see his full face in the viewfinder.

This flattening effect makes moderate telephoto focal lengths — those from about 70mm to 100mm with a 35mm zoom point-and-shoot, and from 55mm to 80mm with an APS model — highly prized for portraits. Because you can fill the frame with a face without getting physically all that close (arm's length or better), you don't get big noses or bug eyes or jutting jaws. (Well, let me just say the lens doesn't make what nature gave people any worse!)

Focal lengths from 70mm to 100mm with 35mm, and from 55mm to 80mm with the Advanced Photo System, are often described as *portrait telephoto,* for the flattering proportions that they bring to tight shots of people.

Telephoto focal lengths are valuable if not essential for other subjects, of course — sports (your sprinting little soccer player), nature (the gorgeous cardinal in the backyard), distant scenes, and candid shots. They're often useful for close-ups because their extra magnifying power lets you stay at a reasonable distance from the subject instead of getting right on top of it for a tight composition. Shooting a skittish butterfly at three feet with your lens set to 105mm is easier than shooting it at one foot with the lens set to 35mm.

When zoom point-and-shoots are set to longer focal lengths, however, several problems can occur. One of them is called *parallax error.* Read more about parallax error, and its remedies, in the sidebar, "When what you see is not what you get."

Getting close at telephoto settings

If you take fairly close pictures with a point-and-shoot zoomed to a long focal length, your subject will end up shifted or even cut off in the actual pictures. To prevent this problem, you must use the viewfinder's *close-up correction marks.*

Close-up correction marks (also called a close-up frame) are a set of lines, or sometimes a corner-shaped bracket, inset within the clear area of the viewfinder window. You should use these marks when you're taking a shot from fairly close to the subject, and/or when you're using a long focal length setting. Here's how.

First, compose the picture as you normally would. Note what's at the top edge of the viewfinder — say it's the uppermost daisy in a flower arrangement. Now tilt or raise the camera up slightly, so that the daisy falls just under the horizontal close-up correction line, or under the invisible line that the corner bracket defines. Then take the picture (see Figure 5-5).

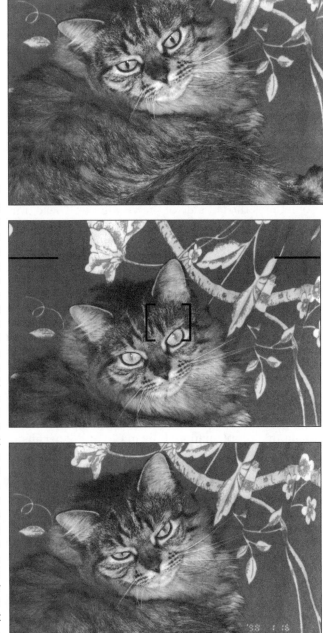

Figure 5-5: Shooting up close with the lens zoomed in can cause a subject to be cut off at the top (top), and sometimes the side. To prevent this, aim the camera up to keep the subject within the viewfinder's close-up correction marks (middle) and then shoot. The subject will be correctly positioned in the print (bottom).

© Russell Hart (3)

If your camera's close-up correction marks include a corner bracket or a vertical line, you may also have to shift the camera slightly to the left before you shoot. This shifting repositions the part of the subject that was at the left-hand edge of the viewfinder so that it's just inside the vertical close-up correction line. But please: Check your camera's manual for details about using its particular close-up correction marks. Instruction manuals almost always have information on shooting close-ups, with illustrations.

Using close-up correction marks is a clumsy business, and they aren't even particularly accurate. (By the way, if your camera is a focus-free model, it probably won't have them because the lens doesn't zoom, and you can't shoot from closer than about four feet anyway.) Some point-and-shoots have a much better system: As you focus close, and/or zoom in to a longer focal length, translucent bands (usually dark, but light in some models) appear at the top and sometimes the left side of the viewfinder. These translucent bands warn you not to put any part of the picture there. This system isn't limited to zoom cameras; my $140 single-focal-length model has it, as do a couple of comparable models. If you like to shoot really close, consider buying a camera with this feature, sometimes called LCD viewfinder framelines or LCD viewfinder correction marks.

Telephoto settings and the lens aperture

Here is one last note on zoom point-and-shoots that offer longer focal length settings. At these settings, the lens aperture gets much smaller, which means that less light reaches the film. The camera may try several things to make up for this lack of light. It may fire the flash, which you may not want — or if the subject is too far away, may not help. Or the camera may set a much slower shutter speed — the length of time the window in the lens stays open. This longer shutter speed increases the risk that shake will blur the picture. (I explain this problem more fully in Chapter 2 because one remedy for it is to use a film with a higher ISO.)

You may have noticed that I keep telling you to break the rules. Well, here I go again. Even though certain focal lengths are good for certain picture-taking situations, no photographic law exists that says you have to follow the focal length rules all the time. Just for the fun of it, zoom to another setting and try a picture there. Wide-angle close-ups of kids' faces, in particular, can make for zany shots — even though they are, technically, taken at the "wrong" focal length for portraits.

Types of Point-And-Shoot Cameras — by Their Lenses

If you read the previous sections in this chapter, now you know your focal-length ABCs, which should help you understand the four broad categories of point-and-shoot cameras — classifications that are based entirely on the camera's lens and zoom focal-length range. These groups are *single-focal-length, compact zoom, standard zoom,* and *long zoom.* Here are a basic rundown and some quick pointers on the use of each type. (If you're shopping for a new camera, also check out Chapter 16.)

The single-focal-length (nonzoom) point-and-shoot

On 35mm models, a nonzoom lens typically has one focal length somewhere between 32mm and 40mm; a 35mm focal length is perhaps most common. On Advanced Photo System models, a nonzoom lens usually falls somewhere between 26mm and 30mm. (All one-time-use cameras are single-focal-length models.) These moderate wide-angle lenses are good for everything from waist-up portraits to fairly wide-open landscape shots. The better models have *fast* lenses that are able to let in more light; you can therefore use them without flash in dimmer light than is possible with most zoom cameras. And virtually all of these models are small enough to fit in a pocket, so you never have an excuse not to take them where you're going.

The major drawback to these cameras is the big-nose effect that you get when you take a close portrait. The funny thing is that many of the *autofocus* models in this group can actually focus quite close (14 or 15 inches is common), so it's tempting to move in. That's fine — for anything but a flattering face.

Following are some of the pluses and minuses of single-focal-length point-and-shoots:

- *Watch out:* Stay at arm's length for portraits.
- *Best choice for:* Traveler, photo diarist, serious shooter who wants a pocket camera.
- *Not so good for:* Frequent portrait shooters, doting parents.
- *Sometimes you see:* A true wide-angle focal length, usually around 28mm or 30mm (on 35mm models), 22mm or 24mm (on Advanced Photo System models). These lenses have a still-wider angle of view, so they are even better for shots of wide-open spaces outside or cramped quarters inside. But they can make the big-nose effect even worse, so arm's length or greater for people!

The compact-zoom point-and-shoot

Compact-zoom models usually have 2X zoom lenses, which means their magnifying power is doubled as you zoom from the shortest to the longest focal length. (See the sidebar, "What's my zoom ratio?") With 35mm models, 35–70mm zooms are the norm in this category. With Advanced Photo System models, 30–60mm is most common. Some very nice cameras in this group are hardly bigger than the most compact single-focal-length models.

A compact-zoom model gives you the very useful 35mm setting; the natural look of a normal focal length; and, at 70mm, a setting that is long enough for a very pleasing portrait. But it does have drawbacks. Toward the long end, the lens admits less light than at the wide-angle position, forcing flash or slower shutter speeds. And you also start to see parallax error with models that can focus pretty close. (Check out the sidebar "When what you see is not what you get," earlier in this chapter, for more on parallax error.)

- ✔ *Watch out:* Flash may be triggered in low light when you're zoomed in, so zoom out to wide-angle when you want to shoot by existing light. And mind the close-up correction marks when you get close to a subject.

- ✔ *Best for:* Traveler, photo diarist, doting parents.

- ✔ *Not so good for:* People who want an even tinier camera or a longer zoom.

- ✔ *Sometimes you see:* Compact zooms that start at a true wide-angle focal length, such as 28–56mm or 28–70mm on 35mm cameras, and 24–48mm on APS cameras. These cameras give you the great advantage of a wider angle of view, plus a longish normal setting at the other end of the zoom range that's pretty good for people pictures.

What's my zoom ratio?

The *zoom ratio* of a lens expresses the relationship between its longest focal length and its shortest. This ratio is usually stated as a factor with a times sign. A 35–70mm zoom, for example, is a 2X zoom because it can zoom to twice its starting focal length; a 40–120mm zoom is a 3X zoom because it can zoom to three times its starting focal length. You can also express zoom ratios proportionally: 2:1 ("two-to-one") and 3:1 ("three-to-one") in the previous examples. If you want to figure out your zoom's ratio, just divide the bigger *mm* number by the smaller one. For a 28–70mm zoom, divide 70 by 28, for a zoom ratio of 2.5X (or 2.5:1). Generally speaking, you should look for a zoom ratio of at least 2:1. Zoom ratios bigger than 2:1 are often considered even more desirable, and camera manufacturers make rather a fuss about zoom ratios in advertising. Most users don't need a zoom ratio bigger than 3:1, though.

The standard-zoom point-and-shoot

The standard-zoom point-and-shoot has come up in the world, with 38–90mm zooms almost universal among 35mm models, and 30–75mm zooms common among Advanced Photo System models. And some 35mm models zoom out to about 120mm (90mm with APS models). Many of these cameras are also quite compact. The standard-zoom point-and-shoot is pretty much the ideal family camera, combining moderate wide-angle, normal, and true portrait telephoto focal lengths. Zooms of this range, though, usually admit a lot less light as you zoom to longer settings — same as compact-zoom models, only worse. And parallax error may be greater still.

- ✔ *Watch out:* The longer focal length settings usually trigger flash in lower light. And if you turn off the flash in that situation, you may get blur due to camera shake.

- ✔ *Best for:* Mom and Dad, general point-and-shooters, portrait enthusiasts.

- ✔ *Not so good for:* People who want a tiny camera or a faster lens.

- ✔ *Sometimes you see:* Zooms that go from true wide-angle to portrait telephoto: 28–90mm on 35mm models and 25–100mm on APS models. This phenomenally useful zoom range is ideal for point-and-shooters — yet is, ironically, the least popular. Go figure.

The long-zoom point-and-shoot

Quite a few point-and-shoots now come with focal-length ranges like 38–135mm, 38–140mm, and 38–145mm. (In the Advanced Photo System, that translates to about 30–120mm.) Unfortunately, their long-zooming lenses admit a *lot* less light when they're zoomed way in, forcing them to set very slow shutter speeds when you're shooting without flash. Translation: The chance of blur is quite high, even if you're using ISO 400 films in decent light. ISO 800 print films should be considered *standard* films for these models — yes, for outdoor, daylight use — if you shoot often at the longest focal length settings. These models also have greater parallax problems than any other kind of point-and-shoot camera, when you take pictures at their longest settings.

A long zoom should come in handy, though, for your budding sports star or your backyard fauna. And you can get really tight portraits with a more comfortable distance between you and your subject. Just be aware of the limitations, and keep in mind that you can often get as tight a picture, and as flattering, at a more moderate tele setting such as 70mm — simply by moving in with your feet. If you're shooting without flash, moving in also lessens the risk of shake-induced blur.

  ✔ *Watch out:* Pack ISO 800 film if you plan to use that longest focal length. Pay particular attention to close-up correction marks or viewfinder warnings.

  ✔ *Best for:* Mom and Dad, gadget enthusiast, outdoor sports fan.

  ✔ *Not so good for:* Anyone looking for a more compact camera, a casual snapshooter.

  ✔ *Sometimes you see:* Translucent LCD framelines in the viewfinder that automatically adjust to show you correction for parallax, which is described in the sidebar "When what you see is not what you get."

After all is zoomed and done, though, what makes you a good photographer is not how many focal lengths your camera has. It's how you use the ones that you have — how you translate your lens's view into your view of the world.

Chapter 6

The Lens and Focusing

In This Chapter

▶ Looking at how your camera focuses

▶ Autofocus versus fixed-focus

▶ Placing your focus point

▶ Locking the focus

▶ Using the infinity lock mode

▶ Commandments of good autofocusing

*F*ocusing was the last great hurdle of camera automation. Automatic film advance, automatic flash, automatic exposure — these amenities have long been a fact of point-and-shoot life. Automatic focusing — *autofocus,* for short — is a more recent innovation. But autofocus was worth the wait, relieving one of the great anxieties of snapshot photography. Autofocus has saved lots of pictures that otherwise would have been lost to the vexing back-and-forth of old-fashioned manual focusing.

So I kind of hate to tell you this, but you — and only you — must make sure that your point-and-shoot's lens is properly focused when you take a picture. I know what you're saying. "There he goes again, telling me I have to do something that the camera does automatically."

I'm the first to admit that a point-and-shoot will take a good percentage of sharp pictures if you just glance through it and snap away. Left to its own devices, your camera will, indeed, focus automatically. It will focus automatically on whatever chance places in its path. But you simply can't leave focusing to chance. That's how bad pictures happen to good people.

The term autofocus is really a misnomer. Power-assisted focus, or maybe computer-aided focus, would be more accurate. Autofocus cameras simply help *you* in carrying out the function of focusing the lens. So this chapter tells you how you can help yourself when it comes to autofocus.

What Is Autofocusing?

So what is focusing, really? People tend to use the term pretty blithely; they at least seem to know that it has to do with making a photograph sharp. Basically, *focusing* is the process of moving the lens in and out until it forms the sharpest possible image of the subject on the film. Focusing is necessary because for every subject at a different distance from the camera, the lens must be at a different distance from the film to create the sharpest possible image.

An autofocus point-and-shoot uses sophisticated technology to measure the distance to the subject. It relays this information to a motor in the lens. The motor then moves the lens to the proper distance from the film.

Though their mechanism is different, your eyes autofocus, too. They do so with such precision and speed, in fact, that you don't even have to think about it. Well, at least until you start needing glasses to find your glasses, or wishing you had arm-extenders to read.

To see how your eyes autofocus, put your hand as close to your face as you can and still see it clearly. Now look right past your hand at a distant object — something across the room from you. Keep looking at that distant object and try to see out of the corner of your eye (that is, without looking directly at it) what your hand looks like. Blurry, isn't it? Now look back at your hand. Again, out of the corner of your eye, see what the far object looks like. Now *it* is blurry. Your eye refocuses automatically when you look at something that's at a different distance — rather like an autofocus point-and-shoot.

When you look through an autofocus point-and-shoot's viewfinder window, though, you don't see that focusing process, even though it's happening inside the camera. The entire scene remains sharp regardless of where the lens actually focuses. For most people, this fact isn't bothersome. But it may be strange for the many photographers switching to a point-and-shoot from an old 35mm *SLR (single-lens reflex)*. An SLR camera's viewfinder allows you to view and compose the subject — and with manual-focus models, to focus it by hand — through the lens itself. You can see one part of the scene become sharp and another become blurry as the lens refocuses, just as you did with your hand and that distant object. But former SLR photographers just have to trust that their point-and-shoot camera is doing its autofocus thing — as they help it along, of course!

Autofocus versus Fixed-Focus

Autofocus is not a necessity for good pictures. Tons of less expensive (under $50) point-and-shoots, and *all* one-time-use cameras, rely on what is often called *focus-free* operation. This term should really be *fixed focus,* because it means that the lens's focus was permanently set at the factory. This fixed setting gives you pretty sharp pictures if your subject is at an average snapshot distance (eight feet or so), and less-sharp-but-acceptable pictures if your subject is a little closer or farther away. But if you get too close to something, it will appear unsharp in your print. With fixed-focus, focus-free cameras, four feet is about as close as you can get and still take reasonably sharp snapshots.

The best way to tell whether you have an autofocus or a fixed-focus point-and-shoot is simply by looking through the viewfinder. If you have an autofocus model, you'll see a small set of marks — often in the form of brackets or a cross shape — in the center of the frame. These marks, called the *focus point,* tell you where the camera is focusing. (Sometimes the focus point is a circle; sometimes a pair of square or rounded brackets; and sometimes lines that intersect to form a cross, not unlike a gun sight's crosshairs.)

If you have a fixed-focus point-and-shoot, its viewfinder lacks the focus point (see Figure 6-1). A fixed-focus camera also lacks the green *focus-OK lamp* found on autofocus models. (See the section "Making sure your focus is locked," later in this chapter.) (Fixed-focus models can, and often do, have a flash-ready lamp, usually red.) The lamp is built into the side of the viewfinder eyepiece or is just inside the eyepiece frame; occasionally it's on the bottom of the eyepiece. Wherever it is, you can see it out of the corner of your eye when you look through the viewfinder.

Still not sure? Camera makers endeavor to promote their products' features, so if your point-and-shoot has autofocus, it probably says so somewhere on the camera or at least on the box. Sometimes camera makers use the initials *AF* to indicate autofocus capability.

If you have a fixed-focus, focus-free point-and-shoot, don't get too close to your subject. You usually need to be at least four feet away from something to make it sharp in the print; anything closer may appear blurry. Check your manual to see what minimum distance the manufacturer recommends.

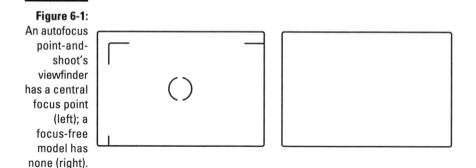

Figure 6-1:
An autofocus
point-and-
shoot's
viewfinder
has a central
focus point
(left); a
focus-free
model has
none (right).

The Focus Point: Where Your Camera Focuses

Autofocus point-and-shoots produce terrifically sharp pictures when you use them properly. But getting sharp results sometimes requires *telling* them where to focus.

The camera automatically focuses on whatever part of your subject the focus point is covering when you press the shutter button. If you're photographing a friend who is six feet away and the focus point covers the friend's face, your camera autofocuses six feet away. If you're photographing mountains that are a mile away and the focus point covers them, then the camera autofocuses, well, way out there. (Beyond a certain distance, everything ends up sharp anyway. "Way out there" in photo jargon is called "infinity," and you can read more about it in Chapter 4.)

You can't assume, however, that the viewfinder's focus point will always fall in the right place. Imagine photographing two friends standing six feet away from you with those mountains in the background. Your friends are smack in the middle of the viewfinder frame. But between the two of them is a little gap, and the viewfinder's focus point falls neatly into it — covering a little piece of distant mountain. Not noticing this little gap, you point and shoot. Guess what happens: The camera focuses on the mountains, and your friends end up unsharp in the print.

That scenario is an example of purely accidental misfocusing. But its more common variation is when you deliberately place a subject off-center in the viewfinder frame. Say you want to compose the shot of your friends and the mountains this way. You ask your friends to stand to the right so that they block less of the background, giving the mountains center stage in your composition. You point and shoot. Guess what happens: The camera focuses on the mountains, because that's where your composition has landed the focus point. Once again, your friends end up unsharp in the print. Call it *tunnel focus.*

The same thing can happen just about anywhere, and on a smaller scale. Say you're photographing your spouse sitting across from you at a restaurant table. If the focus point happens to fall on the far wall, the camera focuses there — not on your beloved.

Unintentional focusing on the background is, along with unwanted camera movement, the main cause of unsharp point-and-shoot pictures. And here's a simple way to avoid it — a photographic one-two punch called *locking the focus.* It's the only sure way of getting the camera to focus on what you consider the most important thing in your picture.

Locking the focus

You should lock the focus any time your composition does not place the viewfinder's focus point on the most important part of the scene you're shooting. Locking the focus means that you deliberately make your camera focus on an important object in the scene — a person, or something interesting in the foreground — and keep the focus locked at that exact distance until you take the picture. Here's how you lock the focus:

1. **Look through the viewfinder and position its focus point on the most important part of the scene — your main subject.**

   In effect, you center that subject.

2. **Press the shutter button halfway down, until the green focus-OK lamp in the viewfinder eyepiece glows steadily.**

   See the next section, "Making sure your focus is locked," for more on the focus-OK lamp.

3. **Holding the shutter button halfway down, reorient the camera so that your desired composition appears in the viewfinder.**

4. **Press the shutter button all the way down to take the picture.**

For example, say you want your main subject to be off-center to the right in your composition. (See Chapter 9 for more on composition.) With those friends and the mountains (see preceding section), you lock the focus by aiming the focus point at your friends (which temporarily puts them in the center of the viewfinder) and pressing the shutter button halfway. Then, holding the shutter button halfway down, you swing the camera left to place your friends off-center to the right (see Figure 6-2). Now press the shutter button the rest of the way to take the picture.

Figure 6-2: To prevent your point-and-shoot from focusing on the background with an off-center subject (top), simply center the subject (middle) and lock the focus by pressing the shutter button halfway. Then pivot the camera to re-establish your composition before pressing the button all the way to take the picture (bottom).

©Mark Harris (3)

You may need to use this technique with vertical composition, too (see Figure 6-3). Say you're standing on a rock to shoot a vertical picture in which your friends are at the bottom of the viewfinder and the mountains in the background are at the top. Your composition causes the viewfinder's focus point to cover the mountains, not your friends — and if you were to go ahead and take the shot, your friends would end up unsharp in the print. But knowing this might happen, you first aim the camera down to place the focus point over one of your friends' faces (which temporarily cuts off the mountains at the top) and press the shutter button halfway. Then, holding the shutter button halfway down, you swing the camera back up to include the mountains and reestablish your desired composition. Now you press the shutter button the rest of the way to take the picture.

Regardless of your composition — centered or off-center — you should always keep your eye on where the focus point lands. Remember those two friends with the gap between them (the ones I describe in the preceding section)? With newfound vigilance, you observe that the focus point has landed in the gap, covering that little piece of distant mountain. To take the picture, you first "aim" the focus point so that it's on one friend's face and then press the shutter button halfway down. Holding the shutter button halfway down, you reorient the camera to center your friends. Then, and only then, do you press the button the rest of the way to take the picture.

Particularly if you're a landscape fan, you may be wondering what happens to distant objects when you lock the focus on closer objects. "If I focus on my friends in front of the mountains, instead of the mountains," you ask, "then won't the mountains be out of focus?" Good question. Here's the important answer.

With most scenes in which you photograph a relatively close object (human or inanimate) in front of a distant background, if you focus on the close object, the background will be reasonably sharp in the print. But the reverse is not true. Focus on the background — those mountains — and the close object simply won't be sharp. I wouldn't worry about why!

Making sure your focus is locked

When you lock your focus, you can't actually see the subject getting sharp in the viewfinder. However, you can verify that your point-and-shoot has autofocused on something by looking at its *focus-OK lamp* (see Figure 6-4).

The focus-OK lamp lights up whenever you press the shutter button halfway. If it glows steadily, it's telling you that the camera has successfully focused. If the focus-OK lamp blinks, or doesn't light, or lights briefly but then goes out or starts blinking, it's telling you that the camera can't focus.

Figure 6-3:
Locking the focus can also be important when you take vertical pictures — here, keeping the camera from focusing on the background (left) with a low main subject (right).

© Russell Hart (2)

Figure 6-4:
The viewfinder's green focus-OK lamp glows steadily to confirm the focus.

More often than not, your camera can't focus because you're too close to the subject. Fix the problem by easing up on the shutter button, stepping back a foot or two, and then pressing the shutter button again. If this tactic doesn't do the job, the autofocus system may be getting tripped up by a difficult subject. See "The Commandments of Good Autofocusing," later in this chapter, for details.

Getting a feel for locking the focus

The idea of pressing the shutter button halfway may sound tricky to you. How do you know what halfway is? How do you avoid pushing too hard when you're just trying to lock the focus and accidentally taking the picture? Manufacturers have anticipated your worry.

On autofocus point-and-shoot cameras, the shutter button is specifically designed for the two-step operation needed to lock the focus. Press it lightly — I prefer to say *press it halfway,* because that's how it feels — and the camera autofocuses, locking the focus on whatever the focus point is covering in your viewfinder. Press it fully — I prefer to say *press it all the way down* — and the camera takes the picture.

Getting the hang of this technique takes a while. You may even waste an occasional frame of film. So practice the autofocus two-step with an empty camera. On some models, you can actually hear the lens quietly click or zip into position when you press the shutter button halfway.

Keep your finger glued to the shutter button. To master its two-step operation, you must lose the worst habit of point-and-shooters: stabbing the button to take a picture. Don't wait for a shot with your finger poised in the air. Your finger should remain in contact with the shutter button before, during, and after you take a picture.

By not stabbing the shutter button, you accomplish two things: First, you lessen the risk that you will shake the camera, which reduces the chance that your picture will be blurred. Basically, you can keep the camera steadier. And second, more crucial to focusing, if you change your mind about where you want to lock the focus, all you have to do is let up on the shutter button a little, re-aim the focus point, and then press the button halfway once again.

Shutter button pressed halfway
(locks the focus)

Shutter button pressed all the way
(takes the picture)

If you move, the focus doesn't

Locking the focus is vitally important to getting consistently sharp pictures. But you should remember that when you have that shutter button pressed halfway, the focus doesn't budge. If you ask your subject to move closer or farther away, or *you* move closer or farther from it to adjust your composition, it's no longer in focus. So, if for any reason the distance to the subject changes after you've locked the focus, you must let up on the shutter button and repeat the focus-locking procedure. Small changes in distance aren't always worth worrying about, however, especially when you're fairly far from the main subject or when refocusing would cause you to lose the moment. Also, if you or the subject moves *sideways,* you needn't refocus.

Zoom before you lock the focus. With most point-and-shoot cameras, locking the focus also prevents you from adjusting the zoom. If you want to zoom in or out after locking the focus, let up on the shutter button, adjust the zoom, and then lock the focus again. (Check out Chapter 5 for more on zooming.)

Infinity Lock: Focusing Far Away

Sometimes you want to make the camera autofocus as far away as possible — and can't. For example, you may want to photograph a distant subject, but worry that the camera will focus on a jumble of detail in the foreground. Or a more common situation — you may just want to take a picture of a scene through a window.

A window may look transparent to you, but most point-and-shoots see it as solid. They focus on the glass, rather than what's on the other side of it.

The solution to this problem is to use your camera's *infinity lock* mode. This mode is also sometimes called *landscape mode* because it works best with subjects that are far away. When you set the camera to infinity lock, it basically overrides the camera's autofocus, setting the lens to focus as far away as it can. (See Chapter 4 for more on the infinity lock mode.)

To make sure that you get correct focus when shooting through a window, the best strategy is to open the window. If this action is impossible — or moving your prize African violets from the window sill would take too long — then use infinity lock (see Figure 6-5), if your camera has this feature. If it doesn't, try putting the camera right up to the glass to shoot — although I suggest testing this method before a picture opportunity happens. Shoot one frame of a distant object through the window and then see whether the resulting print is acceptably sharp. If it is, you can use this technique for future shots.

Widening the Autofocus Horizon

To lessen the chance that your camera accidentally focuses on a background rather than your main subject, point-and-shoot manufacturers have come up with a clever technology called *wide-area autofocusing*. This feature also goes by *multibeam* or *multipoint autofocus*. (See Chapter 4 for more on this feature.)

Generally, wide-area autofocus is sensitive to the central one-quarter to one-third of the horizontal picture frame. This extra spread allows the camera to correctly focus subjects that are a little off-center. If, for example, the camera detects more than one thing within the focusing area (for example, two friends), it focuses on the thing closest to the camera. And if your two friends are an equal distance from the camera, it will focus on them, not the mountain behind them. It's well-suited to *grab shots* — those pictures with which you have just enough time to turn on the camera and snap.

But focusing mistakes are still possible with wide-area focusing. Someone or something may be a little too far to the side for it to catch, in which case the camera focuses on something in the background anyway. And how do you know if it's screwing up? You don't. The little green focus-OK lamp glows steadily, because the camera has focused just fine on something far away.

Figure 6-5: Most point-and-shoots can't autofocus anything on the other side of a window, focusing on the glass instead (left). If you can't open the window to prevent this, set infinity lock (right).

©Russell Hart (2)

So my thinking is, Why take the chance? If you have the time — and you don't need much — always lock the focus. Lock the focus whether your camera has wide-area autofocus or not. (See the section "Locking the focus," earlier in this chapter.)

Some cameras, by the way, let you switch from wide-area focusing to *spot autofocus* — in other words, from multiple focus points back to a single, central one. (See Chapter 4 for details on spot autofocus.) Switching to spot autofocus isn't a bad precaution if focus is extremely critical to a picture. For example, if you think unimportant foliage in the foreground may cause a wide-area autofocus system *not* to focus on something more important in the distance, you can switch to spot autofocus to define the focus more narrowly — to see beyond the foliage. But in most cases, locking the focus and recomposing takes care of things.

The Commandments of Good Autofocusing

You're getting off easy — I'm handing down only nine commandments, not the usual ten! And even if you follow only the first three, you'll get well-focused pictures almost all the time. The first three are super-important; the others are for finessing your particular type of autofocus system.

To get the most from these tips, you need to know whether your camera has an active or passive autofocus system. *Active autofocus* bounces infrared beams off the subject so that the camera can determine the distance to it and set the lens's focus accordingly. *Passive autofocus,* on the other hand, determines the subject's distance by analyzing the image itself and adjusting focus until subject details are as sharp as they can be.

Before you get flustered by these techie-sounding terms, here's a simple way to figure out which one your camera uses — in case you've lost your manual, which should tell you what you've got in the "specifications" section. Outside, in daylight, aim the viewfinder's focus point at a patch of open, featureless sky, no electric wire or clouds allowed. Press the shutter button halfway. If you get a blinking focus-OK lamp (meaning focus is not possible), you probably have passive autofocus. If you get a steady lamp (meaning focus is okay), you have active autofocus.

With all types of autofocus

Here are the three commandments of good autofocusing that should help you get sharp focus regardless of what kind of system you have.

✔ **Thou shalt lock the focus:** Locking the focus should be utterly reflexive. Don't count on multibeams or any other gizmo your camera may have. (Check out the section "Locking the focus," earlier in this chapter, to find out how.)

✔ **Thou shalt watch thy focus-OK lamp:** The focus-OK lamp glows steadily if focus has been achieved and blinks if something is amiss. Quite a few cameras use different rates of blinking to tell you what's up: Fast blinking usually means the camera can't find the focus; slow blinking may mean you're in a special close-up range or that you're just too close. Check your manual to be sure which is which. (For more on the focus-OK lamp, see the section "Making sure your focus is locked," earlier in this chapter.)

✔ **Thou shalt use infinity lock, if thou hast it:** Even if you're pretty sure your camera can focus accurately at great distances, setting infinity lock is a good precaution when you're shooting far-away scenes — but only if there's no important foreground. (For details, see the section "Infinity Lock: Focusing Far Away," earlier in this chapter.)

With active autofocus

When you lightly touch the shutter button of an active-autofocus camera, before you press it all the way down an infrared beam shoots out of a small window on the camera's front. (Infrared is the same invisible light that allows a remote control to operate your TV.) This beam is reflected back to the camera by solid objects, just like visible light. A little window on the front of the camera actually senses this bounced-back beam, and the camera can calculate the angle at which it bounced off the subject or object. From that information, it actually computes how far away an object is and sets the lens to focus at that distance.

Active autofocus has some great *advantages,* which is why you can find it on the vast majority of point-and-shoots:

✔ Active autofocus works in the dark — even pitch black. So it's great for party pictures in dim basement rec rooms.

✔ You don't have to aim a camera with active autofocus at a detail in the subject. It can focus on a blank wall just as well as it can on Uncle Clive's plaid leisure suit — and do so very quickly.

Cleaning your lens

Point-and-shoot cameras get a lot of manhandling — womanhandling, too. In changing film or batteries, sampling a piece of wedding cake, or just holding the camera between pictures, you can easily smudge the lens. And with a big smudge on the lens, you probably won't get sharp pictures. In fact, a smudged lens is a major cause of unsharp results.

So you should inspect your lens routinely, before you take a picture and even as you're shooting an event. To inspect your lens, turn the camera on so that the lens's front surface is uncovered. Hold the camera in your hands so that the surface reflects a strong light source — a window, the sky, a lampshade — and then tilt it slightly back and forth to move the reflection around the lens (see figure). You can spot smudges, accumulated dust, and other crud quite readily this way. Given the small size and recessed position of most point-and-shoot lens surfaces, any smudge is likely to be smack in the middle — the worst place. If you see a smudge, clean the lens.

To clean the lens, you need lens cleaning solution, available in small bottles at your local camera shop. (Never use water or window glass cleaners.) While you're at the shop, pick up some lens cleaning tissue, too. Actually, I find that cotton swabs (sterile, please) often work better than tissue for smaller lenses, but you probably have them at home already.

First, use your breath to blow off the lens lightly. Don't get it wet. If you're particularly fastidious, you can blow off the lens with a photographic blower brush or a can of compressed air; these items are available at camera stores, too. Blowing the lens off before cleaning is important, because it removes any grit or dust that may scratch the lens's surface as you wipe it.

Next, place a drop or two of lens cleaning solution on the end of a cotton swab. Gently wipe the lens surface with the swab, starting in the middle and spiraling out to the edges of the lens. Then, even more delicately, apply the dry end of the swab in the same pattern to polish out any streaks.

Inspect the lens surface again. If smudges or streaks remain, repeat the process. And if the cotton swab doesn't seem to be removing the smudge and/or polishing out the streaks, fold a piece of lens cleaning tissue over on itself a few times, wet it with a few drops of lens cleaning fluid, and use its flattest portion to wipe the lens with a concentric pattern. (If the lens surface is recessed and hard to reach, you can even use a cotton swab to push the tissue around the lens surface.) Repeat the process with dry tissue. You can also use this method to clean the viewfinder window, should it get smudged or accumulate dirt.

And you know active autofocus is bound to have drawbacks, right? Ironically, the biggest of these drawbacks is that active autofocus can focus just about anything. It's indiscriminate, which leads off its *disadvantages:*

- ✔ Active autofocus can focus right past a subject that isn't in the middle of the frame. If Uncle Clive is standing off to the side and you don't first lock the focus on him, your single-minded little robot focuses right on the wall behind him.

- ✔ Active autofocus doesn't have a very long range. The infrared beam that shoots out of the camera is weak; it can't accurately figure the distance to the subject if it's more than about 25 feet away. The limited range usually isn't a problem except with longer zoom lenses, which need to be focused more precisely at far distances.

To make the most of your active autofocus, follow these three commandments whenever you can.

- ✔ **Thou shalt not focus on bright reflections or dull black objects.** Because active autofocus depends on the camera's ability to see the reflection of a dim infrared beam, very shiny objects (or very bright lamps) can overpower the reflection and cause incorrect focus. Likewise, a dull black object (or an actual hole) can swallow up the infrared beam and cause misfocusing.

- ✔ **Thou shalt not confuse thine autofocus with fences.** If you try to take a picture of something on the other side of a fence with an open grid pattern, active autofocus may focus through the fence — then again, it may focus on the fence itself. How can you tell? You can't. If you want to take a picture of something on the other side of the fence, poke your camera through the bars so that the lens, the viewfinder, and all those little windows on the front of the camera are clear.

- ✔ **Thou shalt not focus through glass without infinity lock.** Active autofocus works by bouncing a beam off solid objects. Windows may be transparent, but they're solid. So active autofocus focuses right on the pane of glass, not on your kids washing the dog outside. (See the section "Infinity Lock: Focusing Far Away" for more on taking pictures through windows.)

With passive autofocus

To overcome some of the drawbacks of active autofocus, camera makers equip some higher-priced point-and-shoots with passive autofocus. Passive autofocus works something like your eyes, analyzing what's in plain view. When things are in focus, you can easily tell the difference between light and dark details; when things are out of focus, though, light and dark areas tend to blend together into gray. What passive autofocus does is move the lens until it finds the point at which contrast is greatest — or, to put it in real-life terms, where Uncle Clive's plaid leisure suit has the most snap to it.

Passive autofocus has some nice *advantages:*

✔ Passive autofocus is not limited in distance. It can focus two miles away as easily as two feet away because it doesn't depend on a wimpy beam, the way active autofocus does. That's why you most often find passive autofocus on point-and-shoots with long zooms.

✔ Passive autofocus can focus through glass because it sees through the window to objects on the other side.

Indeed, passive autofocus's single great advantage is that it's particular, unlike that unfussy slob active autofocus. If you aim your viewfinder's focus point at the blank wall behind Uncle Clive and Great Aunt Gretyl, passive autofocus blinks a warning lamp or balks outright — which brings me to the *disadvantages* of passive autofocus:

✔ Passive autofocus can't focus on areas without detail.

✔ Passive autofocus can't focus in the dark because it doesn't have enough light to see — and it can be slow even when it does.

To make the most of your passive autofocus, follow these three commandments whenever you can:

✔ **Thou shalt not place the viewfinder focus point on blank areas.** Passive autofocus must see detail — an area with contrast to it — to be able to focus. If your focus point lands on something featureless — a patch of Aunt Daisy's well-ironed, solid-color dress, for example — the camera either refuses to take the picture or takes a misfocused shot.

✔ **Thou shalt aim the focus point at vertical lines.** Most passive autofocus systems are sensitive primarily (or exclusively) to vertical detail — assuming that you're holding the camera horizontally. (If you're holding the camera vertically, they're sensitive to horizontal detail.) The best thing to aim at with a human subject is the edge of a face, or with closer shots, an eye.

✔ **Thou shalt not focus in the dark.** Passive autofocus needs to see well enough to analyze the sharpness of a detail. While many passive autofocus cameras are equipped with an autofocus-assist lamp (basically, a little built-in red or white flashlight), you're best off shooting in decent light, if it's available. (Turn on room lights if you're in doubt.) Autofocus-assist lamps don't help much beyond 20 or 25 feet.

Chapter 7

A Flash of Inspiration

● ●

In This Chapter

▶ Why you need flash more than you think

▶ How your built-in flash works in autoflash mode

▶ Why use flash outdoors?

▶ Turning off the flash

▶ The connection between flash and film speed

▶ Making indoor flash flashier

▶ Getting the red-eye out

● ●

*T*he pint-sized electronic flash in your point-and-shoot camera is definitely not your father's flash. If you're a baby boomer, your unfortunate
father had to screw a lightbulb-sized flashbulb into a soupbowl-sized metal
reflector every time he wanted to shoot a flash picture of your youthful
achievements. If you have a newer model dad, he probably took his first
photographs of you with flashcubes. Remember those? A simple spring
mechanism rotated the flashcube through four small bulbs — and then you
had to yank out the cube (being careful not to burn your fingers) and attach
a new one.

When it comes to flash photography, there *were* no good old days. Though it
may be smaller than a postage stamp, your camera's built-in electronic flash
just keeps going and going, letting you shoot as many pictures as your film
and batteries allow. And when it comes to improving the quality of your
photography, your flash is a far more helpful and sophisticated device than
the blinding bulbs and rotating cubes of yore.

Yet all the innovation in this itsy-bitsy, teeny-weeny marvel actually simplifies taking pictures with flash. Your camera's flash system fully automates
the exposure calculations that once made flash photography so mind-
numbing and getting good flash pictures such a gamble — and it does this
with remarkable dependability.

Whether you're using a 35mm point-and-shoot, an Advanced Photo System point-and-shoot, or a digital point-and-shoot, your camera will in almost all cases have a built-in flash — and feature flash modes, functions, and icons.

Autoflash: No-Fault Photo Insurance

Whether they pop up, slide out, or just stay put when you turn on the camera (see Figure 7-1), most built-in flash units fire *automatically* when the camera senses there's not enough light on your subject for a good exposure. But this isn't to suggest that you have no creative control. Unless your camera is a very basic model, you have an array of up to five or six flash modes at your command. Most point-and-shoots offer at least three flash modes — *autoflash, fill-flash,* and *flash-off.* Many cameras also offer *slow-sync* and *red-eye reduction* flash.

Figure 7-1: Some built-in flash units pop out when you turn on the camera, but most just stay put.

These various modes make your flash the single most important creative tool on your point-and-shoot. But if at first you feel intimidated by such choices — or if your camera offers a limited number of flash modes, or no choice at all — you must remember this: Left to its own devices, your point-and-shoot camera's thoroughly modern flash will fire whenever it's needed.

When you turn on your camera, it immediately sets itself to autoflash mode. Now, say that you're shooting the kids and dog running through the sprinkler on a bright July day. Your camera's lightmetering system sees all that sun and tells the flash it's not needed. So the flash doesn't fire. (See Figure 7-2.) Follow the inevitable trail of mud back into the house, though, and the camera detects the dimmer light — automatically triggering the flash to compensate. (See Figure 7-3.)

With fast-moving subjects in fast-changing conditions (did I say kids and dogs?), don't worry about setting flash modes. Indoors or out, just turn on the camera and shoot.

© Pat O'Hara

The color of daylight ranges from vivid blue to brilliant red, as this Yosemite
valley landscape shows. Low-angle sun is tinted red by atmospheric particles;
open shade is colored blue by the indirect light from a clear sky. Photographic
film sees these differences more strongly than you do! (Chapter 8)

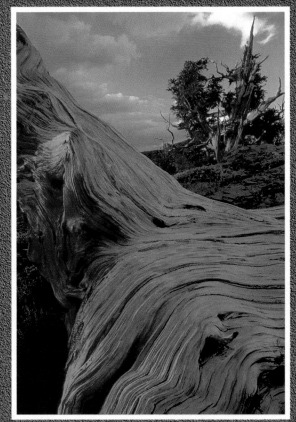

To be a good photographer, you should study how light changes — over minutes, hours, days, or months — and take pictures of those differences. You can study light close to home, or, with a little patience, far afield. Here, the photographer took pictures of bristlecone pines at day's end as a cloud cover cleared and the light changed from diffused (top left) to golden yellow (left) to fiery red (above) in just minutes. (Chapter 8)

© Shellburne Thurber

© Henry Horenstein

The quality of light runs the gamut from hard (top) to soft (bottom). Hard light creates strong shadows and tends to hide detail; soft light can be shadowless and reveals everything. And though the hard sunlight in the shot of the swimmer is intensely colored, overcast conditions can make colors more vivid overall, such as in the blues and greens of the picture of the foal. (Chapter 8)

Color film is most people's film of choice, but many subjects are actually better suited to black and white (top). This window-lit portrait is much more atmospheric in black and white than color (left). Do you agree? (Chapter 2)

© Chris Rainier/SABA

© Mark Harris

Shooting black-and-white film can give your travel photographs a mysterious quality that complements exotic subjects. After establishing a rapport with these New Guinean tribesmen, this photographer asked them to don ceremonial masks — and they did so proudly. (Chapter 13)

On the other hand, color may be essential to a travel photograph. In this striking image, soccer balls offer a dayglow contrast to the drab facade of a Turkish merchant's shop. (Chapter 13)

at 38mm

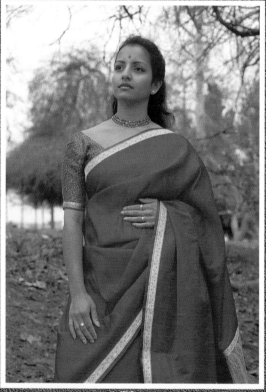

at 70mm

at 105mm

A zoom lens lets you change the subject's size in your picture without changing your physical position. The photographer took all three of these shots from the same spot, with the lens set to 38mm (top left), 70mm (left), and 105mm (above). The longer focal lengths — 70mm through 105mm — are especially good for head-and-shoulders portraits. (Chapter 5)

By taking in a bigger piece of the scene, a zoom lens's shorter focal length settings — also called wide-angle — let you fit more of your subject into the picture when you can't back away any farther. A wide-angle setting (left, 28mm) made possible this dizzying view of old-growth forest. (Chapter 5)

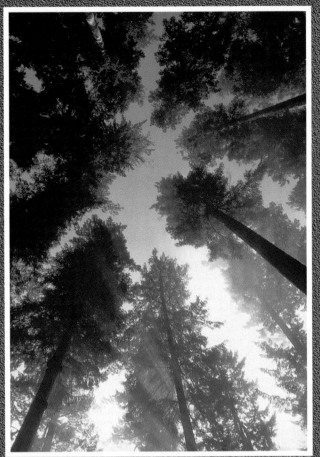

at 28mm   © Pat O'Hara

© Russell Hart

A zoom lens's normal focal length setting can help you eliminate visual clutter. It's especially well-suited to environmental portraiture, as in this shot of an old-fashioned tailor, made at 50mm. (Chapter 10)

at 50mm

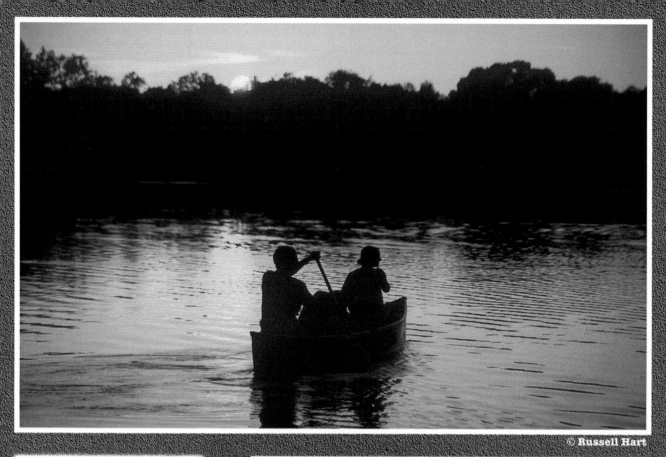

© Russell Hart

A long focal length setting, also called telephoto, lets you fill the frame with a distant subject — here, a canoe way out on a lake, shot from shore. In addition to its magnifying power, a telephoto focal length "flattens" the scene, in this case making the distant trees seem closer to the canoe than they really were. (Chapter 5)

© Russell Hart

For this charming candid of a family card game, the photographer turned off his flash and shot by household light — preserving the familiar feeling of overhead illumination. He used a fast black-and-white film and braced the camera on a shelf to prevent blur. (Chapter 10)

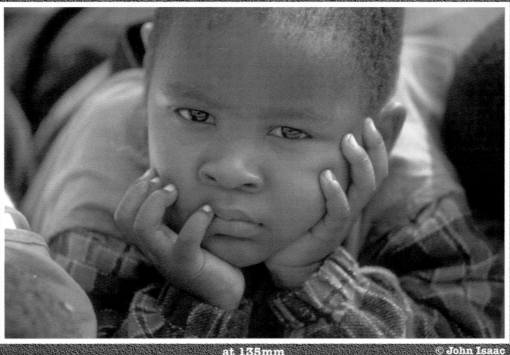

at 135mm   © John Isaac

at 28mm   © Russell Hart

When you want to fill the frame with a face, use a focal length setting of at least 70mm to prevent distortion of facial features (top, a 135mm setting). But when you want to show a subject in his surroundings, a wide-angle focal length setting is ideal (bottom, a 28mm setting). (Chapter 10)

© Dan Richards

When you shoot distant subjects at night with flash, your point-and-shoot doesn't realize that the light can't go the distance — and the result is a totally muddy picture (left). (This is a classic problem in artificially lit sports stadiums.) To get a good picture, use an ISO 800 or faster film, set the flash-off mode, and keep the camera very steady for the shot (right). (Chapter 3)

© Russell Hart

If your home's artificial light is bright and you're using a fast film, your point-and-shoot may not fire its flash — or you may choose to set the flash-off mode to preserve the light's quality. Shooting without flash in artificial light can result in a yellowish, brownish, or reddish cast (left) that your photofinisher may be able to partially correct in a reprint (right). (Chapter 3)

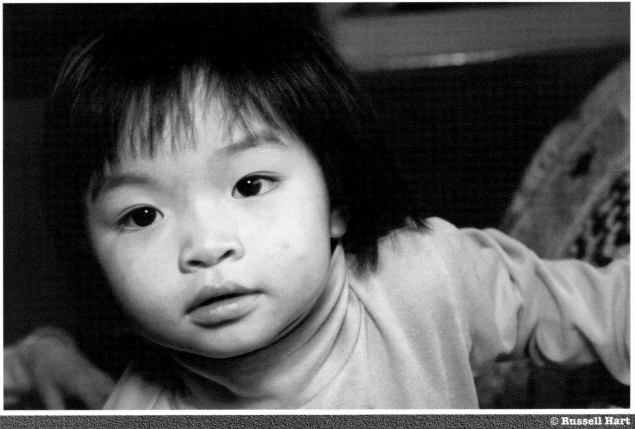

© Russell Hart

Take two — or more. The bottom photograph was taken a few moments after the top one, which isn't a bad photo to begin with. But by taking a second shot, the photographer created a better picture. Not only is the girl's expression more lively and engaged, but the composition is more dynamic — the result of zooming closer, shifting to the side to change the background, and placing the subject off-center. When you keep taking pictures, rather than settling for just one, the subject loosens up — and you do, too, finding new and better ways to frame the shot. (Chapter 10)

If you shoot an off-center subject without first locking the focus, your point-and-shoot may accidentally focus on the background — making the subject unsharp in the print (left). To lock the focus, you simply place the viewfinder's focus point on the main subject (which centers it in the frame, middle) and press the shutter button halfway down. Then you recompose and press the shutter button all the way down to take the actual picture (bottom). (Chapter 6)

APS Classic format © Russell Hart

The Advanced Photo System's choice of three print formats — 4 x 6-inch Classic (left), 4 x 7-inch HDTV (middle), and 4 x 11½-inch Panoramic (bottom) — is a terrific compositional tool, letting you match print shape to subject with a fingertip. But don't think you need to reserve the wider HDTV format for shooting big groups of people, or the Panoramic format for sweeping views! (Chapter 14)

APS HDTV format © Rena Berger

APS Panoramic format © Russell Hart

© Pat O'Hara

Trees seem an obvious candidate for vertical composition in this view of a snowy mountainside. But the vertical format also reinforces the abstract quality snow already lends the scene. (Chapter 12)

© Russell Hart

For this shot of nonchalant sheep (top), the photographer stayed far away from the subject and zoomed his lens to its longest focal length setting. The long focal length combines with shooting from a distance to "stack" the foreground and background — making them seem closer together. But moving in close to a curious cow (right) and using a wide-angle focal length setting, the photographer was able to make the animal large in the frame but still show plenty of background. (Chapter 12)

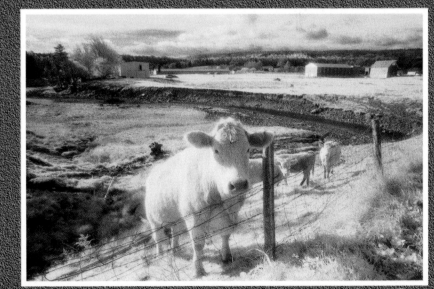

© Russell Hart

Fog is like a sponge that soaks up color, turning an ordinarily multihued subject into a richly monochromatic one. Can you believe that this Great Smoky Mountain forest scene was shot in color? (Chapter 8)

© Pat O'Hara

Strong light needn't create black, empty shadows if a subject has naturally reflective surfaces in it. In this picture — a classic study of shadow patterns — light walls bounced enough light into dark areas to preserve their detail. (Chapter 8)

© Amos Chan

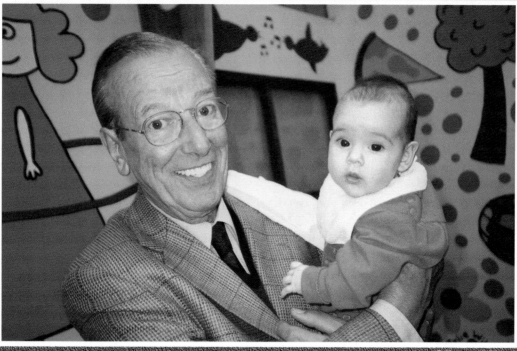

© Russell Hart

Your point-and-shoot's autoflash mode spares you from having to decide whether you need flash, indoors or out. In dim light, it automatically fires the flash (top). In bright light, it keeps the flash from firing (right). (Chapter 7)

© Allen Green

Your point-and-shoot's fill-flash mode is the perfect remedy for people pictures that you must shoot in direct sun, lightening the heavy shadows (right) that can otherwise ruin the photograph. Set fill flash and the flash fires for every shot, even in bright light (far right). (Chapter 7)

Autoflash

Fill flash

Autoflash

Slow-sync flash

When you take night or dim-light pictures with your point-and-shoot set to its autoflash mode, you get very little background detail (left). Setting slow-sync flash mode, if your point-and-shoot offers it, allows more of the existing light to strike the film — greatly improving background detail (right). But the camera must use a slower shutter speed, so hold it steady to keep the background from blurring! (Chapter 7)

When you want to capture the textures created by low-angle light — here, from a setting sun — don't leave your point-and-shoot in its autoflash mode. If you do, the flash may fire (especially with slow ISO 100 or 200 film), lightening nearby shadows and destroying the sense of substance on which a photograph like this one depends. To prevent the flash from firing, set the flash-off mode. (Chapter 7)

Zooming in to a long focal length setting and using slow-sync flash mode were the solution to framing this heron against an intense sunset. The flash automatically brightened the bird, while the camera set a slower shutter speed to capture the background. (Chapter 7)

© John Isaac

Sidelight from a large window illuminates this studious row of Pakistani schoolgirls. To preserve the light's strong, directional quality, the photographer turned off his flash and held the camera steady for the exposure. (Chapter 8)

Warm, late-afternoon light need not be reserved for landscapes or other inanimate scenes. It's terrific for portraiture — formal or candid. (The photographer secretly asked someone off-camera to call to the subjects and took the picture when they were looking away.) (Chapter 10)

© Russell Hart

A change in weather can make what would have been a good picture into a great one. If you're shooting a splendid view, for example, and the skies are in flux, stick around to see what happens. In this Rocky Mountain scene, clouds moved in and bounced colors around, turning the landscape from blue (above) to gold (right). (Chapter 8)

©Amos Chan

©Pat O'Hara

It's simple, but it works: If you want to emphasize the land (or water) portion of a scene, place the horizon line high in the frame by aiming your camera down (top). If you want to emphasize the sky portion of a scene, place the horizon line low in the frame by aiming your camera up (bottom). (Chapter 12)

© Russell Hart

A landscape photograph is usually more interesting if you compose it so that the horizon line is high or low in the frame — anywhere other than the horizontal middle. But as with everything in photography, there are exceptions. For this eerie view of the Dead Sea, the photographer centered the horizon line to reinforce the mirror image. (Chapter 12)

When the family dachshund leapt into a tidal pool for a swim, the photographer grabbed this action shot. But he still had the composure to compose — stooping to a low angle that would bring the dog and rocks closer together in the frame. (Chapter 11)

© Russell Hart

Setting slow-sync flash mode allowed the camera to record room light along with the flash illumination. This mix blurred the birthday boy's clapping hands, adding visual energy to this shot. (Chapter 11)

To avoid blur with action subjects, don't shoot them directly from the side. Photographing from an angle — or even from the front, as in this shot of a budding soccer star — keeps the subject from moving as fast across the frame, making the picture sharper. (Chapter 11)

Blur in a moving subject can evoke speed more powerfully than a sharp rendition. And one way to maximize blur is to shoot in lower light. Just be sure to keep the camera steady if you don't want the whole picture to be blurred. (Chapter 11)

© Mark Ewing

Running water is often best captured with blur. And you can actually get more blur if you put a slower (lower ISO) film in your point-and-shoot, a rare exception to the "use fast film" rule. But when light is dim, as it was in this forest scene, you must securely brace the camera to prevent overall blur. (Chapter 11)

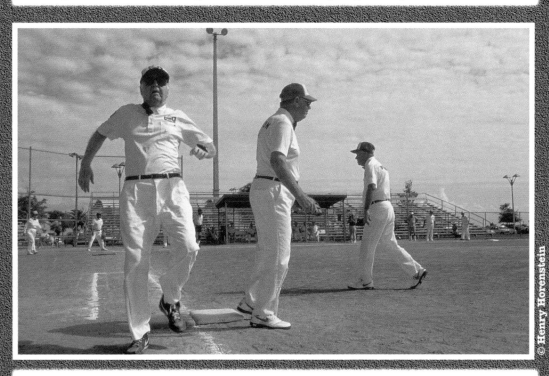

© Henry Horenstein

Action is all around you — and not just in fast-paced sports subjects. Here, the photographer caught minor-league baseball umpires in midstride as they tidied up the diamond. (Chapter 11)

© Pat O'Hara

© Russell Hart

Reflections and silhouettes offer different ways of simplifying a composition. For the picture of marsh grass and cloud reflections, the photographer knelt down to bring the two elements closer together in the frame, for a highly abstract effect (top). And rather than shoot workers installing glass from the front, the photographer photographed them from inside a building's entrance looking out, turning the figures into dark, featureless shapes (bottom). (Chapter 9)

© William Neill

Whether you're photographing a landscape or your wife, placing the subject to one side of the frame, rather than centering it, can make composition more dynamic. In this view of an ancient Yosemite elm (top), the tree's off-center position makes the viewer search what seems to be an empty gray sky on the left — only to find the landmark shape of Yosemite National Park's Half Dome. And in this shot of a Venetian canal (right), the photographer's strong vertical composition and off-center placement of the main subject give equal emphasis to visitor and romantic surroundings. (Chapter 9)

© Allen Green

© Amos Chan

© Mark Harris

You can shoot familiar tourist landmarks more than one way — and your job as a photographer is to find your own way. Here, two photographers took very different approaches to the Eiffel Tower, one a flash-off, tripod-mounted night shot (top), the other a towering view with a wide-angle focal length setting (left). (Chapter 13)

Rainy or overcast weather shouldn't stop you from shooting travel pictures. Here, cloudy and wet conditions created soft, flattering light for this portrait of a North American Indian girl. (Chapter 13)

Ceremonial occasiosns often net you the most colorful pictures — here, an Indian Coorg dancer in her traditional brilliant costume. But when you're traveling, local color is just about everywhere you look. (Chapter 13)

© John Isaac

© John Isaac

A big mistake of adult photographers is shooting children from grown-up eye level. This perspective creates a bird's-eye view of kids — one in which their heads dwarf their bodies. Pictures of kids are usually better when you squat or kneel down to take them, body language that engages kids more fully, too. (Chapter 10)

This 1953 Kodachrome slide has kept its brilliant color for decades, a hallmark of that famous film. Today's color print films are highly fade-resistant, allowing you to get good prints from negatives for many years. But you still have to take proper care of your family's photographic archive. (Chapter 10)

© Jody Dole

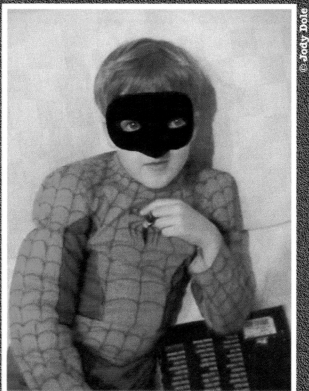

© Jody Dole

These very different pictures were both taken with digital point-and-shoot cameras — no film needed! To create the landscape (top), the photographer used computer retouching software to combine views shot at several different times of day. The boy in costume (left) was reproduced directly from a print made on an inexpensive photo-quality digital printer. (Chapter 15)

© Russell Hart

To photograph this popular tourist market without its usual crowds, the photographer shot early in the morning — before sunrise and after a light rain — with an ISO 400 film. (Chapter 12)

Space is often tight when you're photographing cityscapes, making it difficult to fit full-scale scenes of buildings and streets in the frame. Instead, try shooting representative details such as signs. This bit of neon says it all! (Chapter 12)

© Mark Harris

© Allen Green

Figure 7-2:
In autoflash
mode,
bright light
automatically
tells the
flash not
to fire.

© Russell Hart

Figure 7-3:
In autoflash
mode, dim
light
automatically
tells the
flash to fire.

Watch those fingers. Even autoflash can't do its job if you inadvertently stick your fingers over the flash tube; you get a dark or unevenly lit result. Find a comfortable way to hold your camera without covering the flash, and use this position every time. (Check out Chapter 1 for details on how to hold your camera.)

Autoflash is no-fault photographic insurance. It's just what you need when you don't want to fiddle with the camera while your kids trash the new carpeting. Use it, and you're almost guaranteed a sharp, colorful, well-detailed picture. But here's the surprise: *There are times when you should use flash in bright outdoor light. And there are other times when you should turn the flash off in dim light.* I cover these topics later in this chapter, in the sections "Flash to Fill Shadows" and "Flash-Off Mode: To Flash or Not to Flash."

Button, Button, Where Is the Button?

To make the flash fire outdoors and not fire indoors — or to make it do any of the other interesting things it can do — you need to push the flash mode button. This button is usually marked with a lightning bolt. Repeatedly pushing this button *toggles* you through the flash mode icons, which are displayed on the camera's LCD panel. Get out your camera and try this. If getting out your camera inspires you to take some pictures and you can't figure out how to get back to autoflash, simply turn the camera off and on again. With nearly all point-and-shoot models, doing this resets the camera to autoflash.

If the flash mode button isn't on top of the camera, look for it under a flap or on the back or sides. Different models set and indicate flash modes in different ways. With some models, pushing the flash mode button moves a pointer along printed icons adjacent to the LCD panel. With others, you have to rotate a thumbwheel to select the mode (represented by an icon) that you want. Sliding switches are another, though less common, type of control. I do my best to cover the permutations, but do me a favor: Check your manual! (See Figure 7-4.)

Whatever you push or rotate to choose a flash mode, let the icons be your guide. (See Figure 7-5 for examples of autoflash icons.) And keep in mind — this is important — that your particular camera may display no icon at all when it's in autoflash mode. This is your camera's way of telling you it will take care of things. On other models, the LCD panel displays the actual word *auto,* often paired with a lightning bolt. So if you've taken the camera out of its autoflash mode, you can get back simply by pushing the button repeatedly until auto reappears — or the flash icon disappears altogether! Just remember that the order in which flash modes are displayed varies from camera to camera.

Figure 7-4:
The way you change flash modes depends on your particular point-and-shoot.

Figure 7-5:
Typical icons for autoflash mode.

To make the flash fire with one-time-use cameras, you must press a separate flash-charging button before taking the shot. This button is usually on the front of the camera, as shown in Figure 7-6. With some models, you have to hold the flash-charging button down *while* you press the shutter button. Wait for the flash-ready light to come on before shooting.

Figure 7-6:
With a one-time-use camera, the flash will not fire automatically in low light. You have to press a separate flash-charging button.

Flash to Fill Shadows

With many point-and-shoots, the first push of the flash mode button causes a plain lightning bolt to appear on the LCD panel. If your camera already displays a lightning bolt (and the word auto) in its autoflash mode, this first push may cause the word to disappear, leaving just the bolt. Sometimes the lightning bolt is paired with the words *fill, fill-in,* or just plain *on.* And sometimes it appears with a graphic of the sun (see Figure 7-7).

Thoughtful manufacturers add the sun to remind you that in this mode, which most point-and-shoots call *fill flash,* the flash fires even in bright light.

Some point-and-shoot models call this mode *fill-in flash,* both on the LCD panel and in their manuals. Others use names like *flash-on, anytime flash,* or my personal favorite, *forced emission.* All mean the same thing: that the flash fires every time you take a picture.

Figure 7-7:
Typical
icons for fill-
flash mode.

Why would you want flash when the subject is bright already? To *fill* unwanted shadows with light. High sun in particular creates unattractive hollows under facial features. For example, Great Aunt Gretyl hobbles to your Fourth of July cookout wearing an old-fashioned, wide-brimmed hat. You want to document what could be her last earthly appearance, but the brim of her hat throws her entire kindly face into darkness. Add flash, and that shadow lightens up. Send her the flattering results, and she may bequeath you her classic 1939 Super Kodak Six-20, though you won't be able to find film for it.

Fill flash is really as much a no-brainer as autoflash — and no less automatic in its operation, pumping out the right amount of light for the occasion. You have to select fill flash with the flash mode button, of course. But once you do, you can leave fill flash on, and if you go indoors, it does the job there, too.

And how do you get fill flash if your point-and-shoot doesn't even have an LCD panel with which to display the fill-flash icon? Even cameras with few controls often have a fill-flash button, usually marked with a lightning bolt. But to get fill flash, you must hold down this button *as you're taking the picture.* (It's usually on the side of the camera opposite the shutter button, so you can push it with the fingers of your left hand; see Figure 7-8.) You can do the same thing with one-time-use cameras; see the sidebar "Can a one-time-use camera do fill flash?" later in this chapter.

Figure 7-8:
Simple point-and-shoots having no LCD panel may still offer fill flash. You just hold down a separate button as you take the picture.

Fill flash is also called *daylight sync* or *synchro sun flash* (though if your point-and-shoot's maker uses these terms at all, they appear only in your manual, not on your camera's LCD). The terms refer to the fact that you are *synchronizing* the flash with an exposure for the existing light, thereby mixing the two together. The terms sound retro-techy, but fill flash is actually the more fashionable one.

With some models, the sequence of flash modes may include a setting for backlight compensation. The icon for backlight compensation may be something like a stylized sun, so don't confuse it with fill flash. (If the icon has no lightning bolt, it's not fill flash — in fact, the flash won't fire at all.) Backlight compensation can be useful, but fill flash is a better problem-solver. (See Chapter 8 for more on backlight compensation.)

Fill flash compensates for the inability of photographic film to capture good detail in both the brightest and the darkest parts of some subjects. Though fill flash adds the same amount of light to both highlight and shadow areas, the extra light is more visible in the shadows because shadows are less bright to begin with. This effect actually reduces *contrast* — the difference between the scene's lightest and darkest parts — keeping it within the range of brightnesses the film can record. (You get a free piece of photo jargon — *contrast* — for reading this Technical Stuff paragraph.)

When to use fill flash

Fill flash is a perfect remedy for the small, scattered shadows that can make portraits taken in direct sun so ghastly. Fill flash lightens the eye sockets and nose shadows that would otherwise end up as black as the black hole of

Calcutta (see Figure 7-9). It can help you turn a guaranteed failure into a flattering portrait. Fill flash is mainly an outdoor flash mode, but it even helps with sun coming through a window.

In addition to retrieving eyes from their sockets, fill flash adds *catchlights* to them. Catchlights are tiny, pinpoint reflections of an actual light source — in this case, the flash tube as it fires. Without catchlights, a subject's eyes can look dull and lifeless. Look at any good studio portrait, and you'll find catchlights, created quite deliberately by the photographer.

When you're shooting outdoors in daylight, just leave the camera set to fill flash. Move from sun to shade and back as you shoot, and you'll be pleasantly surprised at the consistency of the results. If you turn the camera off between shots, remember to reset it to fill flash when you turn it back on.

Fill flash is also made to order when the entire main subject is in shadow against a much brighter background (see Figure 7-10). To picture this scenario, think of shooting a portrait under the shade of a gazebo. By flashing your subject, you lessen the difference in brightness between her (the foreground) and the unshaded area outside the gazebo (the background). In these situations, fill flash makes the foreground and background appear more balanced.

When the background is much brighter than the main subject or the light is actually coming from behind the subject, the subject is *backlit*. Some point-and-shoots have the ability, in their autoflash mode, to sense that difference in brightness and fire the flash to compensate for it. These models automatically fire the flash even though the overall light is bright — a condition that would cause most other models to turn the flash off when in autoflash mode.

Figure 7-9: The harsh shadows produced by direct sun can be very unflattering (left). Fill flash lightens those shadows (right) for a more pleasing portrait.

© Rena Berger (2)

Figure 7-10: Subjects in the shade against a bright background are tailor-made for fill flash. Without it (top), you get a dark subject, a washed-out background, or both. With it (bottom), the subject is brightened without sacrificing background detail.

© Russell Hart (2)

This feature is usually called *automatic backlight compensation*. It's clever — a sort of automatic fill flash — but it usually doesn't work with a subject that has scattered shadows. Check your manual to see whether your camera has this ability, but don't think of it as a substitute for setting fill flash.

If your camera has a backlight compensation setting (as opposed to automatic backlight compensation), this setting has nothing to do with flash. Choosing backlight compensation just tells the camera to increase the amount of light reaching the film, to offset the underexposure that backlight may otherwise cause. This feature certainly improves detail in a shadowy main subject (think of the gazebo example I describe earlier in this section), but the price of that gain is a washed-out background. Use fill flash instead of backlight compensation, and you can have it both ways — good detail in both the main subject and the background.

TIP

Can a one-time-use camera do fill flash?

You may think one-time-use cameras, being so basic, offer no choice of modes. But those versions with a built-in flash actually have a second mode: fill flash. Of course, these models don't have autoflash to begin with; when light is dim, you must activate the flash yourself by pushing a button on the front of the camera. (If you don't, you probably won't get an acceptable picture.) But you can also push a one-time-use camera's flash button for *outdoor* shots — portraits in direct sunlight or subjects with their backs to the sun — the same way that you'd set fill-flash mode on a reloadable point-and-shoot. By forcing the flash to fire in these conditions, you lighten dark shadows, which can otherwise mar a portrait, or any other subject within the flash's range. Note that some very simple point-and-shoots operate much like one-time-use flash cameras: They have just one button (or switch) besides the shutter button, which makes the flash fire regardless of the light.

If I seem to be charmed by fill flash, well, I am. Not only does fill flash give outdoor photos a professional look, but it can also save pictures that harsh light would otherwise ruin.

When not to use fill flash

At times, however, fill flash won't have much effect and may do more harm than good. For example, fill flash won't have much effect if your subject is too far away for the flash to "reach." (To find out about your flash's range, read the sidebar "How far will your flash reach?" later in this chapter.) Fill flash won't fill the shadows in a big landscape, for example.

Keep in mind, though, that the loss of effectiveness is progressive. If there are objects in the foreground of the big landscape you're shooting (and as you find out in Chapter 12, including foreground objects in your composition isn't a bad idea), they may benefit from fill flash, so fill-flash mode is worth setting. Fill flash is almost always preferable to using no flash. And outside, *in reasonably bright light,* fill flash has little down side. Even if you goof and use flash from too far away, the scene is well-lit to begin with, so you still get a decent picture. Shooting an indoor subject or a night scene beyond the flash's range, on the other hand, is a real no-no: You get a dark or muddy print with loss of detail.

How far will your flash reach?

Built-in flash units vary in power, affecting the distance range within which they can adequately light a subject. Check your manual's specifications section to find out your point-and-shoot's flash range. (The range is often stated in meters, marked by an *m;* just multiply the number by 3.3 to convert it to feet.) Many of the indoor photos that you take will fall within your flash range, especially if you follow my advice and stick with fast films (check out Chapter 2 for more on film speeds). But another way to increase your camera's flash range is by zooming to a shorter (more wide-angle) focal length. This setting not only allows you to shorten the distance between you and your subject, but also causes the camera to set a bigger lens aperture. And the bigger aperture lets the camera gather more light from the flash.

All that said, you can maximize your fill flash by staying as close to the subject as practical. If your camera is a zooming model, avoid longer focal length settings, which force you to move farther from the subject to fit it all in the frame. Instead, zoom to the shortest focal length setting that the subject permits. A shorter focal length lets you get closer but still fit everything in the frame. (See Chapter 5 for more on the lens and focal length.)

I don't mean to be too cavalier about fill flash. It can actually be harmful when part of a subject's appeal is in its quality of light. Fill flash may destroy that quality. How can you tell if it will? Read the section "Flash-Off Mode: To Flash or Not to Flash," later in this chapter.

Always keep a fresh extra battery on hand. I've been practically begging you to use flash, and flash takes a lot of juice. Heavy flash use reduces the number of rolls a battery can power through your camera.

Flash-Off Mode: To Flash or Not to Flash

If you're a sports fan, you've probably noticed that each big play at a night game ignites a thousand points of flash in the grandstand. Professional photographers joke about the phenomenon, because they know most of those pictures won't come out. They know that there's just no way such a small flash can light a stadium.

Alas, your point-and-shoot has no way of knowing that the subject is too far away to light. It just sees the lack of adequate illumination and flashes blithely away. It pumps out every particle of light it can muster, but just overexposes the heads of the people in front of you, turning them into hairless wonders. Distant sports action ends up darker than the mood of a losing quarterback.

What to do? Just turn the flash off! Don't be shy. Press the flash mode button until the LCD panel shows a lightning bolt slashed through by the universal "no" symbol — a circle around a diagonal line. On some models the canceled bolt may also be accompanied by a moon or star symbol. On a few models you may get no bolt, only the moon and/or star (see Figure 7-11). Whatever the icon, the idea is that you're turning the flash off in dim light — oddly enough, in light that would otherwise cause it to fire automatically.

Your manual probably calls this mode *flash-off*. (If the camera isn't flashing, is flash-off really a flash mode? You made your point.) By turning the flash off, you force the camera to take the picture by the artificial illumination of the stadium itself. So the camera must gather in as much of the existing light as it can.

Flash recycling

No, flash recycling is not the latest form of environmental correctness. After your little flash fires, it takes a moment to accumulate enough juice for another pop. This interval, which can range from a couple seconds to a seeming eternity, is called the *flash recycling* time. It's a major source of aggravation to point-and-shoot photographers who like to take a second shot right after the first, because the camera locks up the shutter button until the flash is pretty much fully recharged.

Some cameras take longer than others to recycle the flash. But if the delay is just impossible, the cause is more often than not a weak battery. Installing a fresh battery is a smart idea if you're planning a people flash blitz, allowing you to quickly take the second or third shot that always seems better than the first. (Check out Chapter 1 for more on batteries.)

By the way, the little orange or red lamp in your viewfinder eyepiece (the green one confirms the focus) tells you whether the flash has

recycled, which is why it's called the *flash-ready lamp* (see figure). It usually blinks when the flash is recycling and stays lit when the flash is ready. More advanced point-and-shoot models may do this with a glowing lightning-bolt icon in the viewfinder, in the dark area just below the frame.

The flash-ready lamp is good to keep your eye on, because if you're taking quick pictures you can shoot as soon as it stops blinking. But you can't hurt anything by pressing the shutter button when the lamp is blinking, since the camera locks up the shutter button until the flash has recycled anyway. If the camera won't let you take a picture, at least you know why — and that you may need to buy a new battery.

Figure 7-11:
Typical
flash-off
icons.

Knowing how to turn the flash off is also valuable because at some events (circus finales, Ice Capades) you may be prohibited from using flash. This restriction is often the case at gymnastics competitions, for example, yet every dismount brings on a fireworks display of flash. These snapshooters probably don't mean to flout the rules. They just don't *know* how to turn off their cameras' flashes. And they almost certainly will be disappointed by their pictures.

I don't mean to suggest that sporting events are the only occasions on which to turn off your flash. Here are some other times and places when and where you should also consider setting the flash-off mode.

- **When you're shooting far-away subjects that would otherwise automatically trigger the flash** — a landscape at dusk, for example. More than a few cameras offer a *landscape,* or *infinity,* mode (sometimes part of the flash mode sequence) just for such occasions. Setting your camera to landscape or infinity mode tells it that it can't light the whole scene, so it turns off the flash for you — usually. If your camera is one of those wacky models that thinks its flash can light a landscape, firing anyway, turn off the flash yourself.

  Keep in mind that a landscape or infinity setting also locks your focus at infinity. If you have things in the foreground, they may end up unsharp.

- **When the quality of light is an essential part of the picture that you want to create.** Say that you're photographing the play of late-afternoon sun across rippling sand. (Forgive the cliché, but I can't argue with nature.) You get in close, for an abstract effect. The light may be low enough to activate the flash in autoflash mode, especially if you're using an ISO 100 film. And flash will probably ruin such a shot by lightening the shadows — both big shadows cast by ripples and tiny ones cast by grains of sand — that provide its eye-catching sense of texture. Interesting, angular, atmospheric light is often low light, and low light is the flash's cue.

  If that's the kind of image you want to create, turn the flash off. And what if you forget? Problem is, you don't always notice the flash firing when you're outdoors. So if you think it did fire, turn the flash off and take another picture of the same thing.

When in doubt about whether to use flash, shoot the subject with and without it. Doing so also gives you two shots for comparison, helping you figure out what works and what doesn't (see Figure 7-12). Please don't be frugal. Saving the cost of one more print is no compensation for a disappointing picture.

✔ **When you're shooting through a window.** If you don't turn the flash off, the reflection of the flash may obscure or obliterate your subject. You can eliminate the reflection by pressing the camera right up to the glass as you shoot. Be warned, though, that doing this may cause the camera to focus incorrectly. The only way to find out whether your camera's focusing is thrown off by shooting through a window is to *try* shooting through a window, and to see how your prints turn out. If your camera can focus correctly, you're in luck. If your camera doesn't focus correctly, try wiping off a clean patch on the window. Better yet, just open the window. (See Chapter 6 for specifics on shooting through a window.)

Figure 7-12:
The flash fired automatically to brighten this shady shot, intensifying some colors but over-powering the soft light and sense of texture (top). Turning the flash off (bottom) preserved these qualities.

© Russell Hart (2)

If you can't get right up to the glass, you can sometimes take a picture through a window with flash by shooting at an angle to it. This method is more likely to work if the window is clean. Shooting at an angle also lets you shoot into a mirror with flash without wiping out your subject.

Keep in mind that turning your flash off can introduce complications. If you're shooting in a dimly lit stadium, especially with a slower film (ISO 100 or 200), the camera may set slower shutter speeds to make up for the inadequate light. With some models, such speeds may be a second or more. These speeds make freezing a moving subject difficult. But just as significant, slower shutter speeds increase the likelihood that hand tremors (which you don't even notice) will blur the image (see Figure 7-13).

Not to worry. I show you ways to deal with shake, which is arguably a more common cause of unsharpness than incorrect focus, in Chapter 2.

Slow Sync Is Not the Kitchen Sink

Slow-sync flash is one of the most useful effects you can get from your point-and-shoot camera. It's also just about the flashiest. Alas, not all models have a slow-sync flash mode, but I think they should. Those that do may call it

Figure 7-13: If your camera withholds flash and sets a shutter speed too slow to counteract hand tremors, it may blur your picture (left). Setting fill-flash mode may give you a sharper picture (right).

© Russell Hart (2)

night or *night flash* or *night scene* or even *night portrait* mode. (More techie-sounding possibilities include *slow-speed sync, slow shutter speed synchro,* and the like.) Slow-sync flash mode's LCD panel icon is usually a lightning bolt paired with a moon or star and occasionally a little head-and-shoulders figure (see Figure 7-14). Sometimes the word slow — even auto slow, since it still does all the calculations automatically for you — accompanies the lightning bolt.

Figure 7-14:
Typical
slow-sync
flash icons.

Slow-sync flash may only be available as part of a subject or program mode that sets other camera functions. For example, you may get red-eye reduction in the bargain, on the assumption that you're photographing people. Check your manual for details.

How can I convey the contribution that slow-sync flash can make to your photography? Get your snapshot shoe box. Now sift out your most disappointing pictures. They're probably something along the lines of a friend or family member posing against city lights or some other lively nocturnal scene. Or at least that's the way you remember it, because the actual picture consists of a washed-out figure in a black void. Photofinishing is a co-conspirator in this ghostly quality. Photofinishing machinery tries to compensate for all that black by making the print, and therefore the main subject, too light. (See Chapter 3 for more on photofinishing problems.)

Take my word for it, slow-sync flash puts an end to this annoying phenomenon. But don't let a starry-looking icon lead you to believe that you can only use it at night. Read on for other good times to use it.

Slow-sync flash mode balances your flash-lit main subject with a dimly lit background in an ingenious way: by combining flash with a slower shutter speed than flash ordinarily needs.

In autoflash mode, the shutter stays open just long enough for the split-second flash burst that lights the main subject. In slow-sync flash mode, the shutter stays open longer so that a good amount of the scene's existing light is recorded on the film along with the flash. Recording more existing light makes the background brighter, because it's often too far away for the flash to affect it.

Lucky for the suburbanites among you, slow-sync flash isn't just for glitzy city lights. Slow-sync flash is also effective indoors, day or night. Use it instead of autoflash, and you get better background detail in your flash shots. Slow-sync flash improves the sense of a room and the other people or things in it (see Figure 7-15).

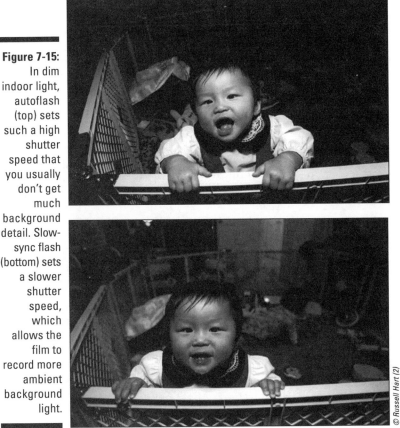

Figure 7-15: In dim indoor light, autoflash (top) sets such a high shutter speed that you usually don't get much background detail. Slow-sync flash (bottom) sets a slower shutter speed, which allows the film to record more ambient background light.

© Russell Hart (2)

Slow-sync flash can also produce a pleasant *warming* of the image — a sort of golden yellow tinge. This effect happens when some or all of the existing light is *tungsten,* meaning from ordinary household bulbs. Tungsten sources also include popular high-wattage halogen lamps, as well as much of the lighting used in malls, galleries, and other commercial spaces. You see the effect of this warming mostly in the background, along with the improved detail, because the foreground (where the main subject is) is dominated by the flash, which your film interprets pretty much the same way as daylight.

The color negative film that you use in your point-and-shoot camera is balanced for daylight — that is, it's designed to produce faithful color in natural, outdoor light. Flash illumination looks pretty much the same to the film as daylight. Tungsten light, on the other hand, looks warmer than daylight to the film — so it contributes a yellowish tinge to slow-sync flash pictures.

If you turn on slow-sync flash in fluorescent lighting (often used in schools, offices, factories, and some stores), you may turn your backgrounds green. Unlike your ever-adjusting eyes, film thinks fluorescent light is green because it has weird gaps in its color spectrum. Personally, I don't mind the effect; the main subject's color is kept clean by the flash, and I'd rather have greenish background detail than none at all. So I guess this effect is a blooper only if you feel differently.

Warming or not, I have to issue a warning about slow-sync flash: Its slower shutter speed increases the chance of blur. Not blur in the main subject, which almost certainly ends up sharp thanks to the quick blitz of the flash, but blur in the background. (This blur is usually more of a streakiness due to subject or camera movement.) If the main subject picks up any blur from slow-sync flash, it usually takes the form of a streaky fringe around its edges.

Personally, I like the effect of the blur. It's arty. It adds energy and a sense of movement to flash pictures. You've probably seen this background blur effect in magazines, because professional photographers have seriously cultivated it, often making it part of their style. How much blur you get depends partly on the technical particulars of your point-and-shoot — for example, how slow a shutter speed the camera is able to set.

If, on the other hand, slow-sync flash gives you too much blur for your taste in normal room light, try a faster film (ISO 400 or 800) — if you're not already using one, as you should be. And make more of an effort to keep your camera steady, bracing yourself against a doorjamb and digging your arms into your chest as you shoot. If your pictures are still too trippy for your increasingly conservative standards, then just go back to autoflash.

Red-Eye Reduction: Getting the Red Out

Yes, your kids can be devils. But that's not why they sometimes have glowing red eyes in your flash pictures. Point-and-shoot cameras are especially susceptible to a photographic affliction called, matter-of-factly, red-eye. Red-eye is the price of a point-and-shoot's compactness: Its flash is so close to the lens that it actually reflects off your kids' (or others') *retinas,* the backs of their beady little eyes. Red-eye is unpredictable, but it's more likely to occur with blue-eyed people in dark environments. Why the camera turns canine and feline peepers green instead of red is best left to those who can actually define the term wavelength.

To lessen the dreaded effect, manufacturers have put red-eye reduction flash capability into all but their most basic point-and-shoots. Alas, these red-eye reduction systems can create more problems than they solve. So in this section I explain some ways of circumventing the problems.

Red-eye reduction comes in two varieties:

- ✔ **Preflash type:** This is the most common type of red-eye reduction system, in which the camera emits one or more low-power flash bursts before the final, full-power burst with which it takes the picture.

- ✔ **Prelamp type:** In this type of red-eye reduction system, the camera shines a small white or red lamp at the subject for a second or so before the exposure.

Red-eye is a particular problem in dim light, the light that automatically triggers your camera's flash. In dim light, your subject's pupils dilate, uncovering more retinal surface — and a larger area to reflect the flash.

Whether your camera uses preflashes or a prelamp to reduce red-eye, the idea is the same: Throw light into the subject's eyes, and his, her, or its pupils immediately contract. This effect lessens the retinal area exposed to the final, full flash.

Which type of red-eye reduction system does your camera use? (Have you already lost the manual?) Okay, here's how you tell. Push the flash mode button until your camera's LCD displays the icon for red-eye reduction. With some models red-eye reduction is separate from the flash mode menu, activated by its own button (which is an excellent idea, for reasons I discuss later). Push this button once to make the icon (see Figure 7-16 for some examples of red-eye reduction icons) appear on the LCD panel.

Figure 7-16:
Typical red-eye reduction icons.

Now point the camera at something dim and press the shutter button halfway, just until the red or orange flash-ready and green focus-OK lamps in the viewfinder eyepiece come on. If nothing happens other than the customary click or zip of the lens focusing, you probably have the preflash type of red-eye reduction. (One sure sign of the preflash type is a double lightning bolt.) If a little lamp lights up on the front of the camera or inside the flash tube and stays lit as you keep the shutter button pressed halfway, you probably have prelamp red-eye reduction. Some such lamps may not light up until you push the shutter button all the way, so you may have to waste a picture to find out. Wasting one picture is worth it if you discover that you do, indeed, have prelamp red-eye reduction.

I have a minor grudge against built-in red-eye reduction. So for my own, personal red-eye reduction system, I take a Sharpie — one of those marks-on-anything pens — and carefully blot out any offending red eyes. Afraid of making your kids look like Betazoids, those black-eyed telepaths on Star Trek? Can't bear to darken your daughter's baby blues? Ask your friendly neighborhood photo dealer for a red-eye-retouching pen, which neutralizes the unwanted red instead of simply covering it, preserving a semblance of natural eye color. This type of pen even comes in a green-eye version for kitty.

Why do I have a grudge against red-eye reduction systems? Because they can make you miss important pictures, for a couple of reasons. This is especially true of the preflash variety.

Preflash red-eye reduction systems

Red-eye reduction systems that work by preflash(es) can cause two problems.

- First, your subject may mistake the preflash(es) for the actual picture, and look or turn away. This ruins the shot, of course.

- Second, even if you tell your subject to expect the preflash(es), he may not know what to do with himself during the lag between the preflash(es) and the final flash (again, the flash for the picture itself). In that seemingly interminable time, the lively moment you sought to capture when you pressed the shutter button can turn into an awkward, self-conscious stare.

Watching the perfect picture slip away as your camera puts on a light show is a frustrating experience, to say the least. Some red-eye reduction preflash systems fire a rapid and very distracting series of up to ten or so bursts before they take the picture.

So particularly if your red-eye reduction system is of the preflash sort, I suggest that you don't use it. As if to acknowledge the problem, some manufacturers relegate red-eye reduction to a separate button, so it's not part of the usual flash mode sequence. You can turn it off and on, or combine it with other flash modes, at your discretion. Thank you very much, but I'd rather have a good picture with red-eye (and fix it with my Sharpie, if need be) than a crummy picture without red-eye.

Prelamp red-eye reduction systems

Prelamp red-eye reduction systems are sometimes — and only somewhat — better than the preflash type. The little light may actually serve as an attention-getting birdie, but if it's bright, it may also make your subject squint. The light may delay the picture just as much as a preflash system does, because it needs to stay on for a second or so to have an iris-closing effect — and it doesn't have much of one even then. But at least people won't think that you've taken the picture, and turn away.

To maximize the effect of prelamp red-eye reduction systems, have your subject look directly at the little light until the picture is taken.

If your camera turns on its red-eye reduction light when you press the shutter button halfway, you can control this delay simply by maintaining that pressure. (Because this action also locks the focus, just be sure that the viewfinder's focus point is on the main subject when you do it; see Chapter 6 for details.) Then when you see the expression or moment that you want, press the shutter button all the way, and the camera should take the picture without much delay.

By the way, if red-eye reduction is part of your standard flash mode sequence, it is essentially a variation of autoflash. (Certain models may even call red-eye reduction something like *Auto-S* — not to be confused with the silent S-Auto mode.) The camera can turn the flash on and off as needed, giving you red-eye reduction in the bargain.

However, some models trigger red-eye reduction even in their slow-sync mode (or night flash mode — whatever it's called on your model). The assumption (fair enough) is that, because slow-sync is used in dim light, red-eye is likely. Unfortunately, if the camera relies on preflash(es) for red-eye reduction, you can't have the pleasure of slow-sync flash without an annoying blitz. I've actually seen cameras with two slow-sync flash modes, one with red-eye reduction preflash and one without. That's a nice touch.

If you're shopping for a new camera and red-eye reduction is important to you, don't let me stop you. Maybe try to find a model with a prelamp system, or a system in which other flash modes aren't saddled with red-eye reduction, so you have more control. And remember that no point-and-shoot red-eye reduction system always eliminates red-eye. That's why they call it *reduction,* silly.

To lessen red-eye without resorting to your camera's red-eye reduction setting, open the curtains, roll up the blinds, and/or turn on more room lights — anything to get your subject's pupils to close. Oh, and take more pictures of people *without having them look at the camera.* Such pictures may be more interesting anyway.

One final note: If you're playing with your flash modes (tsk, tsk), keep in mind that most cameras cancel your selection when you turn them off. They reset themselves to autoflash mode every time you turn them on. (A few expensive models may set the flash mode you were last using, in which case you have to reset them to autoflash yourself.) Some models even reset to autoflash after *each* shot, depending on which other flash mode you choose, *even if you keep the camera turned on*. Shot-by-shot resetting can be a pain, for example, if you're shooting indoors and want to use slow-sync flash for all your pictures. You'd have to set slow-sync flash mode for each and every shot.

Of course, the idea behind having the camera automatically reset itself to autoflash is to rescue folks who forget to change the flash mode when shooting conditions change. But you know better now, right?

Part III
The Art Part

The 5th Wave   By Rich Tennant

"Add some interest to the shot by putting the partridge in the foreground."

In this part . . .

Part III is a pushbutton-free zone. In this part, you discover two valuable but unappreciated pieces of photographic equipment: your eyes and your legs. And you find out how to use them, photographically of course.

You find out that for good composition (putting just the right piece of the subject on film) you must unlock your eye and let it roam your point-and-shoot's viewfinder frame. You find out that you should let your legs roam too, moving in and out from the subject, shifting from side to side, squatting or scrambling up on something — anything but just standing where you are and zooming. Equally important, this part asks you to contemplate the very substance that your eyes were made to perceive, and without which there'd be no photography: light. It asks you to notice the way light turns everyday things into extraordinary things. Are the right light and thoughtful composition all you need for good pictures? Almost!

Chapter 8

The Light Fantastic

In This Chapter

▶ Waiting for the right light

▶ Studying changing light

▶ Comparing hard light and soft light

▶ Exploring the direction and color of light

▶ Looking for sweet light

▶ Compensating for hard light

▶ Shooting in specific kinds of light

*E*very year when fall gives way to winter, I notice the light changing in my house. As the surrounding trees shed their shield of leaves and the world tilts away from the sun, light seems to come through windows at different angles, illuminating corners of the house that have been dark for months. The cat stakes out new patches of sun. The light loses the white-hot color of summer, picking up a warmth that belies the cold weather to come.

Light is ever-changing. It changes from minute to minute, hour to hour, month to month. It changes when the weather changes and when the season changes. Experienced photographers take advantage of those changes. They wait until the end of the day to shoot, for example, when the sun colors things red; or for night to pass so that they can shoot by the suffused light of dawn; or for a storm to leave color-enhancing wetness or a blanket of snow in its wake; or for the midwinter days when a clear sky turns the weak sun's shadows blue. If you want great light in your pictures — something more than a good subject — you may have to wait for it, too. But you have to know what you're waiting for — the characteristics of the light you want — and how, if need be, to modify them. That control is what this chapter is about.

How Light Creates Mood and Atmosphere

Realistically speaking, most photographs that you take must be shot when you see them, not one minute later. These pictures — the off-the-cuff shots of friends, family, and events — are of moments, and the light in them is secondary to the subject. When your middle-aged sister attempts a hand-stand in the living room, you grab your camera as fast as you can and shoot. (At least that's what I hope you do.) You don't stop to worry about the light. In fact, in such situations your flash is probably doing most of the lighting anyway. (Having light *in* your camera is a great thing!)

But some photographs — or should I say photographic possibilities — are as much about light as they are about their subjects. Your husband may occupy the same easy chair every Sunday morning, but one day the light on him may seem different — a beam of warm sunlight from the window raking across the side of his face, making the texture of his skin stand out in a masculine way.

Raking light is light that scrapes across a surface at a steep angle, making its texture stand out. Outdoors, it's especially noticeable at the beginning and end of the day, when the sun is low in the sky.

The light on your husband's face may, indeed, be something new: the effect of a change of season, a felled tree, curtains opened for the first time in weeks. Or maybe you just haven't noticed it before. That's the thing about light: You tend to take it for granted. And if you want to be a good photographer, you can't do that.

To be a good photographer, you should *study* light. Your apartment or house, and your yard or neighborhood, are perfect places to begin. Don't just look at *objects;* look at how the light describes them differently as it changes over the course of a day. The tree across the street may start out looking delicate and ethereal by morning fog; pick up bold, angular contrasts within its branches as the weather clears and the sun gets higher in the sky; and then take on a rosy glow in the setting sun's last rays.

Those changes illustrate what are, really, the three overriding features of light: quality, direction, and color.

The quality of light

Photographers like to describe light's quality in a tactile way: hard or soft. *Hard light* is direct from the source, undiffused. The sun on a clear day produces hard light; a bare lightbulb in your basement produces hard light. If you think of light as being made up of individual rays, hard light's rays head straight for the subject from the light source.

A *light source* is where the light that directly illuminates your subject begins. In the case of the sun or a household bulb, the light source is the actual producer of the light; in the case of a window or a skylight, the light source directs the light.

Recording the changing character of light

To study how light changes, choose an out-door subject that receives a reasonable amount of light throughout the day. Pick a day that you don't expect to be entirely cloudy and take pictures of the subject every couple of hours throughout the day. Photograph the subject from the same position each time; leave marks on the ground for your feet, if possible. After you get your prints back, line them up and study the changes. You'll have a time-lapse sequence that says more about what light can do than anything I tell you here!

One way to capture changes in light automatically is to use an advanced feature variously called an intervalometer, interval timer, or time sequence mode (see Chapter 4). This feature is basically a built-in timer that automatically fires the camera at set intervals, without your having to attend it. If your model is so equipped, you can use it for your study of lighting changes. Find a secure, stable place to set up your camera — a table in your backyard or the sill of an open window overlooking the street — and then set your camera to shoot at one-hour intervals over the course of the day.

Soft light, on the other hand, is scattered light. Instead of reaching the subject directly from the light source, its rays pass through things and bounce off surfaces to surround and envelope the subject. The light on an overcast day is soft, scattered by clouds; the light in open shade on a sunny day is soft, bounced in by the clear blue sky; the light from a ceiling full of office fluorescents is soft.

Shadows are your main visual clue to the quality of light. Hard light pro-duces dark, hard-edged shadows (see Figure 8-1). Soft light produces paler, soft-edged shadows, or none at all (see Figure 8-2).

Manipulating hard light (which I tell you how to do in the section "Coping with Hard Light," later in this chapter) has but one purpose: to make it softer. Hard light is intriguing, but soft light is the ideal, photographically speaking. Indeed, most studio shooters, whether portraitists or product photographers, go to great pains to make the illumination from their studio lights gentle. Soft light is usually more flattering to both people and things. And it's much easier to work with, photographically, than hard light.

The direction of light

Within a given scene, some shadows are cast by the subject on adjacent things — Rover's shadow on the grass beneath him, for example. And some are cast by the subject on itself — the shadow of someone's nose on his cheek.

© Russell Hart

Figure 8-1:
Hard, direct
light
produces
strong
contrasts.

© Russell Hart

Figure 8-2:
Soft,
indirect
light can be
virtually
shadowless,
creating a
delicate
quality.

The direction and/or angle of the light determines where those shadows fall. A low sun throws that nose shadow sideways, across the cheek; a high sun throws it down, toward the lips. A high sun throws Rover's shadow down, on the grass beneath him; a low sun throws the shadow sideways, across the grass.

Light striking the subject from the side is called *sidelight.* Light striking the subject from above is called *toplight.*

You're much more aware of light's direction with hard light than with soft, because hard light's shadows are more distinct. In fact, soft light with no shadows visible is often called *nondirectional* light.

Work with the shadows. When a subject casts a long shadow on the ground, for example, consider including the whole thing — making it a part of your composition (see Figure 8-3).

The color of light

If you've ever watched the pale yellows of a spring sunrise or the ruddy reds of a winter sunset, you know that light has a range of color. With natural light, this variation has to do with weather and other atmospheric conditions. Early and late-day sunlight, because it strikes your patch of earth at a more glancing angle than at high noon, must pass through more atmosphere. And the more atmosphere it passes through, the more airborne particles, dust, water vapor, and even pollution act as a sort of color filter.

But that filtering effect extends to cloudy days, too. A layer of overcast, in addition to greatly softening sunlight, gives it a cool, sometimes bluish quality (more noticeable in prints than when you actually observe it). And the light in open shade on a clear day is bluer still because it's cast by an expanse of open sky. Foggy conditions can actually make a subject almost colorless, for an interesting monochromatic effect in your print.

Indoor light from household fixtures — tungsten bulbs and halogen lamps — is a different story. Most film reproduces indoor light with a usually pleasant yellowish-brown warmth. (See the section, "Artificial light," later in this chapter.) And fluorescent light actually comes out green, for technical reasons I won't trouble you with.

Indeed, light doesn't just contribute its own color to a scene, but actually picks it up from the environment. My favorite tree, for example, is a sugar maple right outside my daughter's window. Every fall it turns a brilliant yellow, and her room turns with it. When sunlight hits the leaves and bounces back through the window, it's magnificent. I turn off my camera's flash and take pictures of it — not of the youthful clutter of my daughter's room, just of the glorious, palpable yellow light.

Figure 8-3:
If the scene you're shooting contains interesting shadows, make them a part of your composition. Here, the photographer placed the figures to the right so that he could include their shadows.

© Russell Hart

Coping with Hard Light

A long-retired photographic adage held that to take pictures in direct sun, you should keep the sun over your shoulder — in other words, behind you, slightly above you, and to the side. The advice always struck me as ridiculously limiting. It seems to suggest either that you take pictures only in one direction or that you move your subjects around — and that you don't much care what's in the background.

Neither photographic subjects nor the sun are as cooperative as that old adage seems to assume. Usually you can't move the things you want to photograph, and moving people can ruin a picture's spontaneity. Picture possibilities present themselves all the time, not just when the sun is over your shoulder. But that old adage does have a kernel of photographic wisdom in it. Sun hitting a subject from roughly the same angle at which you're taking the picture (over your shoulder) minimizes the size and number of heavy shadows on it. This nearly frontal light is somewhat more flattering to human subjects than overhead sunlight, which creates heavy, unattractive shadows under noses and in eye sockets. In either case, hard sun tends to bleach out color.

Shooting in direct sun

Picture opportunities, of course, rarely wait for ideal lighting conditions. And you don't always have the time to wait for better light either. But several simple, quick techniques can help you tone down harsh daylight: adding fill flash, increasing the exposure, and using reflectors. (See "Preserving detail in hard light" for more on these techniques.)

Avoid letting sunlight or any direct light source (a floodlight, for example) strike the front surface of your lens when you take a picture. This causes stray light to bounce back and forth inside your lens, not only creating streaks and bands but often fogging the entire image — giving it a washed-out appearance (see Figure 8-4). You will see sunlight striking the front of the camera right through your viewfinder; the scene will appear washed out, with streaky reflections crossing through it. This ruinous effect is called *flare*.

If you want to shoot toward the sun, position yourself so that a tree, roof, or other object outside the picture area blocks the sun, in effect shading the lens. Or hold the camera with only your right hand as you shoot, using your left hand to shade the lens. (Be careful not to get your hand in the picture.) If you want to include the sun itself in the picture, some flare may be unavoidable, depending on the quality and construction of your lens. But you can minimize the flare by choosing a vantage point from which the sun is partially obscured by a tree branch, telephone pole, road sign, or other picture element. It also helps to use your point-and-shoot's fill-flash mode (see Chapter 7), which adds frontal light to the subject.

Preserving detail in hard light

The patterns created by hard sunlight can be unattractive or confusing. Perhaps the worst thing about hard light, though, is that in extreme cases, photographic film may not be able to record detail — that is, tone and texture — in both the areas that are directly sunlit and those that are in shade. Even when film *can* record detail in both sunny and shady parts of a scene, the print that you get may contain only one or the other.

Highlights are the lightest and/or brightest parts of a photographic subject — those sunny areas, for example. *Shadows* are the darkest or most shaded parts of the subject. You can also use these terms to describe the lightest and darkest parts of the print itself, and the difference between them is known as *contrast*. If that difference is great, the subject or print is said to be *contrasty*.

Figure 8-4: Shooting with the sun behind the subject may allow direct light to strike the lens surface — causing picture-fogging flare (left). To prevent this problem, shift your position to block out the sun and set fill-flash mode (right).

© Peter Kolonia (2)

When you actually *look* at a subject with brilliant highlights and deep shadows, you're able to see detail in both areas. When you gaze at the highlights, the lens aperture in your eyes — that is, your pupils — gets smaller. But the instant your gaze shifts to the shadows, your pupils open wider to let in more light. Unlike a point-and-shoot camera, which must choose one and only one aperture for a picture, your pupils change their size continuously as you scan a scene. What's more, in lower light the "film speed" of your retinas (the light-sensitive back of the eye) is, in effect, increased. Your eyes and brain are a much more flexible system, when dealing with difficult light, than are your point-and-shoot and the film inside it. (See Chapter 2 for more on the lens aperture.)

Modern color print film goes a long way toward capturing detail in bright highlights and dark shadows — an ability notoriously lacking in color slide film (see Chapter 2). But even if your developed color negative contains both shadow and highlight detail, the print itself may not. The photofinishing machinery may have to choose between one or the other because it can give the paper only one overall blast of light. By contrast, I can go into my darkroom and give the print a little more light here, a little less light there — and by doing so, keep detail in both highlights and shadows. Your minilab, with its 500-plus prints-per-hour system, cannot stop to do that. (See Chapter 3 for more on photofinishing.)

Don't despair: Here are several ways to trick your color print film (and your prints) into keeping both highlight and shadow detail *when you're taking the picture*. I describe them here in order of their effectiveness and convenience.

Use fill flash

Fill flash lightens the subject's shadows without significantly lightening the highlights. (I won't get into the physics of this effect here.) It brings shadows and highlights closer together. But keep in mind that fill flash helps only with subjects that are fairly close. When a subject exceeds the flash's outdoor range — perhaps 10 or 15 feet — fill flash doesn't make much, if any, difference. You can't use fill flash to lighten shadows in a landscape or a big building. (In those cases, you just have to wait for better light!) But you *can* use fill flash to lighten the unflattering shadow on the side of someone's face or the distracting shady spots in your prize bed of roses. To improve the range of fill flash, stick with ISO 400 film. (See Chapter 7 for more on fill flash.)

Increase the exposure

First things first, increasing the exposure may be hard to do with your particular point-and-shoot camera — and fill flash, which you almost certainly *can* do, is generally a better remedy for hard light. But unlike fill flash, increasing the exposure works whether the subject is near or far — and its effect *can* make a difference with that building or landscape. However, unlike the other two techniques that I describe in this section, increasing the exposure works only with color print film.

Increasing the exposure simply causes more light to strike the film than the camera would otherwise allow. This effect tends to reduce the negative's overall contrast and, specifically, to lighten shadows in the print.

✔ You can adjust the exposure with the camera's *exposure compensation* control, if your model offers this feature. (This process is usually an easy pushbutton affair; see Chapter 4 for details.) I suggest increasing exposure by at least half an EV (an *EV* is a standard "chunk" that extra exposure is measured in), and in really hard light, one EV.

✔ If your camera doesn't have exposure compensation, it may have *backlight compensation*. You ordinarily use backlight compensation when the light is coming from *behind* a subject, a situation that may otherwise cause underexposure. (See "Backlight," later in this chapter.) But because backlight compensation usually increases the exposure by about 1.5 EV, it can add considerable shadow detail and also lower the negative's contrast. (Unlike exposure compensation, it has only one setting.) That's a lot of extra exposure, so try shooting one picture with backlight compensation and one without so that you can compare them and make mental notes for the next time.

Here's one final note about increasing the exposure to cope with hard light. If the folks at the minilab or other photofinisher make a print that's washed out, ask for a reprint — and don't let them blame it on an overexposed negative. In most cases, the *print* just needs more exposure. (Negatives from one-time-use cameras are often quite overexposed, and they print fine.) Adjusting the print settings just takes extra time on the part of the technicians. (See Chapter 3 for more photofinishing tips.)

Use a reflector

A *reflector* is a white or shiny surface that you use to bounce light into the subject's shadows and thereby lighten them. A big piece of white poster board will do; get it at a good stationer. Foam core is a better idea; it's a white-surfaced, Styrofoam-filled art board that is both lightweight and rigid. You can usually find it at art supply and hobby shops. You can also use a bedsheet or other white cloth, but you may need to attach it to a board for rigidity and control.

To use a reflector, place it on the side of the subject *opposite* the light source (for example, the sun) so that your subject is between the light source and the reflector. For example, if the sun is to the right of your subject, you would place the reflector to the subject's left. Adjust the reflector's distance from the subject and its angle until you see a visible lightening of shadows. Don't move it too close to the subject or you may lose the sense of shadow altogether; remember, shadow is important in defining the light's quality and direction and the subject's shape and textures. Also, be sure to keep the reflector outside the actual picture area. You may need an assistant (a kid looking for something to do?) to hold it in just the right position.

You'll be amazed at the way a reflector lets you control the balance of highlights and shadows. It can even fix overhead sun: Placed underneath a person's face, it immediately fills in those shadowy "holes." And a reflector is great for close-ups, too. I know one nature photographer who habitually tears paper out of his field notebooks and places it around the edges of his close-up subjects, just outside the picture area, to brighten small shadows. Needless to say, this technique doesn't work with large-scale subjects; you can't use a reflector when you're shooting a landscape, unless it's specifically to fill a shadow in the immediate foreground.

You can wrap your reflector in aluminum foil or silver mylar (available at art supply and hobby shops) to make it bounce light more efficiently. Covering the reflector allows you to use it at a greater distance from the subject. You can even substitute gold mylar to warm up shadows.

Reflectors are everywhere — and if you're clever, you can take advantage of them. A sandy beach bounces light up into people's faces, softening hard sun's shadows and often making beach pictures better than you expect. (For a stronger fill effect, have people kneel or sit in the sand so they are closer to it.) Snow has the same effect. If you have the ability to move a human subject around, in fact, you can use nearby white or light surfaces — a stucco wall or a sheet hanging out to dry — to fill unwanted shadows quite effectively.

Capturing Light at the Right Time

Some pictures that are about light are about *momentary* light — light's more fleeting effects. A familiar landscape can be transformed when the sun breaks through a stormy sky and sends out shafts of dramatic light. Or for a short time in the spring, at a certain time of day, the sun may glint off a window and fill your yard's shadows with an interesting bounced light. Like most pictures of people, pictures of such lighting effects are hard to anticipate — and when you see them, you've got to act fast to capture them on film.

But for other pictures, you *can* — and should — wait for the right light. Say you're staying at a hotel overlooking the Grand Canal of Venice or (my preference) a tent on Lake Superior. Both spots command a spectacular view, and you want pictures of them for posterity. You may think that the things in the scene are what make it great: the bobbing gondolas below, or the breathtaking stand of white birch that surrounds your tent. And they do make the scene good, but content alone does not make the photograph great. You have to think about *light* to make the picture as great as its subject.

Midday blues

If you shoot your scene in the middle of the day, you're likely to be disappointed. If the day is sunny, you'll probably get strong shadows, which can give the scene a disjointed, hard-to-read appearance. The direct light also may make colors look less intense than what you remember, when you get the pictures back.

Well, yes, I tend to dump on the poor old midday sun. Don't get me wrong: It *can* be a very interesting light source if handled with care. I've taken pictures of mid-Manhattan buildings with midday sun, for example; it throws ornamental detail into high relief — a sharply defined, three-dimensional appearance. If you wait much later in mid-Manhattan, the great buildings on the city's famed north-south avenues start to block the sun, which travels perpendicular to them. Even with some subjects in nature — valleys and canyons, hillsides and riverbeds — if you shoot too early or too late, you don't get any sunlight in them at all. And high noon is just about the only time, for example, that you can get decent pictures of slot canyons — those narrow, water-sculpted gorges of the American Southwest. The sun can't get inside them any other time!

Generally, though, experienced photographers stay away from midday sun. Needless to say, it can be as bad for portraiture as it is for landscapes, creating harsh, unflattering shadows in eye sockets and under the nose.

Shooting early or late in the day

You're usually better off taking such pictures at the beginning or end of the day — when the light is more angular, less harsh, and warmer.

Outdoor photographers have a special name for the warm-colored, low-angle light that they get early and late on a sunny day: *sweet light*. In fact, many of these photographers take a photographic siesta in the middle of the day, shooting only at its beginning and end!

Your sweet-light photograph needn't be a landscape or a grand view. You can wait for sweet light to do a portrait session in your backyard, or to capture that gnarly detail of your old oak, or to take those close-ups of flowers you've been meaning to shoot.

For sweet-light shooting, use a fast film — preferably ISO 400.

Cloudy is beautiful

A lot of inexperienced photographers avoid cloudy days like the plague. They think the light is drab. They're wrong. By lowering contrast and softening or eliminating shadows, cloudy days bring a special delicacy to subjects. They let subjects' colors and tones speak for themselves, without being drowned out by direct sun.

When I first started taking photography seriously, I would actually *wait* for cloudy days. I preferred their range of close tones — sort of like adding in the minor keys on a piano. Cloudy days also solved some darkroom headaches by keeping contrast under control. Cloudy days can do the same for your commercial prints — provided the printing is a good job. If it's not, cloudy light can make a subject look even worse. Use a reliable photofinisher! (See Chapter 3 for more on choosing a good photofinisher.)

Cloudy days can actually *intensify* colors. Pictures of flowers (see Figure 8-5) or fall foliage are often more vivid in overcast than in direct sun. So if you're on a leaf-peeping trip and the day is cloudy, don't worry, be happy!

When you can't count on clouds to soften hard sun for a portrait, take your subject into open shade. You can find it under a tree, beside a house, under a beach umbrella, and so on.

Shooting in Special Kinds of Light

People don't spend all their time in the great well-lighted outdoors, of course. (Well, a few do.) For most people, light more often comes from various nooks and crannies: windows, open doors, skylights, electric lamps, overhead fluorescent bulbs. And light often comes at odd angles, too — from the side or from the back or even from below your prospective subjects. These specific kinds of light call for different ways of shooting, as I now describe.

Window light

Window light can be hard or soft: direct beams of sun or indirect, scattered rays. Either way, it's beautiful. Having to squeeze through the window's rectangle and enter a room from one side gives light a striking directional quality and rich shadows, even when the light outside is shadowless. Studio photographers covet north-facing windows in particular, because they're lighted by an open sky and rarely get direct sun. North light, they call it.

Window light offers a unique photographic lighting opportunity, one worth exploring to avoid the monotony of indoor flash shots. Rather than blast away with flash, try bringing indoor subjects — a newborn or a vase of flowers — over to a window for pictures (see Figure 8-6.) Or go ahead and set up a more formal portrait session beside a window. For best results getting your subject fairly close to the window is important. The light is brighter there. And because moving closer makes the window's area larger relative to the subject, the light is softer overall, helping keep shadows lighter.

Figure 8-5: Soft overcast is often the best light for photographs of fall foliage and flowers, avoiding the washed-out highlights direct sunlight can cause.

© Russell Hart

Keep your eye on shadows created by window light. The difference between them and the bright, highlighted parts of the subject can be even more extreme than outdoors because there's so little scattered light indoors, in a dark interior, to fill in shadows. (There's a lot more scattered light outdoors.) This lack of scattered light can make the print have either washed-out highlights or dark, empty shadows.

Here are a few ways to prevent this effect, and you can combine most of them to suit your purposes:

- ✔ **Turn up the room lights as much as possible and/or move a lamp closer to the subject on the side opposite the window.** This adds light to the shadows, though keep in mind that it appears as a *warm* light in the print because of the way your color print film sees artificial light. (See the section "Artificial light," later in this chapter.)

- ✔ **Angle your subject slightly *toward* the window, so that the light strikes the subject not directly from the side but a bit more frontally.** With a portrait, this positioning allows more window light to spill into the shadowed side of the subject's face and body. Better yet, simply ask your subject to look toward the window.

- ✔ **Use a reflector.** Placed on the room side of the subject (the side opposite the window) outside the picture area, the reflector bounces the window's light back into the subject's shadows. (See the section "Use a reflector," earlier in this chapter.)

Figure 8-6:
For flattering window-light portraits, bring your subject close to the window, use fast film (ISO 800), and turn off your flash to preserve deep shadows.

© Russell Hart

✔ **Use fill flash to lighten window shadows, but use it only if the light on your subject is direct sun.** Flash usually overpowers indirect window light, destroying the sense of its angle and quality. If the flash fires on its own, set the flash-off mode and take another picture. (See Chapter 7 for more on using fill flash.)

✔ **Use a fast (high ISO) film.** A fast film is especially important if you're shooting by indirect window light. The slower (lower ISO) the film, the longer the shutter speed the camera sets — increasing the risk, already substantial in such low light, that blur will ruin your picture. I suggest an ISO 800 film for this purpose, ISO 400 as a bare minimum. (See Chapter 2 for more on different types of film.) And a high ISO film doesn't excuse you from holding the camera as steady as you can. Brace the camera on something if you want to play it safe. (For tips on steadying your camera, see the sidebar "Steadying your camera.")

✔ **Manipulate the window's treatments.** Sometimes you can change the quality of window light just by doing so. If the window has translucent curtains or translucent blinds, you can use them to soften direct sun. If it has horizontal or vertical blinds, you can adjust them to create interesting slitted patterns of sunlight or to control where the light falls. If your window is bare, you can cover it with layers of wax paper or tracing paper to diffuse sunlight. Even a dirty window can add interesting texture and pattern to the light!

Artificial light

Indoor light — the illumination from household lamps and ceiling fixtures — may seem to be a light of mere convenience, but it has a photographic quality all its own. Because your color print film is actually designed to produce the most accurate color in daylight or with flash, it sees the light from tungsten and halogen bulbs as very warm in color. Pictures taken by such artificial light end up with a yellowish or brownish-yellow cast — an effect that can be quite rich.

The strength of that effect depends heavily on photofinishing because automated printers can partially correct the yellowish cast. Some correction is good; otherwise, the effect may be so brown that the print lacks a sense of color. If this happens, ask for a reprint. (See Chapter 3 for more photofinishing tips.)

To shoot exclusively by household light, you may have to turn off your flash by setting the camera's flash-off mode. Otherwise, your flash may fire automatically and overpower the light. (See Chapter 7 for details.) Use an ISO 800 or even faster film so that the camera sets shutter speeds high enough to counteract blur due to hand shake. In fact, with an ISO 800 film the camera may not fire the flash anyway because the film has enough light sensitivity for a good exposure. (See Chapter 2 for more on film speeds.)

Steadying your camera

When you're shooting in fairly low light — whether by a window, by artificial indoor light, or at dusk outdoors — your point-and-shoot may have to set a fairly slow shutter speed to get enough light to the film for a good exposure. In fact, some point-and-shoot cameras are able to set shutter speeds as slow as a quarter or a half a second, or even longer. A slow shutter speed means that if you don't hold the camera steady, your pictures may be ruined either by a visible blur or (almost worse) just an annoying lack of sharpness — an effect called shake.

In low-light situations, advanced photographers sometimes resort to *tripods* — three-legged collapsible supports that not only keep the camera steady but allow you to control composition and your point of view more precisely. You can even use tabletop tripods — miniature versions that must be used on elevated surfaces and that let you angle the camera in any direction. But other (free) steadying strategies exist as well.

One is simply to steady your arms against your body, specifically, pushing your upper arms into your chest as you shoot. At the same time, you can spread your legs widely, turning yourself into a "bipod" — a human tripod. Or, if a vertical surface is near your shooting position — for example, a wall or door frame — you can lean against it as you shoot.

Finally, if you can find a table, chair, ledge, or shelf that suits your point of view, you can rest the camera on it as you take the picture. However you brace the camera, be sure to press the shutter button smoothly — no stabbing motion allowed. You can also set the camera to self-timer, take your hands off, and have the camera fire by itself, as I describe in Chapter 4.

On the other hand, you may *want* to mix warm tungsten light with flash illumination, as I describe in Chapter 7. Set your camera to its slow-sync flash mode, or if it doesn't offer slow-sync, to fill-flash mode. Set these modes even if the flash is firing on its own (that is, in its autoflash mode) because it will otherwise overpower the existing light. (Again, stick with ISO 800 film.) Mixing flash with tungsten light creates an interesting two-toned effect in which the foreground (the main subject) is mostly lighted by flash, and the background (where the flash doesn't reach) is mostly lighted by existing light. Even when you're mixing flash with room light, make an effort to hold the camera steady; it sets slower shutter speeds indoors than it would set outdoors.

Finally, if your room is lighted just by fluorescent lamps, I would avoid shooting with room light alone. Fluorescent light ends up green in pictures, though again, the photofinisher may be able to correct this cast a bit in printing. If I really want background detail in interior shots and the light is fluorescent, I set my camera to its slow-sync flash mode; this setting tends to limit the effect to a greenish tinge in the background. If your flash isn't firing — a good possibility, given how bright fluorescent light can be — you should force it to, either with slow-sync or fill-flash mode. These settings lessen or eliminate the green cast.

Backlight

Backlight is just what it sounds like: light coming from behind a subject. Sometimes it's the main light source; in this case, a subject is said to be backlit. Backlight can be beautiful, defining a subject by glancing off its sides and/or throwing it into shadow (see Figure 8-7). It's the classic light for silhouettes. But backlight is also one of the most difficult kinds of light for a point-and-shoot camera to deal with.

The problem, usually, is that the camera sees lots of light in a backlit scene even though the main subject is shadowy. So it chooses an exposure that may not get enough light from the main subject to the film. The result is a print in which the main subject is too dark — unless you do, indeed, want a silhouette. If you don't, here are a couple of ways to prevent or minimize the effect.

Figure 8-7: Backlight can add tremendous drama to a photograph (left). Minutes after the first shot, the sun had dropped behind the mountain (right), making the subject flat and much less interesting.

© Pat O'Hara (2)

✔ **Move closer to the subject, or if you have a zoom lens, zoom in tighter so that the subject fills more of the picture area.** By cutting out more of the surrounding area, you lessen the peripheral light that can throw off the exposure. The problem with this approach is that it may cramp your compositional style — forcing you to compose more tightly than you'd like.

✔ **Set your camera's fill-flash mode.** (See Chapter 7 for details.) By brightening the main subject, the added flash helps balance it with the brighter background. A few more sophisticated point-and-shoot models may actually fire the flash on their own when they detect that the middle of the scene (the main subject) is significantly darker than the surrounding areas. Fill flash works only if a backlit subject is within the flash's range.

✔ **Set backlight compensation, if your camera offers it.** Backlight compensation does its job regardless of the subject's distance. Many cameras have this feature (see Chapter 4); it forces the camera to increase the exposure, improving the sense of detail in the main subject. (The increase is about 1.5 EV — photospeak for about 150 percent extra exposure.) A few more advanced models provide automatic backlight compensation when they detect that the center of the picture area is substantially darker than the surrounding areas.

The problem with backlight compensation is that it gives as much extra exposure to the background as the foreground. The resulting print may in turn lack background tone or detail — a penalty you don't suffer when you use fill flash to fix backlight. Depending on the properties of the light, backlight compensation may also cause light to spill over and around the edges of the main subject, making it appear somewhat flat or foggy. Fogginess is a special risk with backlit subjects because you are often shooting *into* a light source such as the sun, which can result in flare.

Chapter 9

Composition 101 (Suitable for Framing)

. . . .

In This Chapter

▶ Should you follow the rules?

▶ Closer is better . . . usually

▶ Moving before zooming

▶ Relating foreground and background

▶ Shooting low, shooting high

▶ Why you should shoot verticals

. . . .

*1*f you've ever visited an art museum, you know that a painting is never shown without a frame. Yet even if it's full of gilded frills, a frame is more than just decoration for the painting it contains. It makes a statement. A frame says that the image within it (unless the image is totally abstract) is a slice of life carefully cut by the artist. A frame also declares that inside its boundaries, your eye is under the artist's control.

Whether or not you put it in a fancy frame, a photograph really comes with its own built-in frame — the picture's edges. Your camera's viewfinder tells you where those edges fall within the scene you want to capture. You adjust the edges' placement simply by moving the camera around (aiming it up, down, or sideways); by moving yourself around (getting closer or farther away, or moving to the right or left); and/or by zooming (if your camera has a zoom lens). (For more on using the viewfinder, see Chapter 5.)

Framing the subject is an important part of *composition* — the way you squeeze, shape, and cajole reality into that little rectangle, which of course eventually becomes your print. But framing isn't the *only* part of composition. Other simple and effective techniques can improve your composition, from shooting the subject at an unusual angle to setting up depth-enhancing relationships between the scene's foreground and its background. I explain these techniques in this chapter.

Composition Rules

Composition is the sum of all the visual tricks a photographer uses to make a picture pleasing and/or challenging to the eye. It starts with where you place the edges of the frame — basically, what section of a scene you choose to put on film. But composition also includes how you lead the viewer's eye around the picture; how you control interrelationships between elements of the scene; and the ways in which you emphasize one part of the scene over another.

Composition is especially important in photography because, unlike painting, you can't invent or rearrange reality. (Well, unless you're very good at digital manipulation; see Chapter 15 for details.) As a photographer, you have to work with what's out there — with the physical facts of the scene in front of you. But those facts can be interpreted and presented in different ways.

If you've come to this chapter in search of cut-and-dried formulas for good photographic composition, though, you may be disappointed. Composition is an endeavor in which anything goes — if it works. It amazes me how regularly and effectively good photographers violate all the visual conventions handed down from painting and other graphic arts. One is the *Rule of Thirds,* which dictates that the most satisfying compositions are those in which important elements (especially the main subject) fall along a grid of lines that divides the scene you're shooting into vertical and horizontal thirds. I don't believe this rule is worth the paper it's often written on, so you don't find it in this book. Besides, the great thing about photography is that experimenting with composition is cheap. For the cost of a few frames of film and a handful of 4 x 6-inch prints, you can compose your subject in various ways — and then decide which of them works best when you get your pictures back.

So in this chapter I suggest several experiments to get you thinking about composition. Composition is worth thinking about, because when it's good, it can make a huge contribution to the quality of your photographs. And I mean good, not great. Every shot can't be a compositional masterpiece, nor does every subject warrant a lot of thought. But you can train yourself — your eye, really — to put that frame around your subject in an interesting and appropriate way, and to apply ideas that help you present the subject in a visually satisfying form.

Aiming versus Framing

Most photographers use a camera's viewfinder like a gun site. Basically, they center whatever they're shooting. (Shooting is the right word: The viewfinder might as well have crosshairs in it.) This mistake is understandable. Photographers get so caught up in the moment they're trying to capture that they forget they're also putting a frame around it.

The classic example of this compositional no-no is in people pictures. When most photographers look through the viewfinder, their eye is immediately drawn to the subject's face, and locks there. The face ends up dead center in the frame, with empty space above the subject's head.

For better composition when you're photographing people, place heads near the top edge of the viewfinder frame, not in its center. To do so, you must aim the camera slightly down. (For more on photographing people, refer to Chapter 10.)

But whether you're shooting people or things, to compose effectively you need to see and use the entire viewfinder area — to unlock your eye from what first caught your attention, whether it's a face or a big red barn. Every time you look through the viewfinder to take a picture, scan its edges. (If you have an autofocus point-and-shoot, remember that the little marks in the middle are for focusing, so don't let your eye settle there.) Notice the distance between things in the scene and the edges of the viewfinder frame — whether those things are far away from the edges, just touching them, or cut off by them.

Composition is much easier if you think of it in terms of creating relationships between the edges of the viewfinder frame and things in the scene. You can point the camera up to place a landscape's horizon line near the bottom edge of the viewfinder frame, for example, so that the horizon will be low in the picture. You can swing the camera to the side to place a person closer to the right- or left-hand edge of the frame, so that the person will be off-center in the picture. Or you can point the camera down to place a face closer to the top of the frame — a simple adjustment that includes more of the subject's body in the picture.

Keep your eye close enough to the viewfinder eyepiece so that you can see the entire frame. If you don't, you may end up with composition that is unexpectedly off-center, that includes things in the picture that you don't want, or that leaves too much space and extraneous detail around your subject.

A word to digital point-and-shoot users: Many models allow you to compose with a TVlike color LCD screen on the camera back. This screen forces you to hold the camera away from your face to shoot pictures, which not only is somewhat awkward, but also increases the risk that your hand shake will blur the picture. If your particular digital model also has a regular viewfinder such as those found on film cameras — that is, it also lets you compose by looking through a small window on the camera's back — then turn off the LCD screen and compose with the regular viewfinder instead. This not only makes composition easier, but saves on batteries!

If, when you scan the viewfinder frame, you see a lot of space between your main subject and its edges, then you can probably make this conclusion: The subject is too *small* in the frame. Which brings me to one of the most important things you can do to improve your composition and your photographs as a whole: Filling the frame.

Filling the Frame

A famous photojournalist, Robert Capa, once said, "If your pictures aren't good enough, you're not close enough." (Alas, he got a little too close to his subject, war.) Getting closer to your subject — and in doing so, making it bigger in the frame — is often the simplest, most powerful way to add drama to a picture. Getting closer lessens or eliminates extraneous detail, gives more emphasis to your main subject, and even improves a picture's sense of depth.

If you have a nonzooming point-and-shoot, getting closer is the only way to make the subject bigger in the frame (see Figure 9-1). If you have a zoom model, though, you can zoom in to make the subject bigger. And with some situations, zooming in is the *only* way to make the subject bigger. One is when you physically can't get any closer to your subject — for example, because a fence blocks you or you'd fall down a cliff. With other situations, zooming in is just the *best* way to make the subject bigger. One example is when moving closer would call too much attention to your picture-taking, causing you to lose a spontaneous moment or to scare off a skittish subject

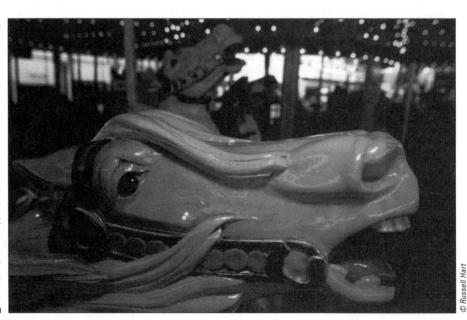

Figure 9-1: One easy and important way to make your pictures more exciting is by filling the frame — and usually the best way to do this is to move closer to the subject.

© Russell Hart

(deer in the backyard). But most of the time, moving in to make a subject fill the frame produces a more interesting picture than zooming in. (See Chapter 5 for more on filling the frame.)

Zooming versus Moving

Zooming is fun. Unfortunately, the fun of it (and the ease of just standing there and looking through the viewfinder as you rock the zoom switch or push the zoom buttons) seems to have convinced point-and-shoot photographers that zooming is the main way to control composition. It absolutely, positively is not! Zooming in and out is no substitute for composition. Real composition requires two legs. In my opinion, legs are the most important compositional tool you have. They let you squat or kneel for a low-angle shot, stand on your tiptoes for a little extra height on the subject, inch to the side, or — most important — walk toward or away from the subject.

The worst thing you can do, compositionally speaking, is to stand where you are when a subject catches your eye and zoom to compose. It's very unlikely that the position you happen to be in is the best one for the picture.

If your point-and-shoot has a zoom lens, recruit a cooperative friend or family member — someone who'll stay put while you take a few pictures of him or her. Place your subject against an interesting background so that you can include a fair amount of detail along the edges of the viewfinder frame. Zoom your lens to a focal length around 70mm. (If you've got a 35-70mm model, just zoom it to its longest setting; if your model zooms longer than 70mm, any middle position around 70mm or a bit beyond is fine.) Compose so that your willing subject fills a pretty big part of the frame. Then take a picture.

Next, zoom your lens to its shortest focal length; on most point-and-shoots, this will be 35mm or 38mm. Setting a shorter focal length gives the lens a wider angle of view, so you get more of the scene in the picture — and as a result, the person will be smaller. Look through the viewfinder and move closer until he or she is *the same size in the frame* as in the first, farther shot. Now take another picture.

When you get your prints back, compare them. You'll be surprised: The closer shot (the one taken at 35mm or 38mm) will actually show *more* of the background than the shot taken from farther away (the 70mm version). Oddly enough, the farther you get from the main subject, provided you keep zooming in to keep it the same size, the less and less background detail will be included in the picture (see Figure 9-2).

Figure 9-2:
For this pool portrait, the photographer first shot at 70mm (top) and then 35mm (bottom), moving closer to keep the little girl the same size in the frame. The 35mm setting shows much more of the surroundings — without making the main subject any smaller.

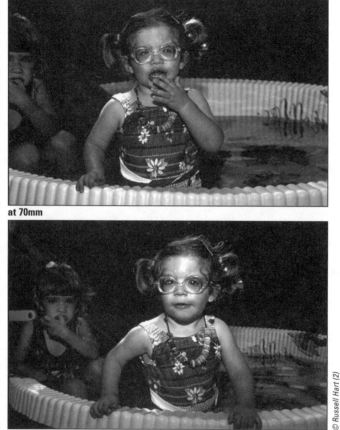

at 70mm

at 35mm

© Russell Hart (2)

TIP

If your background is cluttered, showing less of it may actually be a good thing. In that case, zoom in tight to your subject. But in my opinion, photos that show the subject's context (its surroundings and background) are usually more interesting and valuable than photos that don't. This is especially true if you're taking pictures more for memory's sake than for art's sake. So when I'm shooting with a zoom camera, I tend to stick with shorter focal length settings and I get as close to the subject as I can.

Again, you can't always get physically closer to a subject. In that case, go ahead and zoom in. Better to have your subject fill the frame, even if you have to zoom to do it, than to have it be too small.

If you do the experiment I describe earlier in this section, you'll notice something else. The closer, wide-angle shot — the one that shows more of the background — also makes the objects in the background look smaller, relative to the subject, than they do in the zoomed-in shot. Technically, this is because the lens has less magnifying power at a wide-angle setting (35mm or 38mm) than it does zoomed in (at 70mm). But you can think of it this way: The lens has to make things in the background smaller to squeeze more of them into the shot!

You may also notice a flip side to this effect. Zooming in for a shot does more than just show less of the background. If you zoom to a longer focal length in combination with physically moving — in this case, moving *back* to keep the subject the same size in the frame — you change the size relationships between the main subject and things in the background. You make the individual elements in the background seem larger than they would have been if you'd shot from a closer distance with a wider-angle focal length.

If you want to emphasize a specific object in the background — especially something that is pretty far away and might end up very small compared to the main subject — backing up and zooming in is the way to do it. The extra magnifying power you get when you zoom to a longer focal length makes background objects appear bigger (see Figure 9-3).

Figure 9-3: The photographer first shot at 70mm (left) and then 105mm (right), backing up to keep the man the same size in the frame. This reduced the visible background but increased the apparent size of the distant building.

at 70mm   **at 105mm**

© Mark Harris (2)

By combining changes in focal length (zooming to different settings) with changes in your physical position, you exert tremendous control over the size relationships between foreground and background. But again, you have to *move* to do this. Simply zooming in and out produces no changes in that relationship.

Balancing Foreground and Background

As you compose a photograph, always keep in mind that a print reduces a three-dimensional subject to a flat plane, lessening the sense of depth your eyes and brain provide. But one way to restore that sense of depth is by choosing a shooting position from which you can include interesting foreground elements — objects in the near distance (see Figure 9-4).

Including interesting foreground elements is especially important when you're photographing scenes without people close by. If you're photographing a landscape, for example, try to compose so that natural or manmade things — a tree branch, plants, rocks, or a portion of an architectural structure — occupy part of the foreground. Photographers sometimes call this approach *near-far composition.*

If you want to include foreground objects to enhance the sense of depth in your pictures, use as short a focal length setting as possible. On 35mm zoom point-and-shoots, this setting is usually 38mm or 35mm; some models may offer a 28mm setting. On Advanced Photo System zoom models, the shortest setting is usually 30mm, 26mm, or somewhere in between; a few models may offer a 24mm or 21mm setting. These shorter focal lengths provide the wider angle of view needed to take in both foreground and background. Another tip: If you're having trouble fitting both a near object and a distant one (or the horizon line) in the frame, try shooting from a lower angle — even a squatting position — to bring them visually "closer."

Single-focal-length (nonzooming) point-and-shoots are often especially well-suited to creating strong near-far relationships. This is because their one focal length is often shorter than the shortest focal length on a zoom point-and-shoot — as short as 30mm (and occasionally 28mm) on 35mm models, and as short as 24mm (and occasionally 21mm) on Advanced Photo System

Figure 9-4:
Add depth
to a land-
scape by
composing
with
interesting
objects
in the
foreground.
Here, a
tourist's
sunhat
makes a
stark view
of tidal flats
much more
appealing.

© Russell Hart

models. Also keep in mind that vertical composition (see the section "Rotating the Frame: Horizontals versus Verticals") can make it easier to create near-far relationships, especially if the close object is sitting on the ground — a rock, tree stump, or a cluster of flowers, for example.

One visually pleasing variation on the idea of near-far relationships is to frame a more distant subject with something in the foreground — to create a sort of frame *within* the photograph (see Figure 9-5). You can do this with window frames, doorways, arches, or natural elements. Scout around for these prospects before you shoot a subject.

If your frame-within-a-frame is very dark, which is often the case when you're shooting an outdoor scene from inside, through a window or door, you can brighten it by setting your point-and-shoot to its fill-flash mode. (See Chapter 7 for details.) If you choose to leave your frame-within-a-frame dark, keep in mind that if it occupies a large area of the picture, photofinishing machinery may make the print too light. In this case, you should ask for a darker reprint. (See Chapter 3.)

Figure 9-5: Composition can often be improved by framing a more distant subject with foreground elements, either manmade (left, an archway) or natural (right, silhouetted trees).

© Amos Chan

© Pat O'Hara

Composing Off-Center

One tried-and-true compositional technique that works with nearly any kind of subject, from people to landscapes, is to place the main subject off-center in the frame rather than centering it (see Figure 9-6). Set up your shot so that a person standing in front of the scene is off to one side in the picture, for example, and the other side can be entirely devoted to the background — allowing you to show a bigger swath of it, or to give the background more visual weight. The visual imbalance created by this type of composition also gives the photograph a more energetic quality than does a centered composition, which tends to create a static feeling.

If your point-and-shoot is an autofocus model and you use off-center composition, be sure to lock the focus on the main subject before shooting. (See Chapter 6 for details on locking the focus.) Locking the focus before establishing your final composition prevents the camera from focusing on the background and keeps the main subject sharp.

Figure 9-6:
Instead of
centering
this passing
amusement
park
gondola, the
photographer
composed
so that it
was on the
right side of
the frame.
This off-
center
position
lends the
background
more
importance.

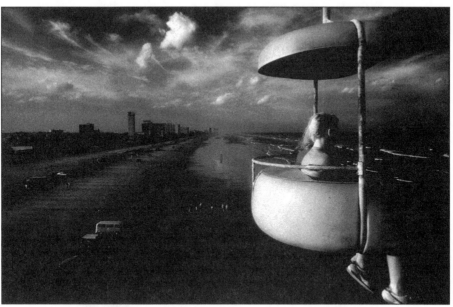

© Russell Hart

Changing Your Angle

Moving sideways one way or the other before you take a picture is something you do almost instinctively, if only to be able to photograph your
subject from the front. But chances are you don't give much thought to
moving up and down — to changing the *height* from which you shoot. You
probably take nearly all your pictures from your own standing eye level,
whether it's 5'2" or 6'2".

But no photographic rule commands that eye level is the best height from
which to shoot a subject. In fact, it often isn't. For example, pictures of kids
are usually much better when they're shot at a kid's eye level (see Chapter 10).
And many other subjects benefit from being shot from a position lower or
higher than eye level (see Figure 9-7).

A low angle can make an ordinary-sized subject look monumental, sometimes comically so. It also tends to minimize receding planes — a field, a
floor, a basketball court. And a low angle radically changes the relationship
between the main subject and its background. Photograph your kids from
your own eye level in the backyard and you'll probably get mostly grass, and
all the junk in your yard, behind them. Lie down on the ground and aim the
camera up at them, though, and the background will probably be trees, sky,
or (if you're not so lucky) the upper half of the neighbor's house. In fact,
shooting from a low angle can actually simplify a subject by putting sky or
trees behind it instead of the usual ground-level clutter.

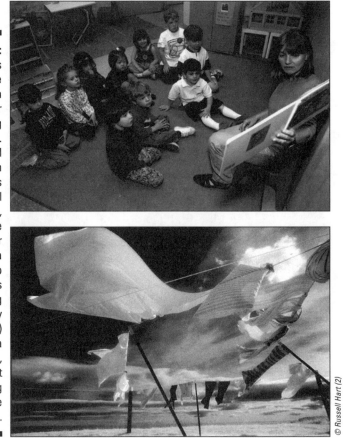

Figure 9-7: Pictures don't have to be taken from your standing eye level. To show all the faces in this preschool class (top), the photographer stood on a chair; to place this blowing laundry (bottom) against a dark sky, he shot while lying on the ground.

© Russell Hart (2)

But a high angle can simplify a subject, too. In particular, it lessens the overlap of objects at different distances; it literally helps you see over one object to the next. Even a little extra height — standing on a rock or a chair — can accomplish this, and with indoor shots produces a much different look than you're accustomed to getting. For outdoor shots, you may even want to shoot from a second-floor window, stand on a car, or (if you're limber enough) climb up a tree. This extra height gives you a clear shot of a large group of people, for example, because you can literally see behind the people in front. A good wedding and party trick! (See Chapter 12 for more on using high or low angles to control the position of the horizon line.)

Shifting Sideways

Shifting sideways to take a picture does much more than simply let you shoot a subject from a more head-on position. If you've ever gotten back a picture in which the subject's head seems to be sprouting a tree or impaled by a telephone pole, a sideways move would have been the preventive medicine for that photographic affliction.

Small shifts in your lateral position — a mere few inches — can prevent objects at different distances from overlapping in confusing and unattractive ways. Bigger moves — a couple of feet — can entirely change a subject's background. A quick shift to the side can replace a cluttered or drab background with one that's simpler and more colorful.

As with all such movements, it's imperative that you carefully study the subject through the viewfinder as you change your position. The viewfinder is your canvas.

Rotating the Frame: Horizontals versus Verticals

There are a few reasons why photographers shoot many more horizontal pictures than vertical ones. One reason is lack of thought — reinforced by the fact that a camera is usually easier to hold and operate horizontally than vertically. Another reason is that most of the things you photograph are themselves more horizontal than vertical, from landscapes to groups of people. I say *most,* because lots of subjects can benefit from vertical composition. In fact, photographers shoot way too few vertical pictures.

Pictures of individual people are usually better as verticals than horizontals. So if you're photographing an individual, unless there's a compelling reason for horizontal composition, turn the camera on its side and shoot a vertical. (Read on for reasons to shoot horizontals.) For a head-and-shoulders shot, composing vertically rather than horizontally eliminates unnecessary background on either side of the subject and also lets you fill the frame more fully with the subject.

When you shoot vertical pictures of people with flash, try to hold the camera so that the flash is at the top. Because most built-in flash units are to the left of the lens (from the photographer's behind-the-camera perspective, of course!), this usually requires that the shutter button, and your right hand, be at the *bottom* of a vertically held camera.

Orienting the camera this way causes light from the flash to strike the subject from slightly above the lens angle, rather than below. This effect is usually more flattering to people, especially when you're shooting from a fairly close distance. (See Chapter 1 for specific suggestions about holding the camera.)

Vertical composition is also useful when you're trying to set up a near-far relationship in a photograph. (See the section "Balancing Foreground and Background," earlier in this chapter.) Why? Because the camera "sees" a wider swath of the scene in its long dimension than its short. But beyond that, vertical composition can also lend a certain abstract quality to your pictures, simply by showing a piece rather than the whole of a subject. It's more unexpected, and more surprising, than horizontal composition, given that the overwhelming majority of pictures taken are horizontals.

So even when your first inclination is to shoot a horizontal picture, consider vertical composition. (All it takes is a quick turn of the camera!) Instead of backing up for a horizontal shot that includes the whole subject — a building, a landscape, and so on — try shooting a vertical section that crops the subject at either side of the frame.

If you have an Advanced Photo System point-and-shoot, try taking verticals in the 4 x 7-inch *H* print format. The extra inch of height over the usual 4 x 6-inch size makes *H* verticals fun both to shoot and to look at. But with a little thought, you can even shoot vertical panoramas.

And what about horizontal composition? I certainly don't have to convince you to use it; it is composition's default orientation. It can be more effective, however, if you place the main subject off-center — that is, on one side or the other of the frame. As I explain in the section "Composing Off-Center," earlier in this chapter, this not only makes your composition more dynamic, but allows you to set up more interesting relationships between foreground and background.

Working the Subject

Sometimes you have just one shot at a subject — literally. Whether it's the expression you've been waiting for in a portrait, a telling gesture in a candid, or an instant of spectacular light in a landscape, the moment you capture is the picture you want, even if right after you shoot it, a better way of composing it occurs to you. My advice: Don't lose the moment because you're fiddling with composition.

On the other hand, the more attention you pay to composition, the more good composition becomes second nature. And when composition becomes second nature, you can have things both ways — capturing the moment *and* composing it in a visually appealing and meaningful way.

Fortunately, not all subjects are so transitory that they limit you to one picture. Now, there are subjects (even those static enough to allow more than one shot) with which only one way of composing clearly seems best: where only one combination of distance from the subject, shooting height, zoom setting, and, of course, framing seems to bring all their elements together in the most effective way. Other times, the right composition isn't always immediately apparent. So when the time is available and the subject isn't going anywhere, try to shoot it in as many different ways as possible. You won't know what's best until you get your prints back!

Choose a favorite subject — no, not your spouse or children, but an inanimate one that won't protest, or blink, or get bored. An old gazebo in the local park? A favorite tree? Even your new sports car. Get a short roll of film and devote it to this experiment. Now shoot the entire roll on your chosen subject.

First, shoot the *whole* subject. Shoot it from up close with a wide-angle focal length setting and from farther away with a longer, zoomed-in setting. Shoot it from different horizontal positions, and from low and high angles, if possible. Shoot it horizontally and vertically, centered and off-center. Then move in or zoom in for details, and shoot a bunch.

When you get your prints back, compare them. Does one composition stand out? Do a couple? Did you have a sense that those shots would be the best ones? If so, then maybe next time you can trust your visual instincts and shoot fewer pictures. But I bet there are some surprises — that some of the prints you like are of variations you didn't have much hope for. The point is that those subjects for which one shot is the perfect shot are rare. If you want the best results, shoot more pictures!

Part IV
Don't Stop, I'm Shooting

The 5th Wave   By Rich Tennant

IT WAS THE WORST POSSIBLE TIME FOR CORRINE TO GET HER EYELASH CAUGHT IN THE VIEWFINDER.

"These are Maasai warriors people, so remember, no pictures!"

In this part . . .

This part is the part of particulars — particular subjects, that is. Whether you prefer people, landscapes, sports, architecture, or nature, Part IV is where you discover how best to capture the subjects you love to shoot. But this part is also where I nag you to take pictures of things that you may not ordinarily photograph — the everyday scenes around you.

People get the lion's share of attention here. But if sports subjects are your game, you find out that keeping a ball in the air isn't that hard, with a little timing and a fast film. If landscape is more your speed, here's where you discover that a little deliberation (of the visual sort) goes a long way. And because I hope photography gives you a new reason to get away, travel gets its own chapter. Travel is the ultimate photo op, a Whitman's Sampler of visual delights.

Chapter 10

Capturing Your Life on Film

● ●

In This Chapter

▶ Sharing pictures

▶ When to shoot?

▶ Expression and gesture

▶ Candids versus formals

▶ Making candids tell a story

▶ Picking the right zoom setting

▶ Pictures at parties and weddings

▶ Photographing kids and pets

▶ The Say Cheese syndrome

▶ Photographs as family history

▶ Ten lame excuses for not taking your camera along

● ●

*W*ant to get a sense of the importance of photography to ordinary people? Hang out at your local photo shop. You find customers standing by the sales counter, or sitting in their parked cars, as they pore over the package of prints they just picked up. You may have beeped at some of them on the street — they're the ones whose cars don't move when the traffic light turns green. They're trying to sneak another look at their pictures before the light changes, too excited to wait until they get home.

Don't be too hard on them. They're you.

That package of prints is a gift, and the photographer who shot them is like a child tearing at ribbons and wrapping paper. Why? Because photographs give you your life back — returning you again and again to its best moments and feelings. By letting you go back, photographs make your memories much more vivid. And when photographs are really good, they surprise you by showing familiar things in a new way.

In this chapter, I first look at the whys, whens, and wheres of capturing your life on film, mostly around your home and in your neighborhood. Then I talk about simple, but effective, techniques to get better people pictures — whether pushing the right mode button or just knowing the best way to capture a fleeting expression.

Why Take Pictures?

For most people, the obvious answer to the question "Why take pictures?" is "to preserve a moment in time," and photographs are momentary by nature. But why, in an era of moving video and 3-D computer effects, do still photos — flat, frozen images — remain so deeply satisfying? Perhaps because they leave something to your imagination, allowing your mind to animate the image from its own rich databank. In this sense, photographs are genuinely interactive, to use that big buzzword — more real than the multimedia, multisensory representation of videotape or computer screen.

That view sounds a little highfalutin, so I'll come back down to earth: Most of all, photography is just plain fun. The act of taking a picture, because it recognizes the importance, charm, or joy of a moment, adds energy to an event or experience (see Figure 10-1). Picture-taking makes people pay attention, and this is especially true of people pictures. People rally for the camera. If your subjects don't willingly pose, they often pretend they don't know you're there, playing along with your attempt to get candid photos. They understand the importance of their participation. Taking candids — purportedly unposed pictures of people — is, in truth, a team sport.

Candid shots, by definition, are pictures taken when people are unaware of the camera, or at least indifferent to its presence. But how do you keep pictures "candid" at events like parties or formal gatherings, where people are very much aware of the photographers all around them? Here are some tricks to try:

✔ **Take pictures of people when they're posing for someone *else's* camera.** You'll probably shoot a little to the side of the "official" photographer; this position actually can give you a more interesting angle on faces than the usual eye-contact pictures. If you shoot from way to the side, you can "stack" faces and figures in an uncommon way.

✔ **Take pictures before people have a chance to pose.** When you photograph a group of people, snap away before the group has a chance to organize itself; people look more animated and relaxed. Then, for the same reason, keep shooting *after* the official picture.

✔ **If your subjects start posing for you or looking at the camera, tell them to ignore you.** They usually do. If they don't, go away and come back in a few minutes.

Figure 10-1:
The very act of taking a picture adds energy to an event or experience.

© Russell Hart

Pictures Are for Sharing

While photographs indeed help you preserve and energize your life, you may find other, more practical reasons to continue shooting in this video-crazed world. First is that photographs let you share your life conveniently with others who aren't a daily part of it. Even if you could fit a videotape into your wallet, you'd need a VCR to show off pictures of your kids, your spouse, or your significant other. A photograph is compact and you can show it off immediately. You don't have to play it, except in your mind!

Sharing photographs takes many forms. Sometimes you mail pictures; these days, you can even e-mail them. (See Chapter 15 for more about electronic picture-sharing.)

TIP

Mailing pictures safely

Protect your prints when you mail them. Never put them unstiffened in a regular envelope, because they may get creased, dog-eared, or otherwise distressed in transit. Save thin cardboard from the backs of paper pads, new shirts, and packaging from toys and appliances. Cut the cardboard to size and use it to protect prints you mail. (This way, if recipients want to frame your pictures, they don't have to ask you for a dreaded reprint!)

Most often, though, you share pictures in person, with friends, relatives, or coworkers. Contrary to the old canard that snapshots are inflicted on unwilling victims, people love to see pictures. So don't leave home without them. Carry pictures of your kids, wife, dog, your last vacation, your new car, or your son's baptism.

Get double prints when you have your film processed, especially if you have important pictures on the roll. Sometimes you can get double prints as part of a free promotion; at most they add a couple of dollars to the cost of a roll. And they make sharing pictures much easier: You just give the duplicates away. You end up with two prints of some less good pictures, but it's still cheaper than getting reprints, and less trouble, too!

Just remember that *you* bring the actual memory to that hilarious but fuzzy picture of your toddler with a bowl of spaghetti on his face. You can sharpen it in your mind, and add the details and context. But the person you show it to has only photographic information to go on, despite your best efforts to fill in the details verbally. Your job is to make the *picture* good enough to convey the meaning or joy of the moment. Of course, you have even more incentive to make your pictures good if you actually give them away. If they're good, people will ask to keep them.

Film Is Cheap

Snapshooters are, to put it charitably, a bit parsimonious when it comes to film. This stinginess is one of the biggest factors working against their photographic success and satisfaction. As any professional photographer can tell you, the first rule of photography is to take lots of pictures.

I'm not suggesting that photographic success depends on the law of averages. But especially with active, changing subjects, the more you shoot, the more likely you are to get that one-in-a-thousand frame (see Figure 10-2). And most subjects are active and changing — kids in motion or facial expressions in a portrait subject. Even a landscape changes in different light. Nobody has perfect photographic timing — the ability to snatch just the right moment every time. There's a good chance that the moment *after* the one you choose to shoot may turn out better — whether due to a subtle change in facial expression or a dramatic shift in a landscape's shadows.

Being generous with film is particularly important when traveling or at special occasions. Why try to save a few rolls on an expensive and long-awaited trip — small change, after all? Why get cheap with film and take the chance that you won't get the most expressive images at a family wedding? Why be penny wise and pound foolish?

Figure 10-2: When you're photographing people — especially more than one person — always take more than one picture. Here, the third shot of three captured the best expressions on both husband and wife.

© Russell Hart (3)

Photography is no different than playing tennis or acquiring computer skills: The more you do it, the better you get. But you need the feedback of prints to understand what you've done, artistically and technically, and to improve on it. And to get prints, you need to shoot film. Film is cheap.

When to Shoot?

When should you take pictures? The simple answer: Anytime and all the time. Many people have the idea that they should save picture-taking for special occasions — unfortunate thinking that goes hand-in-hand with film frugality. Don't just take pictures at your kid's recital, or on trips, or at birthday parties and graduations and weddings. Photography is a visual diary. If you've ever kept a diary, you know that you have to do it every day to keep up. Well, maybe not *every* day — but diary-keepers will tell you that if you miss a week or two, you're in trouble. Memory can fail you.

Life has a rhythm to it. If you only photograph the big events in your life, then your photographic diary won't capture this rhythm. So photograph the seemingly ordinary times, too: a child's lazy summer afternoon in the sandbox, an early morning walk in the fall, a potluck supper with the neighbors, a loved one reading a murder mystery, or — one of the greatest of all family photo ops — the bathing of the dog. These pictures of ordinary times needn't show their human occupants. They might show the day's laundry drying in the wind, the heap of just-raked leaves, or the bowl of particularly luscious fruit on the kitchen table (see Figure 10-3).

Either way, these everyday occasions, places, and things are the ones you might not otherwise remember, because we tend to mark time with "important" events, celebrations, and holidays. I don't have to tell you that, in the rush and clutter of a fully lived life, the quiet times are often the most satisfying. But rest assured: Photographs of quiet times and ordinary subjects don't have to be boring, if you go about taking the pictures the right way.

What You Need for Great People Photos

First, a word about equipment. Believe it or not, your point-and-shoot camera is capable of making people pictures that are every bit as excellent as those taken with fancy "system" SLR cameras, even when professionals are behind them. This is because people pictures — especially candid ones — are more about timing than costly lenses or a clicking-and-whirring motor drive. But you'll find two extremely valuable features in any point-and-shoot you plan to use for people photography:

Figure 10-3:
Shoot the
ordinary.
Light can
transform
familiar
things — a
tomato
sitting on
the kitchen
counter —
into
extraordinary
ones.

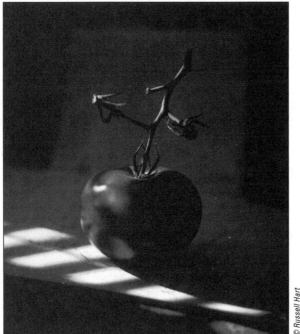

© Russell Hart

✔ **A built-in flash:** Almost all point-and-shoots have built-in flash units, except for the flashless one-time-use models and a few digitals. A flash with a few modes — such as fill flash and flash-off, which allow you to enhance and control the light for more flattering results — is even better. (See Chapter 7 for more on flash modes.)

✔ **A modest zoom lens:** For the best people pictures, a zoom model's lens should go out at least to 70mm, and, for more versatility with candids, to 90mm or 105mm. These longer focal lengths can be particularly useful for tight shots of individuals — again, in order to make pictures of them more flattering. (See Chapter 5 for more on zooming.)

BLOOPER

What about special "portrait" modes, or those very common red-eye reduction flash modes? Not necessary at all. In fact — believe me — they can actually get in the way of good people pictures. In many situations, you should avoid these settings, and you may even want to turn them off if the camera selects them automatically. (See Chapter 7 for more on red-eye reduction.)

What film is best for people pictures? If you read any other part of this book, you already know my answer: ISO 400 color print film. And if you shoot by low light — often the most atmospheric and flattering light for people pictures — you may be better off with ISO 800 film. These fast films offer a number of benefits (see Chapter 2). Use them and you can make sharper *and* more flattering people pictures. Fast films also add background detail to your flash pictures, avoiding the usual dark, empty surroundings. And you get much better pictures of large groups because the increased light sensitivity of these films lets your flash illuminate subjects at greater distances.

Expression and Gesture

Pictures of people certainly benefit from the same properties that make for any good picture: thoughtful and interesting composition, fetching light, and an uncluttered background, for starters. But at the heart of people photography is *expression*. Any photographer who takes pictures of brides or babies for a living can tell you about the importance of expression. For professional portraitists, the difference between an engaging expression and a blank stare is the difference between feast (lots of reprint orders) and famine (*no* reprints!).

Whether you pose your subjects or just snapshoot them, the expression on a subject's face is key. The photograph's viewer looks first at the expression, and only then (you hope) checks out everything else in the picture.

Supporting role: The tripod

A zoom lens and a flash may come built into your point-and-shoot, and may be all you need for satisfying people pictures. But a *tripod* can make a big difference in the quality of your portraits — especially if you like to photograph people in a more posed way by natural light.

A tripod is a collapsible, telescoping, three-legged support for your camera. It has a small bolt on the top; you simply screw the bolt into the small, threaded opening on the bottom of your camera. (Most point-and-shoots have this opening, called a *tripod socket* — but don't buy a tripod if yours doesn't!) You can get a lightweight tripod for $50, and light weight is all you need for a point-and-shoot camera. (Light weight also makes you more inclined to get out the tripod and use it.)

Tripods are especially good if you like to shoot by window light, a magical kind of illumination for people pictures. But in addition to keeping the camera steady, which offsets the increased chance of blur in such light, tripods offer a less tangible benefit: By keeping your camera in a fixed position — which eliminates the need for you to hold and constantly look through it — a tripod actually enables you to interact *more*, not less, with your subject. (Surprised?)

People often feel more comfortable if you look at them *over* the camera, rather than with the camera obscuring your face. In fact, a tripod actually enables you to take pictures without looking through the camera, provided the subject stays in more or less the same place. And a tripod lets you take a series of photos with exactly the same composition. Check with your photo dealer to find out about the available models.

Second only to expression is *gesture:* the way someone uses or places her hands and arms, the way she carries herself, posture, a characteristic slouch. If expression is facial language, gesture is body language. Whether posed or spontaneous, gesture can say as much about a person as expression. And it can say a lot about you as a photographer. A stiff, awkward pose is probably a sure sign you waited too long to take the picture (or, sometimes, not long enough) or that you somehow made the subject feel uncomfortable.

Expression and gesture are fundamental to what are, basically, the two types of people pictures: candids and formals.

A *candid* photograph is an unposed photograph of friends, family members, or others. It shows the subject(s) in the course of spontaneous events, moments, or interactions. A candid may or may not feature eye contact. It can be a picture of someone looking at the camera as he's engaged in an activity or interacts with other people, but before he has a chance to clam up. In a candid, the photographer exerts little or no influence on the subject. Some candids are indeed a slice of life: pictures in which the subject is totally unaware of your presence, until, of course, you give it away with a burst of flash or a click of the shutter. But in any event, you can control the picture by the angle at which you shoot and, of course, the instant at which you choose to take it.

A *formal,* on the other hand, is a portrait made by mutual agreement between the subject and photographer. It often involves carefully positioning the subject relative to a background and light source (see Figure 10-4). You certainly can do formals with your point-and-shoot, as I explain in the section "Getting formal," later in this chapter. But your point-and-shoot camera's ease of use makes it ideal for candids (see Figure 10-5).

Relaxing your subject

Whatever kind of people picture you shoot, the best way to get natural, unforced expressions from your subjects is to be natural and unforced with them. Engage them in real conversation. You may need a little practice at operating the camera and talking at the same time, but remember that your point-and-shoot does most of the photographic thinking for you. So as you photograph your subject, be calm, confident, and upbeat. If you seem too preoccupied with the camera or nervous that something might go wrong, the subject will pick up on your jitters — and you can kiss good expressions goodbye!

Start conversing with your subject by holding the camera down, away from your face, making eye contact as you speak. When your subject replies, lift the camera to your eye and take the picture. (Be sure to have the camera turned on and, if needed, the correct modes set, so you don't have a delay while you stop to fiddle with it.)

Figure 10-4:
A formal portrait is made by agreement with the subject, and often involves a controlled environment — here, placing the boy near a window for a light source and using a dark cloth as a background.

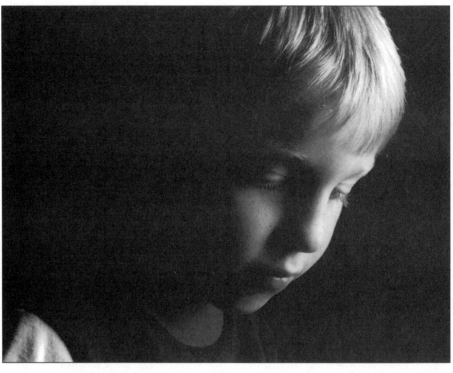

© Peter Kolonia

Figure 10-5:
A candid photo is an unposed shot of people — here, toddlers drawing. Contrary to what you might think, a candid is often better with eye contact.

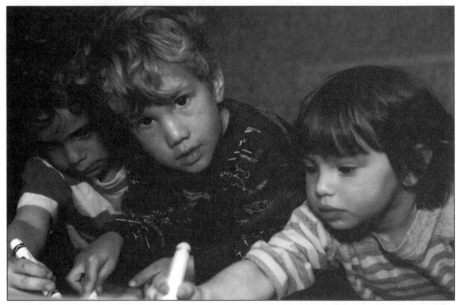

© Russell Hart

Shooting weddings

For people who like people pictures, weddings are made in heaven. All the generations of a family are in one place; everybody looks their finest; one and all are in an upbeat mood: No wonder so many guests show up with camera in hand. You've probably been one of them. Because the opportunities for pleasing people pictures are so great at weddings, consider making your own mini-album to present to the bride and groom after the happy day.

Please don't get in the way of professional photographers who've been hired to produce albums, though. Don't ask them technical questions while they work; don't steal their angle. While the pro may be a better photographer than you, *you* have an inside track: You probably know many of the guests. You know who you should photograph with whom, who's the cutest, the funniest, and so forth. You can use this knowledge to produce an album that may not be as elegant as the one made by the pro, but that has a personal touch the official album lacks. Whether you create an album or not, consider the following:

✔ As always, shoot ISO 400 or 800 color print film.

✔ Look for reaction shots. When the bride and groom kiss at the altar, turn around and shoot Great Aunt Gretyl crying. Leave the kiss to the professional.

✔ Yes, take lots of pictures of giggling kids.

✔ Photograph objects as well as people: the church, the wedding cake, flower arrangements, table favors, and so forth.

✔ When you photograph objects, move or zoom in for details. Try a close shot of the cake — or the cans tied to the bumper.

✔ If you make an album, consider including objects as well as photos. These might include dried flowers, cocktail napkins, or a wedding invitation. Also, art supply shops often have a nicer selection of albums than photo shops.

© Russell Hart

Don't be too bossy with the subject, especially if you shoot candids. Be funny, or if you're not a natural comedian, at least lighthearted. (This makes your sitter more relaxed.)

Nor should you appear to be "sneaking" your shots. Photographing people is, again, a cooperative venture between you and the person you want to shoot. If you loosen up and have fun, your subject usually loosens up and has fun, too. This helps you get better expressions — but you should still take lots of pictures. The best expression could come on the 14th frame of a 24-exposure roll devoted to a single person.

Want proof that your life is full of unexploited photo opportunities? Think about the last few weeks and count the number of situations that involved interesting or funny interactions with or between people. Did you have your camera with you?

Getting formal

What's the difference between candids and formal portraits? The formal is consciously, carefully posed. Formal portraits try much harder than candids to flatter the subject — or at least to make the subject look as interesting as the photographer knows him to be. Formals require the photographer to think more about light, pose, and composition. Done well, a formal can have a classical, painterly feeling.

If you're interested in formal photo portraiture, plan a trip to an art museum. Study portraits by old and modern masters, from Rembrandt to Andrew Wyeth. Note poses — a certain turn of the head, the position of hands — and the way light defines features and contours. (If you don't live near a museum, borrow some art books from your local library.) Try some of these posing ideas in your formal portraits.

The most important prerequisite for formals is patience — with yourself, not your subject. Don't be surprised if your first few attempts are disappointing. That's normal. A formal portrait isn't brain surgery, but it takes a while to develop an eye for what works and what doesn't. Your technique may improve sitting by sitting, but you may want to start by practicing on a (patient!) loved one who doesn't mind being used as a guinea pig. (Forget children. They have enough trouble sitting still for a candid shot, let alone a formal!) Here are some ideas:

  ✔ **Background:** Set up a backdrop perpendicular to an interior window — that is, extending into the room at a right angle from one side of the window's frame. A dark sheet, blanket, or tablecloth works well; just avoid patterns. (You have to figure out a way to support the backdrop, perhaps tacking it to the window frame and hanging the other side over a lamp.)

✔ **Lighting:** The light from the window should be soft and indirect. (Direct sun is usually too harsh, though if you set your camera's fill-flash mode you can soften it considerably.) If the light causes features to cast objectionable shadows across the face, reposition the subject if possible, angling the subject's face more toward the window. Consider lightening shadows with a *reflector,* a big sheet of white paper or cardboard (or just a big sheet). Place the reflector outside the picture area and angle it so that light bounces back into the subject's shadows. A good trick: Have your subject tilt her head up, so light strikes the face more completely. (And another: Shoot outdoors on a cloudy day, with something dark behind your subject.)

✔ **Camera angle and orientation:** Choose your camera angle with care. For tighter portraits (faces or heads and shoulders), place the camera at your subject's eye level, or even slightly lower. A portrait subject is usually, though not necessarily, best suited to vertical composition.

✔ **Posing:** Coax your subject into a comfortable but typical pose, maybe even modeled after a portrait painting you admire. In group portraits, individuals shouldn't cluster so tightly together that they can't move, nor should they spread out so loosely that they don't seem to form a group. Try to set up a structure that leads the viewer's eye from one member of the group to the next. If this setup seems too difficult, try arranging the group in order by height, with the tallest people in the center and smaller people flanking them on the sides. Mix sexes, too. The idea is to create a uniform composition and to keep your subjects' faces relatively close together, not all over the picture area (see Figure 10-6).

✔ **Clothing:** If possible, dress your subject in neutral tones that complement, but don't blend into, the background. Avoid patterns, bright colors, and pure white or black. Choose textured fabrics like velvet or corduroy, if possible. If you're shooting a group and you have any say in the matter, dress everyone in colors of the same family (that is, all bluish or all warm-tone colors).

✔ **Film:** Along with your usual color print film, consider shooting with black-and-white chromogenic film (see Chapter 2). Black and white brings a timeless, classic look to formal portraiture.

Possibly the easiest way to create a formal portrait is turn the subject into a *silhouette* — a dark shape with a much lighter background. Shoot the subject directly against a window or open door with cloudy sky behind him; avoid including prominent latticework or sashes. You have to make up for not seeing the subject's expression by shooting in profile or at an angle that creates a recognizable shape. You may also want to have the subject hold something that's associated with her and easily readable in silhouette — a pipe or hat, for example (see Figure 10-7). Now here's the weird part: Set your camera to its fill-flash mode, but cover the flash with your finger as you fire. This causes the needed underexposure of the figure. Then ask your minilab to make the prints extra dark.

Figure 10-6: For this Christmas portrait, the photographer arranged his subjects to create a close group — you guessed it, in the shape of a Christmas tree!

© Peter Kolonia

Figure 10-7: Shot against a bright, cloudy sky, this silhouette is especially effective because the woman is holding an easily identifiable rose.

© Peter Kolonia

Photographing staged events

You may get some of your best people pictures during staged or semi-staged events — school plays, ballet class performances, or wedding ceremonies, for example. But at these occasions, people often consider a flash intrusive. It can ruin the mood, distract the performers, and drain your camera's batteries — all for no photographic purpose.

Why? Because the people onstage may be out of flash range. Few point-and-shoots can light anything beyond 20 feet with their built-in flash units. What's more, the stage (or altar) may be pretty well lit, and flash may be unnecessary to get the shot.

However, your camera may *think* that flash is needed because the area around the performers in a staged event is often quite dark. So you should set its flash-off mode. Just be sure to use a fast film; I suggest at least ISO 800 film in these situations, especially if you're zooming in, which is likely. The faster film lets the camera set a higher shutter speed, reducing the chance that hand shake will blur the picture. But you should still place your camera on something secure like a tripod (or an empty seat) and gently fire its release so that you don't jiggle the camera. Resist shooting until the on-stage action comes to a standstill. If you shoot while the performers move, they could appear as blurs in your picture.

Planning your candids

Candid photography may bring to mind totally spontaneous pictures — basically, shooting from the hip. You see a scene or expression worth capturing, so you pull out your camera, aim, and fire. While this approach to candids can sometimes yield good results — and point-and-shoot cameras are certainly meant for such spur-of-the-moment photography — seemingly spontaneous people pictures are usually best made with planning and forethought.

First, you need to identify the times of your life that lend themselves to great pictures and make sure that you have a camera on hand for them. Any time family, friends, and acquaintances gather, seize the opportunity. You don't need to wait for a big holiday or a milestone event like a wedding, christening, or bar mitzvah. You'd be surprised at how many great people pictures you can make during a card game, both of the group and of individuals. Then you have the traditional gatherings for sports and games — participatory or spectator, live or televised. When people come together, photography is fair game. Depending on how your family and friends feel about it, even more somber occasions may be appropriate for photography. They are, after all, a part of your personal history.

The best unposed candids, ironically, take planning. Following are some strategies that can help you capture better candids:

✔ **Before family and friends converge, plan your tactics.** If the pretext is a game of cards, set up the table next to the window or some bright lamps, in case you want to shoot without flash for more natural-looking light. You may never lift the camera to your eye — that's okay, too — but you're ready for a shot if you get the urge.

✔ **When people arrive and get settled, analyze the scene and its players.** Who's the most expressive and gestural? Who's in the best light? Who's against the nicest background? If you want to photograph anyone in particular, seat or rearrange people so that person has the best light or the best background.

✔ **Once you determine the most likely candidates, find a shooting position that gives you unobstructed views of them.** When you're in position, sit or stand back and observe your subject — and keep in mind that it's best to start shooting slowly. Don't startle or annoy people with your camera. Fire off a few frames just to get everyone accustomed to the camera. Take your first pictures as "jokes."

Organize a game that requires some physical involvement (basketball or Twister) with the purpose of photographing it. Shoot both when the action is in high gear and during the quieter moments. You may be surprised at the number of keepers you get!

Successful candids require good observational skills. To get good unposed shots, you must wait for them to happen, anticipate them, and seize them when they present themselves. Lying in wait requires some discipline, but once you start, it's fun. In fact, you may be surprised at what you learn about the people you think you know — family, friends, and acquaintances — by watching them in the hope of nabbing a good candid photo. You can get so wrapped up in watching people, in fact, that you forget to photograph them!

All that said, nobody has perfect photographic timing. The expression or gesture or interaction that caught your eye may not be the exact one that ends up on film. What's more, while you concentrate on rather unexpressive Uncle Clive, Great Aunt Gretyl may have one elderberry cordial too many and start doing her famous impressions of long-gone family members — and you're missing them! Good candids sneak up on you. And because taking a candid is often such a delicate matter, you really don't know what you've got until you get the prints back. Moral? Don't wait for the perfect shot. Shoot a lot of film and have fun (see Figure 10-8).

Make candids tell a story

One good way to go about taking candid photos is to make your pictures tell a story. The obligatory, for-the-record shot of family gathered around the Thanksgiving table or Christmas tree serves perfectly well as a historical document, but not much else. More satisfying are groups of pictures that illustrate how the family lives and interacts. Photographic storytelling can reveal much about the character of a family and its individual members.

Figure 10-8:
When you photograph large groups of people, make a special effort to take lots of pictures. Getting a good expression on every face is next to imposs-ible — but the more you shoot, the closer you come.

© Russell Hart (3)

What do I mean by storytelling? Imagine going on a family vacation to a beach resort. Naturally, you get pictures of Johnny buried in the sand and Ginny shrieking her way through amusement park rides. But there was more to the vacation than that. There was the planning stage, when Mom and Dad sat around the kitchen table picking through brochures. Then the drive to the resort, with its spats and diner stops. And how about the misadventure you had when you pulled off the wrong exit? And, of course, the accommodations, grand or grimy. If you have the composure to photograph these sometimes less-than-splendid experiences, the pictures will make your photo albums that much richer over the years.

Candids and backgrounds

It may be the last thing on your mind when you're trying to capture Great Aunt Gretyl's best impression, but you need to pay some attention to the backgrounds of your candid photos. Try to keep them simple. You generally don't want too much activity going on behind your subject; the classic error is to have something "growing" out of someone's head — a backyard tree, a telephone pole, the flowers on the mantel.

Remember that even though your eye and selective attention filter out such visual intersections, a photographic print only reinforces them by squashing them together on a flat plane. So when you frame your candids, scan the area behind the subject for any such conjunctions. If you spy any, all you usually need to do is shift yourself a little to the side.

Another thing to watch out for is your candid subject's distance from the background. With indoor flash photographs, a background that's fairly far from the subject can end up completely dark in the print, and even worse, may trip up the photofinishing machinery into making the person's face too light — a ghostly visage in a black void (see Chapter 3).

Here are some ways to prevent both the visual clutter and the dark backgrounds that can mar your candids:

- ✔ **Fill the frame more fully with your candid subject.** Physically move in closer or zoom in to a longer focal length that makes the subject appear bigger. Getting closer reduces the amount and importance of the background and focuses attention on the person. Important: If you're shooting a single person, use vertical composition to cut down the amount of "empty" space on the sides of the frame.

- ✔ **Make your background closer.** Shift your position to the side so that a nearby wall or other element falls behind the person. (Shoot at a bit of an angle to the wall to avoid casting unattractive flash shadows on it.) Of course, by moving, you may not end up with the direct angle on the person that you initially wanted — so call out to get her to look your way!

✔ **Ask the subject to move.** Move the person to a position in which the background will be closer or more interesting. If you make this request, though, you probably should wait to shoot again until he forgets about you.

✔ **Use your point-and-shoot's slow-sync mode with flash pictures in which the background is unavoidably far away.** This mode (see Chapter 7) causes the camera to set a slower shutter speed — that is, to keep the window in the lens open for a longer time — so that the film records more of the existing light, most visibly in the background. But this effect really works only if you use fast (ISO 400 or 800) film, and if the light level (from either household bulbs or windows) is reasonably bright to begin with. Turn on some extra room lights to be safe.

If light levels are bright enough to let you shoot by existing light, your strategies may change. In fairly bright interiors, the background is often bright enough for the film to record, with no black void effect. So the background can be as far away as you like — sometimes, the farther the better. Having the background far away makes it more out of focus — more blurred. And a blurred background has the wonderful effect of placing emphasis where you want it, on your sharp subjects (see Figure 10-9).

Figure 10-9: When light is bright enough to shoot without flash, a distant background can actually be a plus. At longer focal length settings (here, 135mm), the lens throws it out of focus, emphasizing the main subject.

© Peter Kolonia

Dramatically out-of-focus backgrounds are easier to get when you zoom your lens to its longer focal length settings (see Chapter 5). But just remember that the longer the focal length, the greater the chance that camera shake (caused by your hand movement) will blur the whole image. And the longer the focal length, the greater the chance the flash will fire, if your camera is set to autoflash mode. If this is the case, you may want to turn the flash off, or zoom to a wider-angle setting and move closer to your subject.

Use Flash for People Pictures

Of all the features on a point-and-shoot camera, the built-in flash may be the single most important for making better people pictures. Each flash mode, including flash-off, delivers excellent results in the right circumstances. Your flash can create light where none exists, making portraits possible when you otherwise wouldn't have been able to make them. It can soften harsh light on the faces of your portrait subjects by filling in shadows in eye sockets and under the nose or chin. It can also offset the image-marring effects of strong backlighting. For details on using flash for people pictures, see Chapter 7.

Zoom Settings for Portraits

If your point-and-shoot has a zoom lens, it probably starts out at wide-angle focal length settings such as 35mm or 38mm, and ranges out to longer focal length settings of 70mm, 90mm, 105mm, 115mm, 140mm, or even a little beyond. Professional photographers sometimes call lenses having focal lengths around 90mm or 105mm *portrait lenses*. But that doesn't mean you can't take good people pictures with virtually any focal length setting your zoom offers; you just have to know when to use which! Nor does it mean that you can't get good results from a nonzooming model. (See Chapter 5.)

Long focal length portraits

The fastest way to a flattering portrait — especially if it's a close-cropped face or a head-and-shoulders shot — is with a zoom setting between 70mm and 105mm (see Figure 10-10). With Advanced Photo System cameras, a portrait zoom setting works out to about 55mm to 85mm. Longer focal lengths let you move back from your subject but still fill the frame with her. Physically moving back from the face creates more natural-looking — that is, flattering — size relationships among facial features. No one element (like the nose) appears much larger than any other. Long focal lengths are also useful because they let you exclude background details that might distract from your subject. And because they allow you to shoot from a distance, they're ideal for subjects who might not want a camera shoved in their faces.

38mm

55mm

85mm

105mm

Figure 10-10: For the most flattering results with tight portraits — a face or head and shoulders — zoom to focal length settings of 70mm or longer. Notice how the proportions of this man's facial features change with different settings — and the unattractive "big-nose" effect at 38mm!

© Mark Harris (4)

Faking long zoom settings

If your camera doesn't have long zoom settings (only going to 50mm, for example), or if it's a nonzoom model, you can mimic the more natural facial proportions you get with longer focal length settings by stepping back to make your subject smaller in the frame. After you have the film processed, have the negative reprinted at a larger size — 5 x 7 or 8 x 10. Then just trim the print down to the area immediately surrounding the subject.

If you have to photograph someone up close with a relatively wide-angle focal length — your only option if you have a nonzoom point-and-shoot — try shooting them in profile. Because this places all the facial features at about the same distance from the lens, less distortion occurs. Keep in mind, though, that portraits shot in profile don't give you the subject's full expression.

Wide-angle portraits

If long zoom settings are good for people pictures, does that mean you should avoid your camera's wider-angle zoom settings when taking people pictures? No. The bigger swath taken in by wide-angle settings makes them useful when you're shooting big groups or in tight quarters — those holiday pictures in which you try to pack everybody into your dining room. But you can also use wide-angle focal lengths very effectively for portraits of individuals.

You do so simply by keeping your distance from the subject — and using the extra surroundings to create what photographers call an *environmental portrait*. A good environmental portrait makes meaningful use of the subject's familiar context — bedroom, backyard, kitchen, or workplace. This kind of portrait reveals something about how a person lives, works, plays, or even feels. The stuff that collects around a person often reflects that person's character. Such pictures are especially fun if the location is exciting, colorful, eccentric, or busy. This approach to people pictures may be your only option when photographing folks who don't want to be reminded of their wrinkles — something a more close-cropped portrait shot at a longer focal length setting makes all too apparent. (See Chapter 5 for more on wide-angle zoom settings.)

Photographing Children

Parents just can't help themselves. Their kids are the natural targets of their photographic affections. Even childless aunts and uncles — seemingly more sensible people — are party to the obsession. Why do people feel so compelled to photograph children? The answer seems obvious: We find them cute and irresistible. Well, most of the time.

Take pictures of kids not just when they're most charming, but also when they pout or act up (see Figure 10-11). If the face you get is glum or angry, shoot anyway. Your pictures should reflect the emotional variety of your life.

Make an effort, in fact, to photograph kids when they do their utmost to be uncute and utterly resistible. Again, think of photography as the visual diary of your life. Episodes that may not seem to warrant picture-taking, or that you may be disinclined to photograph, take on new meaning and value as each childhood phase passes. Don't censor your photographs before the fact. You will look back at even the greatest annoyances — the artwork on the new wallpaper, the car happily washed with the windows wide open — with amusement and nostalgia, not anger. You'll be glad to have the pictures.

Of course, I don't mean to tell you how to discipline your kids. But sometimes, instead of getting mad, you might try just getting out your camera. You don't want to reinforce bad behavior, but a picture can defuse a situation that may be due more to childish misunderstanding than any challenge to your authority.

People take more photographs of children than of any other single subject. This is ironic, because children are among the most difficult subjects to photograph. They move too fast — from one activity to the next, from one mood to

Figure 10-11: Most kids are moody. So if you live with kids and take the job of photographing your family seriously, don't just shoot them when they're all smiles. Pouting is part of childhood.

© Russell Hart

the next, from one endearing moment to the next. To keep up with them photographically, you need good reflexes — to get out your camera and shoot quickly. Those reflexes come naturally as you take more and more pictures.

And don't just take pictures of your own children. Practice your skills on other kids, the children of friends or family members. Parents will be grateful for the prints you give them. And when you get good, if you want the challenge, you can offer to take pictures at school events and functions.

Know your child — and be ready

Well, of course, you know your child. But you should use that knowledge to plan your photographic strategy. Otherwise, you may curse yourself that in the time it takes to find your camera and make sure that it has film — and put some in it if not — the moment that captivated you has vanished.

You may find certain times of day or certain activities during which you always want to shoot pictures of your children — and regret not acting on that impulse more often (see Figure 10-12). Maybe your little one likes to play catch before dinner, or stage a command ballet performance afterward. Maybe your kids always stop to giggle at a window display, or study a bird's nest, on the walk to school. Be ready to take pictures at these times.

Figure 10-12:
Identify the activities, rituals, or times of day when you find your kids most appealing. Then have your camera ready and waiting, making sure it has enough film for at least a few good shots.

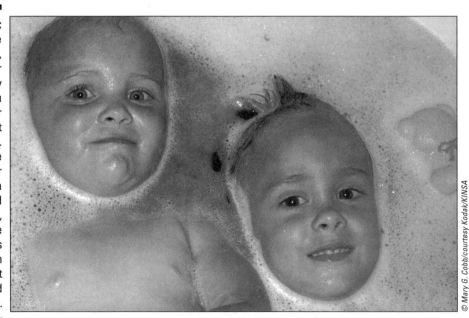

© Mary G. Cobb/courtesy Kodak/KINSA

Study reactions and expressions, too. Maybe you've noticed the look of intense engagement when your child reads a book, clicks through a favorite CD-ROM, paints a picture, or practices an instrument. Or maybe the presence of a particular playmate brings out the *joie de vivre* in your child. Look for the photographic possibilities in your daily or weekly routine. (Doing so may well change and enrich the way you see that routine!) And once you identify these times, have your camera nearby — in your pocket, around your neck, or in your hand.

When you plan your session, check to see whether you're near the end of the roll. If you are, have a new roll handy in case you run out of film. Better yet, if you *are* at the end of a roll — say on the 22nd frame of a 24-exposure roll, or the 33rd frame of a 36-exposure roll — just rewind the film and load a new roll (see Chapter 1). That way — and this bears endless repeating — you won't be stuck reloading film when that perfect photo opportunity appears.

You shouldn't take just one picture; you should take two, three, or more so that you're more likely to get the look or gesture you love. And you may be surprised to see a look or gesture you hadn't even noticed! A camera sometimes sees what you miss. When you get your prints back, pick the one you like best — the one that does the most justice to your own experience. That's the one for the frame, or the album, or to send to friends and relatives.

Now listen to this advice: You shouldn't just wait for the right moment to occur, and then raise the camera to your eye. By then you're usually too late. Put the camera to your eye frequently as your child goes about her business and be ready to press the shutter button at any time.

This idea seems simple enough, but most photographers don't do it. You have to learn to *see* through the viewfinder — to study the subject through it. Only if you see the right expression, gesture, or moment *through the viewfinder* are you likely to capture it.

And as you look through the viewfinder, keep your finger on the shutter button, periodically pressing it halfway down without actually taking a picture. This pressure keeps the flash charged up and prevents the camera from shutting itself down just before a good photo op. (Most models turn themselves off automatically if left unattended for a couple of minutes.)

Nonetheless, your camera may sometimes thwart a fast reaction on your part. The time lag between when you push the button and when your camera actually trips the shutter often seems interminable. Flash charging in particular can hang you up. You can find out more ways to minimize such problems in Chapter 7.

Why not just set the flash-off mode and eliminate the problem altogether? Because if your point-and-shoot fires the flash on its own — something it's likely to do indoors or in dim existing light — chances are you should be using it anyway. Without the flash, you'd have insufficient light for good results.

In fact, if the flash doesn't fire on its own, you might even want to force it to (see Chapter 7). Why? Because the flash helps in other ways, too, when you take pictures of your kids. The flash burst's very brief duration — it can be $^1/_{5000}$ second or even shorter — helps freeze a fast-moving subject. And kids are nothing if not fast-moving.

But if you don't want to use flash, you can get the camera to set a more kid-stopping shutter speed by using a faster film (see Chapter 2). You should use a film of at least ISO 400 speed anyway; to minimize kid blur, use an ISO 800 or ISO 1000 film.

Should kids look at the camera?

You've probably heard self-styled photo experts expound mightily on the matter of kids looking at the camera. Most such experts think that having your subjects even look at the camera, let alone pose, is a bad idea — that it makes for stiff, unnatural pictures. I beg to differ. Pictures in which a child is absorbed in an activity are great. But nothing is better than a spontaneous shot with direct eye contact. Eye contact animates the face. It engages the picture's viewer.

Spontaneity is the key. If you line kids up, of course, they'll start mugging and squirming in no time. In fact, don't try to pose them at all; don't disrupt their activity. Start by taking a few unposed pictures. Then, after the kids get used to you, call out to them to look at you. Shoot as soon as they do. Give them as little time as possible to object or make faces. If they oblige with a good smile, shoot another picture. If they start to act up, and you don't want them mugging, wait to shoot until they're bored by their antics. (Mugging's fun, too.) But either way, keep shooting. The second or third shot, or the fourth or fifth, is often the gem. I've been known to shoot a whole roll (36 exposures) of one situation (and not special occasions, when I'm likely to shoot many rolls). I can't tell you how many times the 36th frame has been the winner.

Even if kids don't get unruly about having their picture taken, they sometimes get hammy. For a while, my daughter offered up the same silly grin and squinty eyes each time I tried to take her picture. Every shot looked the same — the same face pasted onto a different background. She outgrew the habit, and in the interim I stuck with more surreptitious shots. (Currently, she prefers to stick out her tongue for the camera.)

Just one cautionary note about eye-contact photographs: If you set your point-and-shoot's flash system to *red-eye reduction,* which is designed to lessen the devilish-looking red eyes you sometimes get in flash pictures, you may get an agonizingly long delay between when you push the shutter button and when the picture is actually taken. This long delay is particularly true of red-eye reduction systems that use a *preflash* approach, but some *prelamp* systems can also take seemingly forever. If the delay is so long that you're likely to lose the moment, expression, or gesture you want to capture, you're better off shutting the red-eye reduction system off. See Chapter 7 to find out how.

Shoot from eye level — theirs

Perhaps the most common mistake in photographing children is to shoot them from your own eye level. An adult's-eye view turns kids into big faces with foreshortened little bodies. Get down on their level to take your pictures (see Figure 10-13). I repeat: Legs are your most important photographic tool. The pictures you shoot this way not only have less distortion, but also make the viewer feel more involved with the subject.

Figure 10-13:
Stoop to kid's-eye level for pictures of children. This both prevents distortion and engages your subject more fully.

© Mark Ewing

Photo fashions for photogenic kids

A couple of styling suggestions about photographing kids: If you have the chance, dress the kids in clothes that aren't distracting. Don't let a baby-clothes maker's oversized logo take the attention off your child (unless, of course, you plan to enter that company's photo contest!). Keep clothes simple, not too brightly colored or heavily patterned, so that they don't compete with delicate skin tones. Soft, textured clothing is often a good choice because it gives a feeling of substance to clothes without being distracting.

Also, consider having toys around, both to hold the child's interest and as props. Choose them with care, though. They shouldn't be big, brightly colored, or plastic. Wooden blocks are a classic choice.

And one final note about photographing your kids: As they get older — as the infatuation with a newborn and the fascination with a toddler mellow into familiar love — you may find yourself taking fewer and fewer pictures of them. Don't let this happen, if only for your kids' sake. Your pictures will become a big part of their family history. As they grow up and their heads get filled with the minutiae of adult responsibility, your pictures will serve as the main catalyst for their memory. So make that record as complete as you possibly can. Your kids will thank you.

Photographing Pets

Pets are more stalwart photographic subjects than kids, or grownups for that matter. They don't groan "Oh, no, not again!" when you raise the camera to your eye. They don't make funny faces or deliberately stick their tongues out to thwart your photographic endeavors. (Dogs pant, of course.) While they can be just as active as kids — and as much of a photographic challenge when they speed around — they also actually *like* to take naps. Nap time is a good time to get pet pictures.

Otherwise, though, many of the same photographic techniques that apply to taking photos of kids work with pets, too. (See "Photographing Children," earlier in this chapter.) Be sure to get down to their eye level. Unless you have a pet llama or a horse, pets are even lower to the ground than kids.

With cats and dogs, you can get easier eye-level pictures by snapping them when they perch on a window sill or, if allowed, a favorite chair.

Your pet no doubt has some distinctive behavior, often comical (see Figure 10-14). My old family dog used to study ants, nose inches from the ground, head cocked to one side for a one-eyed microscopic view. (It was a perfect opportunity for a ground-level shot.) Our new cat likes to lie flat on her back on our bedroom carpet with her legs straight up in the air, staring at us upside down. Photographing interesting and amusing pet behaviors is a kind of substitute for the fact that animals don't have a child's range of facial expression, at least to human eyes. Pet pictures may otherwise have a certain sameness to them. Their context — environments, behaviors, settings, and so on — becomes especially important.

Figure 10-14:
Pets are great photographic performers. Knowing her dog's fondness for chocolate chip cookies, this photographer set the stage (milk and all) and lay in wait with her camera.

© Annette Feuz/courtesy Kodak/KINSA

For the same reason, you should show pets interacting with family members. They are, after all, a part of the family. These pictures can, of course, be candid: playing fetch, chasing a string, getting a tummy rub. Or they can be more posed — a pet in your arms or on your lap.

I think that making eye contact with pets is just as important as with kids. (See the section "Should kids look at the camera?" earlier in this chapter.) Call out to them when you're ready to take the shot. With pets, expression is almost entirely in the eyes. Indeed, a true dog or cat person will tell you that the eyes are the window to a pet's soul.

Unfortunately, that soul may seem to come from the dark side when flash turns those eyes red — or green, as often happens with pets. Red-eye and green-eye are a special problem with pets (see Chapter 7). With cats in particular, the large area of their eyes relative to their faces compounds the problem. You can use your camera's red-eye reduction system to lessen the effect. But depending on your particular system, there's a long delay between when you press the shutter button and when the picture is actually taken. This delay can cause you to lose the moment you wanted to capture. And pets aren't in the habit of waiting around. You find better remedies for this problem in Chapter 7.

Photographs as Family History

Photographs have become icons of human events and achievements: a spacesuited Neil Armstrong on the moon; John-John Kennedy saluting his slain father; a World War II sailor planting a kiss on a female celebrant in Times Square; a craggy Abraham Lincoln just days before his assassination. Indeed, our sense of recent human history revolves around photographic images.

The same is true on a personal level, the level of *family* history. Photographs passed on from one generation to the next — of ancestors in their Sunday best, the grandparents' homestead, mother as a young bride, yourself as a pinkish newborn — are imprinted as much in your head as on the paper that backs them. With such images, in fact, separating what's in the mind from what's in the photograph itself is hard. Memory and photograph become inextricably linked.

So when you feel too lazy to get out your camera, motivate yourself with the reminder that any picture you take could end up becoming a family icon — an important piece of family history. Your photos are more likely to become icons, however, if they capture the essence of a family member, a family tradition, a family place, or a family experience. And *you're* more likely to capture that essence if you work harder at being a photographer.

People — family and friends, children and parents — probably get most of your photographic attention. And your people pictures will usually have more visual impact if you fill the frame — that is, move close or zoom in to make the subject occupy a large part of the picture area. But sometimes, for the sake of history, stepping back is important — both literally and figuratively. By stepping back, you show your subject in *context* (see Figure 10-15).

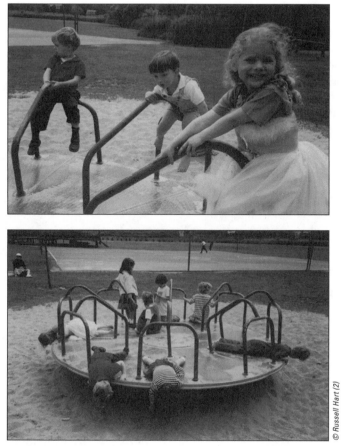

Figure 10-15: Moving close (top) is an important way to get better pictures. But you can provide a valuable sense of context with a "wide" shot, too (bottom).

© Russell Hart (2)

When you photograph the kids romping with the dog in the backyard, for example, take a few pictures that show the *whole* backyard, with its occupants smaller in the frame. When you photograph Fido in his favorite chair, take a few pictures that show the whole living room. And after you shoot that tight photo of your five-year-old on the first day of school, back up and take another that shows as much of the school as possible.

For that matter, you don't always need to include people in these pictures of important places. The backyard, the living room, or the school is a fine subject in itself, especially if you take care to compose the photo in an interesting and meaningful way, in interesting, even beautiful, light.

Consider your house, if you own or rent one. If you take pictures of its exterior over the months and years, you have an incremental record of its changes — seasonal patterns of light and foliage, the growth of trees and plantings, new paint. In fact, try shooting at least one picture from the same position each time, for a sort of time-lapse effect.

Photographing your possessions

Sharing your life and preserving your memories may be the most compelling reasons to take photographs. But there are practical reasons, too — uses that may not even occur to you. Looking for a shower head to match your bathroom faucets? You can't bring the faucets to the store, so bring pictures of them with you instead. A tree fall on your garage, heaven forbid? Take pictures of the damage from every angle, *right away*, in case your insurance company has any questions about it after the debris has been cleared.

In fact, photographing all your most important or valuable earthly belongings is a good idea. If your home or apartment burns or is burglarized, the pictures are the proof of possession you present to the insurance agent — more convincing evidence than your mere verbal vouching. (Oh, and keep those pictures of your possessions in a safe, fireproof place; see Chapter 3 for more on storing negatives and prints.)

Your home's interior — whether apartment or house — goes through similar changes over the months and years. As you rearrange the furniture, acquire new things, repaint and remodel, you alter the feeling of the rooms. Document each phase, especially if you plan to make changes. Think about how an old photograph of a room in a former house can evoke powerful memories and feelings from its time. Think about how kids' rooms change with the growth and youthful fascinations of their occupants.

Neighborhoods change likewise. Whether you live in the city, the suburbs, or the country, make regular pictures of familiar street corners, back alleys, storefronts, shortcuts, the view of neighbors' yards. These pictures become especially meaningful if and when you move to a new home, a new neighborhood, or a new city or state.

At first, such photographs may not seem as interesting as pictures of people, and taking them might seem a bore. But if you have the right attitude, you won't find the task boring at all — nor are the pictures strictly for the historical record. A carefully considered, well-made photograph of a seemingly ordinary object or place can transform it, letting you see it in a new light, sometimes literally. Light is particularly transforming: In the right light, even the most mundane subject can look astonishingly beautiful. (For more on lighting, see Chapter 8.) In this and other ways, photographs give you a better appreciation of the world that surrounds you — and might just be history in the making.

Party pix

It goes without saying that some of the best opportunities for people photography happen at parties. Whether a wedding reception, birthday bash, or New Year's Eve celebration, party time is a perfect time to get out your camera and fire at will. Here are some important pointers for party pictures.

✔ Photograph party preparation and cleanup. Get shots of the nicest food spreads before guests gobble them up, and the decorations before they're trashed. Afterward, present the pictures as gifts to the hosts.

✔ Concentrate on the most animated groups but make portraits of individuals, too.

✔ Look for groups that seem to hold together visually. Avoid groups with individuals whose backs are to the camera or who block the camera's view of others in the group.

✔ If the gathering is a rare or once-in-a-lifetime event — a family reunion, for example — try to photograph everyone there. If you leave someone out, you may regret it later.

✔ Bring appropriate family and friends together for loosely posed group portraits.

✔ Suggest making a group shot of everyone there.

✔ For better background detail with indoor party shots, set your point-and-shoot to its slow-sync mode, if possible, or if it doesn't offer this, fill-flash mode.

✔ Always have double sets of prints made. This gives you one set to give away to the people you photograph, and a second set to keep.

Ten Lame Excuses for Not Taking Along Your Camera (And Why They're Lame)

You may find lots of photo ops around your home and neighborhood, but you'll also want to shoot special occasions and your travels, too. This chapter and Chapter 13 are full of advice about taking those kinds of pictures. Here's a little motivational roster — a few of the many ways you can talk yourself out of taking your camera along, and my rebuttals of each!

1. **The camera's too heavy.** Then buy a lightweight point-and-shoot camera. Or get a padded shoulder strap.

2. **The camera's too big.** Get a pocket-sized point-and-shoot — or buy a one-time-use camera when you get where you're going.

3. **Taking pictures interferes with the experience.** Yes, you have to pause to shoot in the middle of whatever you're doing or wherever you are. This routine becomes second nature. If you don't do it, you'll regret it later, when you have no pictures with which to remember.

_____

4. **The friends I'm with will think I'm obnoxious.** It's your life — and photography is your passion. Send them some flattering pictures of themselves and you'll soon become their official photographer.

5. **Nothing important is going to happen.** You never know. The best photographic opportunities are unexpected.

6. **I forgot to buy film.** Unacceptable. You can buy film almost anywhere. And you should have a few extra rolls in reserve.

7. **My battery is dead.** Sorry. You should always keep an extra battery handy, especially if your camera uses lithium batteries. These batteries may be hard to find, or very expensive, in faraway places. (See Chapter 1 for more on batteries.)

8. **My camera is broken.** It may not be. See Chapter 20 for some trouble-shooting tips. If trying those things doesn't make it work, buy a one-time-use camera for now. Then replace the camera with an inexpensive point-and-shoot.

9. **Photography is too hard.** Nonsense. The automation in today's point-and-shoot cameras nearly eliminates the technical decisions that used to make snapshot photography such a bother.

10. **I'm not artistic.** Let me raise your self-esteem: A few simple tips and techniques can make you a much better photographer than you ever thought possible. That's why you bought this book!

Chapter 11

Snapping Action

. . . .

In This Chapter

▶ Showing action with still photos

▶ Prefocusing ahead of the action

▶ Overcoming your point-and-shoot's time delay

▶ Freezing versus blurring

▶ Using fast film to freeze action

▶ Panning to follow action

▶ Freezing action with flash

▶ Showing action with blur

. . . .

*A*ction photography could just be the most popular and admired form of picture-taking, especially in our sports- and fitness-happy society. But when you think about it, it's really a remarkable contradiction.

Action photography captures *movement* — in *still* photographs! And that's precisely what makes photographs of action subjects so compelling. The still photo, by taking one brief moment of a continuing action — be it a pro football play or your budding gymnast somersaulting in the backyard — lets you look at the action again and again. A great action shot is an instant captured for an eternity. In this chapter, I tell you all you need to know to capture action with your point-and-shoot.

You Don't Need Fancy Equipment to Shoot Action

With all due respect to video, I don't think a moving picture crystallizes movement quite the way a good action shot does. Ever notice, in TV sports, what video directors do in instant replays of close plays — like a late throw to first base or a pass caught right on the sideline? They slow down the tape and then stop it outright at the critical moment: the runner's foot touching first base or the receiver's toes staying just inbounds. In other words, they show you exactly the sort of frozen action that a good sports photographer nails for the front page of the sports section.

"Yes," you're muttering, "exactly the sort of picture I don't have a prayer of getting with my Zippymatic Zoom." Wrong. I'm not going to snow you and say that you can get the same results as pros who use high-speed camera equipment. But the most important component of action photography has nothing to do with equipment. It has to do with timing — with anticipating the critical moment and honing your reflexes to hit the shutter button when it arrives! (See Figure 11-1.)

Your Dawdling Point-and-Shoot Camera

Point-and-shoot cameras, though, can have their quirks when you're trying to shoot fast action. You've probably noticed that your point-and-shoot doesn't necessarily fire right away when you press the shutter button, perhaps because the flash needs to recharge some more or because the camera takes a moment or two to focus. But the other problem is that the lens aperture — the window in the lens — isn't very big on most point-and-shoots. So the window has to stay open longer to gather light from the subject, making it hard to stop the action cold.

Figure 11-1: You don't need special high-speed photo gear to capture action. This rafting shot was made with a Kodak Fun Saver Weekend 35 camera — a waterproof one-time-use model.

© Don Cochran/courtesy Kodak

You can often overcome these problems, though, with special action-oriented techniques. Some techniques require a bit of practice. So get ready to shoot a lot of film!

If you plan to practice shooting the same action over and over again, you can save a considerable amount of money on processing by getting the film developed (made into negatives) but not printed. (The usual cost for develop-only orders with 35mm film is only about $2 to $3.) Later, you can look at the negatives and get the best takes printed. If you use an APS camera, you can get the film developed, plus an index print only. (With 35mm, you can get an index print for a couple more dollars, if your photofinisher offers this service.) The index print makes it easier to pick out the good frames. (See Chapter 3 for more on index prints.)

The Anticipation Game: The Art of Prefocusing

To be a good action shooter, you have to keep your point-and-shoot from dawdling when you press the shutter button. The only way to do so reliably is by mastering a technique that may sound weird at first: Set up a photograph completely and be ready to shoot *without* your subject in the frame. Yes, you read that right. And now for the details.

For good action shots, *prefocus* your subject — that is, make the camera focus *before* the subject enters the picture. You could call this technique *surrogate focusing* because you prefocus on something that's at about the same distance, and in about the same light, as your action subject.

Prefocusing is basically the same thing as locking your focus. (See Chapter 6 for more on this.) The difference is that you lock the focus a little ahead of time — before your subject has entered the viewfinder frame. Here's how to prefocus your action subject:

1. **Choose a stationary object that your moving subject will pass by at a close distance.**

   Some possibilities: a tree, a fence, third base, the goalpost, a parked car, even a friend or bystander.

2. **Lock the focus on the object.**

   Center the viewfinder's focus point on the object and press the shutter button halfway down to lock your focus.

3. **While holding the shutter button halfway down, re-aim the camera to establish your desired composition.**

   Compose so that your action subject — skateboarder, runner, and so on — will be entirely within the frame when you shoot.

4. Hold that focus until your subject enters the frame.

5. Push the shutter button all the way down to take the picture.

Prefocusing is a crucial skill in action photography, and every action technique I describe in this chapter requires it. So I can't overstate the importance of prefocusing. But if you haven't fully mastered the basic procedure needed to lock your point-and-shoot's focus, you might have a little trouble with this technique. Now's the time to practice until you have it down pat. For action prefocusing, you should be able to lock the focus and hold it for a good bit of time — maybe as long as 30 seconds. Practice with an unloaded camera until you have a shooting finger of steel!

Those of you with *focus-free cameras* — that is, models with no autofocus capability — don't need to prefocus. But focus-free cameras usually have some firing delay, for other reasons. So most techniques I describe in this chapter apply to these models as well.

You may ask yourself: If I prefocus on some other object, won't my main subject be a little out of focus? Possibly. But if it is, that's a very worthwhile tradeoff. Capturing the action at just the right moment is far more important to the success of an action photo than getting a flawlessly focused picture. If you choose your prefocusing spot carefully, the little difference in focusing distances won't seriously mar your picture. And even in *stop-action* point-and-shoot pictures, you're likely to get a little image blur anyway — though I tell you how to minimize that later in this chapter in "Tips for Better Action-Freezing."

Your actual subject doesn't have to be out of the frame while you prefocus, by the way. Think of a fast-moving gymnast working on a balance beam or pommel horse. If you try to focus on the gymnast, the camera may get fooled — focusing right past the athlete on the opposite wall, for example. Even if the camera focuses properly on the gymnast, you may miss some good action because of the extra time the camera needs to get ready and set. But prefocusing on the balance beam or the pommel horse is a simple matter. Then just hold that focus by keeping the shutter button halfway down and wait for an interesting move.

Don't get the action shakes! You may be so intent on hitting the shutter button fast that you jerk the camera when you take the picture. This can lead to even more blur in your pictures than a fast-moving athlete creates. Get a firm grip on your camera, tuck your elbows in tight against your body — and now *relax*. Concentrate on *squeezing* the shutter button — clench your fist as you fire the camera — rather than *pushing down* on the shutter button. And make sure that your finger never leaves the shutter button, before, during, or after the shot.

Why prefocus?

Chapter 4 explains that pressing the shutter button halfway down gives your camera a rather complex set of electronic instructions. Under the best conditions, these instructions take maybe half a second to get your camera into what you might call "standby" status. (If the flash needs to recharge, this time can stretch out to four or five seconds or more; if the camera can't focus correctly, it won't fire at all.)

A half-second delay doesn't make much difference when photographing your toddler's early steps. He's not going anywhere very fast, so you can lock the focus and snap away pretty comfortably. When the toddler graduates to a tricycle, it's still no problem — you usually have enough time to lock focus as the child wheels by at all of two miles per hour. But when that former toddler gets a two-wheeler, you'll have to set up to take an action shot. Otherwise, you'll end up pressing the shutter button frantically as he comes speeding by, only to get . . . a fine shot of shrubbery.

As action speeds up, that little prefocusing delay becomes impossibly long. I'm not talking 200-mph race cars here. Even people walking at a brisk pace can beat the time delay of a typical point-and-shoot.

So here's the way to snap your budding cyclist: Find a spot along his path that he'll pass close to. For example, if he's pedaling along a dirt trail that goes right in front of your backyard fence, then set up to take a picture *exactly* as you would if he stood in front of the fence. Adjust your framing (with your feet or zoom lens) and then lock the focus *on the fence* (again, by pressing the shutter button halfway) and hold it there. When your bicyclist rides into the frame, press the shutter button all the way down.

Frozen or Blurred Action?

A camera gives you two main ways to convey a sense of action in a still photograph. One is by *freezing* the action — that is, taking a picture within such a short time interval that the subject seems to stop cold. (Indeed, such photos are sometimes called *stop-action* shots.) The other way to convey a sense of action is by capturing the subject's movement across space — in plain terms, *blurring* its motion. These two methods, freezing and blurring, can even be combined in a *single* picture to create what is often the most effective photographic rendition of action of all. I tell you how to do that in "Capturing action with panning" and "Combining stop action and blur" later in this chapter.

Freezing and blurring are really just variations on each other. You can think of the stop-action shot as a thin slice of time: the tennis racquet frozen in midswing with the ball suspended in midair. Blurring, on the other hand, is a thicker slice of time: the tennis racquet and player's arm forming a wide, blurry arc across the picture frame, with the streak of the tennis ball ahead of it.

Freezing action with fast shutter speeds

To freeze action effectively, you need to take as thin a slice of time as possible. One way to do this is with a fast shutter speed. (See Chapter 2.)

The other method of stopping action is to use electronic flash, which illuminates your subject with an extremely short burst of light. Though you can sometimes use flash outdoors for action, the best way to stop action in bright light is with a fast shutter speed.

Different point-and-shoots have different top shutter speeds — that is, the shortest (or, more correctly, the *highest*) shutter speed they can set. Some models can set only wimpy top speeds of $1/250$ second or even $1/200$ second. Others can go as high as $1/700$ or $1/1000$ second. Most current point-and-shoot cameras above the $100 mark have a top shutter speed of about $1/500$ second — not too shabby. This speed is usually high enough to freeze a runner, making his arms and legs motionless in midstride. If the camera can only go as high as $1/250$ second, the runner's arms and legs may show signs of blur.

Manuals ordinarily list a camera's highest possible shutter speed in their specifications section. If you have a camera with a shutter speed no higher than $1/250$ second, you can still use all the techniques I describe in this chapter. Just keep in mind that you may not get *fully frozen* stop-action shots — you may have a bit more blur in them.

You've probably noticed, though, that you can't set the shutter speed on your point-and-shoot. *The camera sets the shutter speed for you.* After all, you bought a point-and-shoot camera so that you wouldn't have to worry about stuff like that, right? So, when you want to shoot action subjects, how do you make sure your camera sets as high a shutter speed as it can? By following the same advice I give throughout this book: Use fast film.

Fast action requires fast film! If you want to stop action, use as fast a film as possible in your camera (see Figure 11-2). Even outdoors, use ISO 800 film. In lower light, or for indoor action, you may want to go with an ISO 1600 color print film, or even an ISO 3200 color print film. Not sure that your camera accepts fast film? Take another look at your camera manual's specifications page to find out. If you don't have a manual, open up the back of your unloaded camera and look in the chamber where the film cassette goes. Do you see four metallic contacts in a row? Then your camera most likely can use films up to ISO 3200 in speed. Only two or three contacts? Then your camera is limited to ISO 400 or 800 films. (For more information on film speeds, see Chapter 2.)

Advanced Photo System users: The fastest APS films available are ISO 400, and all APS cameras accept this speed.

ISO 100 film

ISO 200 film

ISO 400 film

ISO 800 film

© *Russell Hart (4)*

Figure 11-2: The faster the film you use, the better your point-and-shoot will be able to freeze action. With ISO 100 film, this sliding boy is a total blur; only with ISO 800 film is he totally sharp. The moral: Use ISO 800 film (at least) whenever you shoot fast-moving subjects.

Because fast film needs less light than slow film to make a good picture, using it means the shutter — that window in the lens — need not stay open for as long a time. In other words, your camera sets a higher shutter speed, provided the light is reasonably bright to begin with. And this higher shutter speed freezes the subject better.

Using a fast film for action subjects is even more crucial if you like to zoom in with your lens to make the subject bigger in the frame. Why? Because as you zoom in more, the little window in the lens (the lens aperture) gets smaller. And the smaller the window, the longer it must stay open to get the correct amount of light to the film — that is, the slower the shutter speed must be. The slower the shutter speed, the less well the camera can freeze action (see Figure 11-3). So if you like to zoom in close to the action, use at least an ISO 800 film for action subjects — even outdoors in bright light.

Stash the flash! In some bright-light situations, your point-and-shoot camera may automatically fire its flash — even if you've got fast film loaded. The reason? Quite a few models have light meters that are sensitive to backlight or to other kinds of lighting that create prominent shadows in the subject. (See Chapter 8 for more on backlight.) If these light meters detect backlight, they tell the camera to fire the flash to compensate. And as mentioned, this can slow down your shooting, the last thing you want with an action subject. To avoid the problem, just set the flash-off mode.

Once you load up with fast film and get used to the prefocus technique (see the section "The Anticipation Game: The Art of Prefocusing," earlier in this chapter), you're ready for all kinds of daylight action:

> ✔ **The Little Leaguer charging first base:** From a position off the first-base side of the field, prefocus on the base or the ground around it, and the instant the little slugger runs into the frame, fire.

Figure 11-3: Because it makes your point-and-shoot set a higher shutter speed, fast ISO 400 or 800 film (left) freezes moving water better than a slower film (right).

© Pat O'Hara (2)

✔ **Your daughter on the backyard swing:** Prefocus on the part of the swing frame closest to her. When she reaches the apex of her swing — its slowest and most easily frozen point — shoot!

✔ **The swimming pool belly flop:** Prefocus on the deck at the edge of the pool (or the diver herself, if she stops to look before she leaps). When she takes the plunge, fire.

Finding the decisive moment

If you've already taken pictures of fast action like base running or diving, though, you may have noticed a pattern. Your little slugger is already past the bag. Or the belly flop is just a splash — because the diver's already underwater. Even if you prefocus the shot, you *still* have a short delay between when you press the shutter button and when the shutter actually opens for the shot. And that delay can combine with your delay in reacting to the subject's action to make you miss the slice of time you meant to cut.

A slight time delay when taking pictures of your toddler toddling across the backyard probably amounts to half a baby step — not so critical. But with a speeding two-wheeler, it's another story. Say that you prefocused on your backyard fence in anticipation of your cyclist's arrival; if you wait to push the shutter button until the bike is *centered* in the frame, it may be partially *out* of the frame by the time the shutter actually opens.

So the trick is not only to anticipate the moment when your subject will reach the correct position, but to fire *slightly in advance* of it. To get that two-wheeler in the right position, for example, you may have to press the shutter button when it's just halfway into the viewfinder frame. You might try keeping both eyes open as you're looking through your camera — don't squint your other eye closed — so that you can see your action subject approaching out of the corner of your nonshooting eye. You can also prefocus, hold the shutter button halfway down, and look *over* the camera to see when your action subject is approaching. Then look back through the viewfinder at the last second to snap the picture.

Different cameras have different time delays, so you need to listen for the click of the shutter firing. (When you hear the whirr of the motor advancing the film to the next frame, you know the shot is over.) After a while, you get to know the delay of your camera pretty well and know instinctively how much in advance you have to press the button. Remember that your response should speed up with the speed of your subject. You don't need to fire as much in advance for a tentative tricyclist as for that speeding two-wheeler. It takes practice — and you can't really gauge your success with an unloaded camera. You need the feedback of processed negatives or prints.

Tips for Better Action-Freezing

If you use an ISO 800 film for your action shots and get blur even in bright light, you can probably assume that your point-and-shoot just can't set a shutter speed high enough to freeze really fast action. So here are a few special techniques that should help you get the sharpest possible shot — techniques used even by professional sports photographers with their super-high shutter speeds.

✔ **Catch the peak of the action:** When a basketball player jumps up for a rebound, she's moving pretty fast. And when she comes down with the ball, she's moving pretty fast, too. But when she reaches the highest point of her jump, there is a brief moment when she moves neither up nor down — when she's nearly suspended in space. In fact, when films were less sensitive to light and arena lights were less bright, sports photographers waited for such moments because they knew they could get away with the pretty slow shutter speed that they had to use.

For indoor basketball shots, flash is usually a better approach to freezing the action. (I cover flash techniques in the section "Freezing action with flash.") But if you can't use flash, or you want to shoot only by the existing light, you can get pretty good stop action by timing the shot for the top of the jump. (Just be sure to prefocus on the basket.) See the section "The Anticipation Game: The Art of Prefocusing," earlier in this chapter, for more on prefocusing.

What's more, the peak of any action is often the best moment photographically (see Figure 11-4). The moment a high jumper goes over the bar is also the slowest he moves at any point from run-up to landing. (Prefocus on the high-jump bar.) The high point of a springboard diver's trajectory is also the slowest. (Prefocus on the diving board.)

✔ **Shoot action as head-on as possible:** The angle at which an action subject is moving relative to your camera position has a big effect on how blurred it appears in your picture. If you photograph something moving at a right angle to your line of fire, the chance of blur is greatest: Think of how quickly a toddler on a two-wheeler passes from one side of the viewfinder frame to the other. But if you photograph the cyclist coming at you from an angle, her position changes less quickly and the chance of blur is reduced. If you photograph the cyclist coming at you head-on, her position stays more or less the same — she gets bigger in the frame, of course, so mind your distance — and the chance of blur is far less.

Shooting head-on is clearly not the ticket for speeding trains, but it has many safe applications — shooting a little one coming down a playground slide, for example. If you take the picture as he comes down straight at you, you're likely to see less blur than if you take the shot from the side (see Figure 11-5). And you just might get a livelier picture!

Figure 11-4: If you time your shot so that the action is at its peak — in this case, at a leap's high point, before the subject begins to descend — you have a better shot at freezing it. Prefocus so that the camera won't delay.

© Janalee Stock/courtesy Kodak/KINSA

Figure 11-5: To reduce the chance of blur with a fast-passing subject (left), shoot it from an angle (center) or even head-on (right).

© Mark Harris (3)

✔ **Shoot action from a distance:** When you stand beside a road, cars seem to whiz by faster than you can turn your head. But when you look at cars as they approach from a distance, you can follow them more easily. The farther away an action subject is, the less quickly its position changes as it moves. Now, I'm not suggesting that you photograph a track meet from a quarter mile away. But you might keep in mind that photographing runners on the far turn gives you better stop action than if you photograph them right from the edge of the track as they run by you.

✔ **Pan the action:** *Panning* is an action-shooting technique that requires violating one of the sacred rules of still photography: holding your camera steady. Instead, you move your camera along with the subject, actually taking the picture as you do (see Figure 11-6). The idea is to keep the subject in about the same place in the frame, instead of allowing it to move across the frame. If the subject doesn't move across the frame when you take the picture — that is, quickly changing its position — the chance of blur is less.

Capturing action with panning

To envision how panning works, think of riding on a merry-go-round. If you look off to the side and keep your eyes dead ahead, everything goes by in a blur. But if you turn your head rapidly, you can fix on a person or thing and keep it sharp as you speed by. Panning is simply following a moving subject in much the same way, with your camera rather than your eyes.

One visually interesting side-effect of panning is that you often get a little selective blur in the picture, and this can strongly evoke movement. A runner's torso may freeze, for example, but his faster moving arms and legs may be blurred, suggesting his fast pace. A bicyclist might be quite sharp, but her faster moving spokes, pedals, and feet blur, suggesting speed. And,

Figure 11-6: Successful panning — moving the camera as you take the picture to keep an action subject in the same place in the frame — keeps the subject sharp, but causes interesting streaks in the background.

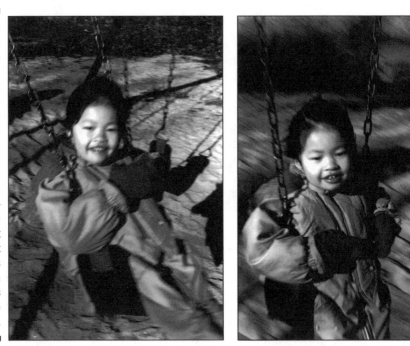

no panning   with panning

© Russell Hart (2)

finally, panning also blurs the background. Background blur creates a dynamic feeling in an action shot, as if you're pedaling right beside that bicyclist. Blur also softens distracting backgrounds, placing more emphasis on the action subject itself.

Here's how you get a panned shot of a moving subject:

1. **Prefocus on an object that your subject will pass in front of and continue to hold down the shutter button halfway.**

   For more on prefocusing, see the section "The Anticipation Game: The Art of Prefocusing," earlier in this chapter.

2. **As your subject approaches, instead of keeping your camera pointed at the original object and waiting for him to pass by, point the camera at him.**

   Now swing your camera to keep the viewfinder glued to him as he moves along, trying hard to keep him in the same part of the frame.

3. **When your subject is right in front of the object you prefocused in Step 1, press the shutter button as you continue to pan.**

   Keep following your subject with the camera even after you take the picture, because this gives you a smooth panning action (sort of like following through on a golf swing).

Expect to blow a few pictures at first. Practice by panning your camera without film. Find a busy road and pan cars as they go by. Don't press the shutter button at first; concentrate on smoothness. Then work on prefocusing and firing the shutter.

One more thing. When you really get the hang of following a moving subject smoothly, you discover that you can actually focus on it *while* you're panning, provided it stays about the same distance away and you keep it in the center of the frame. (Centering the subject keeps the viewfinder's focus point on it, where it needs to be for such on-the-fly autofocus.) So you don't necessarily *have* to prefocus on something else at the same distance. Just follow through with one smooth button press, locking the focus and taking the picture all at once.

Freezing action with flash

Your point-and-shoot camera has a not-so-secret weapon for taking stop-action photos: its built-in electronic flash. Using flash should be your technique of choice for action shots indoors, as well as outdoors in low light or at modest distances.

Be a one-time-use panner!

Those ubiquitous one-time-use point-and-shoots are, as you might have guessed, really not the best kind of camera for action photography. They have only one shutter speed, in fact, and it's a fairly slow one — not what you need for freezing a subject. But that's exactly why you should try panning action with them instead! Any moderately fast-moving subject in daylight — kids running, for example — works well. Just follow the panning techniques I describe in this section and get in pretty tight on your subject. (You won't be able to prefocus, of course, because one-time-use cameras have fixed-focus lenses.)

Electronic flash freezes action very effectively because it is, oddly enough, a slice of time within a slice of time. When you take an ordinary flash shot with your camera set to autoflash — the default setting — the shutter opens up for a brief period that is usually too short to expose the film properly by the existing light. But within that brief time the shutter opens, the flash fires. Electronic flash is basically a very bright spark with a very short duration — $1/1000$ of a second or $1/2000$ of a second on most point-and-shoot cameras. Because the flash lights your subject only for that short spark, it nicely freezes your subject in the picture.

However, you have to worry about three things when using flash for action shots: Distance, distance, and distance. If you're too far away from the subject for your flash to light it properly, you get a weak, muddy picture (see Chapters 3 and 7). And a picture in which you can barely make out your subject doesn't make for much of an action shot. So always use at least ISO 400 speed film, and preferably ISO 800, for indoor flash action. Move in as close as possible to the action, which makes your pictures better anyway. And zoom out to wider-angle focal lengths, which make your lens's window bigger so that it admits more light and gives your flash range a boost.

Other than that, using flash to stop action involves pretty much the same techniques as shooting stop-action pictures in existing light, as described in "The Anticipation Game: The Art of Prefocusing," earlier in this chapter. Prefocusing is particularly important with flash action shots. For one thing, pressing the shutter button halfway keeps the flash charged up. For another, your autofocus camera has to know the distance to the subject to determine the proper flash exposure.

Flash action shots eat batteries! You may have a frustrating time trying to take a series of flash shots with weak batteries, because your camera will take a long time to recycle the flash between shots — preventing you from taking the picture until it does. This delay gets longer the more you shoot. So start out with fresh batteries and bring spares.

Indoor basketball is a good opportunity for flash action. Suppose you want to get a picture of a layup shot or a rebound. You should position yourself off the sideline in such a way that you have a reasonably clear shot of the basket, within the flash range of your camera. As the player moves the ball toward the basket, prefocus on the rim of the basket or the bottom of the backboard. As long as you can hold focus steadily, you can look away from your viewfinder to monitor the action of the game. And be prepared to fire a little ahead of the action. Just remember that you won't be able to shoot at the same pace you do outdoors, because the flash has to recharge. Recharging takes at least three or four seconds between shots.

Don't be a flashing nuisance! School and local league indoor athletics provide good opportunities for action photography, but officials may restrict flash shooting close to the sidelines. Check with the leagues to see whether you need permission. (They might even authorize you to stand in a good shooting spot, if you ask.)

Autoflash is the best flash mode for indoor action shooting. It keeps the shutter open a fairly short time, with the flash providing most or all of the light for the picture. But you might find, if you loaded up with very fast film and are shooting in a well-lit area, that your camera suppresses the flash. In this case, you have to change the camera from autoflash to fill-flash mode.

Showing action with blur

Freezing action is fun, but blur isn't necessarily a bad thing in action shots. A trace of blur in the subject often says *action!* more than a completely frozen effect. And, depending on your point-and-shoot model, you may get some degree of blur whenever you shoot an action subject, even with an ISO 800 film.

If you want even more blur, moving the camera is one easy way to get it — and it doesn't have to be panning movement. You can move your camera against the direction of the action, or at angles to it. You can even jiggle the camera or move it up and down. In other words, *you* can add the blur. If you do it right, the blur will look as if it's somehow the consequence of the subject's movement, not what you did with the camera. Regardless, you get interesting streaky, smeary effects — instant abstraction.

Another simple way to up the amount of blur is switching to a slower film, though this option is a bit of heresy in this book. A slower film makes the camera set a slower shutter speed. If you get good stop-action shots with ISO 400 film, for example, try shooting with an ISO 200 film. Want still more blur? Try an ISO 100 film. And while you're at it, try panning with these slower films.

You can also increase your blur potential *without* switching film, simply by shooting in different light. If you get sharp stop-action shots in midday light, shoot in late afternoon or on an overcast day. Shooting in less bright light usually causes the camera to set a lower shutter speed and ups the chance of blur.

Combining stop action and blur

Can a picture be sharp and blurry at the same time? Actually, yes. And the effect is often more powerfully suggestive of action than either stop-action or blur effects. Better still, most point-and-shoot cameras make it pretty easy to accomplish.

Remember that your camera gives you two basic ways of making an exposure — that is, getting light from the subject to the film. One is to shoot in daylight, or good indoor light, without flash. In this case, you make the picture by the existing light. The other way of making an exposure is to add light — to shoot by flash.

Suppose that you're shooting action pictures in existing light that's okay but not great. You're likely to get at least a little blur. Now suppose that you decide to use flash. The flash's spark freezes the action at that split second, of course. But the film also takes in some of the existing light, recording it as a streaky blur. Voilà — a picture in which one moment of the action is frozen, in the midst of a blur. You can think of it as two pictures taken simultaneously on one piece of film.

When you use flash and get a sharp moving subject with blurry streaks around it, the effect is called *flash ghosting.* I like the effect of flash ghosting — call it blurred sharpness. Flash ghosting adds to the sense of action and can also improve a shot by filling in dark shadows.

Here's how to get flash ghosting in action shots. (For more on specific flash techniques, see Chapter 7.)

✔ **Ghosting with fill flash (flash-on):** Switching your camera to its fill-flash mode (rather than autoflash or flash-off modes) when taking stop-action shots in bright light almost always adds at least a slight ghost. Try the fill-flash mode with runners, or cyclists, or just the kids scooting around the backyard (see Figure 11-7). In fact, try these shots with and without fill flash and compare the results. Remember that you must be close enough to your subject to be within the range of your flash; otherwise, the flash has no effect in the picture.

The slower the film, or the lower the light, the more flash ghosting you see. The camera lowers the shutter speed in these cases to get enough light to the film, making the blurred stuff blurrier still.

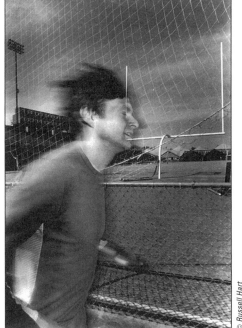

Figure 11-7:
Fill flash froze this runner in his tracks, but the film also recorded existing daylight — creating both a blurry fringe around the figure and a sharp background.

© Russell Hart

✔ **Ghosting with slow-sync flash (night flash):** This mode, which allows the shutter to stay open for a longer time than with fill-flash mode, produces an effect similar to that of fill flash, but with more pronounced blur. Again, the blur is more exaggerated with lower light or slower film; after a certain point, the blurry part of the picture looks more like an abstract painting than a photo. Indoors, you can get heavy-duty art effects with moving subjects, such as people dancing.

✔ **Panning with flash:** You can add flash to any panning picture as long as your subject is within flash range. Just follow the subject with your camera. (See the section "Capturing action with panning," earlier in this chapter.) With fill flash, panning may actually slightly lessen the blur if you do it right. And if you're good at it, you can use panning with your camera's slow-sync (night flash) mode, for very cool effects with subjects like cyclists and rollerbladers.

The Last Word on Action

While your local sandlot softball league or high school track team can provide you with great action photo ops, I hope I haven't given you the impression that action subjects need be limited to sports. The world around you is full of action ready for the shooting. A trip to your local zoo, for example, might net you a leaping monkey or a diving polar bear. Going to a wedding? Take your pocket point-and-shoot with you onto the dance floor, set it to slow-sync flash, and snap away; you'll get some wild and crazy shots, guaranteed. And speaking of formal events, don't forget graduation action shots. No kidding! Almost every graduation has some kind of post-ceremony horseplay, and you can always snap the graduate leaping in the air. Oh, and be sure to bring your weatherproof point-and-shoot along when you take the kids sledding.

One other note: Try not to get so carried away with capturing action that you forget to compose (see Chapter 9 for more on composition). Doing both at the same time takes practice, but even if your subject is fast-moving, you're still putting a frame around it.

In the mode for action

Many point-and-shoots have specialized modes that make action shooting a little easier — though they're no guarantee of good results. I describe these modes in some detail in Chapter 4. But here's a specific look at how you can use these modes for action shooting.

- ✔ **Sports or action mode:** On most point-and-shoot models, this mode simply turns off the flash and sets the motor to continuous film advance mode. Basically, it lets you fire off shots for as long as you hold down the shutter button. But you should know by now when to turn off — or turn on — your flash. And with a well-trained index finger, you can take pictures as fast as in the continuous film-advance mode.

  A few point-and-shoots (Canon *Z* models, for example) employ *continuous autofocusing* when set to action mode. They automatically adjust the focus to follow a moving subject right up to the moment they take the picture, rather than locking the focus at one distance. This feature can help especially in sports with unpredictable action, such as soccer.

- ✔ **Multiple flash (or flash multi):** This mode fires the flash several times during a single

exposure. It can give you interesting effects for gymnastic exercises, dancing, or any other fast movement taking place within a small area.

- ✔ **Multiple exposure (or multiexposure):** This mode prevents the film from automatically advancing to the next frame, so that you can layer several pictures on the same piece of film. It gives you interesting results indoors if you shoot events like gymnastics floor exercises in autoflash mode. Set the camera to multiple exposure and take a shot with the gymnast on one side of the picture frame. Now take another shot with the gymnast on the other side of the frame. (Try not to move the camera between shots.) The result shows the two moments in the same print.

- ✔ **Snap mode:** Snap mode is a fast-firing mode that simply turns off the camera's autofocus, prefocusing the lens at snapshot range — usually six feet or so. You can use this mode for shots of rambunctious kids because you don't have to prefocus at all, but it may limit your ability to set other modes at the same time.

A splash of action

Action photography can sometimes get you pretty wet. Whether you're shooting from a white-water raft or just snapping the kids running through the sprinkler, your camera may get wet, too. The problem is that water and most point-and-shoots don't mix. Camera electronics in particular can get zapped by moisture. If water sports, boating, and singin' in the rain are your idea of a good time, consider buying a weatherproof camera, or even a true waterproof camera.

✔ *Weatherproof* (also known as *splashproof*) means the camera has moisture seals that enable it to get wet, but not submerged. You can use a weatherproof camera in the rain (though not a torrential downpour) and in situations in which you might get splashed — poolside or aboard a cruising boat. A good number of current point-and-shoot models are weatherproof, usually designated with a "drops" sticker on the camera body.

✔ *Waterproof* (also known as *underwater*) means you can fully submerge the camera, usually to at least 10 or 15 feet. Take these models kayaking and white-water rafting, use them in sloppy rain or snow, and shoot at the pool — or should I say, *in* it. (Try the bathtub, too!)

Only a few true underwater point-and-shoots are available. In 35mm, consider the Canon A1, and in the Advanced Photo System, the Minolta Vectis Weathermatic Zoom. (You can also get special waterproof camera "baggies" designed for underwater operation of nonwaterproof point-and-shoots.)

And you can always shoot with one-time-use models. A standard one-time-use camera can take a modest splashing; you only use the camera for one roll of film, after all. And the encapsulated Kodak Fun Saver Sport and Fun Saver Weekend models can go to a depth of 14 feet. These models are a good choice when your wet-and-wild shooting is only occasional.

Finally, remember that some of the best action pictures are of the human drama after an event: an exhausted marathoner pouring water over his head, Little Leaguers mobbing the pitcher after the game-winning strikeout (see Figure 11-8). So don't put your camera down after the action has officially stopped. The game-winning play, after all, can be pretty dull — a called third strike or the deliberate downing of a football to run out the clock. Your reflexes and anticipation as a photographer count after the final buzzer, too!

Figure 11-8: Sports events are full of great moments that aren't about action itself. Here, a racetrack jockey excuses his poor performance to his horse's disgusted owners.

© Henry Horenstein

Chapter 12

Photographing Landscapes

- -

In This Chapter

▶ Finding landscapes nearby

▶ Wide-angle versus telephoto views

▶ Placing the horizon line

▶ Horizontal versus vertical composition

▶ Shooting panoramas

▶ Light and scale

▶ Seasonal changes

▶ Shooting cityscapes

- -

*I*n *my* photographic vocabulary, a *landscape* isn't just a picture of land — of scenery at a distance. It's any image that seems to invite the viewer into an environment. That environment may be full of buildings rather than mountains (a cityscape), or it may be mainly water rather than earth (a seascape). It may even have people in it. (Human figures can do wonders for photographic landscapes, contributing a valuable sense of scale.) But in landscape photography, the place, not its occupants, is the most important thing about the picture.

I have a special fondness for landscape as a photographic genre, because it is, in some ways, a pure visual challenge. You need practice and even skill to get a good portrait, of course, but the picture's success often depends on a subject's willingness to participate in the photographic process. A landscape's success is almost entirely up to you, the photographer: to the way you "frame" the scene, to the physical position you choose, to your sensitivity to light — and even to your patience.

Which isn't to say that a landscape photo's success doesn't depend on the landscape itself. Naturally, a spectacular scene is a great starting point — but the spectacle doesn't guarantee a great picture. And you can make a seemingly ordinary landscape look special simply with your photographic skills and eye. So this chapter offers suggestions not only about how to capitalize, photographically, on gorgeous scenery, but also how to find and shoot interesting landscapes in the familiar world around you.

A landscape photograph is often called a *scenic*. But I think scenic is a less interesting word than landscape; it suggests a picture that is just superficially pleasant. I think a photograph of a scene can be better than this, so I stick with *landscape*.

Landscapes Close to Home

Photographers who live in the middle of the Rocky Mountains or in the wide-open spaces of the Great Plains may seem to have an advantage in creating landscape photographs. And fair enough, landscape-shooting opportunities definitely increase when you travel or go on vacation (see Chapter 13 for more details). But these opportunities are probably a lot closer than you think — maybe even in your own neighborhood.

The key to finding landscapes close to home — whether you live in the city, the suburbs, or the country — is often a simple combination of finding the right vantage point and waiting for the right light. If you live in a tight little neighborhood, finding the right vantage point involves getting a reasonably clear view of, and a little elevation on, the subject. This could mean just shooting from your window. Or it could mean a little scrambling.

Even just a little height on the scene gives it a new, less familiar look. Try parking your car in a good spot for a landscape shot — city or country. Then stand on its hood or roof to take the picture. (Be careful!) Getting that height helps to vertically separate the elements of the scene (especially valuable if you shoot in the confines of a neighborhood or city street). By vertical separation, I mean spreading things out more from the top to the bottom of the picture, so that they don't overlap confusingly in the print.

As for light, if you want to shoot in a city or suburban neighborhood, you should study the way shadows change over the course of a day. Avoid shooting at times when large parts of the scene are cast in shadow. Late daylight is nice for the color it contributes, and it creates interesting long shadows. But late daylight may also elevate the scene's *contrast* — the difference between light and dark parts — which can give your photographs a disjointed appearance. Consider shooting on cloudy days if this seems to be a problem. (See Chapter 8 for more details.)

And then, of course, you have to consider *composition*. The way you frame a landscape subject — which includes not just your vantage point but the focal length you choose — has a powerful effect on how the viewer perceives it. For tips, see the section "Landscapes and Composition," later in this chapter, as well as Chapter 9.

Point and pan: What to do when your lens isn't wide enough

If you can't fit a whole landscape into a single picture, take two — or more. Shoot several side-by-side sections of the scene and then piece the prints together to form a panoramic image.

To create this kind of sectional panorama, first decide how many shots you need to take to span the view you want. Then do a dry run, pivoting the camera from one section to the next as you identify visual cues that can help you match up your shots. A bush or tree can mark where one shot ends and the next begins, but avoid placing important features of the landscape at the edges of a frame. In fact, it's a good idea to slightly overlap the edges of each shot so that you don't have gaps in the final panorama. Then you can simply overlap the finished prints.

Once you figure out the sequence, start on the left side and shoot each consecutive frame as planned. Keep the camera level and rotate your body at the hips so that your point of view stays more or less the same from shot to shot.

This technique gives you a much wider total view than the panorama mode on your camera, if it has one. (A point-and-shoot's panorama mode has a horizontal span no wider than a regular frame; its top and bottom are just cut off!) In fact, if you use a slightly longer focal length setting — say 50mm or 60mm rather than 38mm — the result is more natural looking in its size relationships. You can even shoot a *vertical* for each section (try four or five), for a taller image that includes more sky or foreground. Put enough sections together and you can create a 180- or 360-degree view!

The Lens and Landscapes

Photographers tend to have pretty set ideas about how to shoot landscapes. One idea is that you need a wide-angle lens — the better to take in a landscape's big sweep. You don't. While a wide-angle focal length can play an important role in landscape shooting, other techniques, such as sectional panoramas and telephoto perspective, can produce dramatic landscapes. (See Chapter 5 for more on the lens.)

Some landscape subjects — the big spaces of the American West are a classic example — nearly beg for a wide-angle focal length, which takes in more of the scene when you can't get any farther away (or when doing so would risk a tumble off the cliff behind you!). If you have a zoom point-and-shoot, though, its most wide-angle focal length is probably just a moderately wide 38mm. While this setting works fine for many scenes, it can't do much justice to the Grand Canyon's scale. (The comparable focal length on an Advanced Photo System model would be about 30mm.) In fact, if you're trying to shoot an expansive scene with a 38mm setting (or, with APS, 30mm), you may want to shoot a series of side-by-side views to create a sectional panorama of the scene. (See the sidebar "Point and pan: What to do when your lens isn't wide enough.")

TIP

If you're shopping for a new point-and-shoot and you have a penchant for landscape photos, buy a 35mm model with a lens that starts zooming at a true wide-angle focal length of 28mm rather than the more typical 38mm. (There are a few such cameras out there, from Pentax, Minolta, Olympus, and Rollei.) With the Advanced Photo System, the closest thing to true wide-angle would be a compact model that starts zooming at 24mm or 26mm, rather than the more customary 30mm (see Figure 12-1).

Actually, many single-focal-length (that is, nonzoom) point-and-shoots offer shorter focal length settings than 38mm, or in the case of APS models, shorter than 30mm. Because the shorter focal length lets them take in a bigger swath of the scene, nonzoom point-and-shoots are often better suited to landscape photographs than zoom models. (See the section "Shooting wide-open spaces without wide-angle," later in this chapter.) For example, some 35mm models have 34mm focal length lenses; some have 32mm lenses; some have 30mm lenses. Some even have 28mm lenses, though these tend to be the more expensive "designer" models. In the Advanced Photo System, some single-focal-length models have lenses around 24mm or 26mm, rather than the 30mm at which APS zoom models generally start zooming.

Figure 12-1: For land-scapes, buy a 35mm model that zooms from 28mm (left and right) or an APS model of 26mm or shorter (center).

Capturing more background with a wide-angle focal length

PHOTO OP

A wide-angle focal length does something more interesting than just putting more of the scene on film: It lets you move closer to something to make it bigger in the picture, yet still show lots of background. Basically, a wide-angle focal length lets you change the size relationship between foreground and background, making foreground objects seem larger relative to the background. This effect is useful if you like to photograph people in front of landscapes, but it's even more valuable in confined situations. It not only lets you place more importance on certain parts of the scene, but it also creates the sense of a deeper space.

Setting up "near-far" relationships between the foreground and background of a landscape scene can also reinforce that sense of space. When composing a landscape shot, try to include interesting objects in the fairly near distance — a tree, a rock, an animal. You may want to place these elements to one side of the frame so that they don't detract from the overall scene. (See Chapter 9 for details about this kind of composition.) If you do this, just be sure to lock the focus on a closer part of the scene.

Shooting wide-open spaces without wide-angle

You don't absolutely need a wide-angle focal length to shoot an effective landscape. Many professional photographers even favor longer focal lengths — telephoto settings — for landscape shots. Why? Because longer focal lengths let them *stack* (in a visual sense) elements of the scene that are actually at different distances from one another. That is, longer focal lengths help create the illusion that these parts are closer together than they really are. This effect can give a landscape a flat, graphic quality.

Stacking, also called *compression,* isn't a direct consequence of a longer focal length. It's actually due to the change in perspective you get when you shoot a subject from a greater distance. The longer focal length simply gives you the greater magnifying power (the narrower slice of the scene) needed for this "long distance" shooting. In fact, stacking isn't even an option unless you're pretty far away from the scene to begin with.

If you're shooting in fairly wide-open spaces, you may want to experiment with stacked perspective. Zoom your lens in on a subject as far as it can go — the longer the focal length, the more it enhances the stacking effect — and choose shooting positions from which near and far elements sit side by side. (Be sure to lock the focus on the near element; see Chapter 6 for details.) Keep in mind that you may not see the effect as readily in the viewfinder as in the print, because the print further flattens the subject by reducing it to two dimensions.

When you zoom your point-and-shoot's lens to a longer focal length for a stacked landscape, you increase the risk of blur due to camera shake. (Camera shake is due to the lens's higher magnification; think of looking through shaky binoculars.) Shake is a particular concern in low, late daylight because the camera sets a slower shutter speed, but it can also have an ill effect even in bright conditions. Use a fast (ISO 400 or 800) film to prevent or minimize the problem. (See Chapter 2 for more on film speed and shake.)

Landscapes and Composition

Choosing a focal length is an important part of composition (see Chapter 9). And composition tends to play a bigger role in landscape photography than in people pictures, perhaps because the subject is inherently more abstract — that is, all about shapes, textures, and their physical interrelationships. For similar reasons, creating a feeling of depth is also more important. Placing objects in the foreground is one way to create depth. Another is to look for, and exploit, receding lines in the scene (if they're available). A fence, a stone wall, or a row of trees may cross the scene at an angle, for example, from a close distance to a far one. Such tricks also lead the viewer's eye into the scene (see Figure 12-2).

How to place the horizon line

If you use a wide-angle focal length setting for a landscape shot, its bigger view demands more attention to the position of the *horizon line* — the line in the far distance where the earth meets the sky, or the water meets the sky.

Figure 12-2: A 28mm focal length helped reinforce the sense of depth created by this sunlit sea wall. To enhance depth, look for receding elements and choose vantage points from which they cut across the picture.

© Russell Hart

To put more emphasis on a scene's land (or sea) area, point your camera down to place the horizon line high in the frame. To put more emphasis on the sky, point your camera up to place the horizon line low in the frame.

Most photographers avoid placing the horizon line in the exact horizontal middle of the picture. Doing this leads to a static feeling in a landscape photograph. But you may find, in some cases, that a centered horizon line is the right choice for a subject. A photograph of a mirror image in water, for example, is often more powerful when the line between the real scene and the reflection bisects the image. Photography's rules, as helpful as they may be, are meant to be broken — and broken often!

Move yourself for a better view

Just as important as moving the camera around to adjust the horizon line is moving your body — experimenting with different physical positions. This movement can mean squatting for a low point of view, climbing onto a rock for a high point of view, or moving from side to side.

Using your body as a camera-positioning tool helps accomplish a very important purpose: keeping parts of the scene from intersecting one another in confusing ways. A higher vantage point lets you see over and beyond things in the foreground; a small step to the side can separate two overlapping elements. Remember that the scene is reduced to two dimensions in the print, and overlapping items may look more confusing.

Should you shoot a horizontal? Or vertical?

Most photographers instinctively hold a camera in the horizontal position. This may be because the camera is simpler to operate that way, but also because people's natural field of vision seems to spread sideways rather than up and down. Shooting a landscape reinforces the inclination to make horizontal pictures, because the landscape seems such a horizontal place to begin with. But some of the best landscape photographs are vertical compositions.

Make yourself shoot vertical landscape photographs. Vertical composition can be especially useful if you don't have a very wide-angle focal length on your point-and-shoot. A vertical shot often allows you to set up more interesting relationships between foreground objects and the background.

When to shoot verticals? First, look for vertical elements in the scene. A subject with strong vertical lines often wants to be within a vertical composition (though not necessarily). Vertical composition is also a way to get more foreground or sky into a picture, simply because your camera takes in a bigger swath in the frame's long dimension than in its short. All that said, sometimes a scene with strong *horizontal* lines can make an interesting *vertical* composition — by virtue of the way the edges of the frame abruptly chop off the lines.

Choosing a Landscape Print Shape

With some landscape scenes, the familiar 35mm frame shape and Advanced Photo System "Classic" format just seem to leave too much stuff on the top or the bottom. In such cases, you may want to try a more elongated print format — changing the actual shape of the print you get back.

A print shape for wider scenes

One way to get a different sized print is with the *H print format* offered by Advanced Photo System point-and-shoots. To get an *H* print, you simply set the camera's print-format switch or toggle its print-format button from *C* to *H,* and the viewfinder automatically marks the more elongated frame shape. You compose the shot within this shape, and when you take the picture, the camera automatically records your choice on the film. When the prints are made, the photofinishing machine automatically spits out a 4 x 7-inch print, rather than a 4 x 6-inch print.

When you switch to an *H* print, you don't just get a different shape to work with; you also get a little more of the scene on the right and left of the frame. When you want more on the sides and less on the top (the opposite of a haircut), the extra is helpful.

A print shape for panoramic views

You can also choose the *panoramic format,* which is available in both 35mm and the Advanced Photo System.

A *panorama* is a photographic image that is usually at least twice as long (wide) as it is tall. The stretched-out shape can create a sense of expansiveness in a landscape photograph (see Figure 12-3).

The standard panoramic print size, whether in 35mm or the Advanced Photo System, is 4 x 11^1/$_2$ inches. (Some photofinishers print panoramas in 4 x 10-inch size.) When you set an APS point-and-shoot's print format switch to *P,* or a 35mm camera's panorama switch to *P,* the viewfinder usually automatically shows the new shape for your composition, narrowing the frame at the top and bottom.

Figure 12-3: Panoramas usually work better if you use a fairly wide-angle focal length setting — here, 28mm.

As with the *H* format, Advanced Photo System cameras record your choice of the Panoramic format on the film, and the print is made to the correct size automatically. (See Chapter 3 for more on printing panoramas.)

Also keep in mind that with the Advanced Photo System, you can have any shot reprinted in any other format — restoring a panoramic picture to the *H* format, for example. All the information is stored in the film. But 35mm cameras crop the image on the top and bottom inside the camera, so you can't go back once you shoot a picture as a panorama.

If you have an autofocus model, your point-and-shoot may have a landscape mode. For tips on using this mode, see Chapter 4.

Adding a Sense of Scale

Landscapes don't have to be devoid of people. In fact, human figures — friends or passers-by — can add an important sense of scale to your landscape photographs. Usually, the scene's much larger elements dwarf the figures (see Figure 12-4).

Including a human figure in a scene is also a way of commenting on it, as if to say "look at this spectacle." Sometimes you have to take figures where you find them — visitors to a national park, for example. With friends or family, you can pretty much direct them to stand where you want (if you don't have an uncooperative toddler). Be careful to choose a position that won't detract from the scene (perhaps on the side), and that isn't so close that it puts too much emphasis on the people.

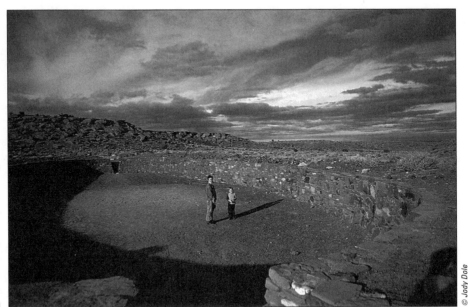

Figure 12-4: Including figures in a landscape photo can add a powerful feeling of scale. Here, figures tell the viewer about the dimensions of a Southwestern Indian ruin.

© Jody Dole

Seeing the Light

Light is the defining ingredient of landscape photography. Because a landscape's forms are so often reduced to curves, lines, patterns, and textures, you're more aware of what light does to it. Landscape photographers favor both early and late daylight because the sun's low angle describes shapes and textures more dramatically and its reddish-yellow color adds warmth. In fact, photographers often call this kind of light *sweet light*. For more about the qualities of light, see Chapter 8.

By the same token, landscape photographers usually avoid shooting in the middle of the day. Midday sun creates deep shadows and harsh contrasts that make a landscape hard to "read," in a photographic sense. But there's an unexpected solution to this problem: overcast. Cloudy skies can make for beautiful landscapes. The clouds create delicate tones and softer contrasts. Of course, to reap those benefits you have to wait for the clouds to roll in. But once they do, you can shoot at just about any time of day!

Exploring Seasonal Changes

A landscape's look changes from hour to hour and day to day, mainly due to changes in weather and light. But landscapes are also profoundly altered by the seasons. Such changes are due in part to changes in growth patterns, from spring lushness to winter barrenness. But even the *quality* of light changes from season to season, as the sun's angle and intensity changes. These differences are worth exploring photographically.

Find a landscape close to home. Choose the best camera position and make mental notes about the exact spot. Shoot the scene when the light is right. Then wait.

How long should you wait? A few months. Wait for the season to change the landscape. Then, when the light is good again, return to the same spot — and take another picture. Wait a few more months, then do it again. Each time, try to frame the subject in the same way. You end up with a time-lapse landscape!

Depending on where you live, one of the most visually remarkable seasonal changes comes in winter: snow. Nothing spruces up a landscape like a fresh blanket of snow (see Figure 12-5). It smoothes contours and enhances textures. It simplifies ordinarily complex scenes by canceling out colors and tones.

Figure 12-5: Snow can turn a familiar landscape into a fantastic one — here, sculpted by the wind. To prevent under-exposure, set backlight compensation or exposure compensation, if your camera offers these modes.

©Pat O'Hara

But snow can also wreak havoc with your point-and-shoot's exposure system. The system sees all that highly reflective white stuff and is fooled into thinking that the landscape is more well-lighted than it actually is. The camera ends up underexposing the film — turning all the white stuff gray in the print (see Chapter 3).

You can prevent underexposure in several ways:

✔ **If your camera has a backlight compensation mode, set it anytime you shoot a scene with a lot of snow in it.** This mode gets extra exposure to the film (see Chapter 8).

✔ **If your camera has an exposure compensation mode, set it to +1 EV or +1.5 EV.** (See Chapter 4.) This mode also adds exposure.

✔ **If your camera has no provision for backlight or exposure compensation mode, try this.** Point the camera at a dark area at middle distance: the shadow of a thick tree trunk, or a dense evergreen bush, or the shaded side of a house or other structure. Press the shutter button halfway and then recompose to include all the snow you want in the picture. This technique will lock in extra exposure. But make sure that the object that you lock focus on is about the same distance away as the main part of your picture.

Perhaps the best insurance against a gray result when you shoot a snowy landscape is simply to use a fast film — at least ISO 400, or even ISO 800. Even if a point-and-shoot camera tries to cut back on exposure when it sees a lot of snow, these films are so light-sensitive that your point-and-shoot's exposure system overexposes the film, compensating for the underexposure that snow's high brightness can cause. (See Chapter 2 for more on film.)

Shooting Cityscapes

Many, if not most, landscapes have manmade elements — buildings, cultivated fields, fences, domesticated animals. They're *human* landscapes. And in a way, cities and towns offer landscapes in which the human element has simply taken over. (Though nothing is as plaintive, photographically, as organic life poking its way through the steel and cement of a city — the lone tree on the corner of a city neighborhood or the leafy trellis on a city rooftop.)

Postcard views have made people think of cities in terms of skylines. But you can't always find (nor is it convenient to look for) a vantage point that encompasses all the big structures of a city. If you do, you probably need to do two things to get a good picture: Zoom your lens to a longer focal length to fill the frame with the buildings and make them seem a tighter cluster and then wait for warm, low-angle light. It's a bit of a cliché to shoot a skyline by setting sun, but the truth is that midday light reveals a skyline for the boring picture that it usually is. I'd never talk you out of a picture. But take my word for this: The most interesting cityscapes are usually taken *in* the city, not outside it!

Time of day is especially important in shooting cityscapes. Buildings in particular can throw large areas into shadow, making the difference between light and dark areas too extreme for your film and print to hold detail in both. But if you're traveling through a city, you may not have the luxury of studying the light and waiting for its best angles — for example, when the sun shoots lengthwise down a narrow city street, throwing its building facades into *high relief* (the effect by which details seem to stand out boldly in three dimensions). If, on the other hand, you're a regular visitor — or, for that matter, work in the city — keep your eye on lighting patterns and changes. And don't stop shooting on cloudy days. By eliminating or lessening the shadows created by a city's structures, they can actually make cityscapes more visually appealing.

Photographing city scenes with a point-and-shoot can pose a more serious limitation than light itself. You may find that your camera's lens — particularly if its zoom starts at 38mm, as many do — simply doesn't have a wide enough angle of view to show all of a building (or row of buildings) from top to bottom. Vertical composition is an obvious strategy here because it gives you more vertical coverage. (See the section "Should you shoot a horizontal? Or vertical?" earlier in this chapter.) But a better approach is not to insist on photographing a building from top to bottom.

Effective cityscapes can often show just a portion or fragment of a building, and its relationship to other buildings and the space around it. In fact, the closer quarters of cities invite you to isolate details of buildings and other elements, instead of trying to show the whole scene. You may even find yourself zooming in tight on things more often with city views than traditional landscapes.

Chapter 13

Have Camera, Will Travel

* *

In This Chapter

▶ Finding out about your destination ahead of time

▶ Testing your camera before you go

▶ Bringing the right film

▶ Taking along the world's smallest tripod

▶ Deciding what to shoot

▶ Capturing local color

* *

*W*hether a round-the-world voyage or a trip to the nearest state park, travel may be the ultimate photo opportunity. From moonlight on the Nile to the neon shimmer of Times Square, getting away from it all provides both new subject matter for your camera and the visual inspiration often needed to make your pictures better.

Who would think of taking a trip without a camera? Memories are the end product of the travel experience, and I can't imagine a better way to recall exotic destinations and exuberant times than with pictures — not postcards, but beautiful photographs steeped in local color. Think you can't make them? Think again. The single, simple trick to better travel photography is planning.

I don't mean just remembering to throw your point-and-shoot in the suitcase. I mean planning your journey specifically with photography in mind. This process includes looking ahead at the weather you may run into; seeking worthwhile photographic sites; bringing along enough (but not too much) equipment and supplies; and foreseeing photographic emergencies. Because logistics — packing bags, getting there, and so on — play such an important part in travel photography, the first part of this chapter focuses mainly on these practical concerns. Then later in the chapter, in "Scenes from a Voyage," I offer specific picture-taking tips. For some intriguing places to go, check out Chapter 19.

Planning Your Trip

If you're plotting a vacation, start by choosing your itinerary, travel times, and even your destination with an eye to photography. This planning will pay off in better pictures. I know professional travel photographers who plan every minute of every day on the road — every shot of every roll weeks in advance.

Now that I have you in a cold sweat about this planning business, relax. You can't be so single-minded. You may have ten whole days away (if that), and photography must wait its turn. You'll also want romance, good food, physical fun, culture, fresh air, sun, and, of course, plenty of sleep. And, yes, some good photos. But most travelers aren't prepared to rise at four in the morning to capture an uncluttered street or the perfect sunrise.

Yet while photography may not be at the top of your vacation "to do" list, it shouldn't be near the bottom, either. The people who get the best vacation photographs do, indeed, plan ahead — incorporating picture-taking into many different travel activities (see Figure 13-1). They don't just ski; they ski and take pictures. (And bring the protective gear that they'll need for their cameras.) They don't just hike; they hike and take pictures. (And first pick up a guidebook to the best local trails.) This approach will net you good fun *and* good photos. Ready to start planning your next trip? Okay, start with getting to the right place — at the *right time,* by reading the next section, "Weather or Not. . . . Finding Out about Your Destination."

Weather or Not. . . . Finding Out about Your Destination

Picking a place to vacation is only the first step toward a great travel — and photography — experience. Now comes the homework part, a modest investment of your time that will pay off with great rewards later. Research the best times to go to your chosen destination. Find out what attractions and activities you want to experience. Here are some ways to get started:

✔ **Get acquainted with your destination's climate.** Will your destination be in the thick of monsoon season when you arrive? If so, consider postponing your trip until the weatherman forecasts better photography. If you go anyway, keep your gear properly weatherproofed as outlined in the sidebar, "Traveling to a rainy or humid destination." Also remember that when the Northern Hemisphere is bathing in summer warmth, the Southern is shivering through winter. Don't arrive in Buenos Aires in July with only T-shirts and a bathing suit!

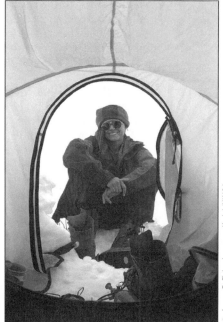

Figure 13-1:
Whether dress-up (left, a Southern Belle in Charleston, South Carolina) or dress-down (right, the photographer's backpacking companion), travel offers terrific photographic possibilities.

© Peter Kolonia

© James R. Fisher/courtesy Kodak/KINSA

✔ **Find out your destination's sunrise and sunset times during the period you'll be there.** Few things are as exasperating as scheduling a vacation in the Scottish Highlands at a time when the sun shines for all of four hours a day. You'll want plenty of daylight hours for outdoor shooting, remember, and will want to know when to catch the best light. After you've figured out when and where you're going, start collecting as many guide books and other resources as you can.

✔ **Establish "must see" (and "must shoot") items.** Find out as much as you can about what's going to be happening during your stay. Visitors' bureau pamphlets list local institutions and upcoming events, as well as contact information. Build your itinerary around photogenic locations and events — state and county fairs, parks, Civil War battle reenactments, museums, rodeos, pageants, and other natural or cultural points of interest. Then make your airline and hotel reservations accordingly.

✔ **Plan day trips and side excursions to flesh out your itinerary.** Even if you're going skiing, for example, I suggest finding out what visual diversions are available in the area surrounding the resort. A photographer friend of mine recently planned a ski vacation over the Christmas holiday, and it rained every day. He was glad the resort had more than its slopes to offer!

You can start your search for information about a travel destination with calls to visitors' or tourists' bureaus. If you're headed to another state, find one through directory assistance in its capital city. If you're off to a foreign country, check with travel agents or in travel guidebooks for the location of the U.S. offices of that country's tourism agencies.

Books, of course, are another great way to research your destination. But they're also a great resource you can carry with you while traveling. And don't forget the Internet. It has become a valuable resource for the traveling photographer — or should I say, the photographing traveler. At its most basic, the Net can give you a fix on your destination's weather. Dozens of online services provide free forecasts, including detailed weather maps for cities and other locations around the world. But the Web offers much more than weather. Say you're traveling to Scotland. Simply by entering the words "Landscape Photography in Scotland" in a Web search engine, you turn up dozens of helpful contacts, not to mention lots of inspirational photos. (See Chapter 18 for information about search engines.)

Deciding What to Bring

As your departure date approaches, you need to start organizing in earnest. Make checklists. Checklists can save the day, and a lot of heartache. Write down everything you hope to photograph, including dates, times, and locations. Write down all the photo supplies you'll need, including film, batteries, and lens cleaning tissue. (While you're at it, list all the non-photographic items you'll need, including passport, maps, visas, medicines, electrical converters, and adapter plugs.) Checklists may seem like overkill, but if you've ever desperately needed a battery or a roll of film and been miles from a camera store, surely you have a sense of their worth.

Traveling to a rainy or humid destination

If you're planning an extended stay in a humid part of the world — a rain forest, perhaps — bring along a *desiccant*. Available in small packets, desiccants draw moisture out of the air. Silica gel is the most common; your local camera shop can probably get it for you. By keeping your camera and film in a plastic bag with the silica gel packet, you protect them from condensation — even fungus. Believe it or not, fungus can eat away both your lens's surface coatings and your film's emulsion.

Another useful item for rainy climates? Protective camera coverings. You can fabricate a "raincoat" for your camera from a plastic bag, or you can buy something more substantial from camera shops or catalog outfits. They sell special plastic shrouds that protect cameras from rain but allow full access to camera controls and the viewfinder.

Taking the right camera

Just about any working camera is capable of great travel shots, if you use it smartly. If the point-and-shoot that you already own has served you reliably, it should work fine for your trip. I'm a firm believer in taking along the camera you know and trust rather than a shiny new model you've never run film through.

You'll still want to tune up your camera before you leave, especially if you haven't used it in a while. Here's what to do:

- **Get fresh batteries for your camera, even if the old ones seem fine.** (You can always save the old ones to use when you get back.) While you're changing batteries, check for leakage; if you spy any whitish residue, clean the inside of the battery compartment with a pencil eraser, as I describe in Chapter 1.

- **Blow out the inside of the camera to remove any dust.** (Try to use canned air from a photo shop, if possible.) Ditto the viewfinder and lens.

- **Check the lens for smudges.** Remove any with lens cleaning tissue or a special lens cleaning cloth. (See Chapter 6 for details.)

If you have two working cameras, I suggest bringing both along. At the very least, pack a couple of one-time-use cameras in addition to your regular point-and-shoot. These cameras are especially handy if you're traveling in conditions hazardous to your normal camera — either nasty weather or places where thievery may occur. And I suggest leaving your good camera at the hotel if you're headed to a beach. Sand and salt water are real camera killers. But waterproof one-time-use cameras can even be taken into the waves.

Whether your camera is a new purchase or an old companion, bring its manual on your trip. In addition, make a "mode map" for yourself. (I tell you how in Chapter 4.) A mode map explains all the buttons and features of your camera in terms that *you* understand.

And don't get stuck without batteries. Many current point-and-shoots take batteries that aren't readily available overseas, or are far more expensive over there. Here's another good general rule: Leave for your vacation with a fresh battery in your camera and bring at least one spare battery for each camera you're packing.

Don't forget to test your camera

I strongly recommend shooting a test roll of film before leaving on your trip. If you have a camera that works properly with slide film (see Chapter 2), that film (ISO 100, please) is the best choice for this test. (Unlike color print film, slide film is very unforgiving — so that if your camera's exposure system is acting up some way, it will be obvious from the slides.) Otherwise, a short roll of ISO 400 color print film will do. Shoot pictures in bright light and in dim light. Shoot pictures with close subjects and with distant subjects. If the camera has a zoom lens, shoot pictures at several different focal length settings. Take flash shots at different distances, too. Try to use every feature on the camera — or at least every feature you think you're likely to use on your trip. If you're going somewhere sunny and plan to take lots of people pictures outdoors, for example, be sure to take some outdoor portraits with fill flash. (See Chapter 7 for more on fill flash.)

As you shoot the roll, listen to the camera. Does it sound "healthy"? If you hear odd noises that you haven't heard before — whining or straining sounds in particular — take heed.

Have your film processed and check the prints (or slides) for sharpness and good exposure. If most of your prints have good color and lots of detail, you're on your way. If, on the other hand, you get back muddy prints (or dark slides) or a lot of fuzzy pictures, you may need to repair or replace your point-and-shoot. Take the camera and test pictures to the folks at a local camera shop or minilab and ask for their advice.

All this testing may seem a bore, but it serves two purposes. First, it lets you discover problems with your camera before, not during or after, your trip. Second, it tests you; you'll be brushing up your camera skills. If your camera has some features that you don't understand, take the opportunity to reread your camera manual — or refer to Chapter 4! If something still confounds you, ask a knowledgeable friend or the clerk at the local camera shop.

Don't succumb to New Camera Syndrome!

In those heady days before a trip, many travelers become convinced that they need a higher-tech, easier-to-use, and sexier camera for their long-awaited vacation. I've heard this sad refrain many times: "I just don't understand why the pictures didn't come out. . . . It's a *new* camera!" Alas, new cameras have been the ruination of much vacation photography. First, new devices can, and do, fail. Second, even if a new camera is working flawlessly, you may not fully grasp its operation. A button may end up doing something very different than you thought it did when you pressed it.

You may still want — or need — to buy a new camera before your trip. If so, buy it at least a few weeks in advance. (See the sidebar "Buying a traveling camera" for some tips.) Run a test roll through it. Then shoot at least two or three rolls more of a variety of subjects. Shoot the types of film that you'll be using on your trip. You'll leave knowing the camera works, and understanding its features. You'll leave with peace of mind.

Buying a traveling camera

Chapter 16 tells you what to look for in a new camera. But if you're shopping with travel pictures in mind, here are some specific things to think about:

✔ Consider a model that has a wide-angle focal length setting (28mm or 30mm on 35mm cameras, 24mm or 26mm on APS cameras), rather than the more common semi-wide-angle (38mm for 35mm cameras, 30mm for APS cameras). Wide-angle focal lengths are great both for sky-spanning landscapes and cramped interiors.

✔ Consider a weatherproof model. It will stand up better to those showers you're bound to get on your vacation and tolerates the inevitable spray on boat rides. If your trip takes you to swimming or snorkeling spots, consider a fully waterproof model.

✔ Consider buying a different type of point-and-shoot if your current camera is in good working condition. If you own a good single-focal-length model, for example, you may want to get a 35mm zoom camera with a 28–70mm or 28–90mm lens. If you already own a good zoom model, you may want to get an ultracompact single-focal-length camera that slips into a pocket.

Film for wanderers

Other things you'll need besides a working camera? Lots of film — especially if you're going abroad. Overseas, even in big cities like London or Rome, you may not be able to find the latest generation of color print films. So don't plan on buying your film over there. When you buy in the U.S., do so at a reputable dealer where film is properly stored. (Too much is at stake!) If you must purchase film on the road, check the expiration dates on the box and try to buy from a store with heavy volume and turnover.

Price is another reason to buy your film in the U.S. In very remote parts of the world, a roll can cost as much as $20 — and it may be way past its expiration date! Keep in mind, too, that in places with heavy tourist trade, such as the Caribbean, film prices are often higher because stores charge what the traffic will bear.

Which film should you buy and how much? As I say throughout this book, you should make ISO 400 film your standard film. But if this vacation is an important one (and what one isn't?), you may want to go with premium ISO 400 film from the major manufacturers rather than your everyday brand. (See Chapter 2 for more on premium films.) Also bring along several rolls of fast ISO 800 film — and consider the film a must if you plan to shoot with long zoom settings. You should even factor in your destination: Bring more ISO 800 film if you're headed for foggy London Town or other spots that are frequently overcast, or if you foresee doing a lot of low-light pictures indoors and out.

In addition to color, consider bringing along a roll or two of chromogenic black-and-white film. (I discuss this film in Chapter 2.) Black and white can reinforce the other-worldly feeling that travel is all about, and shooting it makes you think harder about line, shape, texture, and composition — important matters when you're shooting architecture and landscapes.

How much film to buy? A good general rule is one roll of film for every day you'll be away. I'm talking about long rolls, of course — 36 exposures for 35mm cameras, 40 exposures for Advanced Photo System cameras. Using long rolls means you don't have to change film as often, and that you can carry fewer rolls.

Tripods: Three legs are better than two

Many of the best travel pictures are taken in low light: the sunset from your hotel window, or your traveling companions at an outdoor café at dusk, city lights twinkling behind them. But these pictures won't be sharp unless you keep the camera steady — even if you're using very fast film. In fact, getting sharp results may require you to keep the camera steadier than you can with your hands alone.

Bracing the camera against something helps, of course, but it can limit your shooting position. For this reason, professional travel photographers never leave home without a tripod. I'm tempted to tell you to bring a compact tripod along with you on your travels — but I won't. A tripod is enough of a pain to lug on a hike through a state park, let alone to Bangkok.

So here's an easy-to-stow and inexpensive alternative: the tabletop tripod, also known as a minipod. These little three-leggers fold up smaller than a travel umbrella, weigh under a pound, and are sturdy enough to hold a point-and-shoot steady on a café table, your hotel window sill, or a low wall. (You just screw the tripod's bolt into the threaded hole on the bottom of your camera.) You can even put a minipod on the ground, although this requires lying down to compose the picture. A similar option is the even smaller clamp tripod, which looks like a household C-clamp with a tripod bolt attached. It lets you clamp a camera to a railing, window sill, or table.

When to use a tabletop tripod? Many low-light travel subjects are beyond the range of your camera's flash — a cityscape at night, for example, or distant pyramids at dusk. And you may not want the flash to go off in certain scenes: kids around the campfire or dinner in a romantically lit restaurant. If you don't set your point-and-shoot's flash-off mode, the camera will automatically fire the flash in these cases — destroying the feeling you're after. Solution: Put your camera on a minipod and set the flash-off mode. (See Chapter 7.) When the pictures come back from the lab with their romantic light intact, you may never travel again without your minipod.

When using a tabletop tripod, take the picture with your camera's self-timer (or infrared remote controller, if available) to avoid any blur due to shaky hand contact. (See Chapter 4 for more on the self-timer mode.) A minipod is a great help with dim cathedral and church interiors. Just don't forget to set your point-and-shoot's flash-off mode!

Then for some shots, you may want both flash and existing light — flash to light a dark foreground, a slow shutter speed to get detail in a distant background. Say you're in Paris at night, and you want a picture of your kids in the foreground and the floodlit Eiffel Tower in the background. The best way to get both is with your camera's slow-sync mode (see Chapter 7). The flash will light your children, while a slow shutter speed will make sure that Monsieur Eiffel's handiwork registers on film, too. But will the tower be sharp? If you're hand-holding the camera, quite possibly not. It may end up a blurry smudge in the picture because of camera shake — unless you put your camera on a minipod.

Don't pack it, bag it

Do you really need a camera bag when traveling? It helps. The padding and water resistance of typical camera bags help protect your point-and-shoot, accessories, and other small items. And you can fit in a lot more things than cameras and film: maps, binoculars, sunglasses, and guidebooks, to name a few. Camera bags are also a reminder that you should be shooting. Guess who takes more pictures: The person who carries her camera in a camera bag or the person who carries her camera at the bottom of a suitcase?

When packing film in your camera bag, remove the plastic canisters from the boxes. The boxes take up too much space. If you're bringing more than one type of film, mark the type and speed of the film on the tops of the canisters. And if you're shooting more than one type or speed of film, keep each in separate camera bag pockets. Also keep exposed and unexposed films in different pockets or compartments.

Scenes from a Voyage

What should you photograph in your travels? Answer: As much as you can. Try to take pictures of every new place you go and every new person you meet — even if you don't see anything of particular visual interest. You can't predict what will evoke memories years from now, so get as much as you can on film.

Choosing what to photograph

Here's a good way to go about photographing a new place:

- ✔ **Start with the big and work down toward the small.** When you first visit a town, for example, take a few overall shots, zooming out to include as much as possible. Put family members or traveling companions in these wide shots (filmmakers call them *establishing shots*), but take some without your fellow travelers, too. When shooting traveling companions in front of famous landmarks, buildings, or scenes, vary your camera angle and your companions' stance. For some pictures, ask them *not* to look into the camera and *not* to smile. Change camera orientation, making both horizontals and verticals.

- ✔ **Move in and take some middle-distance shots of your location.** If your wide shot was the entire cathedral, take some pictures of doors, windows, and flying buttresses. Again, try to include people for scale. Unlike wide shots, middle-distance pictures can contain enough detail to tell a story — if you keep your eye open for human interest and even humor. Give clichéd subjects a new look by choosing unusual camera angles. An interesting vantage point can add energy to a quiet subject.

- ✔ **Finally, after you're finished with middle-distance shots, go for the details.** Start with objects. If you're shooting that cathedral, isolate its architectural components — decorative statues, door knobs, or stained glass (see Figure 13-2). Try to pick things that are representative of the larger subject (perhaps even a detail of a priest's robe). Keep your eye out for strong colors, interesting textures, and evocative light.

Don't just wait for *National Geographic* pictures to happen in front of you. They won't. *National Geographic* photographers often spend months in a single location, returning again and again to capture different light, different events, and different seasons. You don't have that luxury, and if you wait for the perfect picture, you won't finish the first roll you put in the camera. I know this from personal experience! What's more, the best pictures are often a complete surprise — not the ones you expect — when you get your prints back.

Shoot signs. They can make great, graphic photos, but they also help identify where you were and what you saw.

Good things to shoot in bad weather

Here's a big secret of professional travel shooters: Bad weather can be good weather, photographically speaking. The sun doesn't have to be shining for you to get great travel shots. Inclement conditions can add instant atmosphere to a photo. So rather than stay in your hotel room in a funk, go out

What to look for in a camera bag

To bag the right camera bag, keep your eye out for the following features:

- **Appropriate size:** Don't buy a bag that's too big. You can get bags specifically for point-and-shoot cameras; they're small, easy to carry, and may even include belt loops for hip- or fanny-mounting.

- **Materials:** Look for good quality, water-repellent materials such as lightweight neoprene or sturdier Cordura nylon. Padded inner walls protect gear from minor knocks, and "closed cell" padding is best because it's waterproof.

- **Pockets:** The more, the better. They should be different sizes and shapes; the best have easy-to-close clip fasteners.

- **Zippers:** Look for heavy-duty plastic zippers with double pull tags, the tags with loops large enough so that you can join them together with a tiny lock. These little locks won't deter serious thieves, but they can prevent spur-of-the-moment pilfering.

- **Shoulder straps:** Important for bigger bags, make sure that they're well padded for your own comfort.

with your camera — protected in a plastic bag or water-resistant case, of course. Night shots in the rain can be particularly beautiful, especially in places with lots of illuminated signage (Picadilly Circus, Times Square, the Ginza). When shooting at night, make sure that you've set your point-and-shoot to its slow-sync flash or flash-off modes (see Chapter 4) and look for interesting reflections.

Overcast is wonderful, too, especially for people pictures. Use the soft light of a gray day to take portraits of your traveling companions or the locals. Even heavy haze and mist can make lovely middle-distance landscapes and street scenes.

Photographing the locals

In some corners of the world, the people are as visually intriguing as the most spectacular landscapes — maybe even more so. Their daily garb and special costumes may be handsomely crafted and colorful, their faces deep wells of character (see Figure 13-3). Their ceremonies can be fascinating, too, if you're fortunate enough to be there for them. But often the easiest and most interesting people to photograph are men and women at work.

When they're working, people wear "public" faces. At work, they're generally less sensitive about being photographed. They may even be delighted that you find their occupation photogenic. The only jobs where this doesn't hold? The police and the military.

Figure 13-2:
After you shoot an overall scene (here, a Japanese marketplace), take some close pictures, too. These pictures help fill in details — and are often the best shots in purely photographic terms!

© Allen Green

Figure 13-3:
The locals may cooperate with your photographic intentions, but pride or even a bit of suspicion may keep them from grinning ear to ear. And that can be better: A solemn expression makes this portrait of a turbaned man a stronger picture.

© John Isaac

In the world's trouble spots, or in more closed societies, avoid photographing anyone in uniform or anything related to the military, including government buildings, border crossings, and even bridges and highways! Take pictures, and you may very well be arrested for spying. Remember that when you're in a foreign country, you're subject to its laws — and even the local American consulate may not be much help if you break them.

Fortunately, most denizens of tourist destinations are used to being photographed, and will be pleased to pose for you. Don't shoot and run, though. Try to establish some sort of relationship with your subject — even a nonverbal one, if language is a barrier. Communicate something about yourself. Try to find out something about them. This interaction pays off in better pictures. Not only will your subjects offer more sincere and friendly expressions, but your pictures of them will be more meaningful to you.

When you're taking pictures in a different culture, be especially sensitive to others' privacy. Try to find out something about local attitudes toward photography *before* you begin shooting; the hotel staff is a good place to start asking questions. In some places, residents simply do not like to be photographed. Take their picture, and they won't hesitate to tell you their displeasure, in ways you'll understand whether you speak their language or not. (You have the questionable option of distancing yourself from them and shooting with a long zoom focal length, but they'll probably spot you anyway.) In other locales, the locals will cooperate only if you "tip" them in advance.

Protecting your gear from theft

You may think your bare-bones point-and-shoot is of such relatively little value that no one would possibly want to steal it. But in less affluent parts of the world, especially big cities, even an inexpensive camera may attract the attention of thieves. Safeguard your camera in the following ways:

✔ Always keep your camera in view.

✔ Write down your camera's serial number and keep it in a safe place. This information can help prove ownership if your camera is stolen and recovered by police.

✔ Keep your camera in locked luggage or in the hotel safe, rather than leaving it out in your room.

✔ Beware of distractions. Thieves often work in pairs, one creating a distraction and the other swiping your camera or camera bag. If someone spills food on you or bumps into you, hold your camera tight.

✔ If your camera is stolen, don't replace it then and there. Cameras are usually more expensive elsewhere than they are in the U.S. Make do with a one-time-use camera until you get home.

Can airport X-rays hurt your film?

In the early days of airport baggage inspection machines, your unprocessed film stood a good chance of receiving a lethal dose of X-rays as it passed through the device — ruining your vacation photos. Today, these machines are better-calibrated and seemingly less likely to cause damage. I know few photographers who have reported film damage from X-rays, but it may take the form of strange coloration, washed-out areas or bands of color, or even just a loss of crispness and color brilliance. But exercising a little caution pays off, especially now that a new generation of more powerful X-ray machines, able to detect plastic explosives, are headed for installation in airports around the world. What can you do?

✔ **Politely ask to have your film hand-inspected at airport security checkpoints — going and coming — rather than have it X-rayed.** Most airports are willing to comply, if begrudgingly. To speed up the process, have your film already removed from its boxes (which you should be doing anyway) and store it in a clear plastic bag for quick inspection.

If you're going to request hand inspection, arrive a little early for your flight. If nothing else, ask for hand-inspection of high-speed (ISO 800) film. It's more vulnerable to X-ray damage.

✔ **Never put film or loaded cameras in your suitcases.** A certain percentage of large pieces of luggage gets hit with harder, potentially more damaging radiation.

✔ **If you think you may have trouble getting unprocessed film back to your destination unharmed, have it processed where you're visiting.** Overseas, look for photo labs that are approved by the major film manufacturers. (See Chapter 3 for more on choosing a photofinisher.)

Two other notes: First, you can buy special lead-lined bags designed to shield film from X-rays. They work, but the blank spot they create on the inspector's monitor may lead him or her to request that you open the bag anyway. And second, the effect of exposure is cumulative: Repeated passes through X-ray machines may build up a layer of "fog" that lessens the color richness and "snap" of your pictures. If you can't *prevent* X-ray exposure, try to *limit* the number of exposures.

Part V
Into the Future: New Age Point-and-Shoots

The 5th Wave   By Rich Tennant

"If I'm not gaining weight, then why does this digital image take up 3MB more memory than a comparable one taken six months ago?"

In this part . . .

Two remarkable technologies are changing the picture in photography, and they're the focus of this part. One is the Advanced Photo System (APS); the other is digital imaging. What makes the Advanced Photo System so powerful is that it's not just about new cameras, though now you can choose from many dozens of APS models. As its name says, APS is a complete system of photography, designed to maximize picture quality and creative control by linking camera, film, and photofinishing.

Special scanners, such as Kodak's new Advantix film drive, now offer direct links from the Advanced Photo System to the computer domain, letting your APS pictures do double duty. For those who want to bypass film altogether, though, digital point-and-shoots capture subjects without film at levels of quality that seem to increase every other week. Either way, you discover a whole new world of things to do with your pictures after you get them into your computer!

Chapter 14

The Advanced Photo System

In This Chapter

▶ Advanced Photo System advantages

▶ Choosing APS print formats

▶ Using the Advanced Photo System viewfinder

▶ The secret behind APS prints

▶ Getting reprints with the APS index print

▶ APS and your computer

A couple of years ago, when the Advanced Photo System was introduced, photographers asked a fair question: If 35mm ain't broke, why fix it? Why, indeed. The decades-old 35mm film format had been revived by the millions of point-and-shoot cameras expressly designed for it, greatly improving the quality of amateur photography. So why bring out another system — the Advanced Photo System?

In a sense, to pick up where 35mm leaves off. Advanced Photo System (APS) point-and-shoot cameras embrace the same decision-free technology that makes 35mm point-and-shoots such a pleasure, from automatic film advance and rewind to autoexposure, autoflash, and autofocus. Their operational details aren't all that different from those of a 35mm model. Flash modes, for example, include the familiar fill flash, flash-off, and red-eye reduction; on better models, you get slow-sync flash and its variations. Most Advanced Photo System point-and-shoots have infinity lock and a self-timer. Upper-crust models have such refinements as backlight compensation, autoexposure compensation, and subject modes. Shooting with an APS point-and-shoot feels pretty much the same as shooting with a 35mm model, which is why this book is as pertinent to the Advanced Photo System as it is to 35mm.

But Advanced Photo System point-and-shoots one-up 35mm models on many counts, both in the increased creative control they afford and in the ways they reduce anxiety about making the camera work. These improvements alone are the focus of this chapter. If you want to find out more about your APS camera's modes, turn to Chapter 4. If you want specifics about APS cameras' lenses, turn to Chapter 5. And if you want to review the way an APS cassette works, turn to Chapter 1. (You can also find a detailed illustration of an APS model there.)

Advanced Photo System Advantages

For all the automation at their fingertips, users of 35mm point-and-shoots still worry about loading that funny-looking 35mm cassette with its perforated film leader. They worry — or don't worry enough — about handling delicate strips of processed 35mm negatives. They wonder how to safely store those awkward strips. And they struggle to figure out which 35mm negative is the right one for the reprint they want.

The Advanced Photo System is an elegant, ingenious solution to those problems — and more (see Figure 14-1). Its sophisticated cassette offers the most foolproof film loading of all time (see the section "Loading Advanced Photo System Film" later in this chapter). Its unprecedented storage and indexing capabilities make keeping track of your pictures far easier than with 35mm (see "Finding the right negative the painless APS way" later in this chapter). And for reasons that this chapter explains, reprinting is much, much simpler. As if that weren't enough, the Print Quality Improvement (PQI) data recorded on the film by many Advanced Photo System cameras allows photofinishing machines not only to make your prints better, but to make them more *consistent*. Before I get into all that, though, I want to tell you about the Advanced Photo System feature that I personally enjoy the most: the choice of *print formats*.

Figure 14-1:
Advanced Photo System point-and-shoots range from one-time-use models (left) to top-of-the-line zoom cameras (right).

Advanced Photo System Print Formats

With 35mm point-and-shoot cameras, your prints come back the same size every time, usually 4 x 6 inches. (You can order the smaller 3^1/$_2$ x 5-inch size, but it has pretty much the same proportions.) The 4 x 6-inch print is a fine shape — a slightly longish rectangle that suits a horizontal landscape or a vertical portrait equally well.

But think, for a moment, about photographers who make their own prints. Most of them don't just use the same shape over and over again. Part of their art is in picking just the right shapes for prints — shapes that are appropriate to what they have photographed. They do this shaping in their darkrooms, of course. But however you go about it, adjusting the shape of a photographic image to complement the subject is called *cropping*.

If you have a 35mm point-and-shoot with a panoramic mode *and* you bother to use it, you're probably familiar with this idea. Set a small, sliding switch to *P,* take a picture, and you get back a print in which the top and bottom of the customary 35mm shape are cropped to create a longer, narrower panoramic image. (See Chapter 3 for more on panoramas.) The problem is that if you forget to tell your photofinisher you've shot panoramas on a roll, those pictures will come back as standard-sized (4 x 6- or 3^1/$_2$ x 5-inch) prints with black bands at the top and bottom. This effect not only causes the image itself to be pointlessly small, but sometimes confuses the photofinishing machinery into making the print too light. You then have to ask that the picture be reprinted as a full-sized panoramic print, usually 4 x 11^1/$_2$ or 4 x 10 inches — and pay accordingly.

Does APS have the right stuff for your picture-taking?

A curious thing about Advanced Photo System pictures is that they're made with a smaller piece of film than that used for 35mm. Most photo experts will tell you that if you start with a smaller piece of film, you're forced to blow it up more to make prints — and print quality suffers. But the Advanced Photo System has proven them wrong. Today's color print films are just so good that you're unlikely to see any difference between APS and 35mm prints.

What's more, the narrower APS film strip also allows the cassette to be smaller, which in turn makes it possible to downsize point-and-shoots using the new system. And some APS models are tiny indeed. My point: If you're looking for a new camera and your interest is piqued by the Advanced Photo System, don't let an "expert" talk you out of it!

The Advanced Photo System is a different story — or picture, should I say. It gives you direct control over the shape and size of the prints that you get back from your photofinisher. Using a switch or button on the camera itself, you select any of three different print shapes and sizes for every shot you take. Advanced Photo System photofinishing machinery automatically prints each shot in the shape and size you choose.

The system's three print formats are called *Classic, HDTV,* and *Panoramic,* indicated on APS cameras with the letters *C,* an *H,* and *P* (see Figure 14-2). They're essentially regular, wide, and wider. Choose *C,* and your picture comes back in the classic 4 x 6-inch print size to which 35mm users are accustomed. Choose *H,* and your picture comes back in an all-new 4 x 7-inch print size that some manufacturers also call Wide or Group, for its usefulness in shooting bunches of people. Choose *P,* and your picture comes back in the size also used for 35mm panoramas, either 4 x 11½ inches or 4 x 10 inches, depending on the photofinisher's equipment.

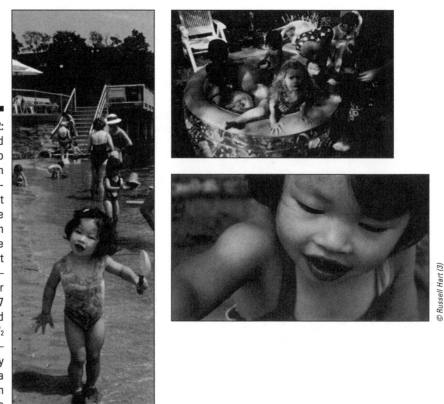

Figure 14-2: Advanced Photo System point-and-shoots let you choose between three different print sizes — 4 x 6 (upper right), 4 x 7 (right), and 4 x 11½ (left) — simply by adjusting a control on the camera itself.

© Russell Hart (3)

What do *H* prints have to do with newfangled TVs?

The Advanced Photo System's HDTV print format is roughly based on the wide-screen shape of high-definition television (that futuristic appliance we were all supposed to have by now). It borrows wide-screen TV's screen proportions, which work out to a 4 x 7-inch print.

The Advanced Photo System's Classic print format actually has the same height-to-width proportion as the standard 35mm format, a shape producing a 4 x 6-inch print.

The height of a Panoramic format print is roughly one-third of its length, which, when printed on four-inch paper, results in a print usually measuring 4 x 11½.

I repeat: You can get a different-sized print for every frame on a roll if you want, or you can use the same format for all the prints on a roll. And you can change your mind afterwards. Curious?

How to select your print format

You usually choose print formats with a sliding or rotating switch near the camera's viewfinder. (The switch may be on the front of the camera with certain models.) Rotating controls are usually located on the camera back to the right of the viewfinder; you move them with your right thumb (see Figure 14-3). Sliding controls may be located either to the left of the viewfinder or on the camera top just above it; you move them with your left thumb or left forefinger. With some models, you toggle through the formats with a pushbutton appearing in one of those places. And, naturally, other cameras may have control variations that I don't mention.

Always set your print format *before* you take a picture. The format that's set when you press the shutter button is the one that the photofinisher uses to make the print.

Figure 14-3: An APS camera's print-format control is usually right beside the viewfinder.

What shape will my pictures be?

Whenever you take a picture with an Advanced Photo System camera, the print format that you select for the shot is automatically recorded on the film with a special code. After the film is processed, the photofinishing machinery reads the code, sizing and trimming the print accordingly. When you're taking a picture, how do you know what piece of the scene will be printed? By looking through the viewfinder.

Whenever you change formats, an APS camera immediately reshapes or marks its viewfinder frame to show you the proportions of the print you'll get. It narrows the frame at the *sides* for a Classic shot. It narrows the frame at the *top* and *bottom* for a Panoramic shot. And it makes no adjustment for HDTV, because that format uses the whole viewfinder area. After the viewfinder is correctly proportioned in this way, you can compose to fit the particular print shape that you've chosen.

Advanced Photo System viewfinders take a couple of different approaches to reshaping the viewfinder, also called *masking* it. Some models actually move the viewfinder's opaque black edges in and out. Other models simply impose dark bands along the right and left edges of the frame for a Classic shot, and along the top and bottom edges of the frame for a Panoramic. These dark edges tell you not to put any part of your desired picture in that area of the frame. The darkening is translucent; you can still see the scene through it. (See Figure 14-4.)

Figure 14-4:
When you choose an APS print format, the viewfinder is automatically masked to show the print shape.

C format   H format   P format

Some less expensive Advanced Photo System cameras use frame lines superimposed within the viewfinder to show you the three different APS print formats. When you look through the viewfinder, you see three different-shaped boxes, formed by lines. The camera doesn't indicate in any way which one it's using. You must check where you've set the print-format control switch and then compose your shot with the corresponding box. You set the switch to *C* and compose with the squarish box if you want a

4 x 6-inch print; set the switch to *H* and compose with the biggest box if you want a 4 x 7-inch print; and set the switch to *P* and compose with the long, narrow box if you want a 4 x 11½-inch print.

Because these models' viewfinders don't tell you which format is set, you can forget to compose within the correct box. The mistake usually happens when your last picture was taken with the *C* or *P* format and you neglect to set the print format switch back to *H*. You compose with the biggest box, thinking you'll get a 4 x 7-inch print. Instead, you get back a 4 x 6- or 4 x 11½-inch print — and important details are often cut off. If your APS camera works this way, make it a habit to check the print format switch before shooting. Fortunately, you can easily correct such mistakes *after* you take the picture. (See the section "How APS lets you change your mind about print shape," later in this chapter.)

By the way, if your APS model's viewfinder uses dark, translucent bands to indicate different print formats, it probably has a pushbutton for setting them. With this type of control, the formats have no click positions, as do sliding or rotating switches. With a sliding or rotating switch, you can set the format without even looking through the viewfinder. With a pushbutton, you ordinarily have to toggle through the different format shapes as you look through the viewfinder — that is, push the button repeatedly until the shape you want appears. (Some pushbutton models may display your chosen format on their LCD panels.)

Which format to choose?

Which print format you choose for a given shot is entirely up to you. *You're* the creative genius behind your Advanced Photo System camera. The best thing I can tell you is to let the subject be your guide. Shooting a vertical head-and-shoulders portrait? Maybe stick with *C*, the 4 x 6-inch print. An expansive landscape? Maybe go with *P*, the 4 x 11½- inch (sometimes 4 x 10-inch) print. Taking a group shot in which all the people don't fit into the *C* frame shape? Switch to *H*, for a bit-wider 4 x 7-inch print. (See Chapter 10 for more suggestions.)

Intrigued by the Advanced Photo System's Panoramic print format? Try shooting *verticals* with it. Orienting a panorama vertically doesn't usually occur to people, but it's great for buildings and other city scenes, fun for full-length portraits, and lends itself to setting up interesting relationships between a scene's foreground and background. Even the *H* format's extra length makes it a great choice for verticals that would be cramped with 35mm. (See Figure 14-5.)

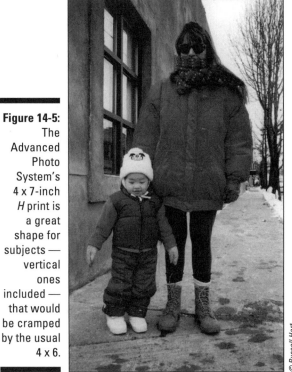

Figure 14-5:
The
Advanced
Photo
System's
4 x 7-inch
H print is
a great
shape for
subjects —
vertical
ones
included —
that would
be cramped
by the usual
4 x 6.

© Russell Hart

In experimenting with Advanced Photo System print formats, don't neglect your camera's zoom lens, if it has one. The combination of changing format and zooming in and out is powerful, giving you unrivaled compositional control. With these two capabilities, you can mix and match cropping and composition in creative ways that were previously impossible with commercial photofinishing.

Set your print format first and then adjust your zoom. Changing print formats after you zoom may cause abrupt cropping of subject details. You can easily rectify this problem, of course, simply by readjusting the zoom and/or moving closer to or farther from the subject. (See Chapter 5 for more on zooming.)

The Advanced Photo System's *H* print is, in a sense, its standard format. (In a technical sense, *H* is definitely the standard format — see the next section, "APS Printing and Reprinting.") I've always rather liked the shape of 35mm pictures, wider than most other amateur and professional film formats. So for me, the still-wider shape of *H* is just more of a good thing. Which isn't to say that I don't switch to *C* when *H* includes a little too much at the edges, or *P* when I want to make a visual statement about long, wide, or tall subjects. The 4 x 7-inch *H* print is also just a nice-feeling size — more generous than a 4 x 6 yet more hand-friendly than a 5 x 7-inch blowup.

But maybe you're more of a strictly snapshooting type and consider changing print formats a bother. If so, just leave your print-format switch set to *H* and get all 4 x 7-inch prints. (For casual shooting, I myself use *H.*) Or, if you prefer the old-fashioned 4 x 6-inch print size, leave the switch set to *C.* Even if the print-format option doesn't jazz you, Advanced Photo System point-and-shoots offer advantages that make them worth having.

HDTV *(H)* format has been the *only* format choice on most Advanced Photo System one-time-use cameras, allowing only 4 x 7-inch prints. But that situation is changing. On many new APS one-time-use cameras, such as the Kodak Advantix Switchable, a sliding switch lets you choose between *H* and Panoramic *(P)* formats — and get whatever mix of 4 x 7-inch and 4 x 11^1/$_2$-inch prints you want.

APS Printing and Reprinting

Having three on-demand choices of print size is exciting — but what if you change your mind? What if you realize, when you get a picture back, that you were trying too hard to squeeze a subject into the Advanced Photo System's Panoramic *P* format? Or that you lopped off the right half of Uncle Clive's face when you used the Classic *C* format? With APS, you can change your mind long after you've actually taken the picture.

You can have any Advanced Photo System picture reprinted in any one of the three formats. Turn that panorama back into a regular 4 x 6-inch print, perhaps restoring sky to a landscape. Or have the 4 x 6-inch print that cut off your Uncle's face redone as a 4 x 7-inch print, and literally retrieve what was beyond the edge — the missing half of Clive's face.

If you think a 4 x 7-inch print — say a vertical portrait — needs to be a little tighter on the top and bottom, then have it reprinted as a 4 x 6. Or if you think the foreground in a landscape that you shot in *H* or *C* is unattractive, then have it reprinted as a *P* — a big, wide panorama!

Keep in mind that with Advanced Photo System photofinishing, you generally pay à la carte — that is, per print. Panoramas cost more than 4 x 7-inch *H* prints, and *H* prints may cost more than 4 x 6-inch *C* prints. So if half your roll is panoramas and half *H* pictures, your processing bill will be higher than if you shot half *H* and half *C* pictures. However, the trend may be toward a flat rate: Some Kodak Premium Processing providers offer a deal in which for about $9 you can get any mix of different print sizes on a 25-exposure roll. Call it a combination platter.

How APS lets you change your mind about print shape

Here's what's behind the Advanced Photo System's reprinting flexibility. Unlike a 35mm panorama, with which the image is actually blocked off by the camera on the top and bottom of the negative, no masking goes on in an APS camera. Each time you take a picture, the entire frame of film is exposed — and all the necessary cropping is done in the printing process. If you select the *H* format for a picture, APS photofinishing machinery uses the entire APS negative (which has the wide-screen proportions that I mention earlier in the chapter) to make the requisite 4 x 7-inch print. If you select the *C* format for a picture, APS photofinishing machinery crops off the short ends of the frame, because they aren't needed for the less-elongated 4 x 6-inch print. And if you select the *P* format for a picture, APS photo-finishing machinery crops the top and bottom of the frame to create a long, narrow print.

The secret to many of the Advanced Photo System's special capabilities is, indeed, invisible. It's a transparent magnetic layer that covers the whole film surface, and remains there after processing. This layer functions much like magnetic audiotape or videotape. Information can be both recorded on it and read from it. In fact, all but basic APS cameras contain a magnetic head for this very purpose.

Print Quality Improvement data is one type of information that may be recorded on the magnetic layer. (See Chapter 3 for details.) The time, the date, and titles are another. And the print format you choose for a particular shot is also recorded on that film frame. With every frame, the photofinishing machinery reads the information the camera has recorded, so that it can make the correct print size, imprint data, and sidestep typical printing problems. (Less expensive APS cameras don't use the film's mag-netic layer to record print format information. Instead, they use light to mark a print format code on the film. But the end result is the same.)

Finding the right negative the painless APS way

If you do change your mind about the format you'd like for an Advanced Photo System picture, you could probably just hand the original print and the rest of your processing order to an experienced clerk and say (for instance), "I'd like this redone as a panorama." She would probably be up to the job. But half the point of the Advanced Photo System is that you yourself can figure out your reprint order, painlessly. To do so, you refer to the *index print* that's returned with your processed film (see Figure 14-6).

Figure 14-6:
The APS index print is a great convenience for reprinting, eliminating the need to look at negative strips to find the correct frame.

Made by digital scanning, the index print (which is usually 4 x 7 inches) is an easy, quick reference for all the shots on a particular roll. Each shot has its own thumbnail image, which shows the full *H* format image that is exposed each time you take a picture. But if you chose the *C* or *P* format for a shot, a rectangle indicating that shape is overlaid on the thumbnail to show the way you chose to crop it — the format in which the picture was actually printed.

If you want to reprint a particular shot (or get a blowup of it) with a different print format, here's what you do. Find the picture on the index print; note its number; tell the clerk, "I'd like number 8 reprinted as a panorama," or, "I'd like number 18 reprinted in the *H* format"; and hand over your negatives. You don't have to squint at negatives to figure out which strip the picture's on, the way you do with 35mm. Why? Because the negatives are coiled inside the film cassette that comes back with your Advanced Photo System order — fully processed! All you have to do is give the cassette to the clerk.

Unlike 35mm cassettes, which are discarded after the film is removed and processed, Advanced Photo System cassettes are reused. After APS film is removed and processed, it is respooled, uncut, back into the same cassette. The cassette is then returned to you with your prints (see Figure 14-7).

Inside the APS cassette, your negatives remain safe from the dust, scratches, and fingerprints that often damage loose strips of 35mm film. The APS cassette bears the same code number as the index print of the pictures it contains. Any time you want reprints, whether in your original format or a different one, you just give the photofinisher the right cassette and the number of the picture's thumbnail from the index print.

Figure 14-7:
APS
negatives
are safely
returned in
the very
same
cassette
you
originally
had in your
camera.

You should keep the index print and the Advanced Photo System cassette together. Special storage units sometimes called *memory keepers* are available for this very purpose (see Figure 14-8). Similar in size to a protective case for a VHS videotape, they contain slots for a dozen APS cassettes and a booklet or sleeve for their corresponding index prints. You needn't worry, of course, if APS prints don't remain with the cassette, because the index print tells you what pictures are on a roll and in what format they were printed. And should index prints and cassettes become separated, you can quickly match them with their code numbers.

Advanced Photo System film comes in different roll lengths than 35mm film. It's available in 15-exposure, 25-exposure, and 40-exposure lengths, with 25-exposure the most popular. The longer the roll, the more thumbnail images must fit on an index print, so usually each thumbnail is smaller. For this reason, some photofinishers can print bigger thumbnails if you shoot shorter rolls.

Figure 14-8:
APS
cassettes
can be kept
with their
match-
numbered
index prints
in 12-roll
Kodak
Advantix
Memory
Keepers.

Loading Advanced Photo System Film

The Advanced Photo System film cassette is more than just a convenient storage vessel. Much smaller than a 35mm cassette, it makes *loading* film a less intimidating business than it is in 35mm. Its special oval shape fits an APS camera's film compartment only one way, so you can't put it in backward. And it lacks 35mm's perforated leader. Loading with the Advanced Photo System is truly "drop-in" — as easy as sliding a VHS cassette into your VCR.

To load APS film, you simply open the film compartment, slide in the cassette, and close the door. (The cassette may ride up a little in the compartment, so just press it down with the door as you close it.) The camera then pushes out the film and winds it to the first frame. That first frame's number is usually the same as the number of exposures on the roll — 15, 25, or 40. Most APS cameras count backwards, telling you how many exposures remain on the roll rather than how many shots you've taken. (For details, see Chapter 2.)

You must use Advanced Photo System film if you're shooting with an Advanced Photo System camera. (Cassettes of 35mm film simply don't fit in an APS model's film compartment, and lack other advanced features needed for correct camera operation.) The same companies that make 35mm film also offer Advanced Photo System film, but they have different product names for it. Kodak's APS film goes by the name *Advantix,* as do the company's APS cameras.

The best way to make sure you're buying and using APS film is to look for the APS logo — a triangular shape with a displaced circular cutout (shown in the margin) and sometimes the words *Advanced Photo System* — on the film packaging and cassette. (The logo also appears on an APS camera's body, usually in front.) Some companies also identify their Advanced Photo System film and cameras with the initials *IX* or *ix,* which stand for *information exchange,* a reference to the system's ability to record to, and read from, the film's transparent magnetic layer. And some companies (notably Fuji) even call the film 24mm, which like 35mm refers only to the film's width. Technically, Advanced Photo System film is designated *IX240,* which combines these ideas, and you may see APS film identified *that* way, too. But for simplicity's sake, find the triangular logo.

If you're wearing your photographic thinking cap, a question may occur to you: Because APS film has no leader, how do you know if a roll has been used? With 35mm, you can tell that a roll's been shot if the leader isn't protruding from the cassette; the leader is pulled inside the cassette when 35mm film is rewound. Because the APS cassette lacks a leader, you might think you can get unexposed, exposed and rewound, and even processed cassettes mixed up. You'd be wrong.

First, if you load an exposed and/or processed APS cassette, the camera won't advance the film. If the camera has an LCD panel, it will just stop and blink the letter *E* (for empty), or sometimes a zero, and/or a symbol of the cassette. Some APS models may physically block an exposed and/or processed cassette, preventing you from inserting it all the way. In either case, you can't inadvertently double-expose an APS roll, or shoot a roll that has already been processed.

These protections are important, but you can also visually check whether an APS cassette is unexposed, exposed, or processed. On one end of the cassette, you find four tiny cutout shapes: a circle, a half-circle, an *X,* and a rectangle. A white indicator appears behind one of these shapes to tell you the cassette's status.

If the circle is white, the roll is unexposed and okay to shoot. If the half-circle is white, the film is half-exposed, and only cameras with the Advanced Photo System's mid-roll change feature (described in "The Mid-Roll Change Feature" in this chapter) will allow you to shoot the rest of it. (Otherwise, you should take it in for processing.) If the *X* is white, the film has been exposed, and you should process it soon. If the rectangle is white, the film has already been processed, and should be stored safely with other processed cassettes. (See Chapter 1 for more on the APS cassette.)

Types of Advanced Photo System Film

Advanced Photo System films come in ISO 100, 200, and 400 color print films, ISO 400 chromogenic black-and-white film, and a couple of ISO 100 slide films.

ISO 400 film is my top recommendation for an all-purpose film, whether in 35mm or the Advanced Photo System. But if you have an APS camera and you find yourself shooting frequently in the Panoramic print format, you may want to compare prints you get with an ISO 400 film and those you get with an ISO 200 film. Why this possible exception to my "Use ISO 400 film for just about everything" rule? Because APS negatives must be blown up more for Panoramic prints than for *H* or *C* format prints. The enlarging greatly magnifies the film's grain texture.

To compare prints, save the end of an ISO 400 roll that's in your camera and buy a short (15-exposure) ISO 200 roll. Find a suitable subject, set your APS camera on *P,* and shoot the last frame(s) of the ISO 400 roll. Rewind and remove the ISO 400 film, replace it with the ISO 200 film, and shoot the same subject. Shoot off the rest of the ISO 200 film, if you like — may as well check it out in the other print formats too — and have both rolls processed. When you get the prints back, choose the best Panoramic print from each roll and mark which speed film you used for it on the back. Then shuffle the two prints thoroughly, so you really don't know which is which.

Now compare the prints — no looking at the backs. Do you see a difference? More important, do you like one or the other better? If you notice anything, the ISO 200 print may have a slightly smoother quality. If you prefer its quality and plan to shoot lots of Panoramic pictures, then you may want to use ISO 200 rather than ISO 400 APS film.

A couple of ISO 100 Advanced Photo System slide films are available. As with 35mm, APS slides are returned in mounts. The mounts are the standard two-inch size designed for 35mm projectors, such as those in the Kodak Carousel line.

If you're curious to try APS slide film, you probably shot slides with your old 35mm SLR camera. Given that experience, you should keep in mind that the picture area of APS slides is much smaller than that of 35mm. If you're projecting your images, you'll have to back the projector away and/or zoom the lens out (if your projector has a zoom lens) to make the projected image as large as what you were accustomed to getting with 35mm. What's more, APS slides are not automatically cropped as are APS prints; the rectangular opening in an APS slide mount is shaped to accommodate the full-frame *H* format.

However, the slide mount is imprinted with your chosen format, and as with APS print films, the index print returned with the roll uses crop boxes on each thumbnail image to indicate the format that you chose for the shot. The index print should make it easier to shape the slide to your intended *C* or *P* proportions with drop-in masks (basically, little cutouts in the shape you want) now in the offing. (For details on shooting slides, see Chapter 2.)

Not all photofinishers provide Advanced Photo System film processing. Of those that do, some can process APS film on the premises. But most send the film out to special processing facilities, which can make the turnaround time for APS photofinishing as long as three or four days. (See Chapter 3 for specifics on APS processing.)

The Mid-Roll Change Feature

The Advanced Photo System has other intriguing features, but you won't find them all together except on a few top-of-the-line models. One interesting option is *mid-roll change,* abbreviated MRC. This unique capability lets you change to a different type or speed of film in the middle of the roll — *without wasting any frames.*

If you want to switch to a different film with a regular APS or 35mm camera, and you haven't reached the end of the roll, you have two choices. You can rewind the roll and "waste" the remaining frames. (Just push the midroll rewind button, remembering that film is cheaper than prints.) Or you can shoot the rest of the roll in a hurry and let the camera automatically rewind it at the end. (You'll probably get some pretty dull pictures.)

With mid-roll change, though, when you push the midroll rewind button in the middle of a roll, you can actually save the remainder of the roll for a rainy day — or a sunny day, depending on the film's speed! Because when you put that half-shot roll of film back into your MRC-capable camera, it actually loads the film and advances it to the first unused, unexposed frame of film. It finds this frame by reading information recorded by the camera on the film's magnetic layer.

If your Advanced Photo System camera has mid-roll change (MRC) capability, rewinding a half-shot roll of film sets the cassette's status indicators to the half-circle symbol. (These indicators appear on the end of the cassette; see the section, "Loading Advanced Photo System Film," for details.) This symbol tells you that the roll contains unexposed frames and that you can reload it later if you choose. But if you put a half-shot roll of APS film into an APS camera that has no MRC capability — even if it has been shot with an MRC model — the camera will consider it an exposed roll and won't advance it.

Why switch film in midroll? I can think of two reasons. Again, you may want to switch to a different film type or speed. Say you're traveling. You're shooting landscapes with an ISO 100 film — against my better judgment, I might add, because I keep telling you to use ISO 400 film! — because you plan to blow them up to display-size prints. (Film with a lower ISO does produce pictures with finer grain, though you probably won't notice unless those blowups are very big indeed!) Then, back at the motel, you want to shoot pictures of your kids splashing in the pool. You rewind the ISO 100 roll, saving it for tomorrow's landscapes, and replace it with an ISO 400 roll. When you set out the next day, just swap rolls again, and the camera will pick up where you left off on the ISO 100 roll. And now that black-and-white and color slide films are available in APS, mid-roll change lets you switch freely between film *types* as well.

The second reason to switch film in midroll is to dedicate particular rolls to specific kinds of subjects. You may save one roll for pictures of parties, another for pictures of school; one for family pictures, another for your arty shots. Or you may reserve a roll for a series of pictures showing the process of constructing an addition to your house.

APS Printing Refinements

Other interesting Advanced Photo System features hinge on the sophisticated interface between the camera and the printing process that APS film affords. For example, the film's magnetic layer can store the time and date you took the picture, if you have a model capable of recording that information. The time and/or date are automatically printed on the *back* of the print, as opposed to 35mm's image-marring approach, "burning" colored numbers into the front of a print with electrical diodes. Called *backprinting,* this feature is a real plus if you've taken on the job of visual diary-keeper.

Likewise, some models also allow you to program in titles — in effect, short captions — for a particular shot. You use the camera's time/date setting buttons, referring to a numerical menu you'll find in your instruction manual. These titles can include such sentiments as "Thank you," "Merry Christmas," and even "I love you." (For details, see Chapter 3.)

Other models even let you specify, with the same pushbuttons used to set the time and date, how many copies you want of a given print — in a sense, allowing you to get reprints in advance for anxious friends and relatives. The APS photofinishing machinery reads your request and makes the extras when it's printing the rest of the roll. You have to set the number of prints you'd like before taking the shot. But if after taking it you decide it wasn't up to par, you can actually cancel your order with the pushbuttons! (You do have to do it right after you take the shot, though.)

And then the Advanced Photo System has some other benefits that are as transparent as the film's magnetic layer, but no less real. Among them is the *Print Quality Improvement* information that many Advanced Photo System cameras record on APS film. The extent of this data varies from model to model, but its purpose is the same: to improve commercial printing by identifying photographic qualities that typically trip it up. The system records, for each and every shot, a set of picture conditions — things like whether flash was used, how much sky fills the frame, and the relative proportion of artificial light in the scene. Using this information, the photofinishing machinery's software can actually avoid the mistakes that are typical of 35mm printing.

The Advanced Photo System and Your Computer

Photo experts like to throw around the term *hybrid.* It's used in reference to photographic systems that combine conventional (analog) and digital technologies. Photo experts sometimes refer to the Advanced Photo System as a hybrid system. They are somewhat misinformed.

Which isn't to say that the Advanced Photo System's designers haven't built in very smart links to the digital world. Take the film's transparent magnetic layer. Though it's currently being used only to record print format, picture-taking conditions, time and date, and so on, it could be used to record and store actual image information. The layer could ultimately serve as the repository for a digital file of the very picture on which it lies — a digital and conventional version of photographs stacked one on top of the other! You could then use whichever version of the photograph suits your particular needs: the negative for reprinting, the digital file for computer retouching or e-mailing.

For the time being, the Advanced Photo System boasts several affordably priced desktop APS film scanners for home computers — models such as Kodak's Advantix Film Drive FD 300. (See Chapter 15.) These ingenious devices are designed to effortlessly convert APS film images into digital computer files. You simply slip your processed APS cassette into a small compartment, close the door, and the unit does just about everything else automatically.

First, the scanner uncoils the entire roll from the cassette, quickly scanning each frame to display thumbnail images of all the roll's pictures on your computer screen. Then it lets you choose an image or images for more detailed, higher-quality scanning. These higher-resolution files can be used for digital retouching with easy-to-use software now available for the purpose. Designed to link directly to your computer, these scanners are even available in versions that accept both Advanced Photo System and 35mm film — though to work with 35mm, you still have to directly handle those funny strips of negatives! (Advanced Photo System "players" — sort of like VCRs for still photos — work in a similar fashion, allowing you to view your APS pictures on a regular TV.)

Of course, if you don't want to invest in a scanner, you can get your Advanced Photo System pictures scanned to a floppy disk or to a Kodak Photo CD or FlashPix CD, just as you would with 35mm film. I describe these services in more detail in Chapter 3. If you're computer-savvy, you can combine such digital delights with your photographic interests in lots of ways. Read Chapter 15 to find out how.

Chapter 15

Photography and Your Computer

· ·

In This Chapter

▶ What your computer can do for your photography

▶ What you need for digital imaging

▶ Getting pictures into your computer

▶ How scanners work

▶ Taking pictures with a digital point-and-shoot

▶ Downloading from a digital point-and-shoot

▶ Rating digital point-and-shoots

▶ Using digital imaging software

▶ Getting pictures out of your computer

▶ Printing digital images

· ·

*1*f you're a personal computer user, you've probably discovered lots of different things you can do with your PC: writing letters, sending e-mail, balancing your checkbook, playing CD-ROMs, visiting Internet Web sites. But chances are you haven't used your computer for any photographic purpose. And why would you? Because with a modest amount of computing power, the right software, and some affordable peripheral hardware, you can enjoy your pictures in ways that surpass just getting prints.

You can e-mail pictures to friends and family. You can transmit pictures to Web sites for any and all to see. You can turn pictures into greeting cards, calendars, and announcements. And maybe most fun, you can retouch and manipulate your pictures — enhancing their color, removing unwanted details, and adding special effects. With computer technology, you can basically accept or reject the reality of your photos. Want to see how your house would look in the latest shade of mauve? Shoot it and repaint it — with your computer.

To do these wondrous photographic things, you first need to get your pictures into your computer. And for that to happen, your pictures must be in a digital form — translated into the same computer language used to store letters and numbers. The main difference is that much more digital information is needed to recreate photographs than letters and numbers. One picture is worth way more than a thousand words — perhaps an entire novel's worth of digital data. Fortunately, you can get your pictures into digital form in a number of ways, ranging from very cheap to only moderately expensive. This chapter gives you an overview of these intriguing options. (For more detail, I suggest you pick up a copy of *Digital Photography For Dummies* by Julie Adair King, published by IDG Books Worldwide, Inc.)

Don't think you have to rush out and buy a digital point-and-shoot — one of the new cameras that takes pictures without film — to get photographs into your computer. Your digital future can begin with the pictures you make with your existing, film-using camera. By *scanning* these pictures (a process that converts them to digital form), you can get even higher-quality results than are possible with digital point-and-shoots. (See "Getting Pictures Into Your Computer," later in this chapter.)

The Digital Details

Whether a digital photograph is scanned from film or captured with a digital point-and-shoot camera, it's made up of tiny, organized little squares called *pixels.* (Pixel is actually a contraction of the term *picture element.*) To picture how pixels work, imagine an intricate mosaic consisting of lots of small tiles. A single tile contains just one color or shade and doesn't offer a clue about what the whole mosaic represents. But when you group the tiles in an orderly fashion, and step back, they blend together to produce a recognizable image.

Likewise, a digital image is formed by thousands, even millions, of tiny, tilelike pixels. Each pixel contains only one color or tone, but when you view the image on your computer monitor or in a digital print, they come together to create a convincing representation of reality.

The minimum amount of digital information needed to store a pixel's tone and color is three *bytes,* a term from the computer language called binary code. You've probably noticed that the ability of computer hardware to handle digital data is described in *megabytes,* often abbreviated MB. That's a million bytes of digital information — and computer files of photographic images are often measured in megabytes.

Getting the right computer for digital photography

Thanks to plummeting prices and phenomenal increases in processing power, you can buy a computer capable of handling and displaying photographic images for $1,000 — monitor included! Here's what that thousand bucks gets you — and what I recommend for photographers with serious computer ambitions.

✔ Pentium or Power PC CPU (central processing unit) that runs at clock speeds of 133 MHz or higher

✔ 4X speed or higher CD-ROM drive

✔ 32 megabytes of RAM

✔ 15-inch or larger color monitor

✔ 28.8 Kbps (kilobits per second) or faster modem (to connect you to the Internet)

✔ 24-bit color video graphics display card

✔ One-gigabyte or larger hard drive

If you want to do your own scanning, retouching, or printing, you should consider the following additional hardware:

✔ Snapshot or flatbed scanner ($100 and up)

✔ Additional RAM memory

✔ Image retouching software (under $50; see the section "Imaging Software: Digital Magic," later in this chapter)

✔ Photographic-quality color printer ($400)

If you have a creaky computer with a puny hard drive and no CD-ROM drive, don't try to upgrade it for photographic applications. A new system — one that is four times as fast, has better features, and comes with a warranty — is actually cheaper! But if you're just lacking in RAM memory or modem speed, an upgrade may do the job. Check with your computer salesperson for details.

A generous amount of *RAM* — random access memory — is needed for your computer to perform photographic functions. RAM is the amount of digital information your computer can actively handle, not to be confused with hard drive storage. Generally, the minimum amount of RAM needed to run photographic software is 16MB. But if you plan to do any retouching on your pictures, you're better off with at least 32MB — and you can double your RAM for as little as $200. If only my brain were that easy to upgrade! (RAM is increased simply by slipping accessory memory boards into your computer's expansion slots; for details, see *PCs For Dummies,* 5th Edition, by Dan Gookin, published by IDG Books Worldwide, Inc.)

Getting Pictures into Your Computer

One way to get digital photographs is to shoot them digitally — that is, with a digital point-and-shoot camera. You then *download* them directly to your computer's hard drive, no film needed. (See the section "Taking Pictures with a Digital Camera," later in this chapter.) But the two other main ways to get pictures into your computer both begin with film — your regular negatives or prints. Negatives or prints can be easily converted to digital form with a process called *scanning*. You can either have your photofinisher do the scanning, or you can do it yourself with an inexpensive computer peripheral called — you guessed it — a *scanner*.

Having your photofinisher scan your pictures

Most minilab and mass-market photofinishers now offer inexpensive scanning services. This is a great way to get started in computer-aided photography without spending money on extra hardware. The scanning service is ordinarily provided at the time you have your film developed and printed, but you can also bring existing negatives or prints back to the photofinisher for scanning.

The photofinisher can do one of several things with the digital files scanning produces, depending on how you want to retrieve them. He can record them on a standard computer floppy disk; he can record them on a special CD-ROM; or he can transmit them to the World Wide Web. (Floppies and CD-ROMs are returned with your processing order.)

Floppy disks

Getting pictures on a floppy allows you to simply pop the disk into your computer's floppy drive and retrieve the pictures just the way you would a text file. The software needed to view the pictures usually comes right on the disk, but you'll need more advanced photographic software to do any further work or manipulation with them.

Kodak Premium Processing, for example, offers two inexpensive "scan to floppy" services: The Kodak Picture Disk, in which an entire roll is scanned to the disk at the time of processing, and the Kodak Picture Disk Plus, in which one image is scanned at a high level of quality to a single floppy. Use the former for pictures that will mainly be viewed on computer screen (e-mailing photos, for example), the latter for pictures from which you want to make good digital prints. The additional cost for scanning a 24-exposure roll to a floppy at the time of processing is usually $5 or $6.

CD-ROMs

If your computer has a CD-ROM drive, consider having your photofinisher put your scanned pictures on a special Kodak CD-ROM — either a Photo CD or a FlashPix CD. You just pop the disk into the drive, but you will need photographic software to retrieve the pictures. Which CD you choose depends partly on your purposes: Pick Photo CD for high-quality printing applications, FlashPix CD for pictures you plan to e-mail or use at smaller sizes in projects such as cards and calendars. The cost of scanning a 24-exposure roll to a CD is a fairly pricey $20 or so. But over half of that is the cost of the CD, to which you can add future pictures — 100 or more total.

The World Wide Web

Besides putting scans of your pictures on a floppy disk or CD, your photofinisher can send them into cyberspace. A number of companies now operate Web sites to which digital images can be directly "uploaded" by the photofinisher. This allows you to look at your pictures online and to invite friends and family to do so. But you can also *download* pictures from the site for use in your computer. (You'll need Web browser software, of course.)

The Kodak Picture Network and PictureVision's PhotoNet, now allied, offer this service through thousands of retail photofinishing outlets. To request it, you simply check off a box on your photofinishing envelope. When you pick up your prints and negatives, you receive a code number that you enter for access to your pictures when you visit the Web site. The cost for this service is about $5 extra per 24-exposure roll (which includes a month of Web display), and you can keep up to 100 photos on the site for an additional $5 a month.

Scanning photos yourself

The cost of photofinishers' scanning services add up over time, so if you're into digital photography for the long haul you may want to purchase your own desktop scanner. These units are generally "plug and play" — totally simple in their installation and operation. They come in models that accept prints, negatives and slides, or both, and cost as little as $100.

Once you install the unit's "driver" software (which comes on a floppy disk or CD-ROM) and hook up the scanner to your computer, you simply insert your print or film into the scanner. The software automatically guides you through and controls the needed steps. The result: an onscreen image for you to manipulate and store.

✔ **Snapshot scanners** are specially designed to turn your photofinisher's standard 4-inch-wide prints (4 x 6 inches, 4 x 7 inches, up to panoramic 4 x 11^1/$_2$ inches) into digital files. Compact and cheap ($100 to $150), they feature a very friendly software interface. You feed prints into them the way you would with a fax machine, and the print is automatically transported through for scanning.

✔ **Flatbed scanners** resemble photocopiers, featuring a flat glass plate on which you place your original. They accept prints and blow-ups up to 8 x 10 or 11 x 14 inches in size, depending on the model; smaller units can cost as little as $100. You can use scanners to digitize documents or nonphotographic images too. (How about scanning those old family photos for retouching?) Combination scanner/printers are available for around $400, and with some models, you can get an accessory adapter that allows you to scan negatives or slides.

✔ **Film scanners** turn negatives or slides into digital files. They're more costly than snapshot or flatbed models — usually $500 and up — but generally offer even better picture quality. Models are available for 35mm or Advanced Photo System film, and several new units accept both 35mm and APS film through the use of an APS adapter module.

Advanced Photo System film scanners such as the Kodak Advantix Film Drive FD 300 (about $350) offer scanning operation in which film handling is as automated as it is with a point-and-shoot camera. You insert the processed APS cassette into a slot, and the scanner automatically unfurls and scans the whole roll, displaying small images of every frame on your computer screen in under 60 seconds (for a 24-exposure roll). Select a picture with the scanner's software, and the frame is automatically rescanned at a higher level of quality.

Taking Pictures with a Digital Camera

The day may come, early in the next century, when most people take their pictures with digital point-and-shoots — eliminating the need for photographic film. If they want prints, they'll either make them at home, on their own digital printers, or have photofinishers make them from digital picture files that they provide on tiny memory cards or disks.

In fact, the technology for this scenario is already in place — and in use. It just needs to get even cheaper, better, and more convenient to become a true mass-market alternative to conventional film and printing. At this point, for the cost of a no-frills digital point-and-shoot (say, $200 to $250), you can get a top-drawer film point-and-shoot. And the cheapest film point-and-shoot will give you picture quality superior to that of the most expensive digital models (those costing close to $1,000). That said, some digital point-and-shoots costing under $1,000 deliver image quality that is more than adequate for a 4 x 6- or even a 5 x 7-inch print. And hey — you don't have to pay a dime for film or processing!

Digital point-and-shoots operate very much like film point-and-shoots, and newer models closely resemble them (see Figure 15-1). They fully automate major camera functions, usually have a built-in flash that fires on its own in low light, and feature a choice of pushbutton- or dial-controlled modes. One noticeable difference is that most, though not all, digital point-and-shoots have an external color LCD — a TVlike screen for composing and reviewing pictures (see the sidebar, "Screen gem: Your digital point-and-shoot's color LCD"). Otherwise, in terms of operation, you pretty much just press the shutter button, and the camera does the rest.

The big difference between film point-and-shoots and digital point-and-shoots is what's inside. Inside a digital point-and-shoot, where a frame of film would ordinarily rest in a regular point-and-shoot, is a special light sensor not unlike the one in video camcorders. The sensor's flat surface is made up of hundreds of thousands, even millions of microscopically small pixels — those tiny digital picture elements I talk about at the beginning of this chapter. These pixels are like little light-gathering windows, and when the camera's lens projects an image of the subject on the sensor, each one captures a different combination of brightness and color. This image is then converted to digital form and saved in the camera's memory. (See the sidebar, "Thanks for the memory: Storing digital pictures.")

Figure 15-1: Kodak's Digital Science DC200 camera looks and feels like a film point-and-shoot, but produces high-quality digital images.

Screen gem: Your digital point-and-shoot's color LCD

On the back of most digital point-and-shoot cameras you find a flat TVlike screen called a color LCD (liquid crystal display). Often hinged or rotatable so that you can keep your eye on it even when you're shooting at weird angles, the color LCD is a multipurpose feature. Here's how it's used. (Refer to Figure 15-2 for an example of a color LCD screen.)

✔ **As a viewfinder:** You can use the color LCD to get a "live" picture of your subject, composing with it the way you do with now-popular video camcorders having external monitors.

✔ **As a playback device:** You can use the color LCD to review the pictures you've shot. In fact, it allows you to check your results immediately — impossible with a film point-and-shoot. You push buttons to move from one picture to the next, and some models can display up to nine or so miniature "thumbnails" at once. You can also use the color LCD to erase bad shots or shots you don't want — immediately, if you like.

✔ **As a control panel:** Many digital point-and-shoot models make their color LCD do double duty for setting camera functions, displaying a "menu" such as that shown by VCRs on your TV screen. Again, you push buttons to scroll through the menu and make choices.

Avoid using a digital point-and-shoot's color LCD as a viewfinder — that is, for composition and shooting. (You can usually turn it off with a button.) Instead, use the camera's optical viewfinder — the little window on the back of the camera — if it has one. The color LCD is hard to see in bright light and forces you to hold the camera away from your face to shoot. (This increases the chance that shake will blur the picture, and makes your arms tired, too!) Using the color LCD to shoot also hugely increases the camera's power needs, forcing you to change batteries much more often. And the batteries can add up, since most digital point-and-shoot models take four AA cells.

Reserve the color LCD for reviewing and erasing pictures. Even if you do this, be sure to use alkaline batteries — at the least. Consider using longer-lived lithium AA batteries, or even rechargeables (see Chapter 1). And whatever type you use, always have an extra set on hand for that inevitable moment when the camera gives out in the middle of a photo op. Finally, if you're shopping for a digital point-and-shoot, choose one that has a regular optical viewfinder as well as the ability to turn off the color LCD.

After you take a picture with a digital point-and-shoot, it must record the picture in its memory. During this time, which can last up to ten seconds, the camera won't let you shoot another picture — however hard you press the shutter button! Newer models take less time, but don't expect to shoot rapid-fire pictures with a digital point-and-shoot camera.

Downloading Photographs from a Digital Point-And-Shoot

So how do you get pictures from your digital point-and-shoot into your computer? With a cable that links camera and computer and special software that controls the process, both supplied with the camera. Transferring pictures in this way is called *downloading*.

Once the software is installed from a floppy disk or CD-ROM (which takes just a few mouseclicks), you connect the cable to the camera and the computer. Then you turn on the camera and computer and fire up the software. With a few more mouseclicks you get a screen filled with *thumbnails,* or small images, of the pictures stored in the camera. You can save some or all of these pictures to your hard drive.

After the downloading is complete, you erase the images in the camera so that you can start shooting again. And once they're on your hard drive, you can view and manipulate the transferred image files with a variety of imaging programs. (See the sections "Imaging Software: Digital Magic" and "Getting Pictures out of Your Computer," later in this chapter, for more about the cool stuff you can do with your digital photos.)

Look for a digital camera that includes a video-out terminal and cable so that you can hook the camera directly to a TV for viewing. That way, you can show off your images on a big screen even if you don't have access to a computer. You can even record photos on videotape and play them back on any VCR.

Imaging Software: Digital Magic

Picture this. You get home from work and suddenly remember that tomorrow is your significant other's birthday — and the card shop is closed. (I hope for your sake you already have the present.) Are you worried? No. You just turn on your computer, click on your digital imaging software, and use it to call up a half dozen thumbnail photos of your sweetheart. You choose the best one and proceed to remove the oak tree that seems to be growing out of his or her head. (You may need to work on your composition; see Chapter 9!) You magnify the image and remove some blemishes. (I won't tell.) You replace that drab sky with a stunning sunset. You key in, with your favorite typeface, "I love you darling, don't ever change." Finally, you send the image by e-mail, use it to create a Web page for all the world to see, or fire up your computer printer to make an old-fashioned card — leaving it on the kitchen table, as if you'd planned things all along.

Thanks for the memory: Storing digital pictures

Once a digital point-and-shoot captures your photograph with its light-sensing "chip," what happens to it? It's stored on the camera's internal memory, much the way your computer "saves" files to its hard drive or floppy disk. Digital point-and-shoots use one of two different types of memory systems to store their pictures: fixed and removable. (Some models may have both.)

Fixed-memory models have memory that's permanently built into the camera. When it fills up with pictures, you have two choices. You can selectively erase unwanted or bad shots (which you do by using pushbuttons and the camera's color LCD) to make room for more pictures. Or you can stop taking pictures and download all the stored shots to your computer's hard drive and then erase the entire memory so you can shoot more. Even if your computer is in the next room, having to do this is at best inconvenient, and at worst can cost you good pictures that you might have gone on to take.

Removable-memory models get around this problem by storing pictures on matchbook-sized memory cards that slip into the camera body (see figure). When a card gets filled up with pictures, you just pull it out and slip in another — basically, like putting in a new roll of film. This way, you can keep shooting, and shoot as many pictures as you have cards for. And when you're good and ready, you can put

the cards back into the camera for downloading. (See the section "Downloading Photographs from a Digital Point-and-Shoot," earlier in this chapter.)

Three different types of digital point-and-shoot memory cards are currently in use — alas, none of them compatible. (It's the old Mac-versus-PC, VHS-versus-Beta thing.) The most common type of these cards is called CompactFlash, used by Kodak's digital point-and-shoots, among many others. Wafer-thin SSFDC cards come in a close second. Each card type comes in different capacities, expressed in megabytes; cards range from 2MB to 48MB. The more megabytes, the more pictures you can fit on the card. But the number of pictures also depends on what picture quality level you set on the camera. (See the sidebar, "Rating digital point-and-shoots.") Memory cards aren't exactly cheap; they can range from $10 to $20 per megabyte, depending on type and capacity. But as with everything else digital, the price keeps dropping.

Which type of memory is best? My advice: Choose a camera with memory capability that fits your shooting requirements. If you don't plan to take more than 20 to 60 photos at a time before returning to your computer, a camera with built-in memory does the trick. If you need to shoot more than 60 photos at a time, opt for a camera with removable memory and purchase a few extra memory cards.

That remedial magic is made possible by digital imaging software. These special photographic programs allow you to perform everything from simple retouching to dramatic special effects on your pictures. And it doesn't matter how you get the pictures into your computer — with a digital camera, from a Photo CD, or by scanning them yourself.

Digital imaging software comes in a huge variety of forms, from simple quick-fix programs that automatically sharpen your pictures and adjust their colors, to super-sophisticated programs that give you a level of photographic control far exceeding what's possible in the conventional darkroom. (The granddaddy of these programs is Adobe Photoshop; for more about it, check out *Photoshop For Dummies* by Deke McClelland, published by IDG Books Worldwide, Inc.)

For your purposes, though, the most useful programs are probably right in the middle — under-$50 software such as Adobe PhotoDeluxe, LivePix Deluxe, or Kodak Picture Easy 3.0. Programs such as these let you do the following things, and more, with your pictures:

- **Retouching:** You can remove red-eye, wrinkles, dust, and scratches; adjust colors that are dull or off; and make pictures brighter or darker.

- **Resizing and cropping:** You can control the size at which pictures will print or be displayed, and reframe the subject to correct compositional errors.

- **Enhancing:** You can introduce special effects such as exaggerated or false color, blurs, textures, or creative distortion; even change a picture's background or seamlessly collage different shots together.

- **Special projects:** You can use straight or manipulated photographs to create greeting cards, calendars, flyers, announcements, invitations, even T-shirt transfers and computer screen savers. Many digital imaging programs also include hundreds of "clip art" drawings and borders for decorating your pictures.

- **Archiving:** You can organize photographs into digital albums and access particular shots with easy indexing systems.

- **E-mailing:** You can send pictures to friends and family — electronically, of course. (See "Getting Pictures out of Your Computer.")

All these programs are self-guiding, and many are truly all-purpose, offering e-mail and printing capabilities in addition to retouching. In some cases, they come free with the purchase of a computer, digital camera, or scanner. But if you can, test drive different programs at your dealer to see what features they provide.

Rating digital point-and-shoots

Thinking about buying a digital point-and-shoot? Consider the following criteria, weighing them against both the camera's cost and what you intend to do with your digital pictures.

Resolution: Basically, the more pixels a point-and-shoot has, the better its picture quality — but the more expensive it will be. Digital point-and-shoot cameras all come with their resolution stated in pixels; check the literature or ask a salesperson.

A digital camera with about 300,000 pixels is said to have "VGA" resolution — quality good enough for viewing on a computer screen. Models in this range are fine for pictures you want to e-mail, transmit to the Web, or incorporate into computer documents, but they're not really up to the task of digital printing. For that task, you need a digital point-and-shoot with close to a million pixels or more. Many new under-$1,000 models have pixel counts well over a million; for this reason they're often called "megapixel" cameras.

Keep in mind that you don't necessarily have to use all of a digital point-and-shoot's available pixels to record a picture. Many models, especially those with high pixel counts, allow you to reduce the number of pixels that actually capture the image. (The camera may only use every second or third pixel, for instance.) This setting, made with pushbuttons, is generally called "low" resolution, as opposed to the "high" resolution of the full pixel count. (Some models may even have a third, in-between setting.)

Why would you want to use fewer pixels for a photograph? Because doing so lets you fit more pictures in the camera's built-in memory, or on its memory cards. But again, you should only use a low resolution setting if your picture quality isn't critical, such as for on-screen viewing.

Compression: Compression is computer jargon for what it sounds like: squeezing a digital file to make it smaller. In the case of a digital point-and-shoot, it means removing less important information from an image to be able to store it with less memory space — and thus to store more pictures. In fact, some models use compression to save memory, while others use lower resolution.

When you open a compressed file on your computer, the image is automatically reconstituted, sort of like adding water to powdered milk. Too much compression, though, and your pictures may not be of high enough quality to reconstitute — especially with a digital printer.

Light sensitivity: With a regular point-and-shoot, you can increase the camera's ability to get pictures in low light simply by using a faster film — that is, one with a higher sensitivity to light. (See Chapter 2.) With a digital point-and-shoot, that sensitivity to light is fixed, a function of the physical size of the tiny pixels. The bigger the pixels, the more light they can scoop up.

Some digital cameras capture photos in low light better than others, but this ability may come at the expense of picture quality. The best advice? Be sure to get a digital point-and-shoot model that has a built-in flash, so that it can add light to the subject when there isn't enough already for a good picture.

Color quality: This is an area best left to computer experts. Even so, digital cameras differ in their ability to render the subject's colors faithfully. They may differ even if they have the same color specifications, which are stated in something called *color bits*. Try to choose a model that has at least 24-bit color.

Getting Pictures out of Your Computer

Whether you retouch them or not, once you get your pictures into your computer, you'll probably need to get them out for various purposes. You may want to share them with friends and family, which you can do either by e-mailing them to computer-abled recipients or transmitting them to a Web site. Or you may prefer to get pictures out of your computer in the form of hard copy — prints, calendars, greeting cards, brochures, or anything else you can output to a digital printer.

E-mailing pictures

If you're one of the millions of people who use computer e-mail — electronic messages delivered over your existing phone lines — then you already have the most important thing you need to send photographs by e-mail: a modem. A modem is an affordable (as little as $100) computer peripheral that converts digital files into a form that can be transmitted by telephonic signals. (New computers often come with a modem built in.)

Because a photograph requires so much digital information to represent, try to use a modem with a "speed" of at least 28.8 Kbps. (The Kbps stands for kilobits per second. Never mind.) The higher the modem's rating, the faster you'll be able to e-mail pictures. Even with a 28.8 Kbps modem going full throttle, transmitting photographs usually takes minutes rather than the seconds required by text files.

You can e-mail photographs using your regular e-mail software and Internet Service Provider. Once pictures are saved as files on your hard drive, you "attach" them to standard e-mail messages just as you would a text document. (Check your e-mail software's instructions if you're not sure how to do this.) Keep in mind, though, that people on the receiving end of your e-mail will need special software to view attached photographs, once they have downloaded the file. This can be the same software you used to view and manipulate the photograph when it was in your computer. But many e-mail programs, Web browsers, and even word processors now have the ability to "open" picture files if they are saved in standard file *formats*. These formats include JPEG, Exif, PICT, GIF, or the new FlashPix — and don't worry about the acronyms. Your photographic software should allow you to save a picture in one or all of these, and most will do so automatically.

Putting pictures on the Web

A number of companies now maintain Web sites on which you can display your digital pictures, sharing them with anyone you invite. Though some of these providers allow you to transmit images directly to the site yourself, using their own photo album and "uploading" software, the most convenient of them are set up so that your photofinisher can scan your pictures and transmit them to the Web site directly. Friends and relatives can even order reprints online, through services such as Kodak's Image Magic. (See Chapter 3 for details, or pick up a copy of *The Internet For Dummies,* 5th Edition, by John R. Levine, Carol Baroudi, and Margaret Levine Young, published by IDG Books Worldwide, Inc.)

Printing digital images yourself

Computer printer technology has become the standard-setter for digital imaging. For less than $400, you can now get a color printer that produces prints that are virtually photographic in quality. But — and this is a big but — to achieve this look you have to begin with a high-quality, high-resolution digital file. Don't expect to get even a very good 4 x 6 print — that old photo-finishing standby — if you're printing pictures from a $200 digital point-and-shoot. To get acceptable quality at 5 x 7-inch size, for example, you need to start with a file of at least a million pixels — even more for larger sizes.

If you buy a printer that you plan to use for your digital pictures, be sure to get one that delivers *photographic quality.*

Digital printers produce prints in a couple of basic sizes. You can get compact models that create prints measuring 4 x 6 inches. And you can get larger models that produce images slightly smaller than the standard $8^1/_2$ x 11-inch paper size. Printers are also distinguished by the technology they use to actually create the image. Here are the most common such types:

- **Inkjet printers** spray microscopic drops of ink onto paper (and occasionally onto other materials like watercolor paper or canvas). Paper is critical: Many papers on the market claim to be the best for producing inkjet photographs, so you may want to experiment with other papers after you try the one supplied by the printer manufacturer.

- **Dye-sublimation printers** are another popular type of photographic-quality printer. These models use a special type of paper and create their color with ribbons rather than ink cartridges. During printing, a special printer head containing hundreds or thousands of microscopic elements heats up the inks on the ribbon in proportion to the detail in the image. The dyes turn to gas, which is absorbed into the paper. The dye-sublimation process is usually slower than inkjet printing because the printer must make at least three passes over the paper in order to transfer the red, green, and blue color dyes in sequence.

The ink used by most inkjet printers isn't waterproof, or even water-resistant — so don't get your inkjet prints wet or store them in a humid environment. Dye-sublimation prints are more water-resistant. With either type of print, though, don't display pictures in locations that receive direct sunlight. You'll be surprised at how rapidly they fade!

Part VI
The Part of Tens

In this part . . .

This part alone is worth the price of admission to *Photography For Dummies,* and proof that good things come in tens — or, in a few cases, elevens and twelves. Like to look at pictures from the comfort of your computer? Open Chapter 18 — and get online. Camera won't shoot? Try the ten things suggested in Chapter 20 — and if the problem is fatal, read Chapter 16. My personal favorite? Chapter 19, a list of great places to take pictures. (It's very personal.) And in Chapter 17, I present ten simple ways to improve your point-and-shoot pictures. Does this whole book boil down to ten tips? You be the judge. Try all ten and see what happens to your photographs!

Chapter 16

Ten Things to Think about When Buying a Point-and-Shoot Camera

In This Chapter

▶ Deciding how much money to spend

▶ Matching the camera type to your subject matter

▶ Deciding whether to buy a digital point-and-shoot

▶ Choosing between 35mm and the Advanced Photo System

▶ Determining the features you need

*I*f you're reading this book, you probably have a camera already. And chances are good that your camera has the right stuff to help you make better pictures — if you bring the right attitude and an intelligent eye to it. But you may decide that to take the kinds of pictures you'd like to take and get the picture quality you want, you have to go out and buy a new point-and-shoot. Your old camera may be a bulky, complicated 35mm single-lens reflex (SLR) that you'd like to replace with something more compact and simpler to operate — a camera that doesn't sit in your closet when you're at home, and stay home when you're off to occasions and on vacation. Or you may have an old 110 camera and are ready to graduate to the immensely better picture quality of a 35mm or Advanced Photo System point-and-shoot.

Maybe you're already using a 35mm point-and-shoot but want to get a new camera (an APS model?) with more features or creative options — extra flash modes or a longer-zooming lens. And some of you may be considering the purchase of a *second* point-and-shoot, perhaps a more full-featured model for specific kinds of subjects, a more pocketable model for go-anywhere convenience, or even a digital point-and-shoot to use with your computer. You may not even be shopping for yourself: The camera may be a gift for a spouse, a parent, a child — or that friend who keeps borrowing *your* camera. Whatever your reasons, this chapter tells you what to think about, and look for, when you're point-and-shoot shopping.

Don't Buy More Camera Than You Need

When you go shopping for your camera, don't let a salesperson talk you into buying more camera than you really need. If you want extra zoom power or added features, naturally you have to pay more. But don't fall for things that a salesperson says you'll grow into, when your intuition and photographic purposes tell you you'll never use them. How often do you really think you would need an *intervalometer,* a mode for time-lapse photography? On the other hand, if such photographic exotica intrigues you, remember that moderately priced zoom models tend to have pretty advanced features anyway, because the point-and-shoot marketplace is so competitive.

Another thing: Visit your newsstand to check out the major photo magazines and their comprehensive buying guides. (I recommend *Popular Photography.*) And most important, ask snapshooting friends which models they've been happy with. (Also see Chapter 18 for Web sites that offer buying tips and camera reviews.)

How Much Do You Want to Spend?

The question of how much you want to spend dictates all other questions. If you want to spend $50 or less, then you can't get a zoom lens — so you don't have to figure out what zoom range you'd like. You'll get a single-focal-length (nonzooming) lens, and you probably won't get autofocus. I think autofocus is worth the extra money; you have to spend more than $50, and more often closer to $100, to get it.

With non-autofocus models (also called fixed-focus or focus-free models) you have to worry about whether you're too close to the subject, because you must ordinarily stay back at least four feet to keep the subject sharp. With autofocus models, you don't have to worry — but you need to help the camera focus in the right place. (Models between $50 and $100 may have primitive autofocus, but I'd hit the $100 mark and get a better system.)

If you're willing to spend closer to $150, you have a choice between a modest zoom camera — perhaps something with a 35–70mm or 38–90mm lens — and a good nonzooming model, which typically has a single-focal-length lens of 35mm or shorter. In many cases, I would vote for the nonzooming model simply because you can do what the zoom does just by moving a few steps closer, and I happen to like the look of the wider angle. (At this price, the nonzooming model's lens will also probably be faster — that is, have a larger window in its lens, the better to shoot by dim light —

and sharper.) Tight portraits are another story, though, as I explain in the section "Do You Want a Zooming or Nonzooming Model?" later in this chapter.

Finally, if you're prepared to spend $250, you'll get a pretty long-ranging zoom — perhaps one that goes beyond 115mm. And models that take you out to 140mm or 160mm may cost as much as $300 to $350, even at a discount. But the waters are muddied here by designer point-and-shoots that cost as much as $1,000 and have single-focal-length lenses. With these models, though, you're paying for professional-quality optics and camera bodies made of metal alloy rather than plastic. And you're paying for style, of course. (One model I can think of even has a sapphire shutter button.)

For simplicity's sake, I'm discussing 35mm point-and-shoot models. Prices for comparably equipped Advanced Photo System (APS) models may be up to 15 percent higher. Also, remember that equivalent APS focal lengths and zoom ranges have lower numbers; a 35mm model's 38–115mm zoom would be the approximate equivalent of an APS model's 30–90mm zoom, in terms of how big it makes the subject on film and/or how much of the scene it takes in. (See Chapters 5 and 14 for details.)

Who Will Be Using the Camera?

Buying a top-of-the-line point-and-shoot for a teenager who just wants it for buddy pictures would be silly. And for a person with artistic yearnings to buy a discount store's blister-pack point-and-shoot would be pointless. The teenager should get the blister-pack model (especially because he is likely to lose or abuse it), or, if parents are feeling more extravagant, an under-$100, single-focal-length model with autofocus. And the artistic type should get the top-of-the-line model for its choice of modes and optical quality, though a gadget-loving snapshooter would be equally happy with such a camera.

The family documentarian can do her job — from shooting at-home candids to snapping family vacations — with a standard zoom model, say one with a 38–90mm lens. A shirtpocket model may make that job easier because it's so portable. Try to match special features to the intended user. A person with poor eyesight may appreciate a special model with an oversized viewfinder window because it's easier to look through. A rugged outdoors type may want a rugged camera — either a waterproof sports model or a weather-resistant, rubber-sheathed one.

What Subjects Will the User Be Shooting?

Most people shoot a variety of subject matter, but some photographers have special passions that call for particular camera models or features. Someone with a penchant for architecture and landscapes, interestingly enough, may be better off using a nonzooming (single-focal-length) model. A typical 35mm nonzooming model has a lens focal length of 35mm or shorter (often 32mm or 31mm, sometimes 28mm), which means the camera has a wider view that takes in more of a big subject than is possible with a zoom model starting at, say, 38mm. (With the Advanced Photo System, typical nonzooming, single-focal-length models have 24mm, 25mm, 26mm, or 28mm lenses; a typical zooming APS model may start out at 30mm, the equivalent of about 38mm in the 35mm format.) Ideal for that architecture or landscape fan: a zooming model that starts at 28mm, which would let him or her shoot the wide view and then zoom in to 70mm or 90mm for details.

Portrait fans, on the other hand, should be using a model that zooms at least to 70mm, because you get a more flattering scale in facial features when you don't have to shoot from too close to the subject. And sports fans — even those whose ambitions extend only to little league — will probably want a camera that zooms to 120mm, 135mm, or beyond, though other drawbacks plague long zooming, as I explain in Chapter 5.

Do You Want a Digital Camera or a Film Camera?

Choosing between a digital or film camera is a cut-and-dry choice: If you're content to store pictures on your computer's hard drive, view them on its monitor, and share them by e-mail (or on Web sites), then a digital *(filmless)* point-and-shoot is just what you need. But if you want hard copies — real prints — a film point-and-shoot beats a filmless one by a mile, in both cost and quality.

You can get prints from a digital point-and-shoot, just as you can print any computer file. But the service costs much more than conventional prints. Even if you invest in a good desktop color printer (now just a few hundred dollars), the picture quality from most digital point-and-shoots is visibly inferior at sizes much larger than 4 x 6 inches; even at that size, with a good model, you'll probably notice some difference in quality. Plus, printing each picture can take several minutes.

What's more, the price that you pay for equivalent features in a digital point-and-shoot is much higher than that of a film point-and-shoot. For the $250 that buys you a top-of-the-line film point-and-shoot with a superzoom, you'll get a lower-end, usually nonzooming *digital* point-and-shoot. (The camera probably won't even have autofocus.) That gap will certainly narrow as digital technology gets better and cheaper. But for the time being, even if you're computer-savvy, a digital point-and-shoot is probably best as a second camera — to complement your film point-and-shoot.

The more pixels a digital camera has, the better its picture quality is — and the more it costs. But if you're only viewing digital photographs on a computer monitor, and not printing them, you're unlikely to see much difference between a model with 300,000 pixels and one with 800,000 pixels. The price difference, on the other hand, can be several hundred dollars! (Check out Chapter 15 for more on pixel counts.)

Do You Want a 35mm Point-and-Shoot or an APS Point-and-Shoot?

The 35mm format is tried and true and delivers incredible image quality with today's color print films. But Advanced Photo System cameras offer a number of advantages over 35mm models. The system's match-numbered cassettes and index prints — processed film stays rolled up in the cassette — make keeping track of your pictures much easier. They also make reprinting a breeze. (See Chapter 14 for details.) And the system's frame-by-frame choice of three different print sizes lets you match print shape to subject, which I especially enjoy. (You can, of course, get 35mm models with a panorama setting.)

If you like big blow-ups, however, 35mm has the quality edge because it's a larger piece of film. And 35mm films are available in a greater variety of types and speeds. In terms of features and operation, though, 35mm and APS models are very similar. So you can't go wrong with either one.

Do You Want a Zooming or Nonzooming Model?

With a nonzooming model, the only way you can make a subject bigger or smaller in the frame is to change your distance from it — moving closer to make it bigger, away to make it smaller. With a zoom model, you can zoom the lens in and out to make the subject bigger or smaller in the frame, in effect composing by zooming. But zooming is not necessarily a good way to compose. Even if you want the convenience of a zoom model, you need to use your legs.

On the other hand, if you have a nonzooming model with a typical 35mm lens, moving in close for a head-and-shoulders portrait may distort your subject — producing a "big-nose" effect. (See Chapter 10 for examples.) Zoom cameras that zip even to a modest 70mm or 90mm help prevent that effect by allowing you to shoot from farther away. If you shoot sports and other far-away subjects, go for an even longer-zooming model, as I explain in the next section, "What Zoom Range Do You Need?"

Most digital point-and-shoot cameras are nonzooming models. Because the digital technology itself is costly to produce, this design keeps the overall cost of the camera down. So you generally have to pay quite a bit extra for digital models with a zoom lens.

If you decide to buy a zoom point-and-shoot, don't buy one with a zoom range less than 2X — less than 35–70mm with a 35mm model, for example, or 30–60mm with an Advanced Photo System model. Anything less than that (for example, 38–50mm), and you're probably better off just moving in and out on your own steam. (See Chapter 5 for more on zoom ranges.)

What Zoom Range Do You Need?

Point-and-shoot makers have been battling to see who can zoom the longest. At the moment, the battle seems stalled at a focal length of about 135mm or 145mm, though at least one model goes to 200mm. But you should consider models that zoom beyond 105mm or, say, 115mm, only if you really need to shoot distant subjects that you can't get any closer to — perhaps boats at sea or a bush leaguer on a playing field. Zooming out to 135mm to capture a face or an overall scene makes little sense. Most of the time, a few steps closer with your zoom at 105mm and you fill the frame just as easily — and without the exceedingly small lens aperture that makes longer zoom settings an even more likely cause of picture-blurring camera shake. (You can find out more about camera shake in Chapter 2.)

In my humble opinion, the most useful of all zoom ranges is also the poorest selling. I'm talking about 28–90mm, a true wide-angle-to-telephoto focal length range. Starting out at 28mm rather than 35mm or 38mm can make all the difference in the world in your ability to capture a broad range of subjects. It gives you a much wider angle of view, so you can take in much more of a scene from a given position.

You can shoot tall buildings in a single bound, for example, without always having to back away so far that something else gets in the way. Or you can fit much more of a tight interior into the frame when your back is against the wall. The same goes for big landscapes: You can't back away much from that canyon rim or scenic pullout to include more of the scene, but if you have a 28mm zoom setting, you won't feel the need as often.

Yet zoom in to 90mm with your 28–90mm zoom, and you've got an ideal setting for flattering portraits. And, of course, you get a bunch of useful focal lengths in between. Alas, as of this writing, only two 28–90mm models remain: the Pentax IQZoom 928 and the Rollei Prego Zoom 90. And but one holdout exists in the 28–70mm category: the compact, clamshell Minolta Freedom Zoom Explorer. (You may find an occasional 28–56mm model, again a 2X zoom.) A hopeful sign: Olympus has introduced a point-and-shoot model that zooms from 28–80mm, the Infinity Stylus Zoom 80 Wide DLX. I can't overstate the value of the 28mm setting: You can't always move back to fit the whole subject in the viewfinder, and when that's the case, the 28mm setting lets you get pictures that you may not get with any other lens.

Cameras of all focal lengths and focal length ranges have been shrinking dramatically. By my thinking, you shouldn't consider a 35–70mm zoom model unless it's fully pocketable, because you can get 38–90mm, 38–105mm, and even 38–115mm models that are hardly any bigger.

What Features Do You Want?

Many cameras suffer from mode overload (see Chapter 4). They have more features than you would ever use. But you don't want to get caught with too few features, either. Look particularly at flash modes. Fill flash is pretty basic these days, but the less common slow-sync flash is also extremely useful, and lower-end models tend not to have it. Having a full range of flash modes actually lessens the need for more advanced features such as exposure compensation and backlight compensation, though these modes do give you extra control with atypical subjects. You may want to avoid models that forcibly combine red-eye reduction with slow-sync flash; even the most basic models seem to have some form of red-eye reduction, however, and it can be next to useless. (See Chapter 7 for more on red-eye reduction.) Refer to the modes with asterisks in Chapter 4 for genuinely useful modes.

Don't be fooled by a point-and-shoot's styling. Some models are handsome and some are out-and-out homely, and you often pay more for good looks. But what matters is that the camera gives you the right lens for your needs and the features that you really want. Pretty pictures are better than a pretty camera.

Is the Camera Comfortable to Hold and Operate?

Take the model you're considering for a walk around the store, just as if you're trying on a new pair of shoes. (Don't buy a camera that the salesperson doesn't let you play with — batteries installed!) Can you get a firm grip on the camera? Do your fingers and thumbs fall naturally into place on surfaces and controls? Is the zoom control easy to operate? Can you hold the camera steady? Does it feel too small or too big in your hands?

Pretend to shoot some pictures with the camera just to see how responsive it is. Is there a noticeable lag between when you press the shutter button and when the camera fires? (Make sure that the flash is fully charged when you assess the camera's responsiveness; the camera won't fire until it is.) If a lag seems to exist, ask to see a different model and compare its shutter button action. Also, operate the zoom control to see how quickly and smoothly the lens zooms in and out. A quick zoom may make getting the shot faster, but it can also require more back-and-forth motion to get the exact focal length and composition that you want.

Is the Viewfinder Easy to Look Through?

On some point-and-shoot models, the viewfinder can be awkwardly placed and physically small. When you raise the camera to your eye, this placement may make finding the viewfinder difficult; you may have to wiggle the camera around to do so. That extra time may cost you the photo op that caught your eye. Also, are the viewfinder's edges easy and quick to see? If the viewfinder is hard to find or to see in its entirety, consider buying a model that has an oversized viewfinder. Designed specifically to help eyeglass wearers see the whole frame better, these models sometimes have the phrase "big finder" in them. However, they may be widely available only in cheaper, nonzooming models, so look and ask around.

Also consider the clarity of the viewfinder. Is it bright and sharp from edge to edge? Overall? If it doesn't seem sharp overall, does it have a *diopter control* (a small dial by the viewfinder) with which to adjust it to your individual vision? In a word, *compare.* Viewfinders can be very different. But, but. . . .

A new camera is like a new car: It takes some getting used to. A camera's viewfinder may seem hard to find at first, but the more you use the camera, the more quickly you can get your eye into position. A button or switch that seems awkward initially will probably, over time, feel more comfortable. No camera can be all things to all people!

Chapter 17

Ten Simple Ways to Make Your Pictures Better

In This Chapter

▶ Capturing the moment

▶ Framing the subject thoughtfully

▶ Using your flash — outdoors!

▶ Getting below — or above — eye level

▶ Shifting your camera position

*I*t really bothers me when people claim they're constitutionally incapable of taking good pictures — that they're not technical enough, not artistic enough, or just don't have access to good subject matter. Forgive me, but they're wrong on all counts.

I always make a case for the rich profusion of subject matter that surrounds each of us, from luminously quiet moments of family life to the play of light in backyards. You simply don't need exotic places or people to make great pictures. And, thanks to point-and-shoot technology, you don't have to be the slightest bit technical to get good picture quality. Exposure, focus, flash — you name it, it's all handled for you, and the results are remarkably consistent.

Which leaves the artistry of photography. Dare I say it? You don't even have to be artistic to take good pictures. You just have to use some visual intelligence. You have to think with your eyes, in a sense. And much of that visual thinking can be reduced to simple notions, a dozen of which I suggest in this chapter. But just to make things even easier for you, I include a condensed version of these tips on the tear-out cheat sheet just inside this book's front cover. Keep it with you when you're shooting and refer to it often. You'll be surprised — *shocked* — at the difference in your pictures!

These pointers apply to *any* kind of point-and-shoot, from fancy "designer" cameras to simple, one-time-use models. You don't have to have a pricey point-and-shoot to make them work for you; you don't even have to have an autofocus model.

Capture the Moment

Not to co-opt Kodak, but most of personal photography is about moments. Keep in mind, though, that moments can be unique or everyday. Don't wait for a specific occasion to take your pictures; find the telling moments in seemingly ordinary events. Also remember that moments are by definition fleeting. To catch that perfect expression or charming interaction, you have to anticipate it — keeping your finger on the shutter button, your eye to the viewfinder, and your patience.

Don't Use the Viewfinder like a Gun Sight

"Shooting" is an apt description of the way most picture-takers compose, placing their main subject dead-center. (There might as well be crosshairs in the camera's viewfinder.) The most common instance of this is the way people's heads always seem to end up smack in the middle of the picture, with empty space above. For people pictures, vertical or horizontal, try placing heads near the top of the picture area.

Photographers often get so caught up in the moment they're trying to capture that they forget they're also putting a frame around it. Thinking about how to frame a subject when you're trying to capture a moment is a little like rubbing your stomach and patting your head at the same time. It takes some concentration! See Chapter 9 for more on composition.

Get Close

Try to fill the frame with your main subject. Most pictures suffer from the subject's being too small. In most cases, the best way to fix this — and the only way, if you have a nonzooming camera — is simply to move in closer. Unless you're shooting a tight portrait, zooming to fill the frame is often not a good idea. (See Chapter 9 for an explanation.) In fact, your own two legs are the most important photographic tool at your disposal: Use them to move in and out, and thus to control the subject's size in the frame.

 If your point-and-shoot is a non-autofocus model — often called a "focus-free" camera — you shouldn't get closer than about four feet from your main subject. If the subject is closer than that, it will probably end up unsharp in the print. The same thing goes for one-time-use cameras.

Shoot from a Low or High Angle

There's nothing sacred about your own eye level. If you've ever stooped to shoot pictures of kids, you know this instinctively. Shooting from a child's-eye level helps you make more intimate contact. And with taller subjects, human or inanimate, aiming the camera up from a low angle can create an interesting monumental effect. (Again, legs are your tool here. Squat!)

 Shooting from a high angle is a little trickier. You may have to get up on a wall or a car hood, or perhaps shoot from a deck or window. But even a little extra elevation on a subject can keep foreground and background elements from overlapping confusingly, and add depth to an image.

Use Flash Outdoors

 Your point-and-shoot automatically fires its flash in dim light, but you shouldn't think of flash just as a way to add light to a subject when there isn't enough to shoot by already. Flash is actually a great idea when you must shoot in direct sunlight, because it "fills" the dark, unattractive facial shadows created by a subject's eye sockets and nose. Flash also helps brighten a "backlit" subject that would otherwise end up too dark.

On the other hand, if an outdoor subject has delicate lighting that you think might be overpowered by flash (rosy light at the end of the day, for example), don't use it. And if you're shooting a landscape, don't bother — it's too far away for the flash to make any difference. When in doubt, shoot pictures with *and* without flash and then compare the final results.

Keep Flash Backgrounds Close

 Otherwise, the print may make your subject appear to be surrounded by a dark void — a background too distant for the flash to light. (Photofinishing machinery worsens this effect, trying to compensate for all that darkness and, as a result, making the main subject too light.) While you're at it, choose a colorful background. And if you don't have the luxury of moving the subject around, two other things can improve background detail. One is to use slow-sync flash mode, if your camera has this mode. (See Chapter 7 for more on flash modes.) The other is to switch to a faster film.

Use a Fast Film

Don't be talked into a print film that has a lower "speed" than ISO 400 unless you plan to make big blow-ups from it. Current fast films — ISO 400 or even ISO 800 — give you prints of exceptionally high quality. And their extra sensitivity to light not only reduces the risk of slow, image-blurring shutter speeds, but lets you shoot without flash in a wider range of existing light. Just as important, it improves background detail in flash shots. Check out Chapter 2 for more on film speed.

Place the Main Subject Off-Center

Whether you're shooting a person or a mountain, try not to center the subject in the viewfinder unless you have a compelling compositional reason to do so. A centered subject makes the picture more static in feeling. A subject placed to one side of the frame usually creates a more dynamic design. Refer to Chapter 9 for more details on composition.

Move from Side to Side

A small shift sideways can make a huge improvement in a picture, preventing objects at different distances from overlapping horizontally and creating visual confusion. Study the viewfinder as you move to see how a change in lateral position can change the relationships among elements of the scene.

Experiment with the Horizon Line

Usually, anything is better than placing a landscape's horizon line midway up the frame. Put it at the bottom instead, and you can emphasize a sky, for a "big" effect. Place it near the top, and you can create a strong feeling of depth.

Take Lots of Pictures

Film is cheap. Photography's great pleasure is that you can learn what works by trying it, for the cost of a frame of film and a 4 x 6-inch print.

Chapter 18

Ten Great Photographic Web Sites

In This Chapter

▶ What you need to visit photography Web sites

▶ Talking shop in photo newsgroups

▶ Finding photo how-to Web sites

▶ Locating equipment-oriented Web sites

▶ Getting your own pictures on the Web

*A*re you wired? I hope so, because the Internet is one of the best places to find out about taking pictures. Thousands of sites on the World Wide Web concern some aspect of photography. Hundreds of those sites are specifically devoted to snapshooting. In this chapter, I describe some of the best of these photo-friendly sites, including a couple that let you get your own pictures online. (See Appendix B for a list of photo manufacturers' Web sites.) You'll need a home computer, browser software, and a modem to get on the Web. For details, check out *The Internet For Dummies,* 5th Edition, by John R. Levine, Carol Baroudi, and Margaret Levine Young (IDG Books Worldwide, Inc.).

If you're buying a modem and plan to visit Web sites containing photography, get a fast one — at least 33.6 Kbps. Online photographs contain much more digital information than text or even graphics, and otherwise take forever and a day to download.

Kodak's Guide to Better Pictures

www.kodak.com/ciHome/photography/bPictures/pictureTaking/
pictureTaking.shtml

An extensive reference geared to snapshooters, this corner of Kodak's massive Web site illustrates picture-taking techniques with hundreds of photographic examples. Start with Kodak's top ten shooting tips (for example, get close, use a simple background, hold your camera steady, and so on). The site also helps you make the best film choices and explains the benefits of different lens focal lengths, camera settings, and accessories.

One of the most complete how-to sites on the Web, this site has a trouble-shooting guide to help you. A comprehensive glossary also complements this book's bits of photo jargon. If you aspire to greater control over your images, advanced advice on exposure manipulation is also proffered.

Although you can view this site with almost any browser, I suggest using the latest version (for example, Netscape Communicator or Microsoft Internet Explorer 4.0) so that you can see all the cool animated effects!

Popular Photography Online

Okay, so Popular Photography Online is not technically a Web site — you have to be an America Online member to get to it. (Just select Keyword and type in **Popular Photography**.) But Popular Photography Online brings all the resources of that venerable real-world magazine to the digital sphere. Find out more about point-and-shoot cameras from senior editor Dan Richards, whose regular column on the subject is the most intelligent and readable in the business. Or check out the latest digital point-and-shoots, smartly reviewed by technology editor and digital maven Mike McNamara. If you have advanced yearnings, read SLR guru Burt Keppler's time-honored column. Camera test reports, buying guides, how-to's on everything from travel photography to close-up shooting, and, of course, great pictures by some of the world's best photographers are all here for the clicking. You can search for information on particular cameras, view pictures from your favorite shooters, or find out more about photographing specific subjects simply by entering a model, name, or topic.

To take advantage of Popular Photography Online's built-in links to manufacturers' Web sites and other photo-related sites, you need to download America Online's browser software. Just follow the onscreen instructions.

The Family Photo Historian

www.geocities.com/Heartland/2878/

This site states its lofty purpose up front. "It is no small task to find, organize, restore, and preserve our photos," says its opening page. "But if it is not done, a valuable legacy will be lost. We must establish a new tradition of The Family Photo Historian." I encourage *you* to be your family's photo historian — and this site provides lots of detailed advice about photographic organization, preservation, and restoration to complement what's in Chapter 3.

Photo newsgroups

While you're online, check out the photo *newsgroups* — public online forums where you can post, bulletin board-style, your most pressing photographic questions and ideas. Use Deja News (www.dejanews.com) to search for them, typing in a photographic term or specific camera model. Or open your Web browser's Newsgroups window and enter any of the following names:

✔ rec.photo.moderated

✔ rec.photo.marketplace

✔ rec.photo.misc

✔ rec.photo.digital

✔ rec.photo.equipment.35mm

✔ rec.photo.equipment.misc

✔ rec.photo.film+labs

✔ rec.photo.technique.art

✔ rec.photo.technique.misc

✔ rec.photo.technique.people

✔ America Online: Keyword *Photo*

Weekly tips on ending photo clutter, offers for free photo-saving product catalogs, and downloadable family tree charts are among this site's many features. The Family Photo Historian also provides suggestions about creating a photographic diary, classifying and sorting photos, and putting together scrapbooks. If you're looking for better ways to cope with important old family pictures, check out the Links page. It connects you with the Web sites of a family tree software maker and a photo lab that restores old black-and-white prints.

This site is supported by advertisements, which are displayed for a few seconds before each page appears on your screen. Don't change the channel: The right page comes up eventually!

Kodak Picture Network

www.kodak.com/go/40

Want to put your pictures on the Web? The Kodak Picture Network makes it easy. When you deliver your exposed film to participating photofinishers, just check a box on the drop-off envelope. After the film is processed and printed, it's scanned and transmitted to the Kodak Picture Network Web site for about $5 extra a roll. When you pick up your order (you keep the negatives, naturally), you're assigned a special code number. After you're home, just fire up your computer, go to the site, enter the number as instructed — and you can see your very own pictures onscreen. You have the actual prints to look at, too, of course, but the real fun is that you can invite computer-ready friends and relatives to the site (just give them the code number) to see your latest masterpieces. Or, if you like, with a few mouse clicks you can e-mail pictures directly to them from the site.

To sample the Kodak Picture Network's goodies, you have to join it. The first three months of membership are free; after that, the charge is $4.95 a month. You join by filling out a simple online form. A membership gets you a continuing online display of 100 pictures. (You're charged a mere penny a month for anything above 100.) You can even use the site to order reprints, which are made from high-resolution versions of the images that you see onscreen; you just pick up the prints at your photofinisher.

To use the Kodak Picture Network, you need to download Kodak's software from the site; it's compatible with Windows 3.*x*, 95, and NT, as well as Macintosh System 7.5 or later. To see which of your local photofinishers offers the service, use the site's dealer locator; close to 40,000 drop-off locations exist. Network members can even use their membership numbers to read Wide Angle, an online magazine on how to get better pictures.

The Mining Company

`www.miningco.com`

Get to the point-and-shoot heart of this huge online magazine by typing **Amateur Photography** into its Search This Site window. You can find both original photo tutorials (many of them seasonal or related to upcoming holidays) and reviews of other photo Web sites (with direct one-click links to them). Some of the material is for photographers who are moving beyond basic snapshooting (you, perhaps?); you can even find stories on darkroom techniques (check the archives). But most articles are just intended to help you take better pictures of your life and/or family. Keep in mind that you can easily get lost in this site due to its sheer size; photography is just one of perhaps 400 subjects. Set time aside to browse it, because its writers are experts in their respective subjects and the content's quality is therefore better than on many sites.

Phil Greenspun's Guide to Point-and-Shoot Cameras

`www-swiss.ai.mit.edu/philg/photo/point-and-shoot.html`

Phil Greenspun is a legend on the Internet. A writer and educator in the computer world, he is also a passionate photography buff. His expansive Web site is oriented mostly toward more serious photographers, but his reviews of cameras and mail-order merchants are unbiased. The point-and-shoot models that he reviews tend to be on the high end, and his writing often assumes that readers have knowledge of more advanced gear or techniques. But if you're looking to get the most camera for your point-and-shoot dollar, this site is one of the best resources online. Be sure to check out the reader-submitted comments; if you have an opinion about your camera, you can even add it here.

For a more comprehensive overview of point-and-shoot cameras, visit photo buff Zhu Hai Qing's site at `www.ee.nus.sg/~zhu/photo/compact/compact.html`.

Collected Visions

`cvisions.nyu.edu`

Created by a New York University photo teacher, this site takes a fascinating and sometimes scholarly look at snapshot photography and how it shapes your memories. It invites you to upload your family pictures for both online exhibitions and inclusion in a digital archive of thousands of such images. (The archive is open to all visitors.) You can even contribute a written essay about the ways that you've been affected by your family's photographs.

Get your pictures ready to upload to this site by using a photofinisher who's able to scan your processed film to a floppy disk. Ask that the resulting digital image files be in *GIF* or *JPEG* format. (GIF and JPEG are simply for different ways of encoding digital information.) After your photos are in the right format, you can submit them to Collected Visions simply by filling out a form and following the site's onscreen directions.

Fodor's Focus on Photography

`www.fodors.com/focus/`

The people who bring you Fodor's travel guides are now online, providing tips specifically for people who travel with their cameras (you, I hope) and want to come back with more than tourist snapshots (you, I hope). A section on getting ready for your trip includes good advice on camera buying and which film(s) to take. For when you're on the road, the guide offers helpful hints for getting well-exposed pictures of tropical beaches, southwestern canyons, autumn colors, animals in the wild, and more. How-to topics include lighting, composition, and people photography.

PhotoNet

www.photonet.com

Here's yet another way to get your photographs online: Bring your film in to any Wolf or Ritz camera shop (or any of PhotoNet's 9,000 participating stores) or mail it to Mystic Color Labs, and ask to have your pictures put on the Web. The extra charge per roll is about $5. PhotoNet gives you a special access code that you can share with online friends and relatives; they can even order copies of your photos on the site and pick up the prints at a participating store near them. Pictures stay online for 30 days, and a small charge gets you additional time. (PhotoNet and the Kodak Picture Network have recently joined forces to create a single online network.)

Photography Information Council (PIC)

www.photoinformation.org

Sponsored by a consortium of photo manufacturers and distributors, the Photography Information Council (PIC) Web site is a terrific complement to those companies' own Web sites — which, by the way, you can get to through direct links in the PIC Site. The site offers both picture-taking tips (many specific to seasons or occasions) and helpful explanations of various photo technologies (35mm point-and-shoot cameras, the Advanced Photo System, and digital imaging among them). Pictures by ordinary snapshooters often illustrate the information. You can even post your pressing photo questions to a special online forum, and they will be answered by PIC or forwarded to the appropriate industry resource. Still prefer hard copy? Call 800-599-5929 for a free PIC brochure.

Chapter 19

Ten Favorite Places to Take Pictures

In This Chapter

▶ Horsing around on Chincoteague Island

▶ Cruising along in Amarillo, Texas

▶ Getting back to nature in Utah

▶ Living it up in Las Vegas

▶ And much, much more!

*H*ow do you pick the top ten photo ops in America, a country with a staggering abundance of visual riches? By making the choices entirely personal. In no particular order, then, here are a few of my favorite places to take pictures. (Actually, I've chosen 12 — I couldn't help myself.) These spots also happen to be great places to just *look*. I mention this because to take good pictures, you have to be in touch with — and moved or amazed by — your surroundings. That's my opinion, anyway.

So before you raise the camera to your eye, study and experience what's in front of you. Look before you shoot. Your pictures will be better for it.

I've tried to choose spots that are accessible yet offbeat, and also to come up with a mixture of subject matter and photographic possibilities. Twelve different states are represented. You find landscapes, cityscapes, wildlife, flowers, roadside art, and architecture, too. But I've also chosen things that are within the reach of point-and-shoot cameras — wildlife that's close enough to capture with a point-and-shoot zoom lens, for example. One last word: Some of these places are fragile, so treat them kindly. As the photographic saying goes, take only pictures, leave only footprints.

Don't take pictures from your car! You will *never* get the best shot.

Chincoteague Island, Eastern Shore, Virginia

Is any image more romantic than a horse on a beach? If you'll settle for a pony, then Chincoteague is the place for you: According to local legend, the area's plentiful wild ponies descend from equine survivors of a sixteenth-century Spanish shipwreck. The animals are so fearless that they actually poke their heads into your car windows as you cruise through the Chincoteague National Wildlife Refuge, which is across a channel from the town of Chincoteague. No need for telephoto lenses here — but do get out of your car to photograph the winsome creatures! The refuge is at the southern tip of Maryland's Assateague Island National Seashore, a 40-mile stretch of beach and uplands where the ponies also roam.

Though you can see Chincoteague's ponies anytime, show up toward the end of July and you'll be able to photograph them taking part in the annual Pony Swim and Auction. Members of the local volunteer fire department *(saltwater cowboys)* herd ponies from the refuge into the water and across the channel to town. (Swimming ponies — what more could you want?) The foals and yearlings are auctioned off to benefit the department, and then the rest of the ponies swim back to the refuge. Chincoteague is just over three hours southeast of Washington, D.C.; for this year's Pony Swim and Auction dates, call the Chincoteague Chamber of Commerce at 757-336-6161.

Local chambers of commerce can be great sources of inside information about an area — and its photographic possibilities. Don't always go by what people at auto clubs say!

Cadillac Ranch, Amarillo, Texas

As you drive west out of Amarillo on Interstate 40, a surreal sight presents itself: in a working grain field, a neat row of ten old Cadillacs buried nose-down in the ground up to their passenger doors, their famous tail fins angled up toward the big sky of Texas. Called Cadillac Ranch, it's Stonehenge for the automotive era.

Created in 1974, the work grew out of a collaboration between oilman and art fan Stanley Marsh (who owns the land) and the Ant Farm, a group of architects in San Francisco. Each car represents a change in the Cadillac's tail-fin design from 1948 through 1964, when the fin had all but disappeared. The monument is designed to be taken in at cruising speed; after all, it sits along the former path of legendary Route 66. But to photograph it properly, you should pull into the service road, get out, and walk around so that you can work its eye-catching angles. (The Caddies' tilt in the ground matches the inclination of the sides of Egypt's Great Pyramid.)

Bryce Canyon National Park, Utah

To choose from among the five national parks that make southern Utah a natural wonder — Bryce, Zion, Arches, Canyonlands, and Capitol Reef — is like trying to distinguish between five perfect gems. But in terms of pure light, Bryce Canyon is the jewel in the crown, so it gets my photographic vote. Technically, Bryce isn't a canyon: It's a red-rock amphitheater, populated by thousands of water-hewn stone spires and pinnacles called *hoodoos*. The Paiute Indians dubbed Bryce "Red Rocks Standing Like Men in a Bowl-Shaped Canyon," but the hoodoos are more fantastically intricate than their matter-of-fact description suggests — more like pagodas, minarets, and temples (note the religious references). The rim approach is reminiscent of the Grand Canyon, but Bryce feels more intimate in scale. Get your camera and walk down into the amphitheater in mere minutes on the Queen's Garden trail or, if you're more ambitious, the Navajo Loop.

In the amphitheater, you discover the best thing about Bryce, photographically speaking: the way its eroded vertical surfaces scatter warm light every which way. Whether you're shooting a deep-green pinyon juniper against a red-rock wall or just a portrait of your companion against a background of hoodoos, the light is matchless. You can even break the old rule against shooting in the middle of the day (see Chapters 8 and 12) because you can easily find soft, reflected light — and open shade is more often warm in its light than cool, as it normally is. Two suggestions, one technical, one meteorological. If you're taking pictures in which light-colored rock fills the frame, consider setting backlight compensation or "plus" exposure compensation (if your camera offers these modes) to prevent underexposure. (See Chapter 8 for more on exposure compensation.) And if you visit Bryce in the winter, hope for a little snow — the icing on the cake.

Drive to the southern tip of the park and hike the Bristlecone Loop (an hour round-trip). Your reward is at the far end of the trail: picturesquely gnarled specimens of the world's oldest living tree, the bristlecone pine. I forget how many millennia these particular wooden Methuselahs have overlooked the Rainbow Point panorama. Photograph them, but don't forget to touch them, too, and imagine what *they* have seen.

Las Vegas, Nevada

From the sublime (Bryce) to the ridiculous, right? Why would I tell you to take pictures in the gambling capital of the world? Because it's the best place to fly to if you want to motor up to Bryce Canyon (Zion is even closer)— and because you'll be there anyway, you should take photographic advantage of its world-famous signage. Whatever you think of the way Las Vegas makes a living, there's no such thing as bad neon, and Las Vegas has the most and the best. If photography is about light and color, then its casinos are rich ground. Just don't blame me if you lose money!

Get out your camera, and you won't be tempted to gamble. (My wife and I may be the only people who've ever spent a night at Caesar's Palace and didn't even drop a quarter.) A good time to shoot is late afternoon, toward dusk, when the neon really starts to stand out but enough daylight still exists to fill in details of buildings and give you a deep blue desert sky. But you can shoot at night, too. Use fast film (ISO 400 or 800), of course. And if your camera's flash starts firing on its own (that is, in autoflash mode), either turn it off or switch it over to slow-sync flash mode to mix in more existing light. If the sign's more than 15 or 20 feet away, though, just turn the flash off. (Check out Chapter 7 for more on flash modes.)

With slow-sync flash or no flash, try a few shots in which you deliberately move or jiggle the camera as you press the shutter button. This action creates colorful streaks and blurs in your prints, often reducing them to abstract patterns. Or try bulb or bulb flash mode, if your camera offers it; keep the shutter button pressed all the way as you move the camera and then release it after a second or two. (See Chapter 4 for more on these modes.) Be sure to visit Glitter Gulch, the older downtown area (north of the familiar "Strip") where casinos aren't also in the hotel business.

You may be able to sneak a few pictures in the casinos, though their gaudy interiors aren't as interesting as their light show come-ons. (Load up with ISO 800 film and turn off your flash!) Keep shooting, though, and you'll be stopped. Management doesn't want a photographic record of its paying customers, in case their gambling is a deep dark secret!

For an all-natural respite from the artifice of Las Vegas — not to mention some very photogenic high-desert scenery — visit Red Rock Canyon, 20 miles west of town. Or look for prehistoric Indian rock art among the flaming-red sandstone of Valley of Fire State Park, less than an hour north off U.S. 15 (the same road that takes you to Zion and Bryce Canyon, which I discuss earlier in this chapter).

White Birch Forest, Pictured Rocks National Lakeshore, Michigan

Yes, the California redwoods are splendiferous. (That's a combination of splendid and coniferous.) But they're nearly impossible to do justice to with a point-and-shoot camera, especially if yours doesn't give you the wide view of a 28mm focal length, as most don't. The big trees are just too big. So if you love trees — and love to photograph them — let me point you somewhere else entirely: to the unsung and largely undeveloped Pictured Rocks National Lakeshore, along the south coast of Lake Superior on the Upper Peninsula of Michigan between the towns of Munising and Grand Marais.

In the park, on the northeastern end of Twelvemile Beach, is a forest of white birch trees that takes your breath away. A forest is dark, right? Not this one. Except for the occasional pine accent, it's solid white and full of light. When birch leaves turn yellow in the fall, it's even more spectacular. Follow the little road off the main (gravel) park road down to the Twelvemile Beach camping area (a fine place to pitch a tent, if I do say so myself) and stop along the way for pictures. Then take a walk on the white-sand beach and notice that Lake Superior feels different than the other Great Lakes, more like an ocean than a lake.

The name *Pictured Rocks* — so photographic — actually refers to the brightly colored, tree-topped cliffs and rock formations that face the lake in the southwestern part of the park. The only way that you can shoot them is from a boat. Commercial boat tours depart regularly from nearby Munising.

The Staten Island Ferry, Battery Park, New York

You get two great pictures — plus a free ride — from the famous Staten Island Ferry. One picture is of the southern tip of Manhattan, which in recent years has amassed quite a few interesting skyscrapers (the World Trade Towers included). The other one is of the Statue of Liberty. You can shoot going and coming (just stay put when the ferry arrives at Staten Island, and ride back), but you may want to take your cruise late in the afternoon, when the sun casts warm sidelight on the buildings and then sets almost directly behind the statue. (Also check out the view up the East River, which includes the famous Brooklyn Bridge.)

Some ferry crossings pass closer to the statue than others; be prepared to zoom. And use fast (ISO 400 or 800) film! Fast film causes the camera to set a higher shutter speed, lessening the chance that choppy water will shake you and blur your pictures. (See Chapter 2 for more on film speeds.)

Paradise Meadow, Mount Rainier National Park, Washington

This alpine meadow positively explodes with wildflowers — lupine, mountain daisy, Indian Paintbrush — from mid-July to the end of August. Parking is easy, and the area's trail system is excellent. If you get a cloudy day, count your blessings: It's usually *better* than direct sun for shooting flowers.

If the sun is shining when you visit Paradise Meadow, choose a small group of flowers and shoot them while a fellow traveler shades them with his or her body. (Shoot them in your own shade, if the angle is right.) This shading lowers the high contrast created by the sun and keeps color from being washed out.

For flower close-ups closer to home, visit regional arboretums and botanical gardens. Great specimens grow year-round in their well-tended greenhouses!

Vietnam Veterans Memorial, Washington, D.C.

Somber monument aside, the Vietnam Veterans Memorial is a place for photographs of people and their emotions — of faces and gestures. If you do take pictures, shoot quickly and quietly, be discreet and respectful, and don't call attention to yourself by using flash. (Flash creates *hot spots* — bright reflections — on the polished black stone anyway.) If the faces in your prints are too light, more than likely the problem is with the photofinishing: The wall's dark tone throws off the machinery. Ask your photofinisher to reprint the picture (see Chapter 3).

At the north end of Arlington National Cemetery, just across the Potomac River from downtown Washington, is the Marine Corps War Memorial — the famous monument of soldiers raising the American flag during the World War II battle for the Japanese island of Iwo Jima. The sculpture, in case you didn't know, is based almost detail for detail on a *photograph* by war photographer Joe Rosenthal.

Lucy the Elephant, Margate City, New Jersey

Over the years, most of my photographer friends have paid their pictorial respects to Lucy the Elephant. Lucy is a six-story wooden building in the shape of an Indian elephant, fully detailed in tin down to the *howdah,* a canopied saddle on her back. Now a National Historic Landmark, Lucy was built in 1881 by a real estate developer to lure prospective buyers to the area. She still contains a real estate office, and now a tavern, and you can tour her insides for a small charge during the summer months. But her magnificent exterior is free for the photographing. You find Lucy at the corner of Decatur Street and Atlantic Avenue in Margate City, just south of Atlantic City on the Jersey shore.

Lucy is big. If you have a zoom point-and-shoot, set it to your shortest focal length (for example, 28mm, 35mm, or 38mm). This wider angle of view helps fit her all in — though you still have to back up quite a bit!

The Santuario de Nuestra Señor de Esquipulas, Chimayo, New Mexico

St. Francis de Asis, an eighteenth-century Spanish colonial church in the New Mexico farming town of Ranchos de Taos, is a photographic icon — its massive adobe buttressing having been the subject of many famous shooters. But tucked away on the "High Road to Taos" (Route 76 out of Española), in the village of Chimayo, surrounded by a juniper-studded adobe court, is a less photographed but equally picturesque Spanish colonial church, the Santuario de Nuestra Señor de Esquipulas. Thousands of pilgrims come for the curative dirt found in a small room behind the altar (a long story), so the church is full of cast-off crutches and religious artwork. A visual spectacle.

Anhinga Trail, Everglades National Park, Florida

Getting close enough to wildlife to photograph it with a point-and-shoot camera is nearly impossible unless you go to a zoo, and then it's not exactly wild. But the Everglades' Anhinga Trail — the first trail inside the park entrance, which is just 30 miles south of Miami — puts you about as close to wild subtropical animals and birds as you'll ever get. You follow raised pathways and elevated boardwalks though a swampy channel of tall marsh grass and open pools; along the way you see submerged and sunning alligators, crook-necked anhingas (black fishing birds) spreading their wings out to dry, and the ancient shapes of gar fish drifting below the surface. You can get reasonably tight shots of some of these exotic specimens with a zoom that goes to 105mm or thereabouts; 135mm or 140mm will, of course, help you fill the frame even more.

Remember that unlike other parks, the Everglades' wonders are subtle and easily missed. Be quiet and watchful (Anhinga is a short trail, so you can linger), and you'll also spy dozens of different water snakes and turtles, and, if you're lucky, the big, brilliant roseate spoonbill. Spindly legged egrets, herons, and storks are everywhere. The best time to visit — and definitely to photograph — is in late winter. (I've always gone in February or early March.) By then, the park's available water has dwindled into small sloughs such as that around Anhinga trail, so the animals tend to congregate there.

Not much more than an hour south of Disney World, in the heart of Florida's citrus country, is a place more fantastic than that famous theme park — and it's all natural. Highlands Hammock State Park (six miles west of the racing town of Sebring, off U.S. Route 27 on State Route 634) is basically a hardwood forest that has been spared fire and hurricanes well into maturity, an island in an otherwise piney sea. It is simply the most primeval place that I have ever been to.

The park's Ancient Hammock Trail winds under a dense canopy created by centuries-old mahogany and hickory trees, but the gem of its easy trail system is the Cypress Swamp Trail. It takes you on an elevated boardwalk through what is essentially a flooded forest of cypress and other spiky, exotic vegetation — through shady swamp where wading birds stalk frogs and fish in slow motion, and quiet pools where alligators swim undisturbed. Definitely use ISO 800 film!

The Salton Sea, Southern California

Twenty miles south of the town of Indio, California's date capital, is one of the largest inland bodies of salt water in the world — and one of the strangest landscapes I've ever seen. Salton Sea waters, diverted decades ago from the Colorado River for recreational purposes, have overtaken many of the human settlements along its shore (which is hugged by a good road). Trailers, houses, boats, and cars sit half-sunken in a mirror of sky-blue water, with treeless pink mountains in the distance. It's a surreal scene, but not to everyone's photographic tastes!

Chapter 20

Ten Things to Try If Your Camera Won't Shoot

In This Chapter

▶ Pressing the right buttons

▶ Reloading the film

▶ Checking your batteries

*N*othing is more frustrating than spotting a picture-perfect subject and being unable to get your point-and-shoot to shoot it. Sometimes the camera just won't turn on; other times, it turns on but does nothing when you press the shutter button. This chapter offers some remedies for both those problems.

If none of these suggestions gets your point-and-shoot shooting, take it to a photo dealer. If the folks there can't solve the problem, your camera may have to be repaired. Just keep in mind that if you have an inexpensive or older model, buying a new one is often cheaper and easier — and also gives you a good opportunity to trade up. Before you buy, though, be sure to read Chapter 16 for some point-and-shoot buying tips.

Even if they're working properly, most point-and-shoot cameras let you shoot *when there's no film in the camera.* So don't go snapping blithely away only to realize — after all those great pictures — that your camera was shooting blanks. If you haven't used your camera in a while, check the little window on the camera's back (35mm models only) to make sure that a cassette is in place. Or check the frame counter, which appears on the LCD panel or in a small, separate window, to make sure that it moves from one number to the next as you fire (both 35mm and Advanced Photo System models). If the frame counter is not moving, the film probably isn't advancing.

One bonus suggestion: If your camera starts up but then acts up, try turning it off and on again. Doing this is a bit like restarting a crashed computer: It sometimes clears the camera's electronics or software chips of whatever is troubling them.

Turn the Camera On Correctly

If your camera just won't start up, you may be pressing the wrong button. Check your manual to find out which button is right. Also, make sure that you're pressing the button all the way in; sometimes you have to briefly hold it down to get the camera to react. Cameras that sport both dials and pushbuttons may start up only when you rotate the main dial to any position other than *off;* if your model has more than one dial, make sure that you're using the right one. And with models featuring sliding front panels, you actually turn on the camera by sliding out the panel to uncover the lens. The panel must click decisively into shooting position. If it slips back in as you clutch the camera to shoot, it turns off the camera.

Reload the Film

If a 35mm point-and-shoot doesn't engage the film properly, it won't let you take pictures. When this problem occurs, the camera usually flashes an *E,* for empty, on its LCD panel. (Models lacking LCD panels indicate this problem by not advancing the film counter to 1, remaining stuck on 0.) Open the camera back, take out the film, and load it again. (See Chapter 1 for specifics.) If you're using an Advanced Photo System model and inadvertently loaded an exposed or already processed cassette, the camera won't let you shoot either. Find an unused roll and load it instead.

Replace the Battery

Even when a battery is too weak to run the camera, it usually has enough power left to display or flash a low battery icon on the LCD panel — again, if it *has* an LCD panel. (For more about this icon, see Chapter 1.) Less expensive models may not have an LCD panel; you may have to press a battery-check button, which lights up a lamp to tell you the battery is okay. Otherwise, with them, the only way to find out whether your battery is the culprit is to change it.

Make Sure the Battery Is Correctly Installed

If a battery is installed backward — that is, with the ends reversed — the camera can't get any juice out of it. If your particular model takes more than one battery, make sure all of them are right; just one incorrectly installed battery out of two, three, or four will put you out of business. (If your camera has an LCD panel, an incorrectly installed battery will cause its display to remain blank.)

You'll find printed or embossed insertion diagrams or symbols inside the battery compartment or cover, and occasionally on the outside of the compartment. They show you which way to orient the end of the battery with the bump on it, which is its positive (+) terminal. See Chapter 1 for details.

Clean the Battery Contacts

If a battery has been sitting in your camera for a long time, miniscule leakage of its acidic contents may have corroded the battery compartment's *contacts* — the metallic points with which the camera draws power from the battery. Corrosion usually leaves a whitish powder, but may not always be visible.

To clean the contacts, get a pencil with a rubber eraser on the end, open the battery compartment, remove the battery, and vigorously rub the eraser against both the top and bottom contacts in the compartment. If your battery goes in lengthwise rather than sideways, rub the eraser against both the far terminal (the one deep inside the camera) and the terminal on the compartment cover or cap. Then blow out the eraser fragments. Now, replace the battery with a new one. A battery that has already leaked is likely to do it again, gunking up your camera all over. Plus, a leaky battery will have lost some of its energy.

If you use your breath to blow out the battery compartment, rather than a blower brush or compressed air, shut your eyes to avoid getting corrosive dust in them. If you use compressed air (available at photo shops), keep the canister upright to avoid squirting propellant into the battery compartment!

Check the Flash-Ready Lamp

If you're shooting in dim light, make sure that the flash-ready lamp is glowing steadily. The flash-ready lamp is either on the viewfinder eyepiece or along the edge of the viewfinder frame as you look through the camera; it's usually red or orange. (Check your manual for its location and color.) If the lamp is *blinking,* the flash hasn't fully recharged — and the camera won't fire when you press the shutter button. (The exception to this is with a one-time-use model, which fires the flash even if it is only partially charged.) Wait to shoot until the flash-ready lamp glows steadily (especially important with one-time-use models!). If the flash takes a long time — ten seconds or more — to charge, you may need fresh batteries.

When your camera starts up, it automatically charges the flash — even when the light is bright — so it's ready in case you choose to use flash to fill dark shadows (see Chapter 7). So if you try to take a picture immediately after you turn the camera on, the charging cycle may prevent the camera from firing when you press the shutter button, especially if your battery is weak. Just wait a few seconds and then try shooting again. If you don't use flash, subsequent shots won't be slowed by flash recycling time.

Step Back from the Subject

If you're too close to your subject, the lens on an autofocus point-and-shoot may not be able to focus it — and if the lens can't focus it, the camera won't fire when you press the shutter button. Most models tell you whether you're too close by rapidly blinking their viewfinder's focus-OK lamp, a little green light in the eyepiece. (Check your manual for its exact location.) If you see this lamp blinking, let up on the shutter button, move away from the subject a foot or two, and then try again. If the focus-OK lamp glows steadily, you should be able to shoot — provided the flash has recycled, of course!

Cameras without autofocus (focus-free models, as they're sometimes called) let you take a picture even if you're too close to the subject. In this event, the picture will be unsharp. Check your manual to find out how close you can get to the subject and remember not to get any closer.

Make Sure Your Digital Camera Has Finished Saving the Previous Picture

This process (much akin to saving a computer file on a hard drive or floppy disk) may take as much as ten seconds or longer after you shoot the picture — a time during which you can't take another. Many models display a special symbol on the LCD panel during the time that they're saving a picture. (See Chapter 15 for details.)

Rewind the Film and Insert a New Roll

It doesn't happen very often, but sometimes film snags on the cassette or the camera. This problem may be caused by physical damage to the cassette, which in my experience is more likely with 35mm than the Advanced Photo System. To rewind the film, push the midroll rewind button. (Check your manual for its location.) See Chapter 1 for details.

Appendix A

Impress Your Friends! A Short Glossary of Photo Jargon

*P*hotography had its own jargon long before the high-tech buzzwords of the computer era. Naturally, more terms come into being as new camera and film technologies are introduced; the Advanced Photo System (look it up!) is responsible for quite a few recent additions. But most of the terms in the following list are decidedly old-fashioned, so they're not just for impressing your friends. Use them with the old-timers at your local photo shop — correctly, of course — and their eyes will light up.

To save space for other important things, I keep the definitions short. Also note that I define only a few essential camera modes in this glossary. For a complete rundown of modes, see Chapter 4.

35mm: The type of film used by most point-and-shoot cameras, which is why they're called 35mm point-and-shoots. It comes in a cassette with a protruding film leader.

Advanced Photo System (APS): Breakthrough camera and film technology that has created a new generation of point-and-shoots, APS offers a choice of three print formats, improved photofinishing, and significant storage and reprinting conveniences.

Angle of view: The amount of a scene taken in by a particular lens focal length. Short focal lengths have a wide angle of view, allowing you to photograph a larger portion of the scene than long focal lengths, which have a narrow angle of view.

Archival: Describes any negative or print storage or display material that won't cause the photographic image to fade, stain, or discolor over time. Acid-free materials are archival.

Autoexposure: The system with which your camera automatically sets the lens aperture and shutter speed to get the correct amount of light to the film.

Autoflash: Flash mode in which the camera automatically decides whether or not flash is needed, turning the flash on in dim light and keeping it off in bright light. It's the default mode of most point-and-shoots.

Autofocus: Automatic focusing.

Backlight: Light coming from behind the subject. When light from behind is the main source, the subject is said to be backlit.

Backlight compensation: Adjustment of exposure to prevent the subject from turning out too dark when light is coming from behind it.

Black-and-white film: Film that reproduces the subject in shades of gray (and black and white, depending on the scene's contrast) rather than in color. Black-and-white film is available in conventional or chromogenic versions.

Camera shake: The unwanted movement passed along to your camera by involuntary hand and body tremors, it's a major cause of unsharp pictures.

Candid: An unposed, spontaneous photograph of a person or group of people.

Catchlights: Tiny highlights (bright spots) in a subject's eyes, caused by reflections of the light source.

CCD (charge-coupled device): The tiny "chip" that is a digital point-and-shoot's equivalent to film. The CCD uses rows of microscopic sensors to measure and record light energy, which is then stored digitally.

Color print film: Film designed to produce a color negative from which any number of color prints may be made.

Color saturation: The relative brilliance with which a film (or print) reproduces the subject's colors. Films that deliver more intense colors are said to have high saturation.

Composition: The process of adjusting framing, camera position, and/or focal length to turn the subject into a visually appealing photograph.

Contrast: The degree of difference between a subject's tones, a function of its inherent shades and colors and also of the quality of light.

Correct exposure: The specific amount of light that must strike a given film to produce the best possible picture quality.

Cropping: Masking or otherwise shaping a photographic image to change its proportions.

Default: A mode, or group of modes, that a point-and-shoot always returns to after settings are changed for a particular shot or roll.

Developing: See *photofinishing*.

Diffused light: Light that has been softened by cloud cover or any other translucent element.

Digital: Pertaining to computer language and operation. A digital point-and-shoot captures and stores pictures without film, for direct use in computer software and printing applications.

DX code: The bar code on the side of a 35mm film cassette that automatically tells the camera what film speed (ISO) to set for correct light metering and exposure.

Exposure: The amount of light that strikes the film when you take a picture. Also, a frame of film — enough for one shot.

Exposure compensation: Found on relatively few point-and-shoots, this capability allows you to manually alter the autoexposure for specific effects and subjects.

Exposure latitude: The range within which a film can tolerate errors in exposure and still produce acceptable results.

Exposure value: Abbreviated EV, always with a plus or minus number attached, it indicates the degree of exposure change with exposure compensation or backlight compensation — for example, +1.5 EV, –0.5 EV.

Fast film: Film with a high sensitivity to light, reflected in its high ISO rating — usually ISO 400 and above.

Fill flash: (Also known as *flash-on*.) Flash mode in which the camera fires the flash for every shot. Fill flash can be used to soften shadows in bright outdoor light by filling them with light.

Film cassette: The small, lightproof housing in which film is supplied, and that you place in the camera to shoot. With 35mm, the film cassette is discarded after processing; with the Advanced Photo System, it's returned to you with the processed negatives inside.

Film leader: The short, half-width strip of film extending from an unexposed 35mm cassette; must be engaged in the take-up spool for a camera to advance the film.

Film speed: The measure of a film's sensitivity to light, film speed is indicated with an ISO number — ISO 400, for example. The higher the number, the more sensitive the film.

Film winding: (Also called film advance.) Moving a roll of film from one frame to the next for each shot, often by built-in motor.

Flash: Your point-and-shoot's tiny but highly useful built-in light source, the flash fires in an action-stopping burst and often has several different modes.

Flash-off mode: A mode in which the flash won't fire regardless of the light level. It may cause the camera to set a slow shutter speed.

Flash-ready lamp: A small light beside the viewfinder window or next to the viewfinder frame, it blinks when the flash is charging and glows steadily when the flash is ready to fire. Usually red or orange.

Focal length: Technical term indicating how wide or narrow a section of a scene the lens includes in a picture (angle of view), and/or how big or small it makes the subject (magnification).

Focal length range: The run of focal lengths offered by a zoom lens. It's specified by the shortest and the longest, in millimeters — for example, 38–90mm.

Focus point: Small brackets, lines, or a circle in the middle of an autofocus point-and-shoot's viewfinder indicating where the camera is focusing.

Focus-free: (Also known as fixed-focus.) Term for point-and-shoots that have no autofocus capability. With these models, the lens's focus is preset at a medium distance that gives reasonably sharp results with any subject about four feet away and beyond.

Focusing: In-and-out adjustment of the lens to make the main subject sharp on the film.

Focus-OK lamp: (Also called an autofocus confirmation lamp.) A small light beside the viewfinder window that blinks when the camera can't focus a subject and glows steadily when correct focus has been achieved.

Formal: A photograph of a person or group of people made by mutual agreement, often with controlled lighting and a set-up background.

Frame: The rectangle that you see when you look through the viewfinder, used for viewing and composing the subject; or one picture's worth of film; or that thing you put your prints in.

Frame counter: The display that tells you how many shots you've taken, or are left, on a roll of film. The frame counter may be located on the camera's LCD panel or in a small separate window.

Frame lines: Light or dark lines or brackets just inside the viewfinder frame that indicate the area of the scene that will be recorded on the film. (Many point-and-shoots do not have frame lines.)

Frame numbers: Numbers printed by the manufacturer along the edges of 35mm film, or by the photofinisher on an index print or the back of a print. Frame numbers allow you to identify a particular negative for reprinting or blowups.

Grain: Tiny clumps of silver crystals that form the photographic image during film development, their pattern is sometimes visible in the print. The faster the film, the more visible the grain — but even fast films are now very fine-grained.

Hard light: Light that creates strong contrast and heavy shadows in the subject, usually from a direct source such as the sun or a lightbulb.

Icon: A symbol representing a specific mode or status, it's displayed on the camera's LCD panel or printed on its body.

Index print: Created by digital scanning, a print-sized sheet of tiny positive images of every shot on a roll. Used for storage, indexing, and reprinting reference.

Infinity lock: Often called landscape mode, this setting causes the camera to focus as far away as possible; especially useful to prevent misfocusing when shooting through windows.

ISO number: See *film speed*.

LCD (liquid crystal display) panel: Found on all but the least expensive point-and-shoot models, it indicates camera status and settings.

Lens: A cylinder of shaped pieces of glass or plastic at the front of a camera, it projects a tiny image of the subject onto the film.

Lens aperture: The window in the lens that lets light through to the film. Your point-and-shoot automatically adjusts this window's size, called the f-stop, to control the exposure.

Light meter: The built-in device that your point-and-shoot camera uses to measure light and determine the correct exposure settings.

Light source: The immediate origin of a scene's light, such as the sun or a window.

Locking the focus: Pressing and holding an autofocus point-and-shoot's shutter button halfway, to prevent the camera from refocusing incorrectly with your final composition.

Long focal length: See *telephoto focal length.*

Midroll rewind button: Used for rewinding a roll of film before it's finished (that is, fully exposed).

Mode: A setting that causes the camera to perform a specific function or operation. See Chapter 4 for detailed definitions of specific modes.

Muddy: Term for prints that are lacking in detail, contrast, and color brilliance (often grayish or brownish).

Negative: Used to make the print, it's the visible form a picture takes after the film is processed. A negative's tones and (with color print film) colors are the opposite of what they were in the subject, but printing reverses them back to their original state.

Normal focal length: Focal length setting — usually around 50mm with 35mm models, 40mm with APS models — that reproduces the most natural-looking size relationships in a scene.

One-time-use camera: A model designed to shoot a single roll of film, it's available in specialized designs, and comes in both 35mm and APS versions. You turn in the camera itself to the photofinisher when the roll is done.

Panorama mode: A setting in which the camera produces an elongated image intended for the creation of a 4 x 10- or 4 x 11$\frac{1}{2}$-inch print.

Parallax error: The difference between what the lens sees and what you see through the camera's viewfinder; especially pronounced at longer focal lengths and with closer subjects.

Photofinishing: (Also called processing.) The business of turning your exposed film into negatives (developing) and your negatives into prints (printing) — or into any other usable, visible form.

Pixels: Short for picture elements, the tilelike bits of color and tone that form a digital image.

Positive: Opposite of negative, used to describe any photographic image that reproduces the subject's original tones and/or colors. A slide is a positive; a print is a positive.

Prefocusing: Same idea as locking the focus, but means using the technique to reduce shutter-button time lag when shooting a moving subject.

Print format: The proportions (height to width) or shape of a photographic print. The Advanced Photo System offers a choice of three print formats, selectable with a control on the camera itself.

Printing: See *photofinishing.*

Processing: See *photofinishing.*

Quartz-date: Term for point-and-shoot models with the ability to imprint the date on photographic negatives; numbers appear permanently on the front of the prints.

Random Access Memory (RAM): The amount of active digital storage in your computer, RAM must be relatively high to allow work with photographs.

Resolution: Technical term for the measurement of photographic sharpness, resolution is lower for digital point-and-shoots than film models.

Rewinding: The process of retracting a roll of exposed film into its cassette before removal from the camera. Motorized on many models, rewinding starts automatically at the end of the roll or when you press the midroll rewind button.

Scanning: The process of translating a photograph (negative or print) into an electronic form that can be used by computers.

Self-timer mode: A setting in which the camera delays taking a picture by a specified interval after you touch the shutter button.

Sharpness: The degree to which clear, distinguishable details of the subject are rendered in a photographic negative or print.

Short focal length: See *wide-angle focal length.*

Shutter button: The button that you press to take a picture. On autofocus cameras, the shutter button also activates and locks the focus when pressed halfway.

Shutter speed: The length of time the window in the lens stays open to let light through to the film.

Single-focal-length: Term for lenses on nonzooming point-and-shoots. Because the focal length cannot be adjusted, you can only control the subject's size in the picture by physically moving yourself and the camera in and out.

Slide film: Film designed to produce a positive transparent image of the subject on the original film itself. Mainly intended for projection or scanning rather than printing, though prints can be ordered from slides.

Slow film: Film with relatively low sensitivity to light, reflected in its lower ISO rating — usually ISO 200 and below.

Slow-sync flash: (Also known as night, night scene, or night portrait mode.) This mode combines flash with a longer shutter speed to improve background detail in low-light flash shots.

Soft light: Light that creates delicate tones and pale or minimal shadows in the subject, such as from a cloudy sky or in open shade.

Telephoto focal length: (Also called a long focal length.) A focal length setting — usually around 60mm (with APS) or 70mm (with 35mm) and beyond — at which the subject is magnified (appears bigger than normal in the frame).

Thumbnails: Small reference images of the shots on a roll, appearing in an index print or on a computer screen.

Toggling: Pressing a pushbutton repeatedly to advance through a menu of modes, in order to choose and set one.

Tungsten light: Artificial light from household bulbs (halogen is a variation).

Viewfinder: Window on the camera through which you see the rectangular frame used to view and compose your subject. (On many digital point-and-shoots the viewfinder is a TVlike color LCD screen.)

Wide-angle focal length: (Also called a short focal length.) Focal length at which the lens takes in a relatively large section of the total scene. Most point-and-shoot zoom lenses start out at a wide-angle setting (38mm, 28mm), and most nonzoom models have wide-angle lenses (35mm, 32mm).

Wide-area autofocus: (Also called multibeam or multipoint autofocus.) An autofocus system in which multiple focus points cover a wider-than-usual area in the middle of the viewfinder. Wide-area autofocus allows the camera to focus subjects that are slightly off-center without the need to lock the focus.

Zoom lens: A lens of adjustable focal length. You zoom to increase or decrease the lens's magnifying power, making the subject bigger or smaller in the frame.

Zooming in: Setting a longer focal length on your zoom lens, to make the subject bigger in the picture.

Zooming out: Setting a shorter focal length on your zoom lens, to include more of the scene in the picture.

Appendix B
Manufacturers, Distributors, and Retailers

・・・

*I*n these days of discount stores, mass merchandisers, and rampant catalog sales, the place you buy a camera (or any other photographic product) may not be much help when you need more information — or when things go wrong. Unless you cultivate a relationship with a friendly neighborhood photo shop, you may need to contact a product's manufacturer or distributor directly.

The following alphabetical list helps you make that contact. This list includes addresses, phone numbers, and Web sites for most major U.S. suppliers of point-and-shoot cameras (35mm, Advanced Photo System, and digital models), plus manufacturers of films, batteries, digital products, and storage and display materials. You even find companies that operate photofinishing networks.

Don't send a malfunctioning point-and-shoot to these addresses without first consulting the camera's maker. Repair facilities are often in different locations than a company's headquarters.

Manufacturers usually have technical or customer service departments that can answer your questions about camera operation, film performance, and other photographic matters. Most can also provide you with a replacement camera manual if you lost yours. Some companies have consumer catalogs of their offerings (ask for one if you're shopping), but if not, they can mail you brochures on specific products. You may even be able to request materials or assistance through the company's Web site, which is also a good source of information.

Adobe Systems, Inc., 345 Park Ave., San Jose, CA 95110-2705; telephone (800) 685-3507 or (408) 536-6000; Web site www.adobe.com. Computer software for photography.

Agfa Division of Bayer Corp., 100 Challenger Rd., Ridgefield Park, NJ 07660-2199; telephone (201) 440-2500; Web site www.agfahome.com. Film, cameras, digital photo products.

Canon USA, Inc., One Canon Plaza, Lake Success, NY 11042-1119; telephone (800) OK-CANON or (516) 328-5000; Web site www.usa.canon.com. Cameras, digital photo products, accessories.

Eastman Kodak Company, 343 State St., Rochester, NY 14650-0412; telephone (800) 242-2424 or (716) 724-4000; Web site www.kodak.com. Film, cameras, batteries, digital photo products, photofinishing.

Epson America, Inc., 20770 Madrona Ave., Torrance, CA 90503; telephone (800) GO-EPSON or (310) 782-0770; Web site www.epson.com. Digital cameras, digital photo products.

Fuji Photo Film USA, Inc., 555 Taxter Rd., Elmsford, NY 10523-2394; telephone (800) 755-3854 or (914) 789-8100; Web site www.fujifilm.com. Film, cameras, digital photo products, photofinishing.

Hewlett-Packard Company, 16399 W. Bernardo Dr., San Diego, CA 92127-1899; telephone (800) 851-1170; Web site www.hp.com. Digital cameras, digital photo products.

Ilford Photo, West 70 Century Rd., Paramus, NJ 07652-1490; telephone (201) 265-6000; Web site www.ilford.com. Film, digital photo products.

JVC Company of America, 41 Slater Drive, Elmwood Park, NJ 07407-1311; telephone (800) 252-5722; Web site www.jvc.com. Digital cameras.

Konica USA, Inc., 440 Sylvan Ave., Englewood Cliffs, NJ 07632-2720; telephone (800) 285-6422; Web site www.konica.com. Film, cameras, digital photo products, photofinishing.

Kyocera Electronics Inc. (Contax, Yashica), 2301 Cottontail Lane, Somerset, NJ 08873; telephone (800) 526-0266 or (732) 560-0060; Web site www.contaxcameras.com or www.yashica.com. Cameras, digital products.

Leica Camera, Inc./Minox, 156 Ludlow Ave., Northvale, NJ 07647-2305; telephone (800) 222-0118 or (201) 767-7500; Web site www.leica-camera.com. Cameras, camera bags.

Minolta Corporation, 101 Williams Dr., Ramsey, NJ 07446-1282; telephone (800) 528-4767 or (201) 825-4000; Web site www.minolta.com. Cameras, digital photo products, accessories.

Nikon Inc., 1300 Walt Whitman Rd., Melville, NY 11747-8518; telephone (800) NIKON-US; Web site www.nikonusa.com. Cameras, digital photo products.

Olympus America Inc., 2 Corporate Center Dr., Melville, NY 11747-3157; telephone (800) 622-6372 or (516) 844-5000; Web site www.olympus.com. Cameras, digital photo products, accessories.

Pentax Corporation, 35 Inverness Dr. E., Englewood, CO 80112-5484; telephone (800) 877-0155 or (303) 799-8000; Web site www.pentax.com. Cameras, digital photo products, accessories.

Polaroid Corporation, 201 Burlington Rd., Bedford, MA 01730; telephone (800) 343-5000 or (617) 386-2000; Web site www.polaroid.com. Film, cameras, digital photo products.

Print File Inc., 1846 S. Orange Blossom Trail, Apopka, FL 32703; (407) 886-3100; Web site www.printfile.com. Archival film and print storage materials and systems.

Ricoh Consumer Products Group, 475 Lillard Dr., Ste. 101, Sparks, NV 89434-8926; telephone (800) 225-1899 or (702) 352-1600; Web site www.ricohcpg.com. Cameras, digital photo products.

Rollei Fototechnik, 40 Seaview Dr., Secaucus, NJ 07094; telephone (888) 876-5534; Web site www.rolleifoto.com. Cameras, digital photo products.

Samsung Opto-Electronics America Inc., 40 Seaview Dr., Secaucus, NJ 07094-1807; telephone (800) 762-7746 or (201) 902-0347; Web site www.simplyamazing.com. Cameras, digital photo products.

The Saunders Group (Silver Pixel Press), 21 Jet View Drive, Rochester, NY 14624-4903; telephone (716) 328-7800; Web site www.saundersphoto.com. Camera bags, accessories, photo books.

Sony Electronics Inc., One Sony Drive, Park Ridge, NJ 07656; telephone (800) 472-7669 or (201) 930-7796; Web site www.sony.com. Digital cameras, digital photo products.

Vivitar Corporation, 1280 Rancho Conejo Blvd., Newbury Park, CA 91320-1403; phone (805) 498-7008, Web site www.vivitar.com. Cameras, digital photo products.

Mail-order retailers

You can order cameras, film, digital products, and accessories by telephone from the following companies, which ship the products directly to you by common carriers. Some have a complete line of photographic products; others specialize, as indicated. A number of these companies also sell photo books, both how-to and coffee table. Call them for a catalog.

Though all mail-order retailers have toll-free phone numbers for ordering, you can also usually order through their Web sites, if you

(continued)

(continued)

prefer. And most offer overnight delivery service, if you need stuff in a hurry.

If you do buy by mail order, know what you want in advance. Not all mail-order companies are prepared to give over-the-phone buying guidance — nor do the people staffing the lines necessarily have in-depth knowledge of the products they sell. Do your research by talking to friends about their cameras, reading photo magazines and buying guides, and visiting both manufacturers and nonproprietary photo Web sites. (See Chapter 18 for suggestions.) And abide by the following tips:

✔ **Avoid imported gray market merchandise, a specialty of mail-order suppliers.** Although gray market photo goods may be of the same quality as domestic goods, they carry a store or international warranty rather than a standard U.S. one. (If you ask, the salesman must tell you that a product is gray market.) If you have problems, getting warranty service may be more difficult.

✔ **Avoid the additional cost of extended warranties.** Although they extend the usual one-year warranty to three, four, or five years, these warranties are serviced by third-party repair companies of sometimes questionable stability *and* ability.

✔ **Don't let the salesperson sell you a different product than the one you want.**

✔ **Keep in mind that *you* may be charged a restocking fee if you return an item.**

✔ **Note that shipping and handling charges increase the bill; ask about them before committing to a purchase.**

✔ **Beware if merchandise is back-ordered; it may be weeks before you receive it.** Try to find a supplier who has the product in stock.

✔ **Always pay with a credit card.** Getting a refund is usually easier with a credit card purchase than one made with a check or money order.

Here are some mail-order retailers; specialized offerings are described.

Adorama Inc., 42 West 18th St., New York, NY 10011; telephone (800) 815-1260 or (212) 741-0052; Web site www.adoramacamera.com.

B&H Photo-Video, 420 Ninth Avenue, New York, NY 10001; telephone (800) 947-9005 or (212) 444-6666, Web site www.bhphotovideo.com.

Calumet Photo, 890 Supreme Drive, Bensenville, IL 60106; telephone (800) 225-8638 or (630) 860-7447. Photo products and books.

Camera World of Oregon, 700 N.E. 55th Avenue, Portland, Oregon 97213-3150; telephone (800) 222-1557 or (503) 227-6008; Web site www.cameraworld.com.

Light Impressions, 439 Monroe Ave., P.O. Box 940, Rochester, NY 14603-0940; telephone (800) 828-6216 or (716) 271-8960. Archival negative and print storage materials, photo albums.

Porter's Camera Store, P.O. Box 628, Cedar Falls, IA 50613; telephone (800) 553-2001 or (319) 268-0104; Web site www.porters.com.

Ritz Camera, 6711 Ritz Way, Beltsville, MD 20705; telephone (800) 52-FOCUS or (301) 419-0000; Web site www.ritzcamera.com.

Samy's Camera, 200 S. La Brea Ave., Los Angeles, CA 90036; telephone (800) 321-4726 or (213) 938-2420, Web site www.samys.com.

Visual Departures, Ltd., P.O. Box 427, Riverside, CT 06878; telephone (800) 628-2003 or (203) 698-0880; Web site www.visualdepartures.com. Collapsible reflectors, specialized photo products.

Index

• Numbers •

2CR5 lithium battery, 14
8 x 10s, 96
8 x 12s, 96
12-exposure rolls, 61
16 x 20s, 96
16 x 24s, 96
24-exposure rolls, 62
25-exposure rolls, 62
35mm film, 10, 375
    cutting negatives apart, 95
    index print, 94
    printing costs, 76–77
35mm point-and-shoot cameras, 10
    advancing film, 22, 24
    automatic film loading, 20
    built-in flash, 168
    captions, 98
    compact-zoom models, 148
    contacts in film chamber, 44
    counting exposures, 24
    date back, 98
    drop-in loading system, 23
    film cassette chamber, 21
    film chamber, 44
    film roll lengths, 58
    film tip mark, 21
    focal lengths, 136
    fogging film, 25–26
    frame counter, 22
    LCD panel, 22, 24
    leader, 20
    lenses, 136
    loading film, 20–23
    long-zoom, 149–150
    manual crank for rewinding film, 35
    mechanical counter, 24
    mistakenly opening camera, 24
    one-time-use, 59
    opening camera back, 20
    panorama format pictures, 96
    panorama mode, 113–114
    picture number, 22
    prewinding, 26
    print size, 313
    pulling too much film out, 22–23
    rewinding film, 23, 35

    setting correct ISO speed, 44
    shortest focal length, 216
    single-focal-length, 147
    spool hub, 21
    standard exposures, 33
    standard-zoom, 149
    take-up mechanism, 22
    take-up spool, 20
    testing color slide film, 44
    typical location of controls, 13
    wide-angle focal length, 284
    winding motor, 22
35mm SLR (single-lens-reflex) camera, 152
36-exposure rolls, 62
40-exposure rolls, 62
223A lithium battery, 14

• A •

AA batteries, 16
    digital point-and-shoot cameras, 17
AAA batteries, 16
action mode, 122–123, 278
    predictive autofocusing, 123
action photography
    blur, 275–276
    combining stop action and blur, 276–277
    composition, 278
    decisive moment, 269
    different topics appropriate for, 277–278
    distance and flash, 274
    electronic flash, 274
    fast film, 266–268
    flash-off mode, 268
    freezing action with fast shutter speeds, 266–269
    freezing action with flash, 273–275
    frozen or blurred action photographs, 265–269
    good examples of, 268–269
    indoor shots and autoflash, 275
    movement, 261
    no fancy equipment necessary, 261–262
    panning, 272–273
    point-and-shoot camera quirks, 262–263
    prefocusing, 263–264, 269
    shooting in advance of action, 269
    squeezing shutter button, 264
    stop-action point-and-shoot pictures, 264

action-freezing photographs, 265–269
   catching peak of action, 270
   electronic flash, 266
   fast shutter speeds, 266–269
   panning action, 272
   shooting from distance, 271
   shooting head-on, 270
   timing shot, 270
   tips, 270–272
active autofocus, 162, 163, 165
   advantages, 163
   bright reflections or dull object focus, 165
   disadvantages, 165
   infinity lock and windows, 165
   pictures through fences, 165
Adobe PhotoDeluxe, 71, 339
Adobe Photoshop, 339
Advantix, 323
Advantix Film Drive FD 300, 328
Agfachrome, 42
aiming *versus* framing, 210–212
airport X-rays and film, 308
alkaline batteries, 16
all-auto mode, 108
angle of view, 57, 375
   describing, 135
Anhinga Trail, Everglades National Park,
   Florida, 369–370
anytime flash mode, 172
aperture, setting size, 127
aperture-priority autoexposure mode, 127
APS (Advanced Photo System), 311–328, 375
   advantages, 312
   backprinting, 327
   captions, 98
   color print film, 39
   computers and, 327–328
   date feature, 98
   film, 313, 322
   finding the right negative, 320–322
   index prints, 94, 320–321
   loading film, 312, 323–324
   memory keepers, 322
   MRC (mid-roll change), 325–326
   panoramic prints, 97
   photofinishing, 319
   portrait telephoto, 144
   PQI (Print Quality Improvement), 92, 312, 320
   print formats, 312–319
   printing refinements, 327
   protecting negatives, 321
   reprints, 319–320, 327
   scanners, 328
   slide film, 325
   storage and indexing capabilities, 312
   time and date, 327
   titles, 327
   types of film, 324–325

APS (Advanced Photo System) film
   index print, 77
   printing costs, 77
APS (Advanced Photo System) point-and-shoot
   cameras, 10
   advancing film, 27–28
   black-and-white film, 50
   built-in flash, 168
   C, H, P switch, 114
   choosing format, 317–319
   Classic format, 314, 315, 316
   color slide film, 44
   compact-zoom models, 148
   fast film, 266
   film cassette, 28
   film cassette size, 27
   film roll lengths, 59
   film-compartment door, 26, 27
   focal lengths, 136
   fogging film, 26
   frame lines, 316–317
   HDTV format, 314, 315, 316, 319
   icons on film cassette, 28
   lenses, 136
   limited range of film speeds, 44
   loading film, 26–28
   long-zoom, 149–150
   masking viewfinder, 316
   minilabs, 75
   MRC (mid-roll change) feature, 36
   no visible leader, 28
   Panoramic format, 289, 314, 315, 316
   reshaping viewfinder, 316
   selecting print format, 315
   shape of pictures, 316–317
   shortest focal length, 216
   single-focal-length, 147
   standard exposures, 33
   standard-size prints, 90
   standard-zoom, 149
   testing color slide film, 44
   typical location of controls, 13
   vertical composition, 222
   verticals with Panoramic format, 317
   wide-angle focal length, 284
   zoom lens, 317
archival, 375
archival materials, 102
artificial light
   fill-flash mode, 206
   mixing with flash, 206
   slow-sync flash, 206
   turning off flash, 205
autoexposure, 375
autoflash mode, 87, 106, 108, 111, 130,
   168–170, 376
   indoor shots, 275
   no icon for, 170
   shutter, 182

autofocus, 151, 376
    accidental misfocusing, 154–155
    active, 162, 163, 165
    defining, 152
    eyes, 152
    focus point, 154–160
    focus-OK lamp, 163
    infinity lock, 160, 163
    locking the focus, 155–157, 163
    making sure focus is locked, 157–158
    multipoint, 120
    overriding, 119
    passive, 162, 165–166
    predictive, 123
    spot, 162
    tips, 162–166
    tunnel focus, 155
    wide-area, 161–162
autofocus cameras, 119
    versus fixed-focus cameras, 153
    focusing far away, 160
    focus-OK lamp, 153, 157, 162
    shutter button, 159
    where camera focuses, 154–160
    wide-area autofocusing, 161–162
autoframing function, 123
automatic backlight compensation, 175
automatic flash, 111
automatically setting modes, 124–125
autozooming function, 123

• *B* •

backgrounds
    balancing with foreground, 216–217
    candid photos, 244–246
    formal photos, 238
backlight, 207–208, 376
    backlight compensation, 208
    fill-flash mode, 208
backlight compensation, 84, 126–127, 199, 376
    automatic, 175
    backlight, 208
    flash, 173
backlit, 174
batteries, 13–19
    AA or AAA, 16
    alkaline, 16
    changing with film in camera, 19
    correct orientation of, 18
    counters and changing, 19
    displaying status, 18–19
    keeping extras on hand, 15
    lithium batteries, 14–15
    loading, 16, 18–19
    power icons, 18

    rechargeable, 16
    recycling itself, 15–16
    removing while storing camera, 19
    travel, 299
battery power icons, 18
better pictures
    capturing the moment, 354
    close backgrounds and flash, 355
    fast film, 356
    flash outdoors, 355
    getting close, 354–355
    horizon line, 356
    moving sideways, 356
    off-center subject, 356
    shooting from high or low angle, 355
    taking lots of pictures, 356
    viewfinder used like gun sight, 354
black-and-white chemical processing, 48
black-and-white film, 46–51, 376
    APS (Advanced Photo System) point-and-
        shoot cameras, 50
    chromogenic, 49–50, 97
    composition, 47
    contrasting with color film, 47
    custom processing, 49
    Ektamax paper option, 50–51
    fill-flash mode, 47
    light, 47
    negatives, 48
    processed in conventional black-and-white
        chemicals, 48
    processing, 50
    processing your own, 49
    slow-sync flash mode, 47
    types, 48–49
black-and-white negatives, printing on Ektamax
        paper, 51
black-and-white one-time-use cameras, 51
black-and-white slide film, 48
blowups, 68, 95–97
blurred-action photographs, 265–269, 275–276
    combining with stop action, 276–277
    different light, 276
    moving the camera, 275
    slower film, 275
Bryce Canyon National Park, Utah, 365
built-in flash, 233
built-in light meter, 125–127
bulb mode, 128
burning in, 91
button cells, 19
buttons
    changing modes, 108–109
    help for pushing, 109
    on point-and-shoot cameras, 105–107
    toggling, 108–109

buying point-and-shoot cameras, 345–352
  35mm *versus* APS (Advanced Photo
    System), 349
  comfort holding camera, 352
  digital or film camera, 348–349
  features you want, 351
  how much you want to spend, 346–347
  more camera than you need, 346
  viewfinders easy to look through, 352
  what photographer will be shooting, 348
  who will use it, 347
  zoom range, 350–351
  zooming *versus* nonzooming, 349–350
bytes, 330

• *C* •

C, H, P switch, 114
C-41 processing, 43, 69
Cadillac Ranch, Amarillo, Texas, 364
camera bags, 303
  features, 305
camera manuals, 13
  travel, 299
camera shake, 376
cameras
  autoflash mode, 87
  batteries, 13–19
  battery power icons, 18
  buying for travel, 301
  cleaning, 88
  continuously taking pictures, 117–118
  displaying battery status, 18–19
  end-sensing mechanism, 59
  exposure compensation control, 199
  fill-flash mode, 47
  intervalometer, 193
  lame excuses for not taking along, 259–260
  LCD panel, 12–13, 18
  leaving film in for extended periods, 60
  lightproof, 12
  loading batteries, 16, 18–19
  loading film, 19–29
  new for travel, 300
  operating remotely, 116–117
  parts of, 12–13
  point-and-shoot, 9–36
  quartz date capability, 19
  remedies when it won't shoot, 371–374
  remote receptor, 116
  removing batteries while storing, 19
  slow-sync flash mode, 47
  steadying, 57
  taking slower film out of, 54
  traveling with right, 299–300
  typical location of controls, 13
  viewfinder, 12

candid, 376
candid photos, 235
  analyzing scene and players, 242
  backgrounds, 244–246
  blurred background, 245–246
  distance from background, 244
  finding good shooting position, 242
  good observational skills, 242
  identifying occasions for, 241
  physical games, 242
  planning, 241–246
  planning tactics, 242
  slow-sync mode, 245
  telling a story, 242, 244
  tips, 228
  visual clutter and dark backgrounds, 244–245
Capa, Robert, 212
captive processing, 78
capturing your life on film, 227–228
  expression and gesture, 234–246
  film is inexpensive, 230–232
  good people photographs, 232–233
  reasons for taking photographs, 228
  sharing pictures, 229–230
  when to take pictures, 232
catchlights, 174, 376
CCD (charge-coupled device), 376
CD-ROMs, scanning photographs to, 333
children
  cameras defusing behavior, 249
  clothes, 254
  difficulty photographing, 249–250
  emotional variety, 249
  eye contact, 252–253
  flash and photographing, 252
  knowing when to photograph, 250–252
  looking at camera, 252
  multiple shots of, 251
  photographing, 248–254
  reactions and expressions, 251
  red-eye reduction, 253
  seeing through viewfinder, 251
  shooting down on, 253
  shooting on their level, 253
  spontaneity, 252
  times of day or activities to photograph, 250
china marker, 94
Chincoteague Island, Eastern Shore,
    Virginia, 364
chromogenic black-and-white film, 49–50, 97
  making prints from, 50
cityscapes, 292–293
  time of day, 293
clamshell cover, 29
cleaning
  cameras, 88
  lenses, 164

close-up correction marks, 144, 146
clothing in formal photographs, 239
cloudy day light, 202
Collected Visions Web site, 361
color filtration, 41
color negatives, 38, 72
    printing, 70
    reddish or reddish-orange cast, 40
color of light, 195
color print film, 38–41, 376
    APS (Advanced Photo System), 39
    balanced for daylight, 184
    C-41 processing, 43
    color filtration, 41
    color of the light, 40
    dyes remembering silver crystal pattern, 54
    exposure latitude, 39
    as forgiving film, 39–41
    hard light, 198–200
    ISO 400 as standard, 52
    ISO ratings, 51
    processing, 43
    quality, 38–39
color prints, things that can go wrong with, 83–89
color saturation, 63, 376
color slide film, 41–46
    APS (Advanced Photo System), 325
    APS (Advanced Photo System) point-and-shoot cameras, 44
    backlight compensation, 127
    bracketing exposures, 46
    brand names, 42
    E-6 processing, 43
    EV compensation, 45
    fill flash, 46
    getting good results with, 43–45
    hard light, 198
    middle-of-the-road point-and-shoot cameras, 45
    precise exposure, 45
    prints from, 43
    processing, 43
    proper exposure, 43
    slide rules and exposure compensation, 45–46
    testing in 35mm and APS cameras, 44
color slides. *See* slides
communicating with photofinishers, 82–83
CompactFlash card, 338
compact-zoom point-and-shoot cameras, 148
composition, 132, 209–223, 376
    action photographs, 278
    aiming *versus* framing, 210–212
    balancing foreground and background, 216–217
    becoming second nature, 223
    black-and-white film, 47
    changing your angle, 219–220
    filling the frame, 212–213
    height, 219–220
    horizontal *versus* vertical pictures, 221–222
    landscapes, 282, 286–288
    near-far, 216
    off-center, 218
    relationships between viewfinder frame and scene objects, 211
    Rule of Thirds, 210
    rules, 210
    shifting sideways, 221
    subject's context, 214
    trying different, 223
    working subject, 222–223
    zooming *versus* moving, 213–216
computers
    APS (Advanced Photo System), 327–328
    compressed files, 340
    digital photographs, 330–331
    downloading from digital point-and-shoot cameras, 332, 337
    e-mailing pictures, 341
    getting pictures into, 332–334
    getting pictures out of, 341–342
    imaging software, 337, 339
    photofinishers scanning pictures, 332–333
    photography, 329–342
    printing digital images yourself, 342
    putting pictures on World Wide Web, 341–342
    RAM (random access memory), 331
    right for digital photography, 331
    scanning photographs yourself, 333–334
    upgrading for photography, 331
continuous wind mode, 117–118
contrast, 63, 197, 376
    fill-flash mode, 173
    landscapes, 282
contrasty, 197
correct exposure, 40, 376
costs
    custom labs, 91
    film roll lengths, 59
    photofinishers, 76–77
CR123A lithium battery, 14
creative modes, 128–129
    bulb mode, 128
    multiple exposure mode, 128–129
    multiple flash mode, 129
cropping, 376
    photographs, 96, 313
custom photo labs, 91

• D •

Dale Labs, 78
dating prints, 98
daylight picture too light or dark, 84
daylight sync flash, 173
default, 377
dessicants, 298
developing, 377
  automation, 69
development, 68
digital, 377
digital photographs, 330–331
  bytes, 330
  FlashPix CD, 99
  Kodak Photo CD, 99
  MB (megabytes), 330
  photo networks, 100
  pixels, 330
  right computers for, 331
  scan-to-floppy service, 99
digital photography, 97, 99–100
digital point-and-shoot cameras, 12
  AA batteries, 17
  built-in flash, 168, 335
  color LCD, 336
  color quality, 340
  compression, 340
  downloading into computer, 332, 337
  extra batteries, 17
  fixed-memory models, 338
  flash and, 17
  focal lengths, 136
  lenses, 136
  light sensitivity, 340
  lithium batteries, 17
  loading film, 29
  memory cards, 338
  rating, 340
  recording picture in memory, 336
  regular window-type viewfinder and color
    LCD, 17
  removable-memory models, 338
  resolution, 340
  storing digital pictures, 338
  taking pictures with, 334–336
  video-style LCDs, 17
digital print restoration services, 71
direct light source, 197
distributors, 383–385
DL123A lithium battery, 14
dodging, 91
double exposures, 129
double prints, 229
drive modes, 114–118
  continuous wind mode, 117–118

interval timer mode, 118
intervalometer mode, 118
multi-self-timer mode, 116
remote control mode, 116–117
self-timer mode, 115–116
sequential self-timer mode, 116
setting to continuous wind, 122–123
step zoom mode, 117
dust on negative, 87–88
DX code, 52, 377
dye-sublimation printers, 342

• E •

E-6 processing, 43
early light, 202
Ektachrome, 42
Ektamax paper, 50–51
electronic flash in action photography, 274
electronic photofinishing revolution, 97, 99–100
e-mailing pictures, 341
emulsion, 68
enlargements, 68, 95–97
  8 x 10s, 96
  8 x 12s, 96
  16 x 20s, 96
  16 x 24s, 96
  flaws, 95
  panorama format pictures, 96
  panoramic prints, 97
  standard sizes, 96
enlargers, 91
environmental portraits, 142, 248
EV compensation, 45–46
EV (exposure value), 45–46
expiration date, 61
exposure, 58, 377
  increasing for hard light, 199–200
  increasing to compensate for backlight,
    126–127
exposure compensation, 377
  color slide film, 45–46
exposure compensation control, 199
exposure compensation mode, 84, 127
exposure control, 43
exposure latitude, 39, 377
exposure value, 377
expressions, 234–246
eyes and hard light, 198

• F •

faces burned out, 86
family history, 256–258
  home interior, 258
  neighborhoods, 258

places, 257
subject in context, 256
The Family Photo Historian Web site, 358–359
fast film, 54, 58, 377
    action photography, 266–268
    APS (Advanced Photo System) point-and-shoot cameras, 266
    larger grain, 54
    negatives, 78
    reducing risk of shake, 56
favorite places to take pictures
    Anhinga Trail, Everglades National Park, Florida, 369–370
    Bryce Canyon National Park, Utah, 365
    Cadillac Ranch, Amarillo, Texas, 364
    Chincoteague Island, Eastern Shore, Virginia, 364
    Las Vegas, Nevada, 365–366
    Lucy the Elephant, Margate City, New Jersey, 369
    Paradise Meadow, Mount Rainier National Park, Washington, 368
    Salton Sea, Southern California, 370
    Santuario de Nuestra Señor de Esquipulas, Chimayo, New Mexico, 369
    Staten Island Ferry, Battery Park, New York, 367
    Vietnam Veterans Memorial, Washington, D.C., 368
    White Birch Forest, Pictured Rocks National Lakeshore, Michigan, 366–367
fill-flash mode, 79, 111, 168, 377
    artificial light, 206
    backlight, 208
    black-and-white film, 47
    capturing good detail, 173
    catchlights, 174
    color slide film, 46
    contrast, 173
    daylight picture too dark, 84
    filling shadows, 172–173
    flash ghosting, 276
    fluorescent light, 206–207
    hard light, 199
    indoor picture has green cast, 86
    maximizing, 177
    one-time-use cameras, 176
    as outdoor flash mode, 174
    person against background is silhouette, 87
    portrait mode, 123
    snowy scene grayish and muddy, 84
    subject in shadow against brighter background, 174
    when not to use, 176–177
    when to use, 173–176
fill-in flash mode, 172

film
    35mm, 10
    airport X-rays, 308
    APS (Advanced Photo System), 313, 322
    black-and-white film, 46–51
    brands to purchase, 62–65
    color negative, 38
    color print film, 38–41
    color slide film, 41–46
    contrast, 63
    correct exposure, 40, 52
    developed into negatives but not printed, 263
    development, 68
    emulsion, 68
    experimenting with different speeds, 55
    expiration date, 61
    exposing with multiple scenes, 128–129
    fast, 54
    fogging, 25–26
    formal photographs, 239
    freshness, 61
    good people photographs, 233–234
    gray-market, 65
    how many frames left on roll, 33
    ISO number, 37, 51
    latent images, 68
    leader, 20, 21
    leaving in camera for extended periods, 60
    loading, 19–29
    low cost of, 230–232
    mail-order, 65
    midroll rewind, 33
    number of exposures to purchase, 58–62
    premium, 63
    prewinding, 26
    prints from, 68–72
    private label, 64–65
    putting new roll in camera before event, 33
    refrigerating, 59, 61
    rewinding, 33–36
    right amount of light to, 40
    saturation, 63
    sensitivity to light, 51
    speeds, 37–38
    standard exposures, 33
    stopping from advancing, 128–129
    store-brand, 64
    storing before processing, 60
    stroboscopic multiple exposure, 129
    travel, 301–302
    types, 37, 38–51
    unusual shooting circumstances, 83
    winding modes, 114–118
film cassette, 377
film cassette chamber, 21

film chamber and 35mm point-and-shoot
    cameras, 44
film leader, 377
film roll lengths
    12-exposure rolls, 61
    15-exposure rolls, 61
    24-exposure rolls, 62
    25-exposure rolls, 62
    35mm point-and-shoot cameras, 58
    36-exposure rolls, 62
    40-exposure rolls, 62
    APS (Advanced Photo System) point-
        and-shoot cameras, 59
    convenience and practicality, 59–60
    costs, 59
    one-time-use 35mm point-and-shoot
        cameras, 59
    personal photographic habits and, 60
    switching between types of film, 61
film scanners, 334
film speed, 51–58, 377
    differences in quality, 55
    experimenting with different, 55
    focal length, 57–58
    graininess, 54
    panoramic prints, 55
    shake, 56–57
    sharpness, 56
film tip mark, 21
film winding, 378
film-compartment door, 26, 27
fireproof safes, 102
fixed-focus cameras, 153
fixed-price processing, 77
flare, 197
flash, 167, 378
    artificial light and, 205
    autoflash mode, 168–170
    automatic, 111
    backlight compensation, 173
    battery usage, 274
    choosing mode, 170–171
    with every picture, 172–173
    fill-flash mode, 168
    filling shadows, 172–173
    firing when needed, 168
    flash-off mode, 168
    freezing action, 273–275
    good people pictures, 246
    how far it will reach, 177
    keeping on, 111
    lessening reddish glint in eyes, 113
    mixing with artificial light, 206
    modes, 168
    muddy prints, 87
    not covering when shooting, 170

off for fast sequence, 122–123
one-time-use cameras, 171
panning with, 277
photographing children, 252
recycling time, 178
red-eye reduction mode, 168
resetting modes, 188
shooting with and without, 180
slow-sync mode, 168
staying within range of, 79
turning off, 112, 178–181
turning on and off, 170–171
flash ghosting
    fill flash, 276
    panning with flash, 277
    slow-sync flash, 277
flash mode button, 170–171
flash modes, 111–113
    autoflash mode, 111
    fill-flash mode, 111
    flash-off mode, 112
    flash-on mode, 111
    night flash mode, 112
    red-eye reduction mode, 113
    slow-sync mode, 112
flash multi mode, 278
flash-off mode, 112, 168, 177–181, 378
    action photography, 268
    complications, 181
    quality of light part of picture, 179
    shooting far-away subjects, 179
    shooting through window, 180–181
    staged events, 241
    when to use, 179–181
flash-on mode, 111, 172
FlashPix CDs, 99, 333
flash-ready lamp, 178, 378
flatbed scanners, 334
floppy disks, scanning photographs to, 332
fluorescent light, 206–207
    color of, 195
    fill-flash mode, 207
    slow-sync flash, 184, 207
focal length range, 139, 378
focal lengths, 135–138, 378
    35mm point-and-shoot cameras, 136
    APS (Advanced Photo System) point-and-
        shoot cameras, 136
    changing, 138
    digital point-and-shoot cameras, 136
    film speed, 57–58
    fine-tuning, 138–146
    including foreground objects and, 216
    long, 135
    long for portrait photographs, 246
    longer, 143

normal, 139–140, 142
numbers, 135
pictures of individuals, 233
point-and-shoot camera types, 135, 136
shake, 285
short, 135
stacking scene elements, 285
telephoto, 139–140, 142–146
trying "wrong," 146
wide-angle, 139–142
wide-angle and portrait photographs, 248
focus
  infinity, 119
  locking, 155–157
  setting closer than usual, 121
  setting manually, 121
  setting to distant range, 119
  setting to medium range, 120
  subjects off center, 161
  wide-area, 120
focus point, 153, 378
  keeping your eye on, 157
focus-free, 378
focus-free cameras, prefocusing, 264
focusing, 152, 378
focusing modes, 119–121
  infinity lock mode, 119
  landscape mode, 119
  macro mode, 121
  manual focus mode, 121
  snap mode, 120
  spot autofocus mode, 120
focus-OK lamp, 163, 378
Fodor's Focus on Photography Web site, 361
fogginess, 208
fogging film, 25–26
  APS (Advanced Photo System) point-
    and-shoot camera, 26
forced emission mode, 172
foreground balancing with background,
    216–217
formal, 378
formal photographs, 235
  backgrounds, 238
  camera angle and orientation, 239
  clothing, 239
  film, 239
  indirect light, 239
  lighting, 239
  posing, 239
  reflectors, 239
  silhouettes, 239
  soft light, 239
  vertical composition, 239
frame, 378

frame counter, 378
frame lines, 131, 379
frame numbers, 92–93, 379
framing *versus* aiming, 210–212
freezing action with flash, 273–275
f-stops, 127
Fujichrome, 42
fuzzy logic mode, 124–125

• G •
gestures, 234–246
glossy paper, 70
good people photographs, 232–234
  candid photos, 241–246
  expression and gesture, 234–246
  film, 233–234
  flash, 246
  formal photographs, 238–239
  photographing children, 248–254
  relaxing your subject, 235, 238
  zoom settings for portraits, 246–248
grab shots, 161
grain, 379
graininess and film speed, 54
gray-market film, 65
grease pencil, 94

• H •
hard light, 192, 379
  color print film, 198–200
  color slide film, 198
  coping with, 196–200
  direction, 195
  fill-flash mode, 199
  increasing exposure, 199–200
  manipulating, 193
  preserving detail, 197–200
  reflectors, 200
  shooting in direct sun, 197
hard-to-print negatives, 82
high key picture, 125
highlights, 197
holding point-and-shoot cameras, 30–32
horizon line, 286–287

• I •
icons, 108–109, 379
Ilford XP-2 film, 50
imaging software, 337, 339
incorrect focus and lack of sharpness, 57
index prints, 77, 320–321, 379
  35mm film, 94
  APS (Advanced Photo System), 94
  storing, 322

indirect light and formal photographs, 239
indoor light, 205–207
  color of, 195
indoor picture has green cast, 85–86
indoor shot has funny overall color, 85
infinity, 119
infinity lock mode, 119, 160, 163, 379
  active autofocus, 165
infinity mode, 179
inkjet printers, 342
Internet and travel, 298
interval timer mode, 118
intervalometer, 193
intervalometer mode, 118
ISO 100 color print film, 53
ISO 200 color print film, 53
ISO 400 Advanced Photo System film
  panoramic prints, 55
ISO 400 color print film, 53
  exceptionally fine grain, 54
  as standard, 52
ISO 800 color print film, 52, 53
ISO numbers, 37, 379
ISO ratings, 51
ISO speed, 44

• *K* •

K-14 processing, 43
KL123A lithium battery, 14
Kodachrome
  K-14 processing, 43
  processing, 43
Kodak Advantix Black-and-White+ 400 film, 49
Kodak Elite Chrome, 44
Kodak Gold line of film, 63
Kodak Photo CD, 99
Kodak Picture Disk, 332
Kodak Picture Disk Plus, 332
Kodak Picture Easy Software, 71, 339
Kodak Picture Network, 100
Kodak Picture Network Web site, 333, 359–360
Kodak Premium Processing, 48, 72
  APS (Advanced Photo System) film
    processing costs, 77
  scan-to-floppy service, 99
Kodak Royal Gold film, 63
Kodak T-Max T400 CN film, 50
Kodak Tri-X Pan film, 48
Kodak's Guide to Better Pictures Web site,
  357–358
Konica VX Pan 400 film, 50

• *L* •

lame excuses for not taking camera along,
  259–260
landscape mode, 119, 160, 179
landscapes, 281
  capturing more background with wide-angle
    focal length, 284–285
  cityscapes, 292–293
  close to home, 282
  cloudy skies, 290
  composition, 282, 286–288
  contrast, 282
  H print format, 288
  horizontal or vertical shots, 287–288
  lens, 283–285
  light, 290
  moving yourself for better view, 287
  near-far composition, 285
  panoramic view shapes, 288–289
  photographing, 281–293
  placing horizon line, 286–287
  pointing and panning, 283
  print shapes, 288–289
  seasonal changes, 290–292
  sectional panoramas, 283
  sense of scale, 289
  underexposure and snow, 292
  wide-angle focal length, 283
  wide-angle lens, 283
  wide-open spaces without wide-angle focal
    length, 285
  wider scene shapes, 288
Las Vegas, Nevada, 365–366
late light, 202
latent images, 68
LCD (liquid crystal display), 106, 379
LCD panel, 12–13, 18, 106
LCD viewfinder correction marks, 146
LCD viewfinder frame lines, 146
leader, 20, 21, 377
lens aperture, 39, 40, 379
lens cover, 29–30
lenses, 379
  35mm point-and-shoot cameras, 136
  angle of view, 57, 135, 138
  APS (Advanced Photo System) point-
    and-shoot cameras, 136
  cleaning, 164
  digital point-and-shoot cameras, 136
  focal length, 57
  landscapes, 283–285
  magnification, 57, 135
  portrait, 246
  setting aperture size, 127

shading from sunlight, 197
telephoto, 143
wide-angle, 136
zooming, 57
light
black-and-white film, 47
capturing at right time, 201–202
cloudy days, 202
color of, 195
direction of, 193, 195
early or late, 202
hard, 192, 196–200
landscapes, 290
midday, 201
momentary, 201
mood and atmosphere, 191–195
nondirectional, 195
quality, 192–193
raking, 192
recording changing character, 193
right amount to film, 40
shadows, 193
shooting in special light, 202–208
sidelight, 195
soft, 193
source, 192
studying, 192
sweet, 202, 290
toplight, 195
light meter, 43, 125–127, 379
reading small area of scene, 125–126
light source, 379
lighting
formal photographs, 239
tungsten sources, 183
lithium batteries, 14–15
AA size, 17
digital point-and-shoot cameras, 17
keeping extras on hand, 15
LivePix Deluxe, 339
loading batteries, 16, 18–19
loading film, 19–29
35mm point-and-shoot camera, 20–23
APS (Advanced Photo System), 26–28,
323–324
digital point-and-shoot cameras, 29
leader, 20
locking the focus, 155–157, 163, 379
changing distance to subject, 160
making sure focus is locked, 157–158
off-center composition, 218
practice, 159
too close to subject, 158
wide-area autofocus, 162
zooming before, 160

long focal lengths, 135, 380
long-zoom point-and-shoot cameras, 149–150
loupes, 95
low-light shots, 115
Lucy the Elephant, Margate City,
New Jersey, 369

• *M* •

macro mode, 121
magnification, 57
describing, 135
mailing photographs, 229
mail-order film, 65
mail-order photofinishers, 76, 78
mailers, 76
printing costs, 77
reprints, 90
scan-to-floppy service, 99
mail-order retailers, 385–386
manual, 13
manual backlight compensation mode, 126
manual focus mode, 121
manufacturers, 383–385
mapping modes, 109
mass-market labs, 72–73
low cost, 73
making prints lighter or darker, 81
no personal service, 73
printing costs, 77
reprints, 90
scan-to-floppy service, 99
matte paper, 70
MB (megabytes), 330
media safes, 102
memory keepers, 322
metering modes, 125–127
aperture-priority autoexposure mode, 127
exposure compensation mode, 127
manual backlight compensation mode, 126
spotmeter mode, 125–126
midday light, 201
middle-of-the-road point-and-shoot cameras, 45
midroll rewind, 33
midroll rewind button, 380
minilabs, 74–76
APS (Advanced Photo System) point-and-
shoot cameras, 75
enlargements, 96
making prints lighter or darker, 81
printing costs, 77
relationship with, 82
reprints, 90
The Mining Company Web site, 360

modes, 107, 110–129, 129–130, 380
  automatically setting, 124–125
  canceling settings, 129
  changing, 108–109
  creative, 128–129
  drive, 114–118
  flash, 111–113
  focusing, 119–121
  mapping, 109
  metering, 125–127
  number on average camera, 111
  print-format, 113–114
  subject, 122–125
momentary light, 201
moving *versus* zooming, 213–216
MRC (mid-roll change) feature, 36
  APS (Advanced Photo System), 325–326
muddy, 380
muddy prints, 79, 84
  causes, 79
  flash and, 87
  flash pictures beyond range of flash, 79
  grainy, 79
  lacking detail, 79
  learning from mistakes, 83
  muted colors, 79
  poor contrast, 79
  taking pictures in too dim light, 79
  underexposure, 79
multibeam autofocus, 161
multiple exposure mode, 128–129, 278
multiple flash mode, 129, 278
multipoint autofocus, 120, 161
multi-self-timer mode, 116

• N •

near-far composition, 216
  frame within photograph, 217
  landscapes, 285
  vertical composition, 222
negatives, 68, 380
  black-and-white film, 48
  cutting apart, 95
  dust on, 87–88
  fast film, 78
  fill-flash mode, 79
  finding for reprints, 92–93
  fingerprints, 93
  frame numbers, 92–93
  good, 78–79
  hard-to-print, 82
  locking focus, 78
  multiple ways of printing, 81
  nose grease, 88
  picture restoration, 71
  preserving, 102
  protective sleeves, 94
  staying within flash range, 79
  thin, 79
  unsleeved, 93
  viewing problems with, 83
  washing hands before touching, 93
night flash mode, 112, 182
night mode, 182
night portrait mode, 182
night scene mode, 182
nighttime flash shot muddy, 86–87
nondirectional light, 195
normal focal lengths, 139–140, 142, 380
nose grease, 88

• O •

off-center composition, 218
one-time-use 35mm point-and-shoot cameras
  film roll lengths, 59
one-time-use point-and-shoot cameras,
  10–12, 380
  fill flash, 176
  flash, 171
  focus-free operation, 153
  outdoor use, 12
  panning, 274
  pros and cons, 11
  single-focal-length, 147
  travel, 299
outdoor shot has great sky and dark ground, 89
overriding autofocus, 119

• P •

panning, 272
  action photography, 272–273
  difficulties, 273
  with flash, 277
  one-time-use point-and-shoot cameras, 274
panorama format pictures in 35mm point-
  and-shoot cameras, 96
panorama mode, 113–114, 283, 380
panoramic prints, 113–114
  APS (Advanced Photo System), 97
  enlargements, 97
  film speed, 55
  ISO 400 Advanced Photo System film, 55
  landscapes, 288–289
  printing costs, 77
Paradise Meadow, Mount Rainier National
  Park, Washington, 368
parallax error, 143, 380
party pictures, 259
passive autofocus, 162, 165–166
PQI (Print Quality Improvement), 320

people against colored background have weird cast, 89
person against background is silhouette, 87
pets
  eye contact, 255
  eye-level pictures, 254
  interacting with family members, 255
  interesting and amusing behaviors, 255
  photographing, 254–256
  red-eye and green-eye, 256
Phil Greenspun's Guide to Point-and-Shoot Cameras Web site, 360–361
Photo CDs, 333
photo kiosks, 90, 100–101
photo networks, 100
photofinishers, 67–68
  alerting about panorama format pictures, 96
  being firm and reasonable with, 83
  busy labs, 80
  color filtration, 41
  communicating with, 82–83
  costs, 76–77
  dating photographs, 98
  doubles service, 73
  dust on negative, 88
  finding good, 80–81
  fixed-price processing, 77
  FlashPix CD, 99
  having specific complaints, 83
  "house" film brands, 78
  Kodak Photo CD, 99
  learning from mistakes, 83
  looking at negative with, 82
  mail-order, 76
  mass-market labs, 72–73
  minilabs, 74–76
  photo networks, 100
  printing on glossy paper, 70
  printing on matte paper, 70
  problems with prints from, 41
  reprints, 90, 92–95
  scanning pictures, 332–333
  scan-to-floppy service, 99
  showing you problem, 83
  store-brand, 73
  test prints, 80–81
  types, 72–78
  warning about unusual shooting circumstances, 83
  word of mouth, 80
photofinishing, 38, 68, 380
  APS (Advanced Photo System), 319
  development, 68
  multiple prints of negatives, 71
  photo kiosks, 100–101

  printing, 68
  prints, 68–72
  reliability, 69
photographic Web sites
  Collected Visions, 361
  The Family Photo Historian, 358–359
  Fodor's Focus on Photography, 361
  Kodak Picture Network, 359–360
  Kodak's Guide to Better Pictures, 357–358
  The Mining Company, 360
  Phil Greenspun's Guide to Point-and-Shoot Cameras, 360–361
  PhotoNet, 362
  PIC (Photography Information Council), 362
  Popular Photography Online, 358
photographing
  children, 248–254
  landscapes, 281–293
  pets, 254–256
  possessions, 258
  staged events, 241
  TV screen, 124
photographs
  archival materials, 102
  automatically zooming for pictures, 117
  blowups, 68
  candid, 235
  candid shot tips, 228
  captions, 98
  changing positions and angles of, 137
  composition, 132, 209–223
  contrast, 197
  contrasty, 197
  cropping, 96, 313
  dating, 98
  delay in shooting, 115–116
  deterioration, 101
  developing and printing automation, 69
  digital form, 330–331
  double exposures, 129
  drying and cracking, 101
  enlargements, 68
  fading, 101
  as family history, 256–258
  fast sequence, 122–123
  formal, 235
  getting into computers, 332–334
  good people snapshots, 232–234
  grab shots, 161
  high key picture, 125
  highlights, 197
  horizontal *versus* vertical, 221–222
  mailing, 229
  mildewing, 101
  multiple delayed shots, 116
  natural-looking rendition, 142

(continued)

photographs *(continued)*
no flash, 122–123
one at a time at specific intervals, 118
party pictures, 259
picture restoration, 71
portrait telephoto, 144
portraits, 123
preserving, 101–102
reasons for taking, 228
red-eye, 184
relaxing your subject, 235, 238
reprint costs, 77
reprinting problem, 41
scanning, 97
scanning to CD-ROMs, 333
scanning to floppy disks, 332
scanning to World Wide Web, 333
scanning yourself, 333–334
shadows, 197
sharing, 229–230
staining, 101
storing in shoeboxes, 102
subject backlit, 174
subject in context, 256
subjects at a distance, 142–146
sunlight, 102
taking with digital point-and-shoot cameras,
     334–336
taking your picture, 123–124
time exposure, 128
weddings, 237
when to take, 232
photography
computers, 329–342
travel, 295–308
PhotoNet, 333
PhotoNet Web site, 362
PIC (Photography Information Council)
     Web site, 362
picture mode. *See* subject mode
picture restoration, 71
pixels, 330, 380
point-and-shoot cameras, 9–36
35mm, 10
all-auto mode, 108
APS (Advanced Photo System), 10
autoflash mode, 106, 108, 168–170
batteries, 13–19
batteries recharging, 15–16
battery power icons, 18
built-in flash, 233
button cells, 19
buttons, 105–107
buying, 345–352
changing batteries with film in, 19
changing modes, 108–109

clamshell cover, 29
compact-zoom, 148
counters and changing batteries, 19
covering the flash, 31
defaults, 106
dials replacing buttons, 106
differing shutter speeds, 266
digital, 12
displaying battery status, 18–19
DX code, 52
exposure control, 43
extending lens, 30
faking long zoom settings, 248
fill-flash mode, 168
flash mode button, 170–171
flash modes, 111–113
flash multi mode, 278
flash-off mode, 168
focal lengths, 135, 136
focus-free models, 119
getting good results with slide film, 43–45
good people photographs, 232–233
holding, 30–32
LCD panel, 18, 106
lens aperture, 40
lens covers, 29–30
light meter, 43, 125–127
loading batteries, 16, 18–19
loading film, 19–29
long-zoom, 149–150
mapping modes, 109
middle-of-the-road, 45
mode icons, 108–109
modes, 107–108, 110–129
multiple exposure mode, 278
multiple flash mode, 278
number of modes on, 111
one-time-use, 10–12
panoramic mode, 283
quartz date capability, 19
quirks for action photography, 262–263
reading film bar code, 52
red-eye reduction mode, 168
removing batteries while storing, 19
rewind button, 33, 34
right amount of light to film, 40
shutter button, 31, 32, 106
shutter speed, 39, 40
single-focal-length, 137, 147
slow-sync mode, 168
snap mode, 278
sports or action mode, 278
standard-zoom, 149
tripod socket, 234
turning off flash, 16
turning on and off, 29–30

types, 10–12
types by lenses, 147–150
underwater, 279
variations of rewinding film, 35
waterproof, 279
weatherproof, 279
widest lens aperture, 39
Zarkon mode map example, 110
zoom lenses, 233
zooming models, 31
Popular Photography Online Web site, 358
portrait lenses, 246
portrait modes, 123
  fill flash, 123
  good people pictures, 233
portrait photographs
  long focal length, 246
  wide-angle zoom settings, 248
  zoom settings, 246–248
portrait telephoto, 144
portraits, 123
posing formal photographs, 239
positives, 380
possessions, photographing, 258
PQI (Print Quality Improvement), 92, 312
prefocusing, 380
  action photography, 263–264, 269
  focus-free cameras, 264
  importance, 265
premium film, 63
preserving
  negatives, 102
  photographs, 101–102
prewinding film, 26
print formats, 380
printers, 342
print-format modes
  C, H, P switch, 114
  panorama mode, 113–114
printing, 68, 381
  automation, 69
  color negatives, 70
  digital images yourself, 342
  on glossy paper, 70
  on matte paper, 70
prints, 68–72, 70
  8 x 10s, 96
  8 x 12s, 96
  16 x 20s, 96
  16 x 24s, 96
  burning in, 91
  captions, 98
  dates on envelopes, 94
  dating, 98
  daylight picture too dark, 84

daylight picture too light, 84
dodging, 91
dust on negative, 87–88
enlargements, 95–97
faces burned out, 86
glossy paper, 70
indoor picture has green cast, 85–86
indoor shot has funny overall color, 85
marking envelopes, 94
marking with grease pencil, 94
matte paper, 70
muddy, 79
nighttime flash shot muddy, 86–87
objections to, 83
obtaining good, 78–79
outdoor shot has great sky and dark
    ground, 89
people against colored background have
    weird cast, 89
person against background is silhouette, 87
photofinishers and problem prints, 82–83
reprints made from, 90
saying something is wrong with, 83
scratches through picture, 88
snowy scene grayish and muddy, 84
things that can go wrong with, 83–89
private label film, 64–65
problem prints, 83–89
  daylight picture too dark, 84
  daylight picture too light, 84
  dust on negative, 87–88
  faces burned out, 86
  indoor picture has green cast, 85–86
  indoor shot has funny overall color, 85
  nighttime flash shot muddy, 86–87
  outdoor shot has great sky and dark
      ground, 89
  people against colored background have
      weird cast, 89
  person against background is silhouette, 87
  scratches through picture, 88
  snowy scene grayish and muddy, 84
problems with prints from photofinishers, 41
processing, 68, 381
  black-and-white film, 50
  color print film, 43
  color slide film, 43
  Kodachrome, 43
  mail-order film, 65
program image mode. See subject mode
protective camera coverings, 298

● **Q** ●
Qualex, 72
quartz date capability, 19
quartz-date, 381

• R •

raking light, 192
RAM (random access memory), 331, 381
rechargeable batteries, 16
red barn effect, 89
red-eye, 184
 dim light, 185
red-eye reduction flash, 184–188
 good people pictures, 233
 photographing children, 253
 preflash type, 185, 186
 prelamp type, 185, 186, 187–188
red-eye reduction mode, 113, 168
reflectors, 200
 formal photographs, 239
 hard light, 200
 window light, 204
relaxing your subject, 235, 238
remedies when camera won't shoot, 371–374
 battery installed correctly, 372–373
 checking flash-ready lamp, 373–374
 cleaning battery contacts, 373
 digital camera finished saving, 374
 making sure film is in, 371
 reloading film, 372
 replacing battery, 372
 rewinding film and inserting new roll, 374
 stepping back from subject, 374
 turning camera on correctly, 372
remote control mode, 116–117
remote receptor, 116
reprinting problem photographs, 41
reprints, 90, 92–95
 APS (Advanced Photo System), 319–320, 327
 finding negatives for, 92–93
 made from prints, 90
 mail-order labs, 90
 mass-market photofinishers, 90
 minilabs, 90
resolution, 381
retailers, 383–385
rewind button, 33, 34
rewinding, 381
rewinding film, 33–36
 problems, 34
Rule of Thirds, 210

• S •

Salton Sea, Southern California, 370
Santuario de Nuestra Señor de Esquipulas, Chimayo, New Mexico, 369
saturation, 63
scanners, 334
 APS (Advanced Photo System), 328

scanning, 381
 photographs, 97
scan-to-floppy service, 99
scenic, 282
scratches through picture, 88
Seattle FilmWorks, 78
self-timer mode, 115–116, 381
sequential self-timer mode, 116
shadows, 193, 197
 direction of light, 193, 195
 window light, 204
shake, 285
 film speed, 56–57
 magnification and, 57
sharing photographs, 229–230
 double prints, 229
sharpness, 381
 film speed, 56
 lack due to shake or incorrect focus, 57
shoeboxes, storing photographs in, 102
short focal lengths, 135, 381
 See also wide-angle focal length
shutter
 autoflash mode, 182
 customized opening, 128
 slow-sync flash, 182
 staying open longer than usual, 112
shutter button, 31, 32, 381
 holding halfway down to lock focus, 155–157
 squeezing, 264
shutter speed, 39, 40, 381
sidelight, 195
silhouettes and formal photographs, 239
single-focal-length, 381
single-focal-length point-and-shoot cameras, 137
 autofocus models, 147
 near-far relationships, 216
 one-time-use cameras, 147
skylines, 292–293
slide film, 381
slide projection equipment, 41–42
slide rules, 45
slides
 color slide film, 41–46
 hand and tabletop viewers, 42
 mountings, 42
 as positive transparency, 42
 projection equipment, 41–42
 viewing test slides, 44–45
slow film, 381
 smaller grain, 54
slow shutter speed synchro mode, 182
slow-speed sync mode, 182

slow-sync flash, 181–184, 382
  artificial light, 206
  better background detail, 182
  dimly lit backgrounds, 182
  flash ghosting, 277
  fluorescent light, 207
  fluorescent lighting, 184
  increasing chance of blur, 184
  shutter, 182
slow-sync mode, 47, 112, 168
  candid photos, 245
snap mode, 120, 278
snapshot scanners, 334
snow
  scene grayish and muddy, 84
  underexposure, 292
soft light, 193, 382
  direction, 195
  flattering, 193
  formal photographs, 239
source of light, 192
special light, 202–208
  artificial light, 205–207
  backlight, 207–208
  window light, 203–205
spool hub, 21
sports mode, 278
spot autofocus mode, 120, 162
  along with spotmeter mode, 126
spotmeter mode, 125–126
  along with spot autofocus mode, 126
SSFDC cards, 338
staged events, 241
standard-size prints, 90
standard-zoom point-and-shoot cameras, 149
Staten Island Ferry, Battery Park,
    New York, 367
steadying cameras, 57
step zoom mode, 117
stop-action photographs, 264, 265–269
  combining with blur-action, 276–277
store-brand film, 64
store-brand photofinishing, 73
street shooting, 120
stroboscopic multiple exposure, 129
subject, backlit, 174
subject modes, 122–125
  action mode, 122–123
  fuzzy logic mode, 124–125
  portrait mode, 123
  take my picture mode, 123–124
  TV mode, 124
sunlight
  photographs, 102
  shading lens, 197
  shooting in, 197

surrogate focusing, 263
sweet light, 202, 290
syncro sun flash, 173

• *T* •
tabletop tripods, 302–303
take my picture mode, 123–124
take-up spool, 20
telephoto focal lengths, 139–140, 142–146, 382
telephoto lenses, 143
  flattening or compressing scene, 143–144
  parallax error, 144
  portrait telephoto, 144
telephoto settings
  getting close, 144–146
  lens aperture and, 146
test prints and photofinishers, 80–81
testing cameras for travel, 300
thin negatives, 79
thumbnails, 337, 382
time exposure, 128
toggling, 382
  buttons, 108–109
toplight, 195
travel
  avoid photographing, 307
  bad weather, 304–305
  batteries, 299
  black-and-white film, 302
  buying camera for, 301
  camera bags, 303
  camera manuals, 299
  cleaning camera lens, 299
  climate, 296
  day trips and side excursions, 297
  deciding what to bring, 298–303
  dessicants, 298
  detail shots, 304
  dusting out camera, 299
  establishing shots, 304
  film, 301–302
  flash and existing light, 303
  fresh batteries for camera, 299
  how much film to purchase, 302
  Internet, 298
  local attitudes to photography, 307
  middle-distance shots, 304
  must shoot items, 297
  new cameras, 300
  one-time-use cameras, 299
  photographic supplies, 298–303
  photographing locals, 305–307
  photography, 295–308
  planning photographs, 296
  protecting gear from theft, 307
  protective camera coverings, 298

(continued)

travel *(continued)*
  rainy or humid destination, 298
  research, 298
  sunrise and sunset times, 297
  taking the right camera, 299–300
  testing cameras, 300
  tripods, 302–303
  what to photograph, 303–307
tripods, 128, 234
  tabletop, 302–303
  travel, 302–303
tungsten light, 382
tungsten sources, 183
tunnel focus, 155
TV screen, photographing, 124

• U •

underexposure and muddy prints, 79
underwater, 279
unsleeved negatives, 93

• V •

Vietnam Veterans Memorial,
    Washington, D.C., 368
viewfinder, 12, 382
  aiming *versus* framing, 210–212
  changing picture in, 132–134
  changing picture with zoom lens, 132–133
  close-up correction marks, 144, 146
  composing from, 211
  difference in actual photograph from, 143
  filling the frame, 212–213
  flash-ready lamp, 178
  focal lengths, 135–138
  focus point, 153, 154–155
  frame edges, 132
  frame lines, 131
  parallax error, 143
  placing heads near top edge, 211

• W •

waterproof, 279
weatherproof, 279
weddings, 237
White Birch Forest, Pictured Rocks National
    Lakeshore, Michigan, 366–367
wide-angle focal lengths, 139–142, 382
  capturing more landscape background,
      284–285
  depth, 140
  exaggerating objects or people in
      foreground, 140
  landscapes, 283

shooting wide-open spaces without, 285
wide-angle lenses, 136
  landscapes, 283
wide-area autofocus, 120, 161–162, 382
  locking the focus, 162
window light, 203–205
  reflectors, 204
  shadows, 204
  tripods, 234
windows, shooting pictures through, 160
World Wide Web
  putting pictures on, 341–342
  scanning photographs to, 333

• Z •

zoom lenses, 233, 382
  APS (Advanced Photo System) point-
      and-shoot cameras, 317
  background objects appearing bigger, 215
  cameras without, 137
  changing angle of view, 138–146
  changing picture in viewfinder, 132–133
  control lever or buttons, 132–133
  filling the frame, 212–213
  fine-tuning focal length, 138–146
  focal length range, 139
  getting close at telephoto settings, 144–146
  identifying, 132
  normal focal length, 142
  parallax error, 144
  tele control, 134
  telephoto settings and lens aperture, 146
  testing at different focal points, 213
  when to zoom, 139
  wide control, 134
  wide-angle focal lengths, 139–142
  zoom ratio, 148
  zooming in *versus* zooming out, 133–134
zoom ratio, 148
zooming in, 382
zooming in *versus* zooming out, 133–134
zooming lens, 57
zooming out, 382
zooming *versus* moving, 213–216

There's an easier way to do more with pictures

YOUR ONLINE RESOURCE

WWW.DUMMIES.COM

Discover Dummies Online!

The Dummies Web Site is your fun and friendly online resource for the latest information about ...*For Dummies*® books and your favorite topics. The Web site is the place to communicate with us, exchange ideas with other ...*For Dummies* readers, chat with authors, and have fun!

Ten Fun and Useful Things You Can Do at www.dummies.com

1. Win free ...*For Dummies* books and more!
2. Register your book and be entered in a prize drawing.
3. Meet your favorite authors through the IDG Books Author Chat Series.
4. Exchange helpful information with other ...*For Dummies* readers.
5. Discover other great ...*For Dummies* books you must have!
6. Purchase Dummieswear™ exclusively from our Web site.
7. Buy ...*For Dummies* books online.
8. Talk to us. Make comments, ask questions, get answers!
9. Download free software.
10. Find additional useful resources from authors.

Link directly to these ten fun and useful things at
http://www.dummies.com/10useful

For other technology titles from IDG Books Worldwide, go to
www.idgbooks.com

Not on the Web yet? It's easy to get started with *Dummies 101*®: *The Internet For Windows*® *98* or *The Internet For Dummies*,® 6th Edition, at local retailers everywhere.

Find other ...*For Dummies* books on these topics:

Business • Career • Databases • Food & Beverage • Games • Gardening • Graphics • Hardware
Health & Fitness • Internet and the World Wide Web • Networking • Office Suites
Operating Systems • Personal Finance • Pets • Programming • Recreation • Sports
Spreadsheets • Teacher Resources • Test Prep • Word Processing

IDG BOOKS WORLDWIDE
BOOK REGISTRATION

Register This Book and Win!

We want to hear from you!

Visit **http://my2cents.dummies.com** to register this book and tell us how you liked it!

- Get entered in our monthly prize giveaway.

- Give us feedback about this book — tell us what you like best, what you like least, or maybe what you'd like to ask the author and us to change!

- Let us know any other *...For Dummies*® topics that interest you.

Your feedback helps us determine what books to publish, tells us what coverage to add as we revise our books, and lets us know whether we're meeting your needs as a *...For Dummies* reader. You're our most valuable resource, and what you have to say is important to us!

Not on the Web yet? It's easy to get started with *Dummies 101*®*: The Internet For Windows*® *98* or *The Internet For Dummies*®, 6th Edition, at local retailers everywhere.

Or let us know what you think by sending us a letter at the following address:

...For Dummies Book Registration
Dummies Press
10475 Crosspoint Blvd.
Indianapolis, IN 46256

...FOR DUMMIES™

BESTSELLING BOOK SERIES